ALL STAR WESTERN FEATURING JONAH HEX

ISSUE #14 COVER SKETCH BY ARIEL OLIVETTI

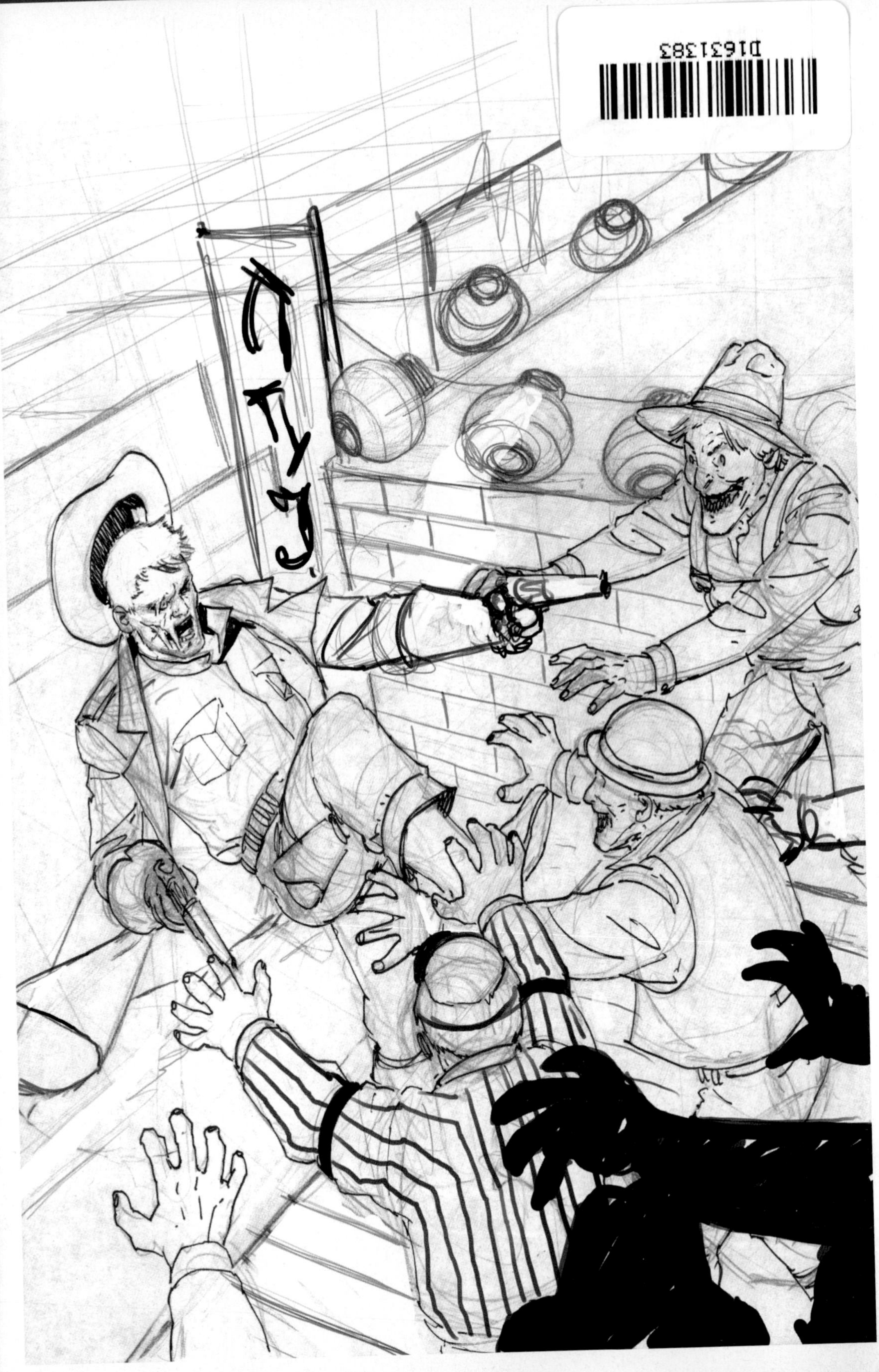

ALL STAR WESTERN FEATURING JONAH HEX

JEKYLL AND HYDE DESIGN SKETCHES BY MORITAT

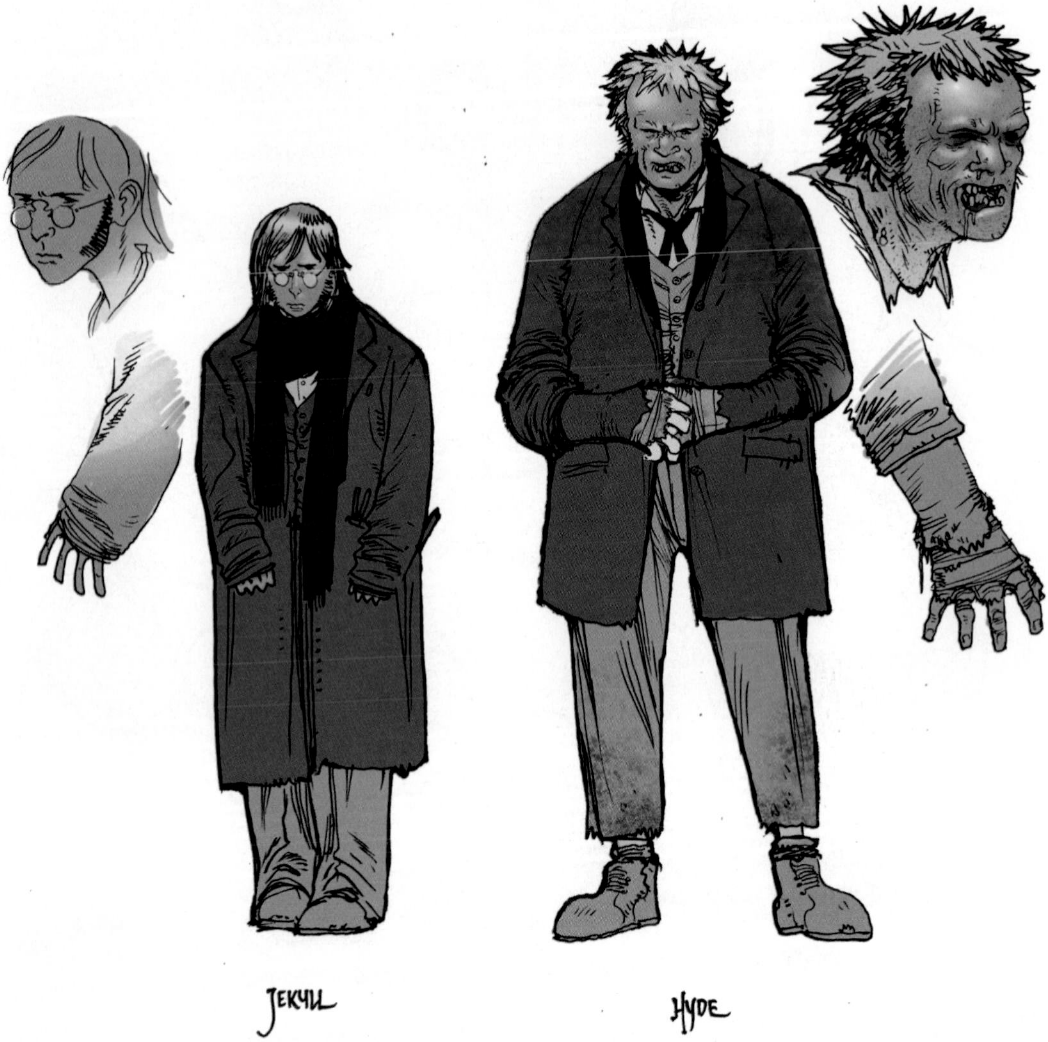
JEKYLL
HYDE

I THINK THIS IS THE REFERENCE
MR. SIMONSON USED FOR THE NURSE FOR 015

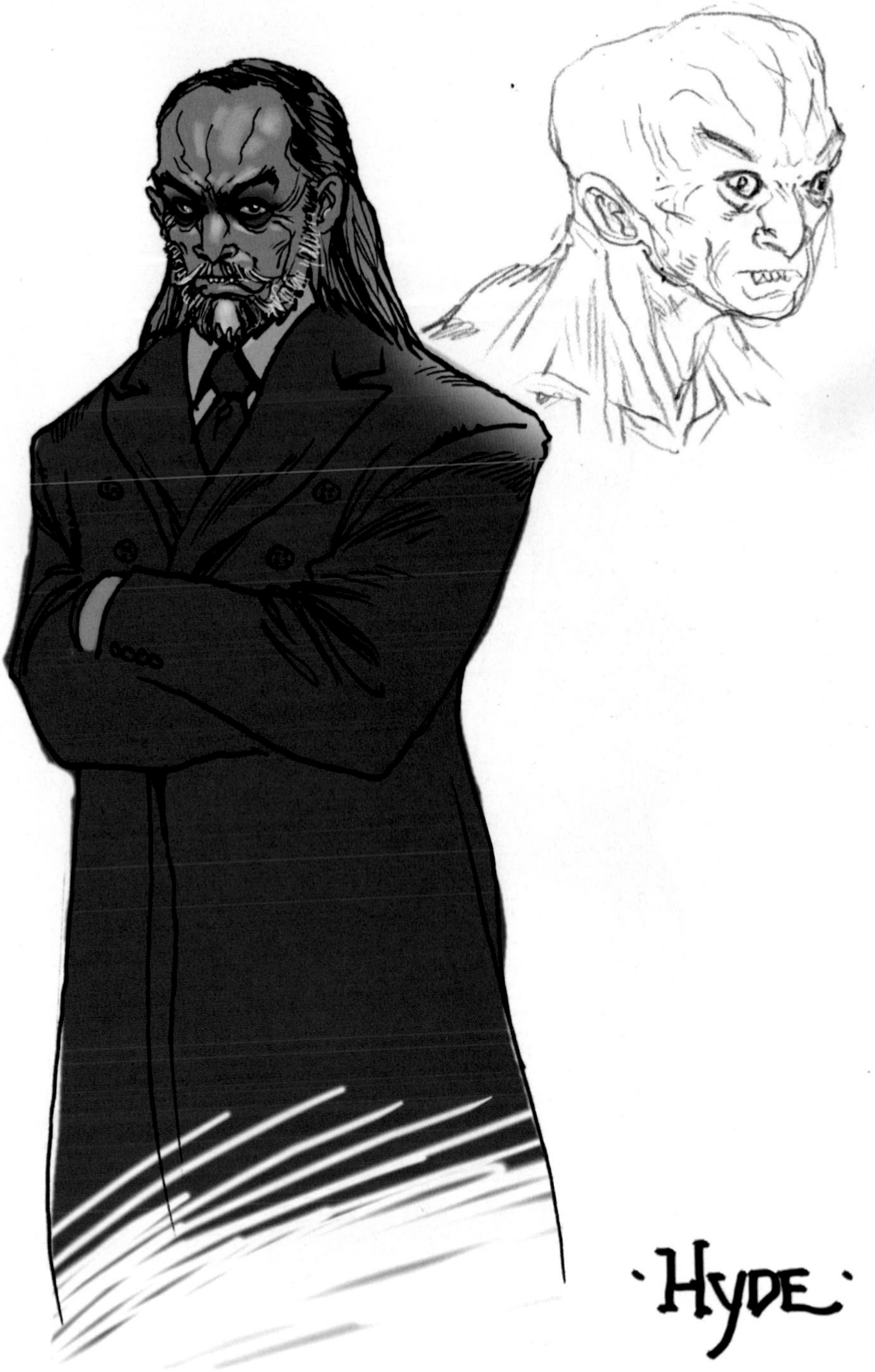
·HYDE·

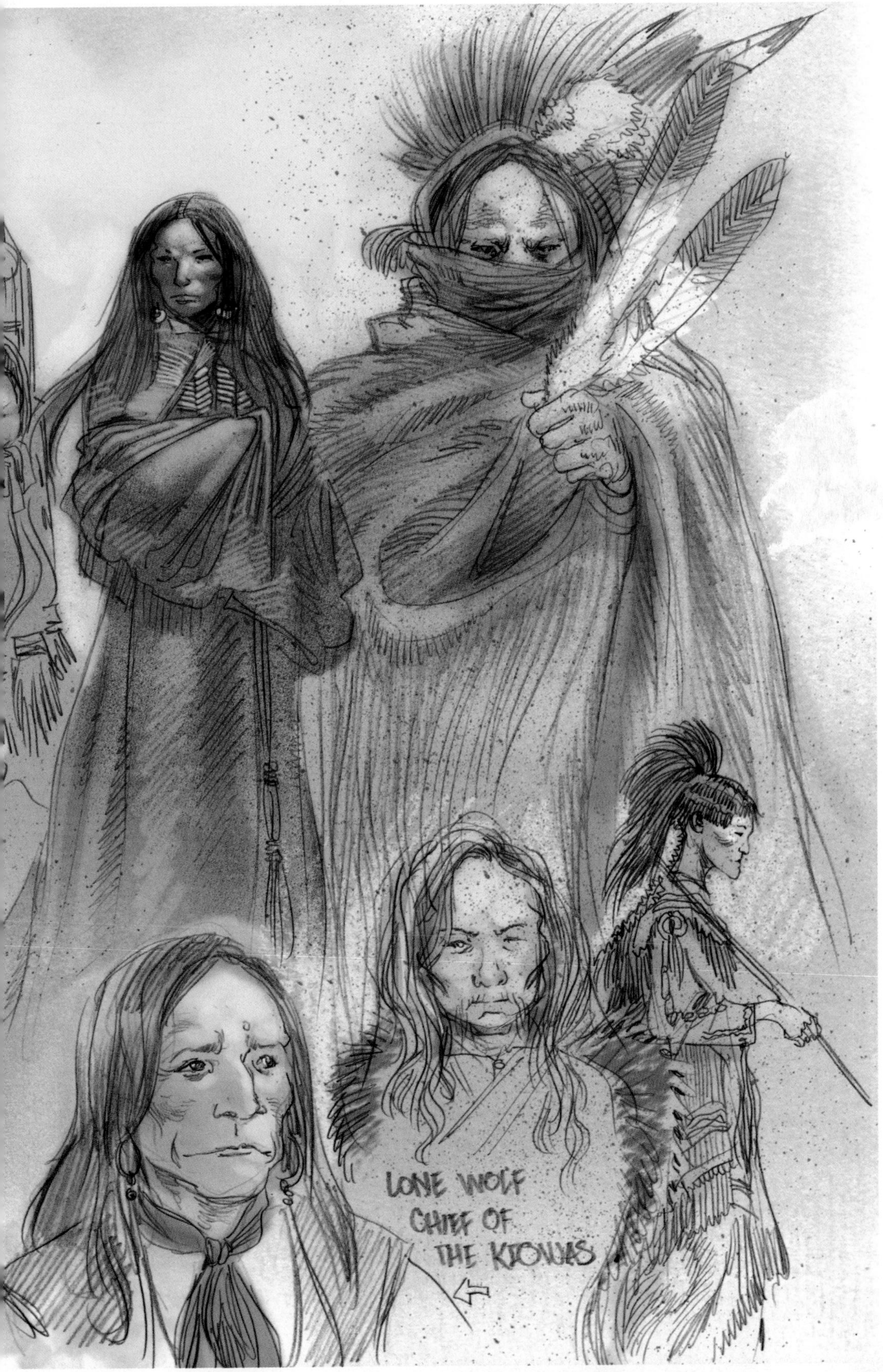
LONE WOLF
CHIEF OF
THE KIOWAS

ALL STAR WESTERN FEATURING JONAH HEX
TOMAHAWK DESIGNS BY PHIL WINSLADE

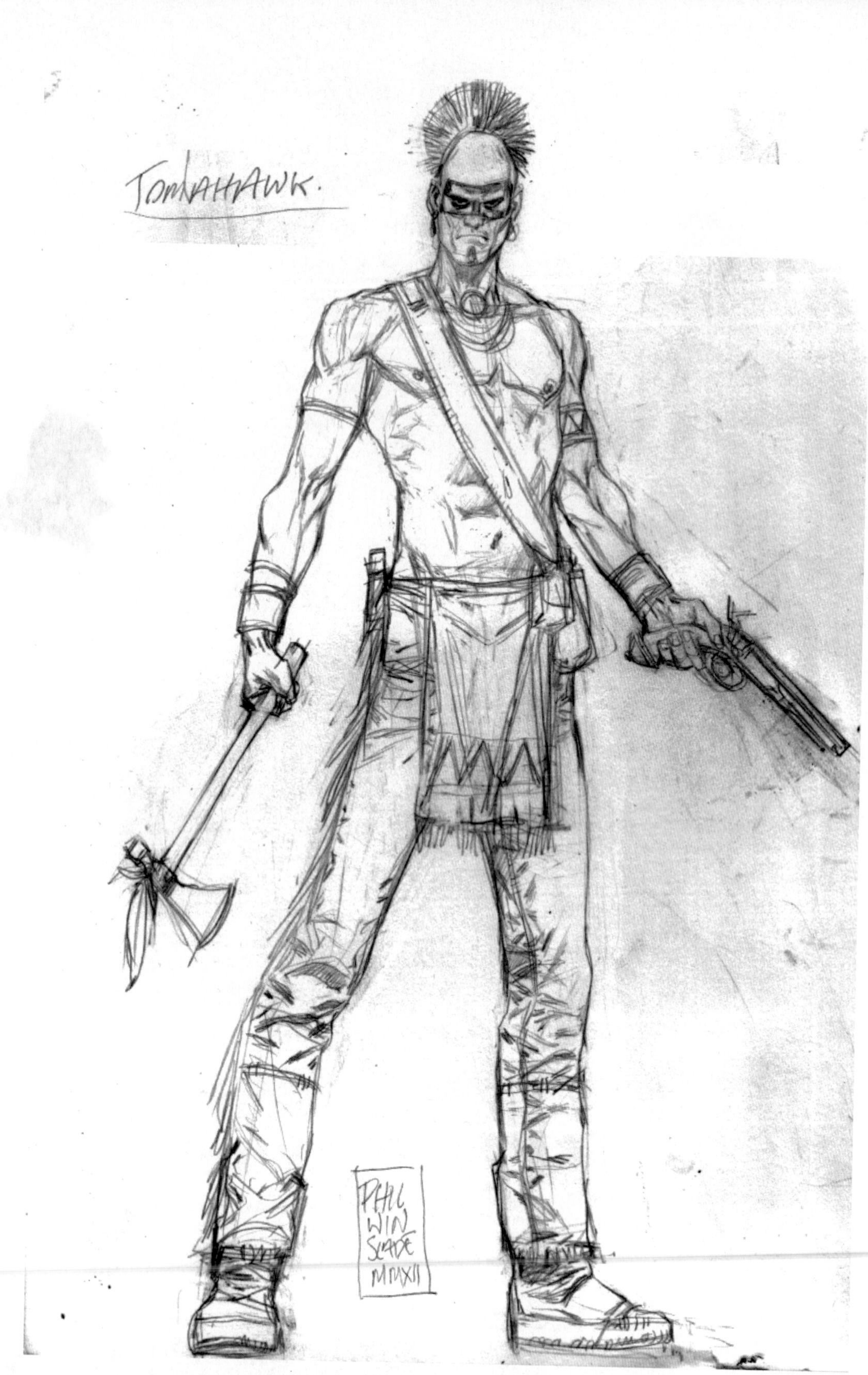
TOMAHAWK.
PHIL WIN SLADE MMXII

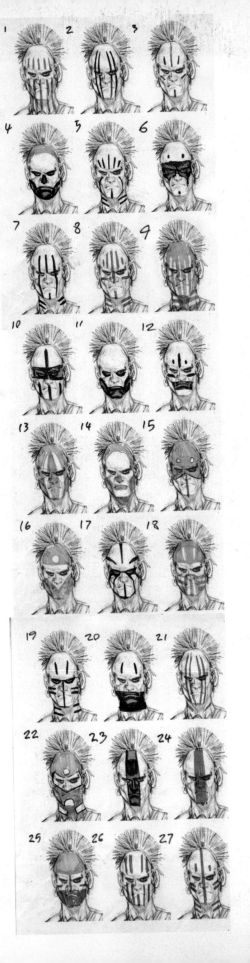

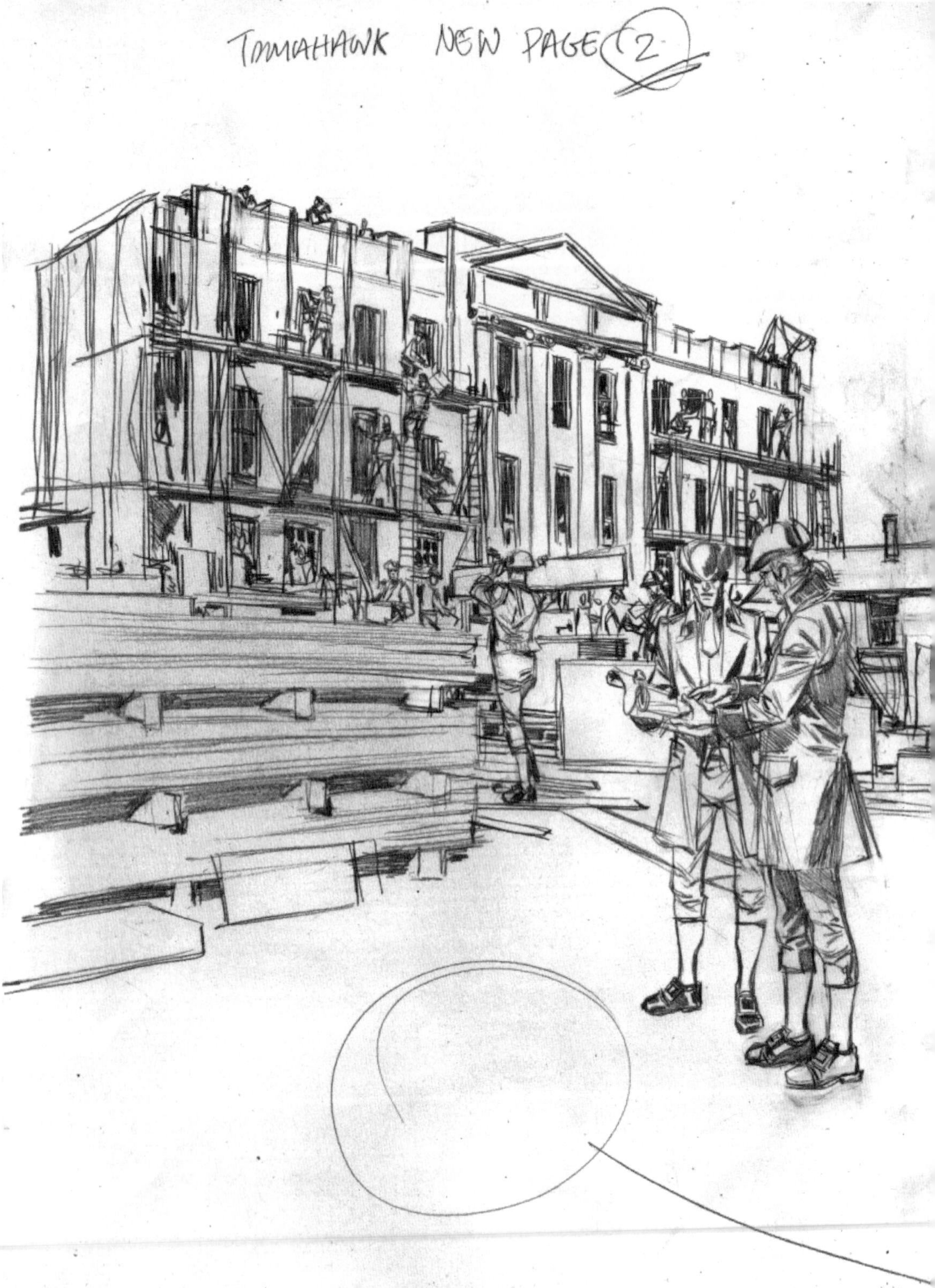
TOMAHAWK NEW PAGE 2

GRAPHIC FIC Hex
Palmiotti, Jimmy.
All Star Western. Volume 3, The
Black Diamond Probability /

2013026274

10/14

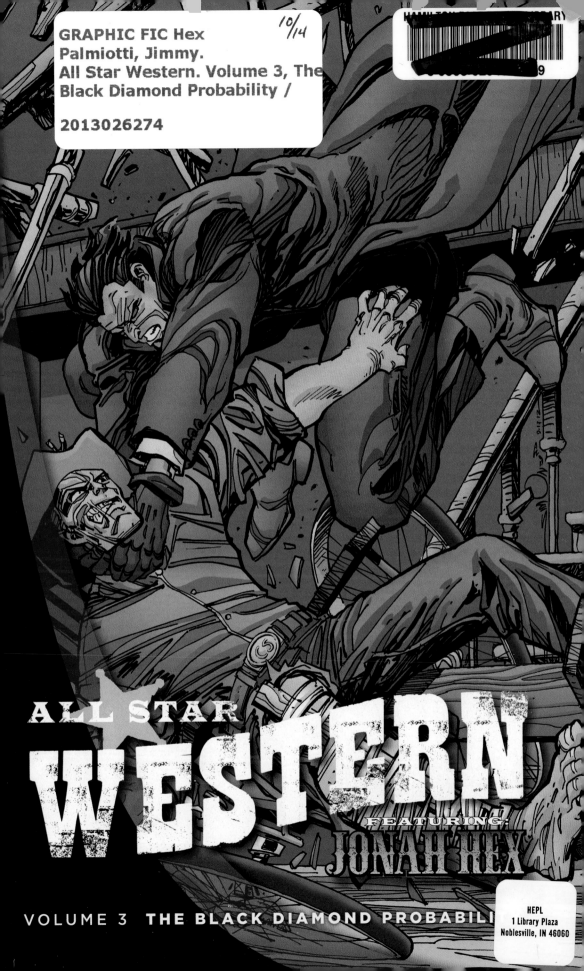

ALL STAR WESTERN

FEATURING: JONAH HEX

VOLUME 3   THE BLACK DIAMOND PROBABILITY

HEPL
1 Library Plaza
Noblesville, IN 46060

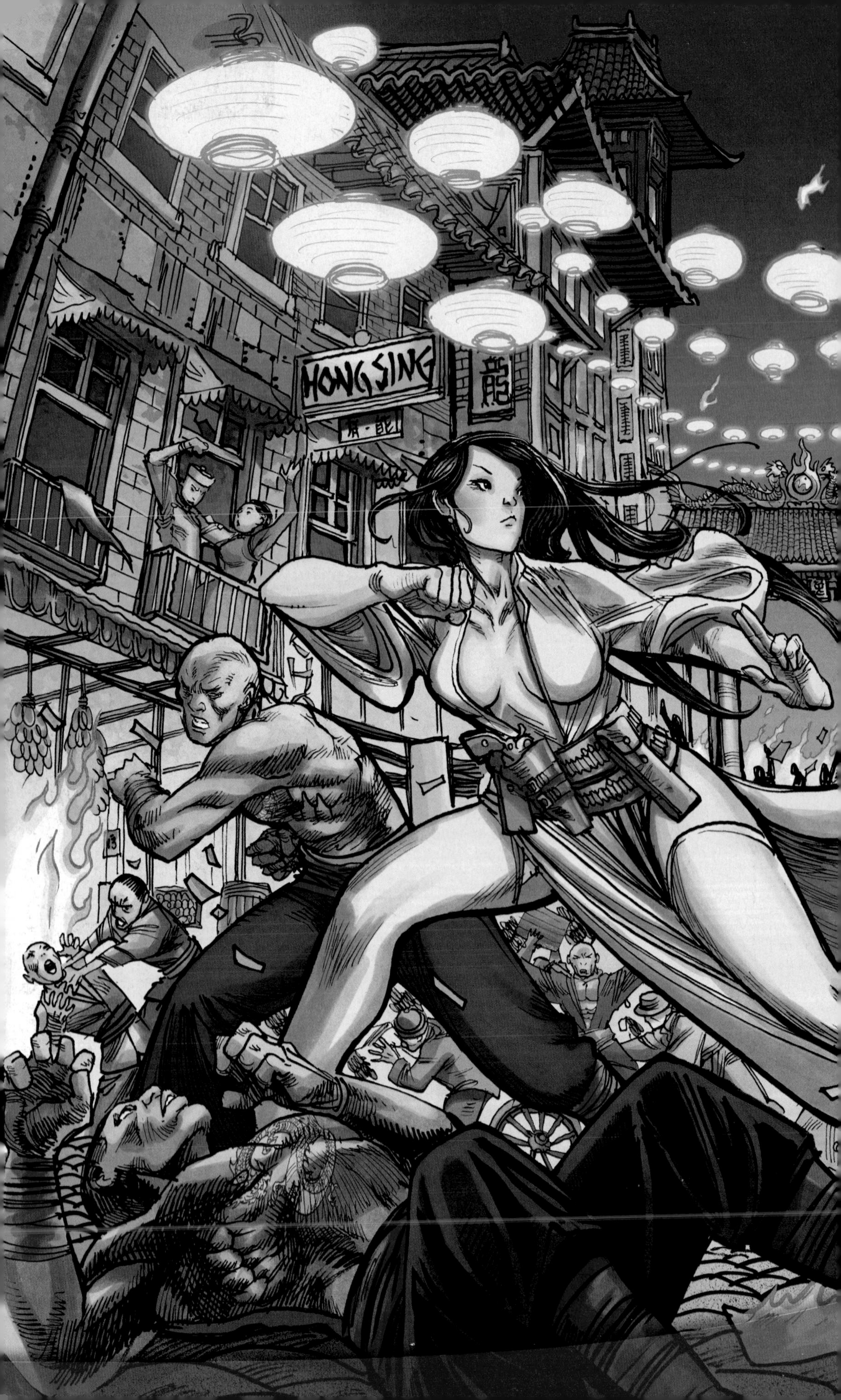
HONG SING

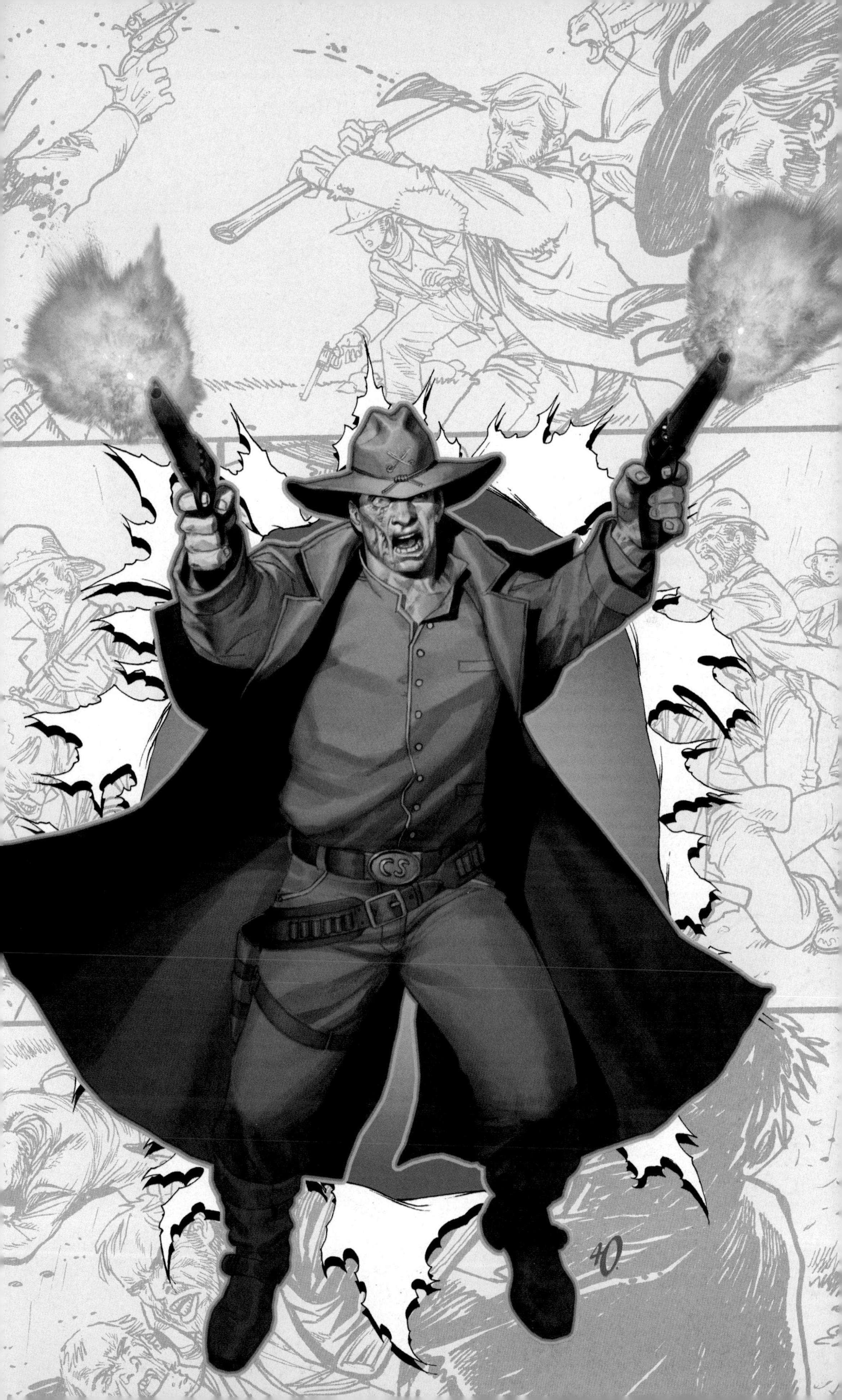

JIMMY PALMIOTTI & JUSTIN GRAY writers MORITAT artist cover art by ARIEL OLIVETTI

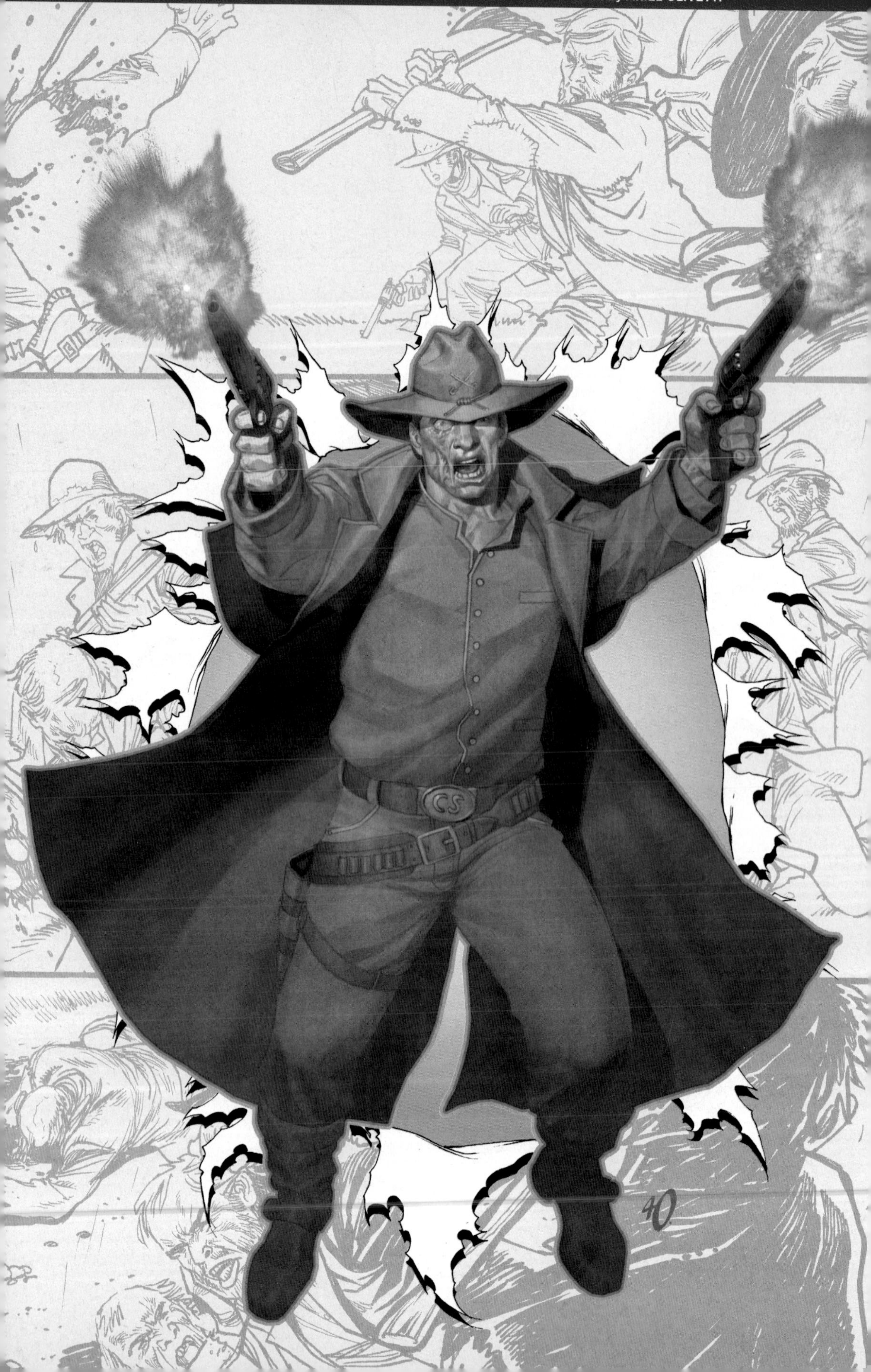

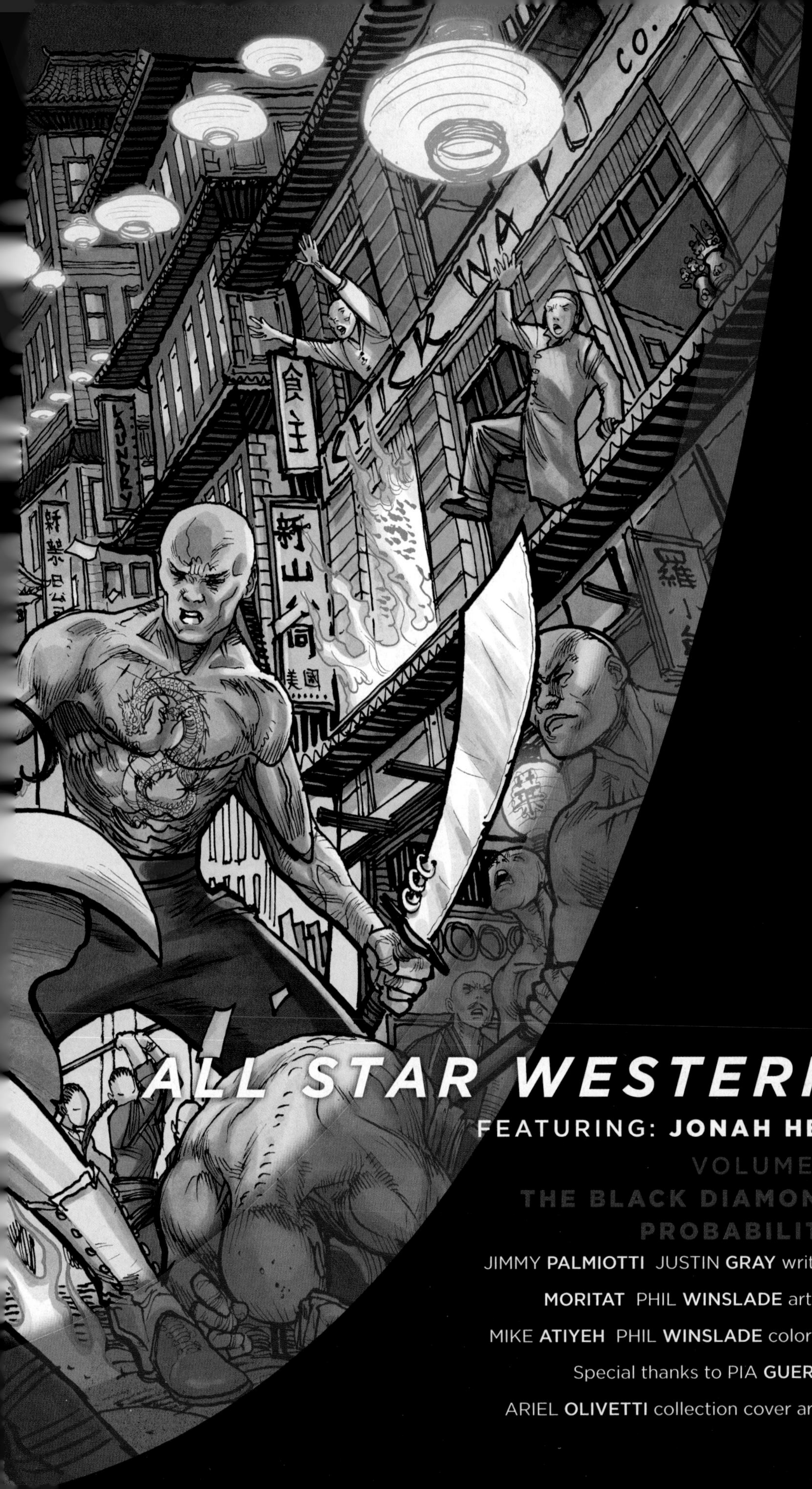
LAUNDRY
CO.

ALL STAR WESTERN

FEATURING: JONAH HEX

VOLUME 3

THE BLACK DIAMOND PROBABILITY

JIMMY **PALMIOTTI** JUSTIN **GRAY** writers

MORITAT PHIL **WINSLADE** artists

MIKE **ATIYEH** PHIL **WINSLADE** colorists

Special thanks to PIA **GUERRA**

ARIEL **OLIVETTI** collection cover artist

JOEY CAVALIERI Editor – Original Series KATE STEWART Assistant Editor – Original Series
ROWENA YOW Editor ROBBIN BROSTERMAN Design Director – Books ROBBIE BIEDERMAN Publication Design

BOB HARRAS Senior VP – Editor-in-Chief, DC Comics

DIANE NELSON President DAN DIDIO and JIM LEE Co-Publishers GEOFF JOHNS Chief Creative Officer
JOHN ROOD Executive VP – Sales, Marketing and Business Development AMY GENKINS Senior VP – Business and Legal Affairs
NAIRI GARDINER Senior VP – Finance JEFF BOISON VP – Publishing Planning MARK CHIARELLO VP – Art Direction and Design
JOHN CUNNINGHAM VP – Marketing TERRI CUNNINGHAM VP – Editorial Administration
ALISON GILL Senior VP – Manufacturing and Operations HANK KANALZ Senior VP – Vertigo & Integrated Publishing
JAY KOGAN VP – Business and Legal Affairs, Publishing JACK MAHAN VP – Business Affairs, Talent
NICK NAPOLITANO VP – Manufacturing Administration SUE POHJA VP – Book Sales
COURTNEY SIMMONS Senior VP – Publicity BOB WAYNE Senior VP – Sales

ALL STAR WESTERN FEATURING: JONAH HEX VOLUME 3: THE BLACK DIAMOND PROBABILITY
Published by DC Comics. Copyright © 2013 DC Comics. All Rights Reserved.

Originally published in single magazine form in ALL STAR WESTERN FEATURING: JONAH HEX 0, 13-16 © 2012, 2013 DC Comics.
All Rights Reserved. All characters, their distinctive likenesses and related elements featured in this publication are
trademarks of DC Comics. The stories, characters and incidents featured in this publication are entirely fictional.
DC Comics does not read or accept unsolicited ideas, stories or artwork.

DC Comics, 1700 Broadway, New York, NY 10019
A Warner Bros. Entertainment Company.
Printed by RR Donnelley, Salem, VA, USA. 10/4/13. First Printing.
ISBN: 978-1-4012-4399-9

Library of Congress Cataloging-in-Publication Data

Palmiotti, Jimmy, author.
All Star Western. Volume 3, The Black Diamond Probability / Jimmy Palmiotti, Justin Gray, Moritat.
pages cm
"Originally published in single magazine form as ALL STAR WESTERN 0, 13-16."
ISBN 978-1-4012-4399-9
1. Graphic novels. I. Gray, Justin, author. II. Norman, Justin, illustrator. III. Title. IV. Title: Black Diamond Probability.
PN6728.A425P37 2013
741.5'973—dc23
2013026274

SUSTAINABLE
FORESTRY
INITIATIVE
Certified Chain of Custody
At Least 20% Certified Forest Content

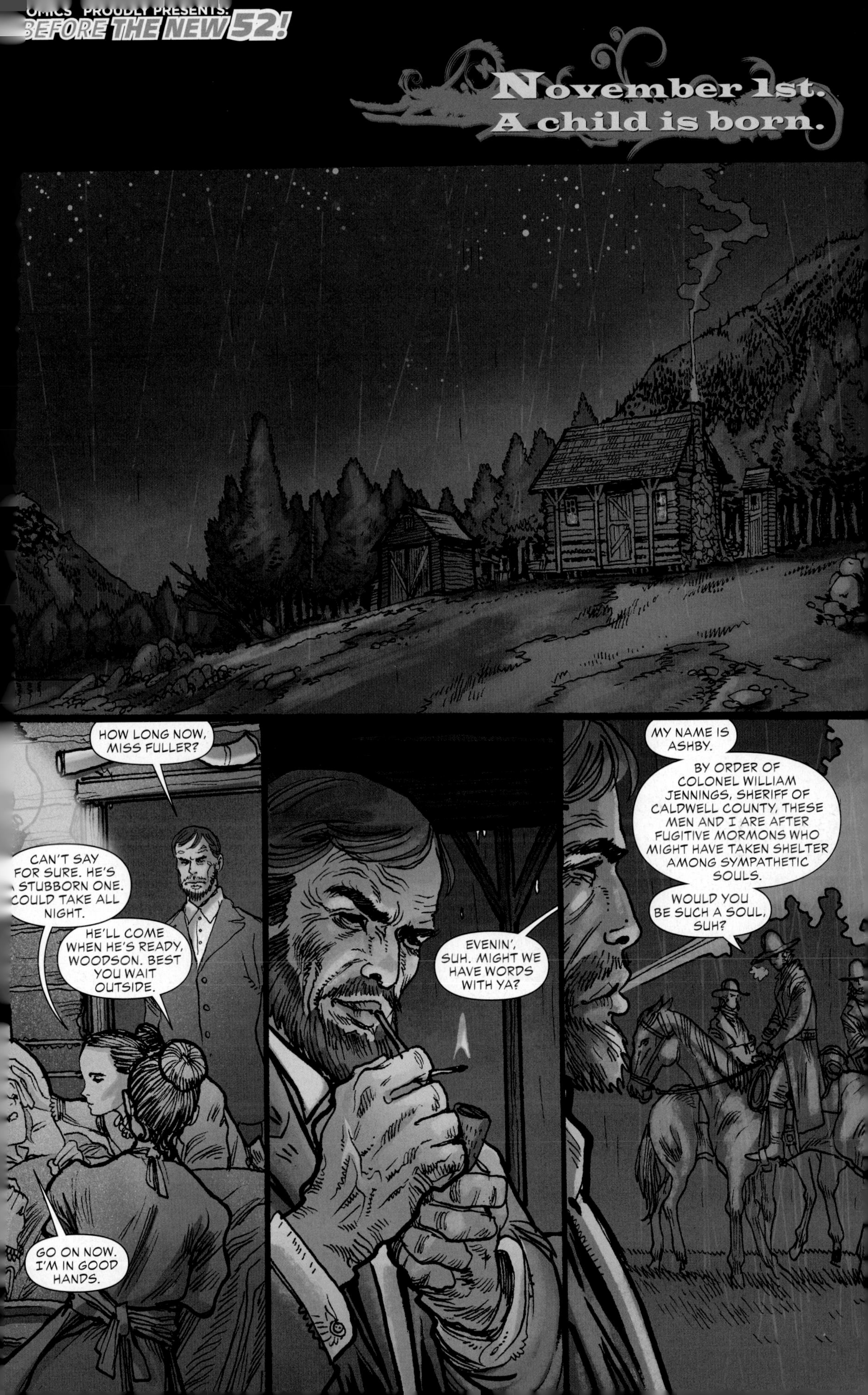
OMICS PROUDLY PRESENTS:
BEFORE THE NEW 52!
November 1st.
A child is born.
HOW LONG NOW, MISS FULLER?
CAN'T SAY FOR SURE. HE'S A STUBBORN ONE. COULD TAKE ALL NIGHT.
HE'LL COME WHEN HE'S READY, WOODSON. BEST YOU WAIT OUTSIDE.
GO ON NOW. I'M IN GOOD HANDS.
EVENIN', SUH. MIGHT WE HAVE WORDS WITH YA?
MY NAME IS ASHBY.
BY ORDER OF COLONEL WILLIAM JENNINGS, SHERIFF OF CALDWELL COUNTY, THESE MEN AND I ARE AFTER FUGITIVE MORMONS WHO MIGHT HAVE TAKEN SHELTER AMONG SYMPATHETIC SOULS.
WOULD YOU BE SUCH A SOUL, SUH?

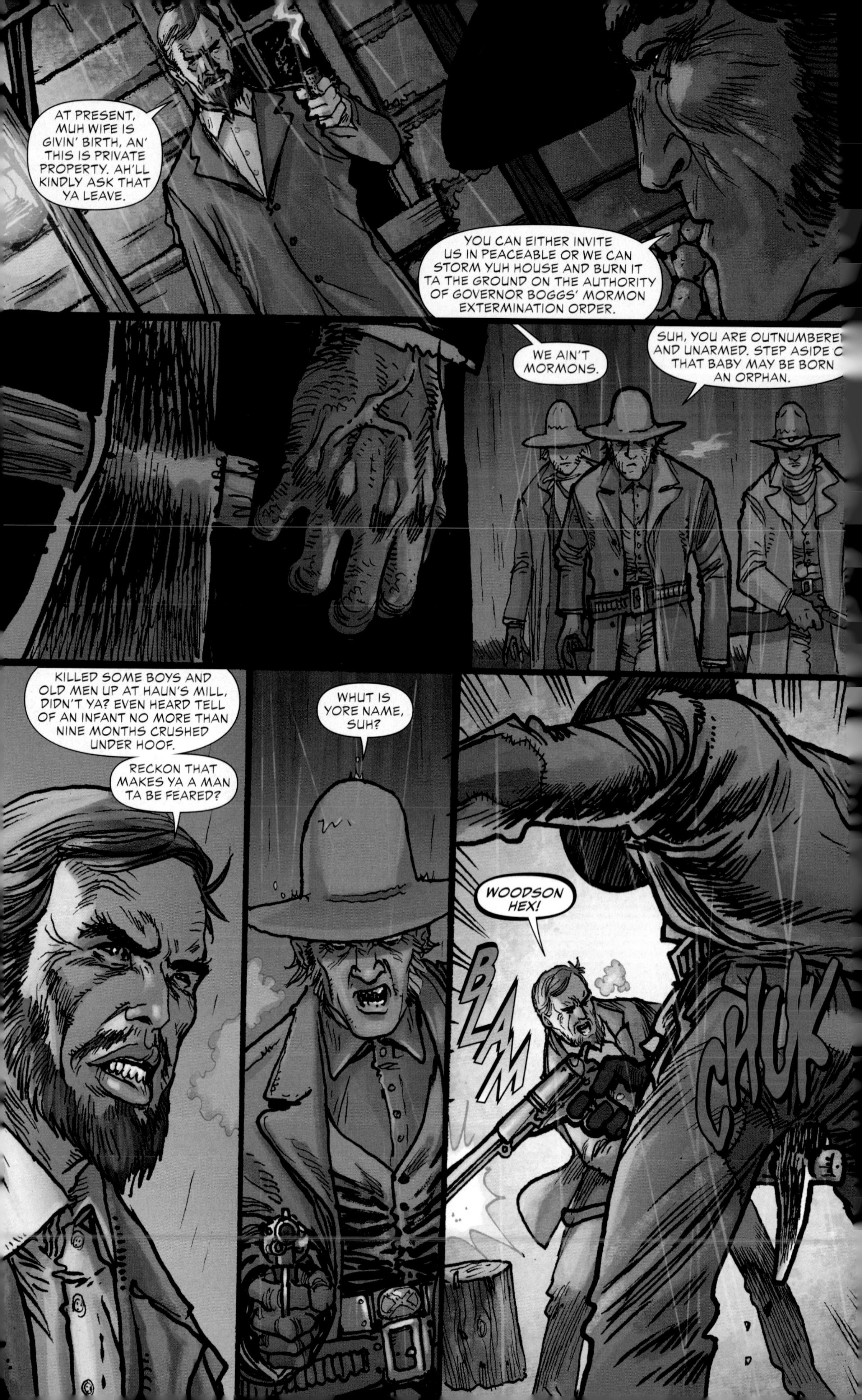
AT PRESENT, MUH WIFE IS GIVIN' BIRTH, AN' THIS IS PRIVATE PROPERTY. AH'LL KINDLY ASK THAT YA LEAVE.
YOU CAN EITHER INVITE US IN PEACEABLE OR WE CAN STORM YUH HOUSE AND BURN IT TA THE GROUND ON THE AUTHORITY OF GOVERNOR BOGGS' MORMON EXTERMINATION ORDER.
WE AIN'T MORMONS.
SUH, YOU ARE OUTNUMBERED AND UNARMED. STEP ASIDE OR THAT BABY MAY BE BORN AN ORPHAN.
KILLED SOME BOYS AND OLD MEN UP AT HAUN'S MILL, DIDN'T YA? EVEN HEARD TELL OF AN INFANT NO MORE THAN NINE MONTHS CRUSHED UNDER HOOF.
RECKON THAT MAKES YA A MAN TA BE FEARED?
WHUT IS YORE NAME, SUH?
WOODSON HEX!
BLAM
CHUK

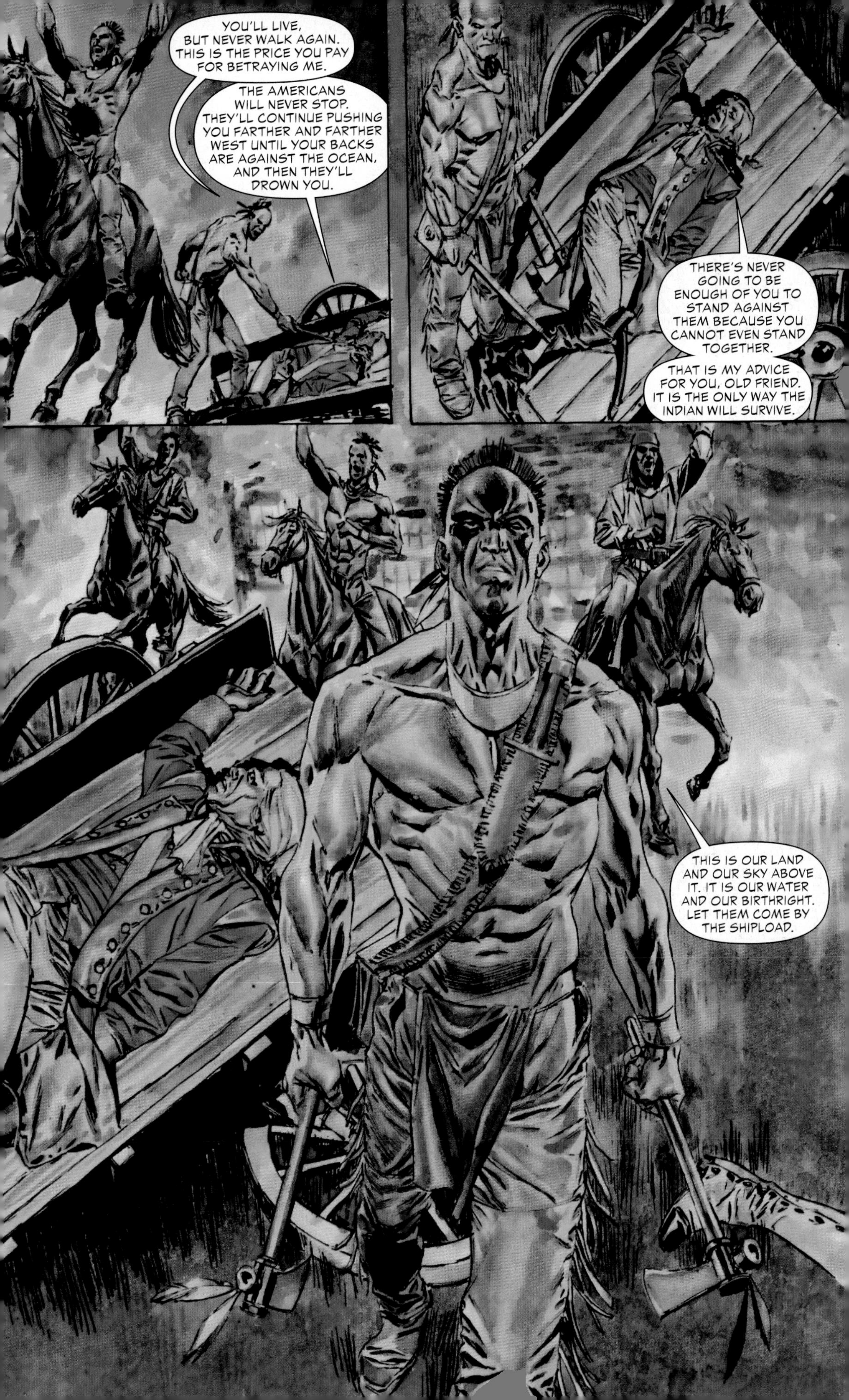
YOU'LL LIVE, BUT NEVER WALK AGAIN. THIS IS THE PRICE YOU PAY FOR BETRAYING ME.
THE AMERICANS WILL NEVER STOP. THEY'LL CONTINUE PUSHING YOU FARTHER AND FARTHER WEST UNTIL YOUR BACKS ARE AGAINST THE OCEAN, AND THEN THEY'LL DROWN YOU.
THERE'S NEVER GOING TO BE ENOUGH OF YOU TO STAND AGAINST THEM BECAUSE YOU CANNOT EVEN STAND TOGETHER.
THAT IS MY ADVICE FOR YOU, OLD FRIEND. IT IS THE ONLY WAY THE INDIAN WILL SURVIVE.
THIS IS OUR LAND AND OUR SKY ABOVE IT. IT IS OUR WATER AND OUR BIRTHRIGHT. LET THEM COME BY THE SHIPLOAD.

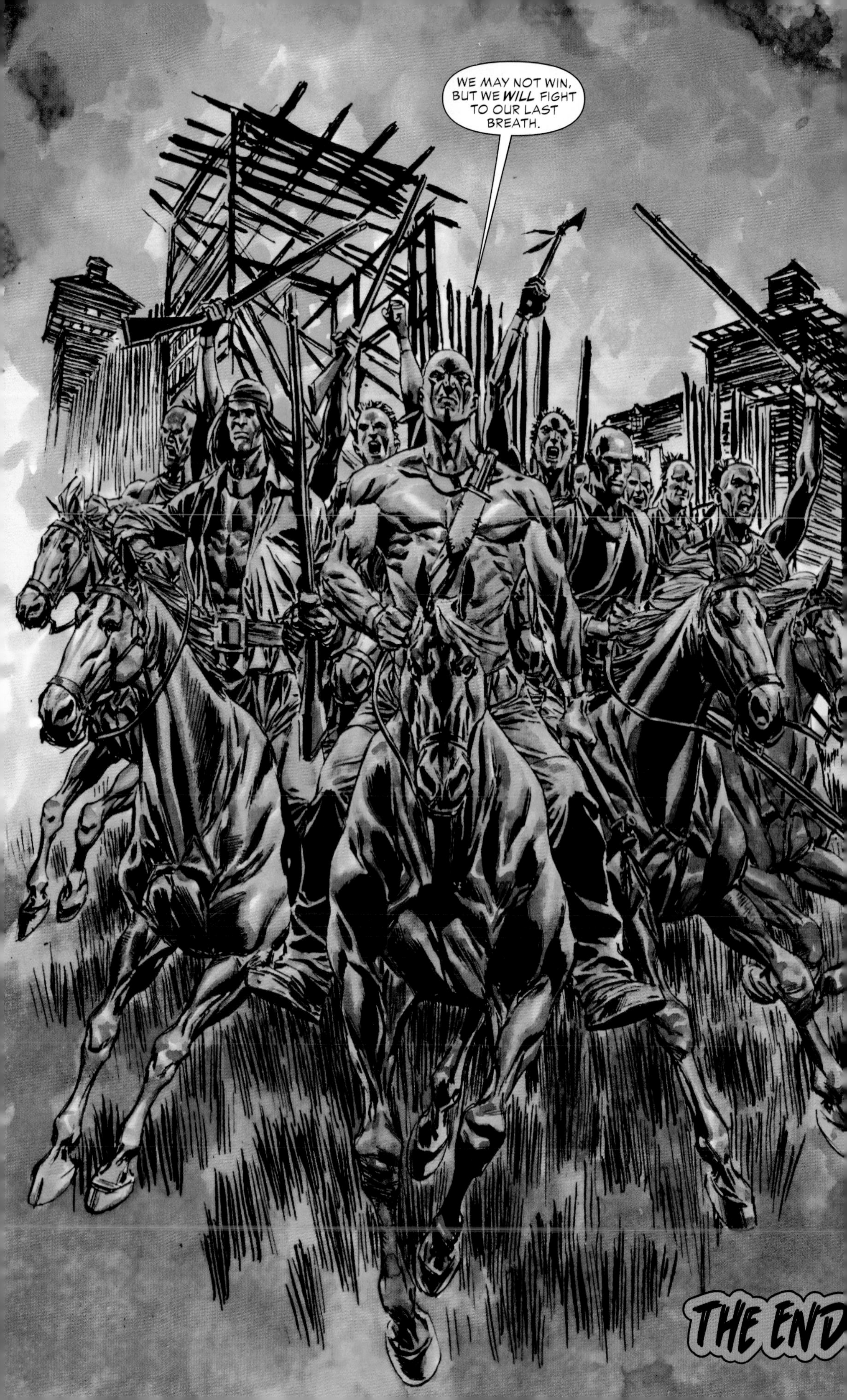
WE MAY NOT WIN, BUT WE *WILL* FIGHT TO OUR LAST BREATH.
THE END

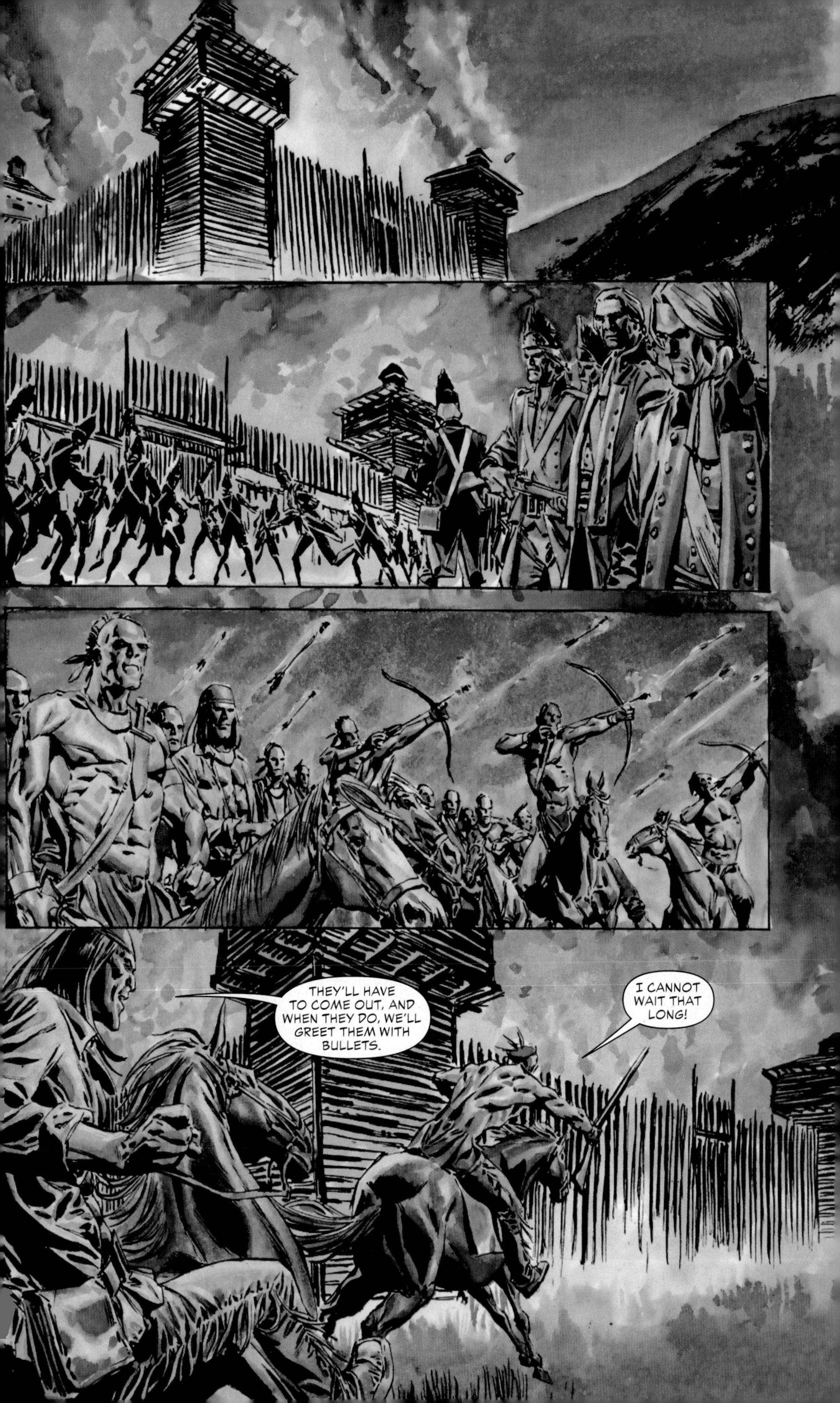
THEY'LL HAVE TO COME OUT, AND WHEN THEY DO, WE'LL GREET THEM WITH BULLETS.
I CANNOT WAIT THAT LONG!

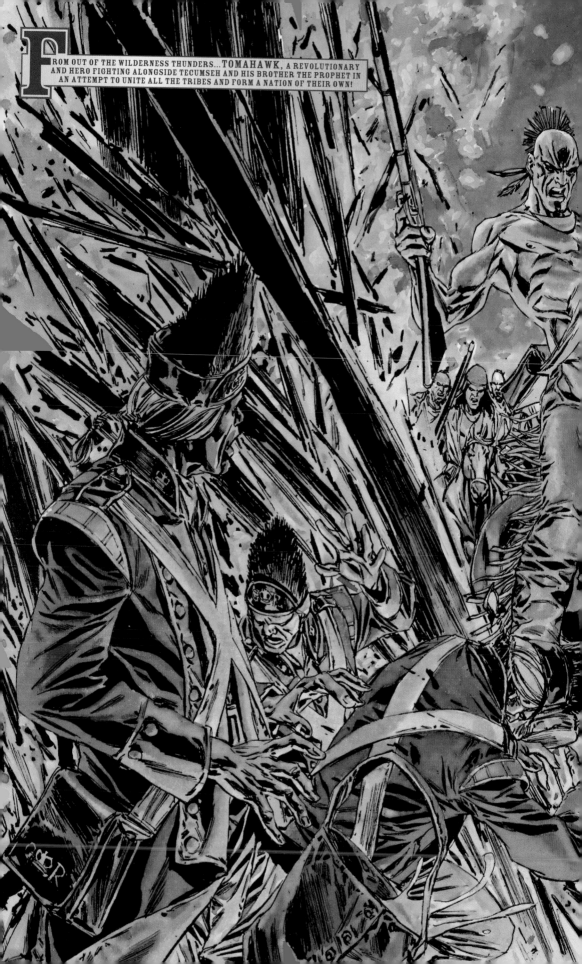

FROM OUT OF THE WILDERNESS THUNDERS...TOMAHAWK, A REVOLUTIONARY AND HERO FIGHTING ALONGSIDE TECUMSEH AND HIS BROTHER THE PROPHET IN AN ATTEMPT TO UNITE ALL THE TRIBES AND FORM A NATION OF THEIR OWN!

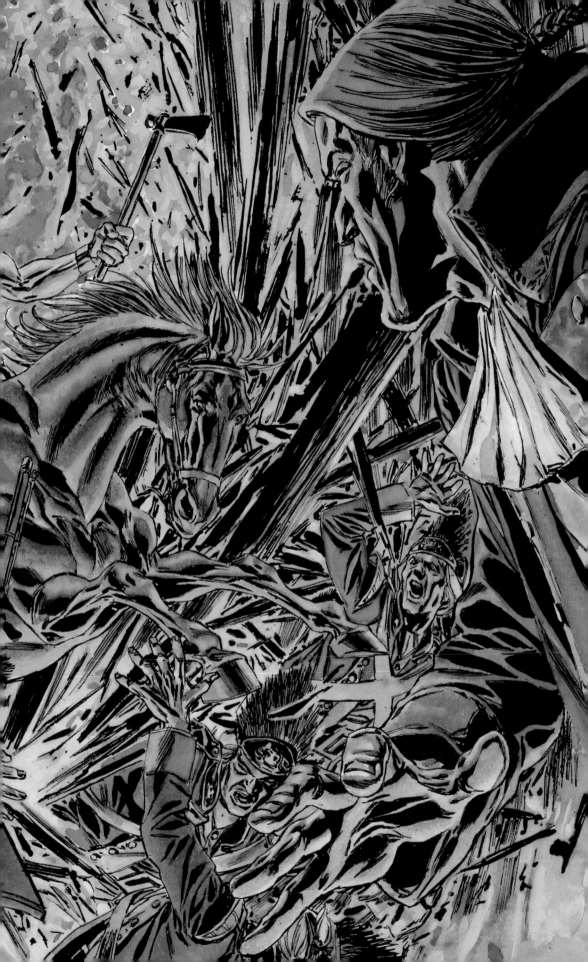

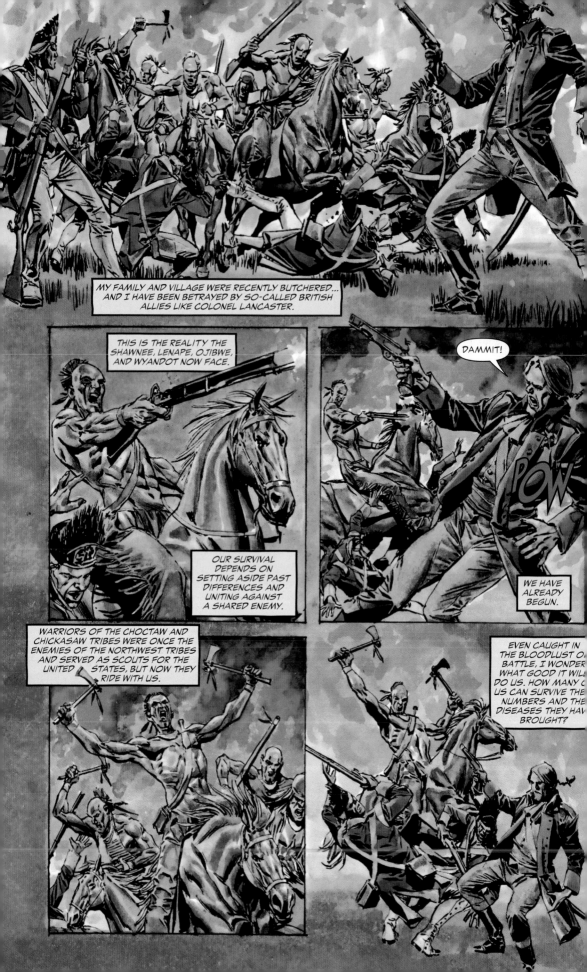

MY FAMILY AND VILLAGE WERE RECENTLY BUTCHERED... AND I HAVE BEEN BETRAYED BY SO-CALLED BRITISH ALLIES LIKE COLONEL LANCASTER.

THIS IS THE REALITY THE SHAWNEE, LENAPE, OJIBWE, AND WYANDOT NOW FACE.

OUR SURVIVAL DEPENDS ON SETTING ASIDE PAST DIFFERENCES AND UNITING AGAINST A SHARED ENEMY.

DAMMIT!

POW

WE HAVE ALREADY BEGUN.

WARRIORS OF THE CHOCTAW AND CHICKASAW TRIBES WERE ONCE THE ENEMIES OF THE NORTHWEST TRIBES AND SERVED AS SCOUTS FOR THE UNITED STATES, BUT NOW THEY RIDE WITH US.

EVEN CAUGHT IN THE BLOODLUST O_ BATTLE, I WONDER_ WHAT GOOD IT WIL_ DO US. HOW MANY _ US CAN SURVIVE THE_ NUMBERS AND THE_ DISEASES THEY HAV_ BROUGHT?

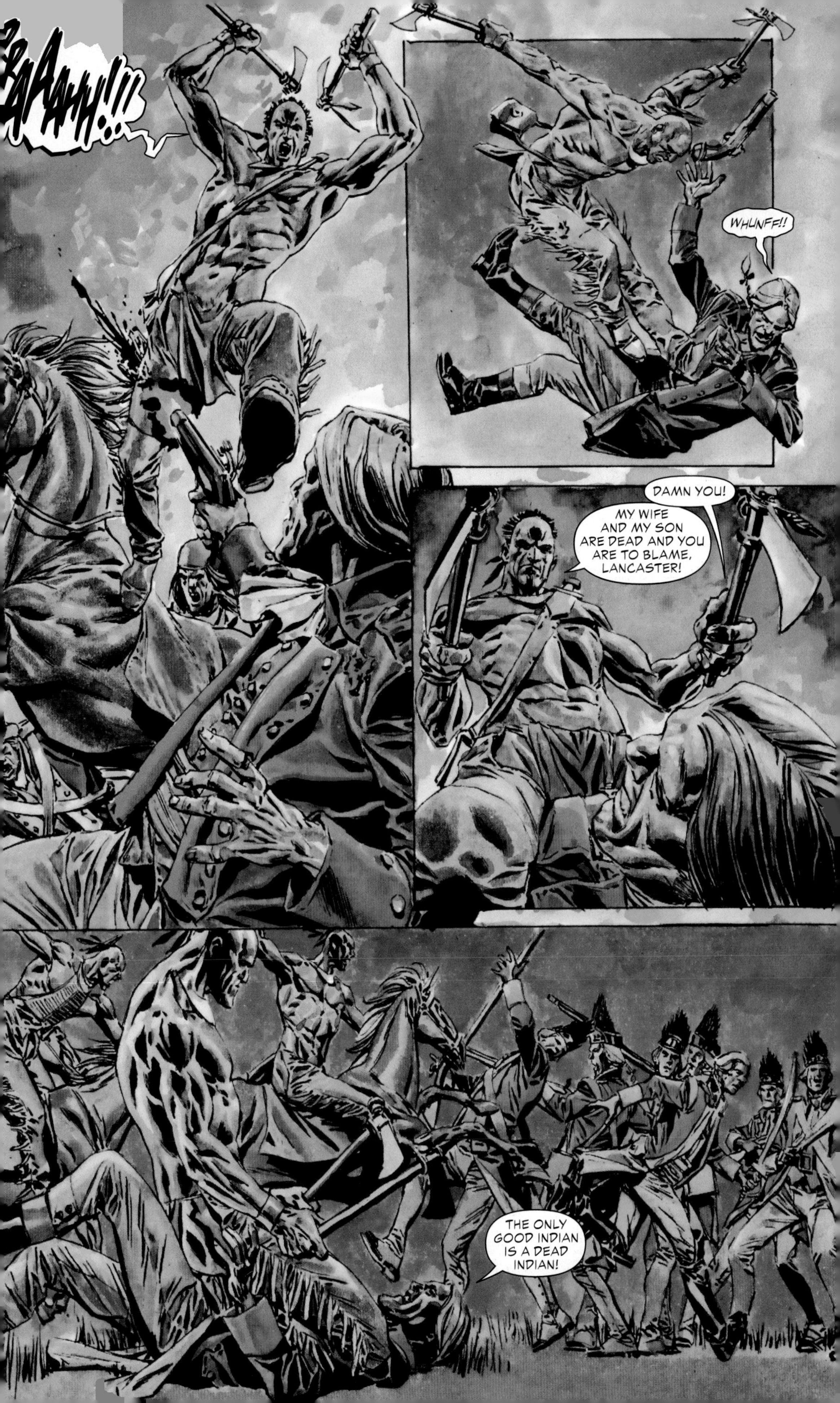

YAAAHH!!!
WHUNFF!!
DAMN YOU!
MY WIFE AND MY SON ARE DEAD AND YOU ARE TO BLAME, LANCASTER!
THE ONLY GOOD INDIAN IS A DEAD INDIAN!

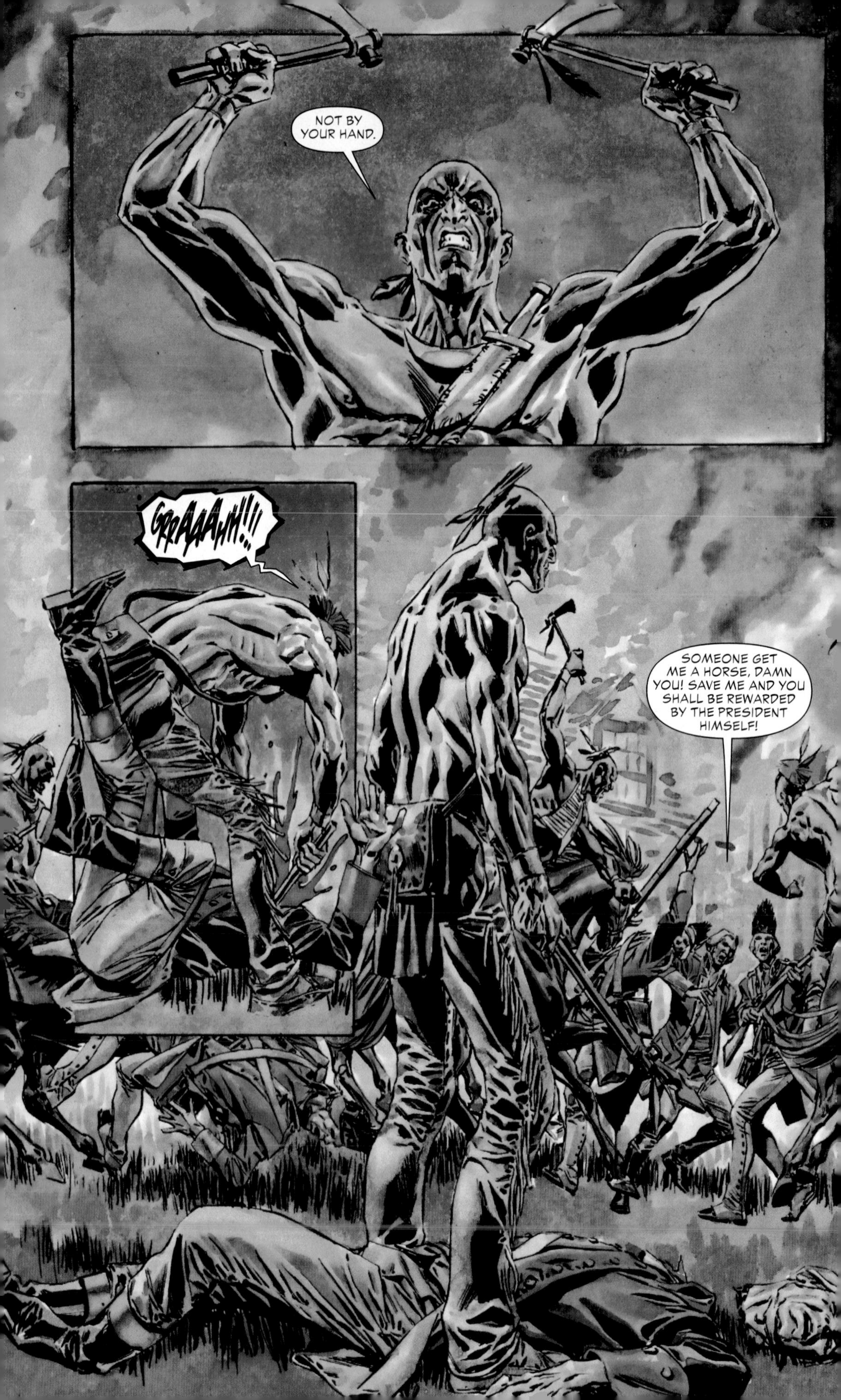
NOT BY YOUR HAND.
GRRAAAAHH!!!
SOMEONE GET ME A HORSE, DAMN YOU! SAVE ME AND YOU SHALL BE REWARDED BY THE PRESIDENT HIMSELF!

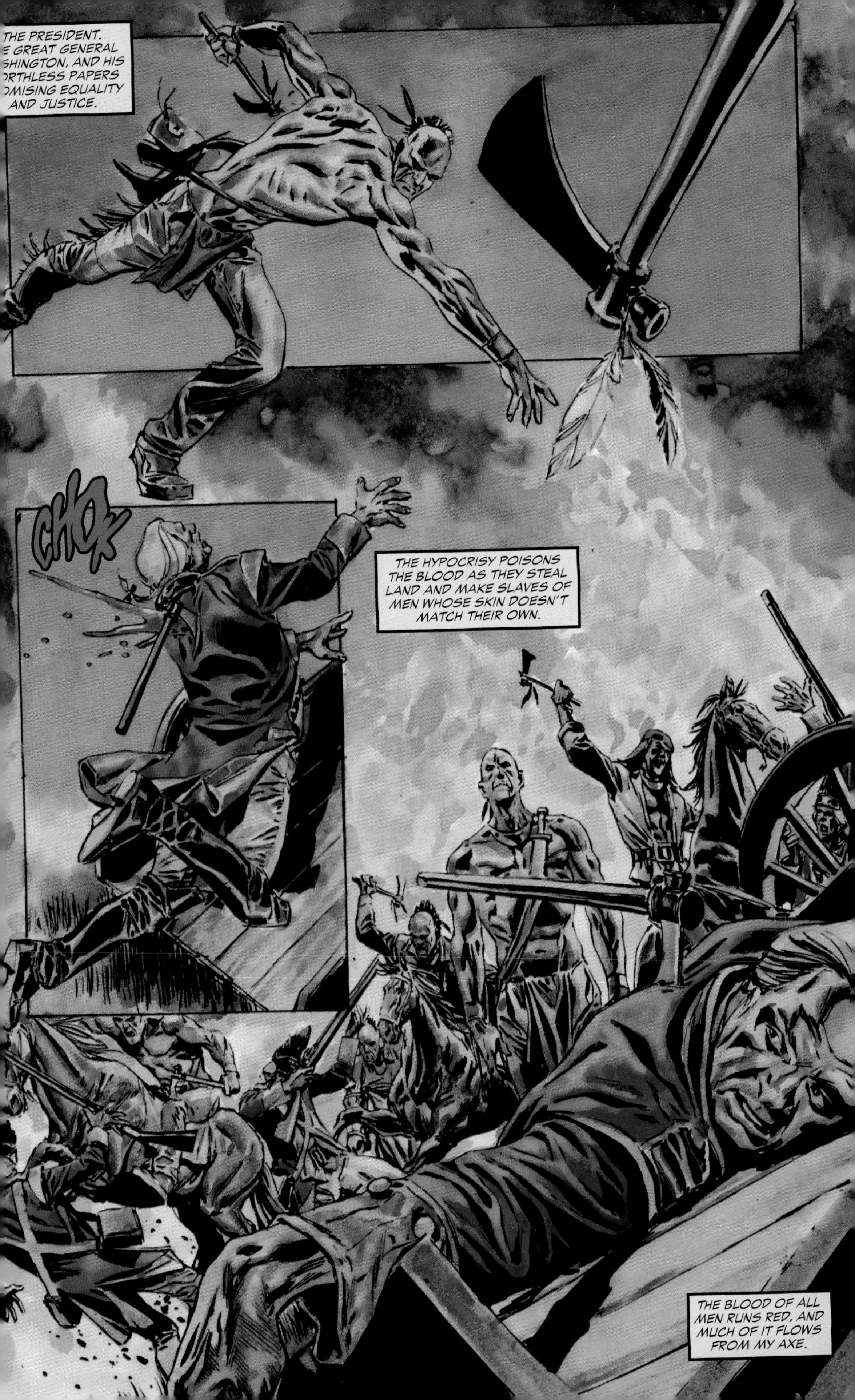
THE PRESIDENT.
E GREAT GENERAL
SHINGTON, AND HIS
ORTHLESS PAPERS
OMISING EQUALITY
AND JUSTICE.
CHOK
THE HYPOCRISY POISONS THE BLOOD AS THEY STEAL LAND AND MAKE SLAVES OF MEN WHOSE SKIN DOESN'T MATCH THEIR OWN.
THE BLOOD OF ALL MEN RUNS RED, AND MUCH OF IT FLOWS FROM MY AXE.

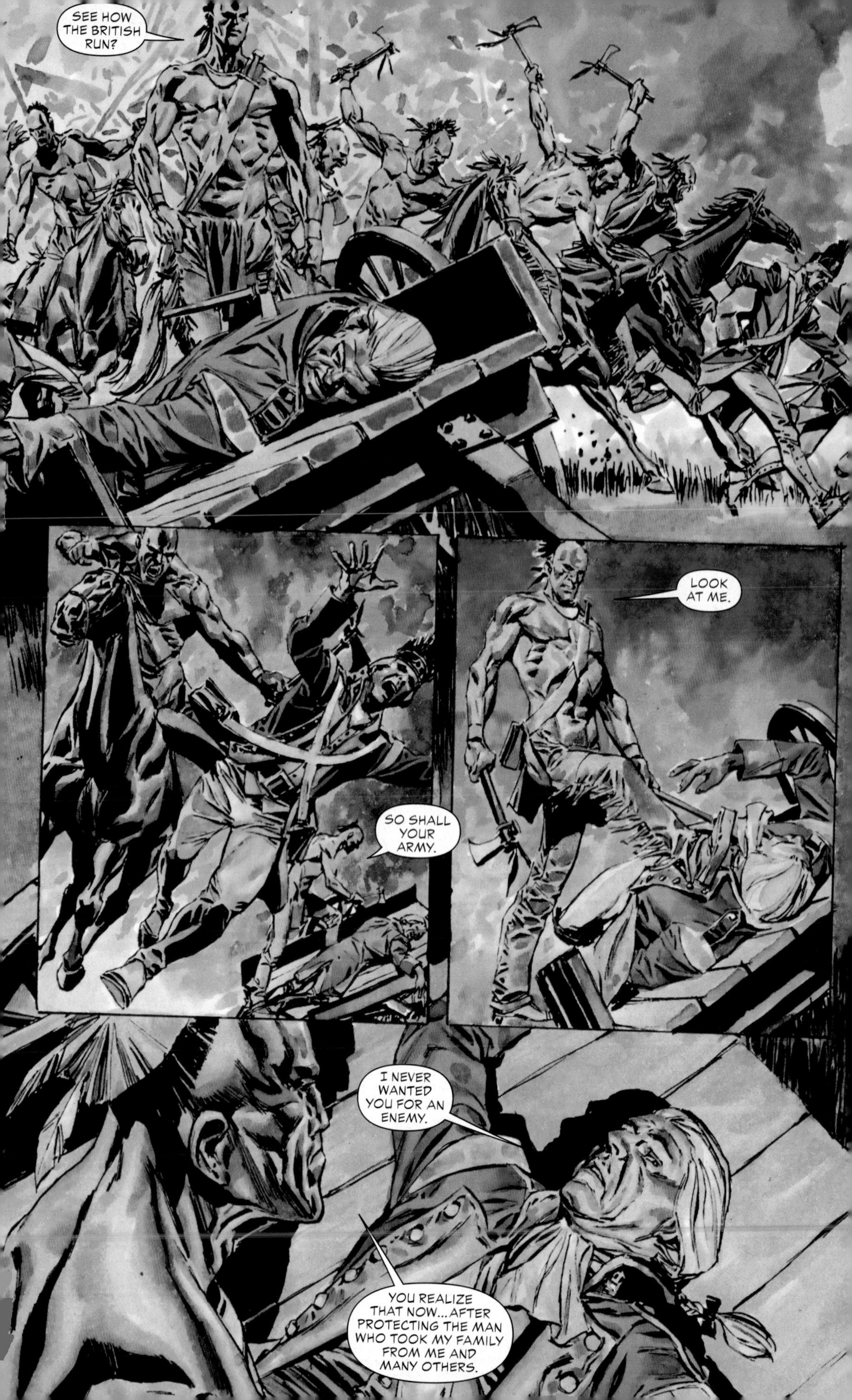
SEE HOW THE BRITISH RUN?
SO SHALL YOUR ARMY.
LOOK AT ME.
I NEVER WANTED YOU FOR AN ENEMY.
YOU REALIZE THAT NOW... AFTER PROTECTING THE MAN WHO TOOK MY FAMILY FROM ME AND MANY OTHERS.

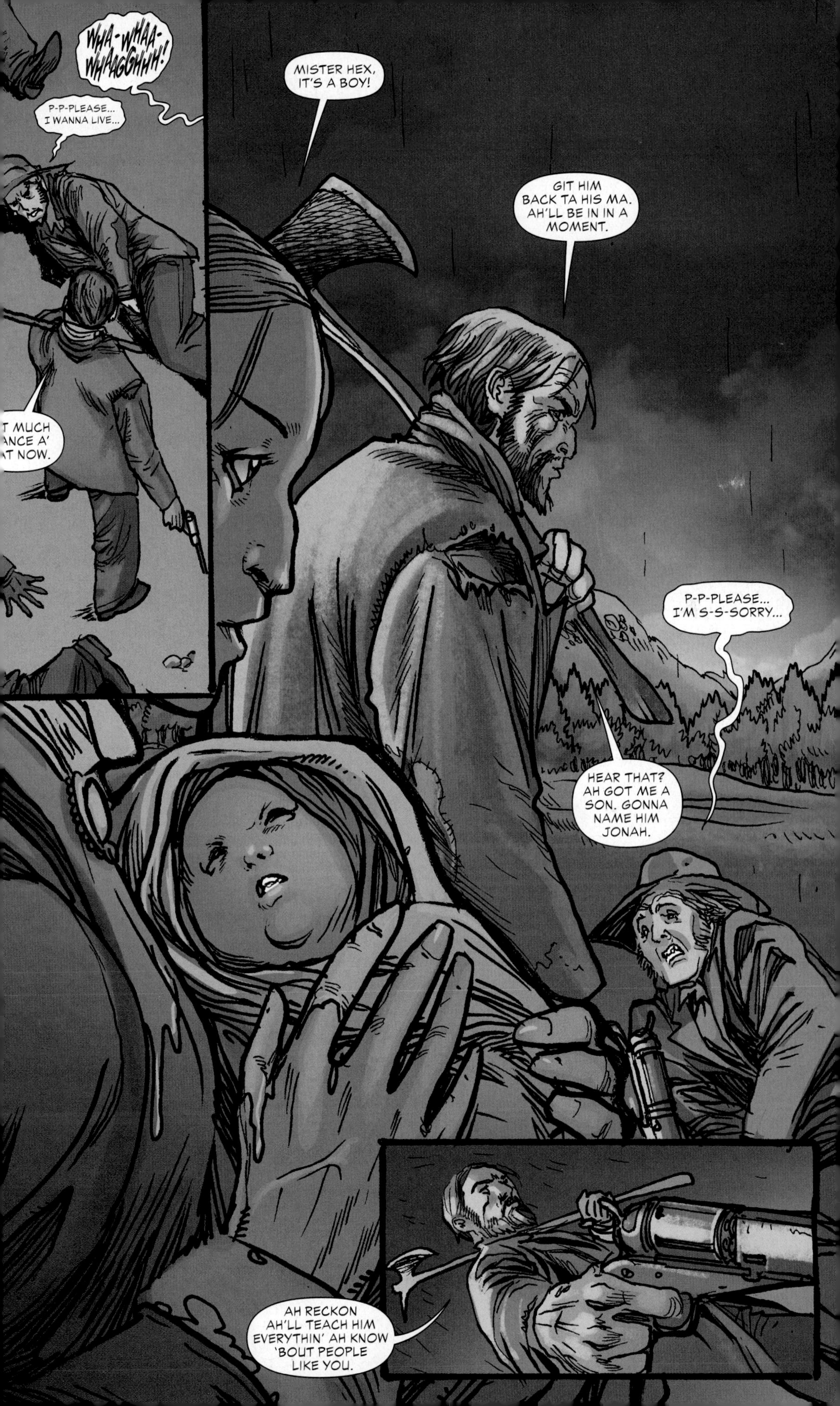
WHA-WHAA-WHAAGHHH!
P-P-PLEASE... I WANNA LIVE...
T MUCH ANCE A' AT NOW.
MISTER HEX, IT'S A BOY!
GIT HIM BACK TA HIS MA. AH'LL BE IN IN A MOMENT.
P-P-PLEASE... I'M S-S-SORRY...
HEAR THAT? AH GOT ME A SON. GONNA NAME HIM JONAH.
AH RECKON AH'LL TEACH HIM EVERYTHIN' AH KNOW 'BOUT PEOPLE LIKE YOU.

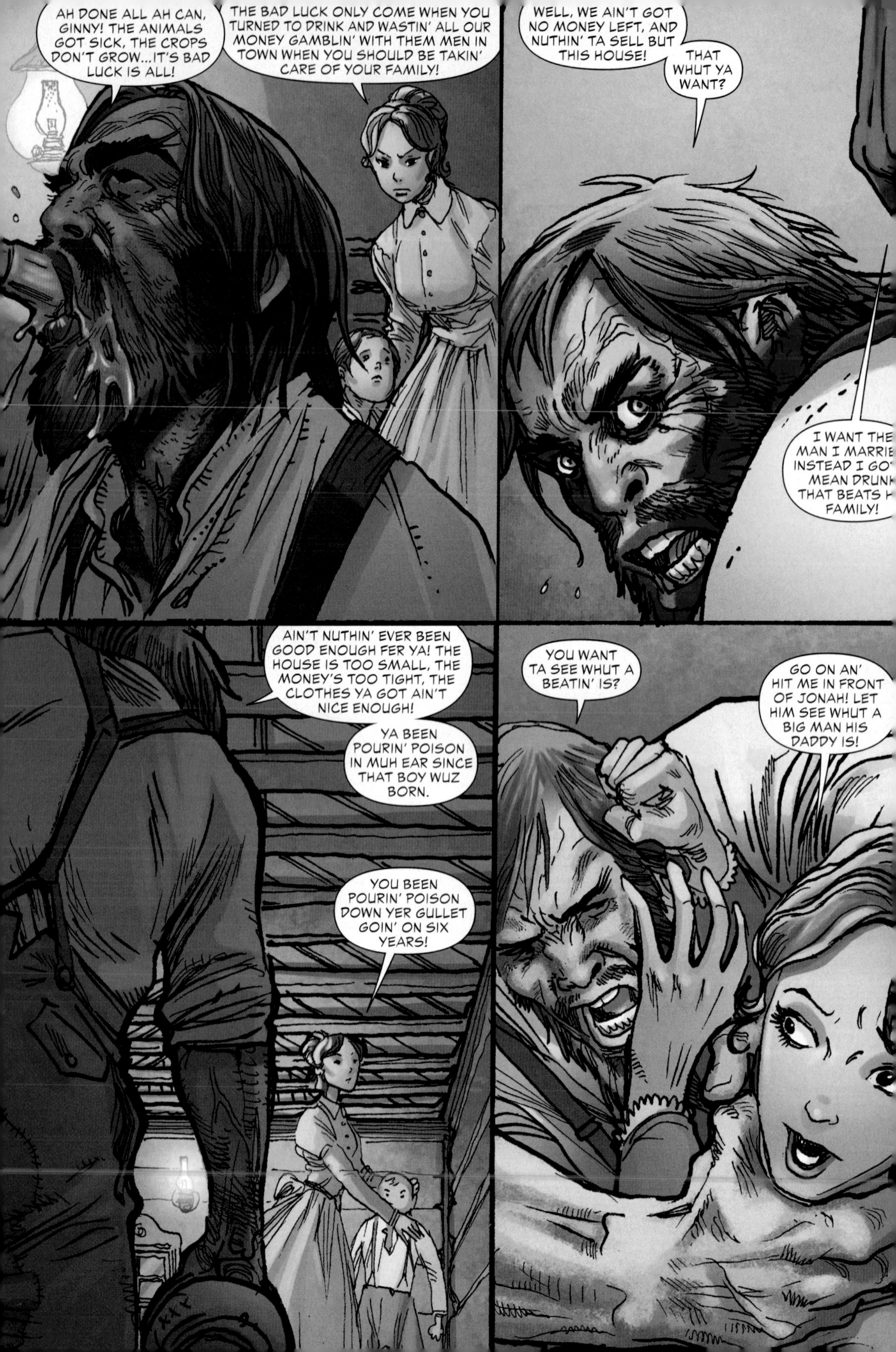
AH DONE ALL AH CAN, GINNY! THE ANIMALS GOT SICK, THE CROPS DON'T GROW...IT'S BAD LUCK IS ALL!
THE BAD LUCK ONLY COME WHEN YOU TURNED TO DRINK AND WASTIN' ALL OUR MONEY GAMBLIN' WITH THEM MEN IN TOWN WHEN YOU SHOULD BE TAKIN' CARE OF YOUR FAMILY!
WELL, WE AIN'T GOT NO MONEY LEFT, AND NUTHIN' TA SELL BUT THIS HOUSE!
THAT WHUT YA WANT?
I WANT THE MAN I MARRIE INSTEAD I GOT MEAN DRUNK THAT BEATS H FAMILY!
AIN'T NUTHIN' EVER BEEN GOOD ENOUGH FER YA! THE HOUSE IS TOO SMALL, THE MONEY'S TOO TIGHT, THE CLOTHES YA GOT AIN'T NICE ENOUGH!
YA BEEN POURIN' POISON IN MUH EAR SINCE THAT BOY WUZ BORN.
YOU BEEN POURIN' POISON DOWN YER GULLET GOIN' ON SIX YEARS!
YOU WANT TA SEE WHUT A BEATIN' IS?
GO ON AN' HIT ME IN FRONT OF JONAH! LET HIM SEE WHUT A BIG MAN HIS DADDY IS!

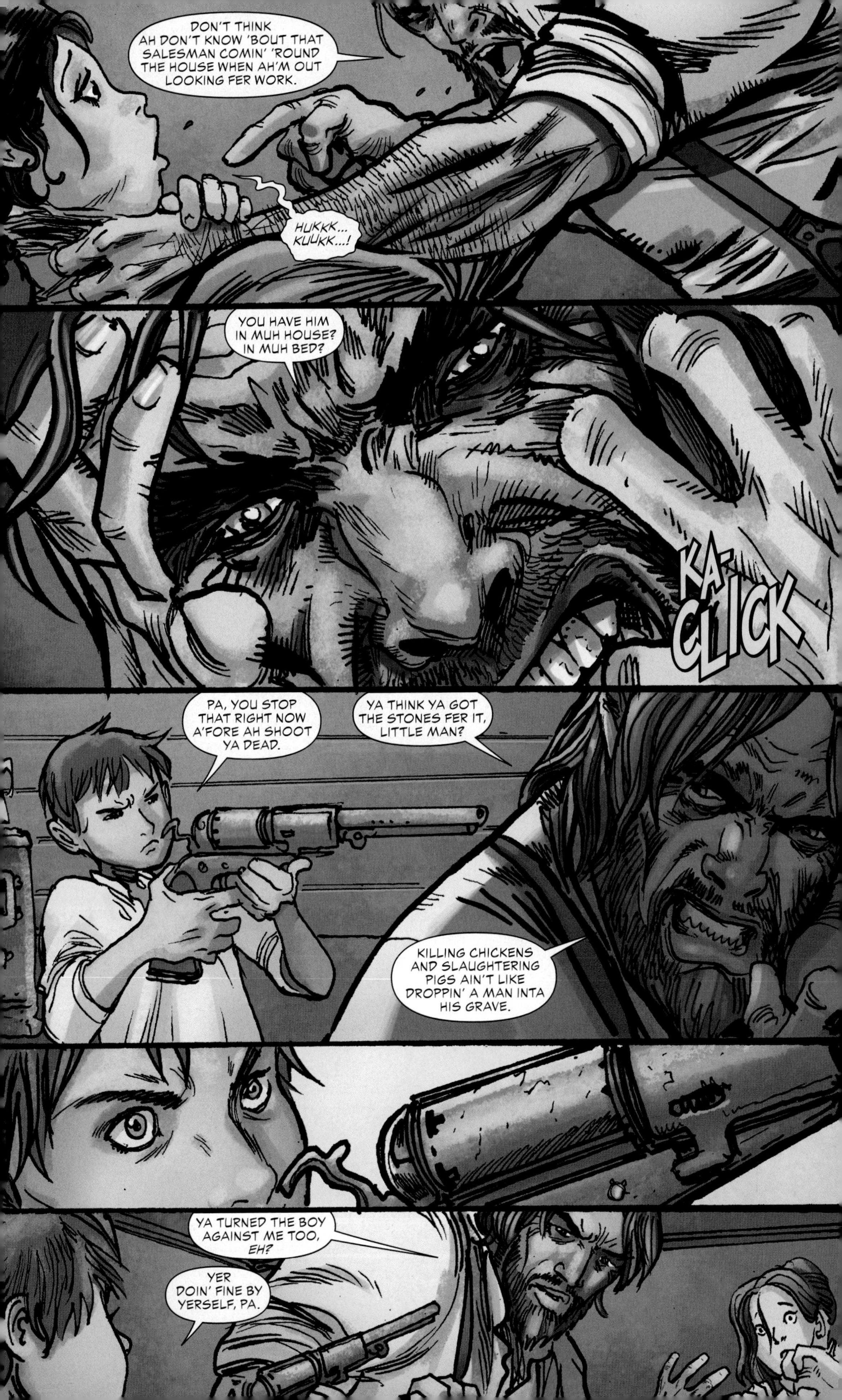
DON'T THINK AH DON'T KNOW 'BOUT THAT SALESMAN COMIN' 'ROUND THE HOUSE WHEN AH'M OUT LOOKING FER WORK.
HUKKK... KUUKK...!
YOU HAVE HIM IN MUH HOUSE? IN MUH BED?
KA-CLICK
PA, YOU STOP THAT RIGHT NOW A'FORE AH SHOOT YA DEAD.
YA THINK YA GOT THE STONES FER IT, LITTLE MAN?
KILLING CHICKENS AND SLAUGHTERING PIGS AIN'T LIKE DROPPIN' A MAN INTA HIS GRAVE.
YA TURNED THE BOY AGAINST ME TOO, EH?
YER DOIN' FINE BY YERSELF, PA.

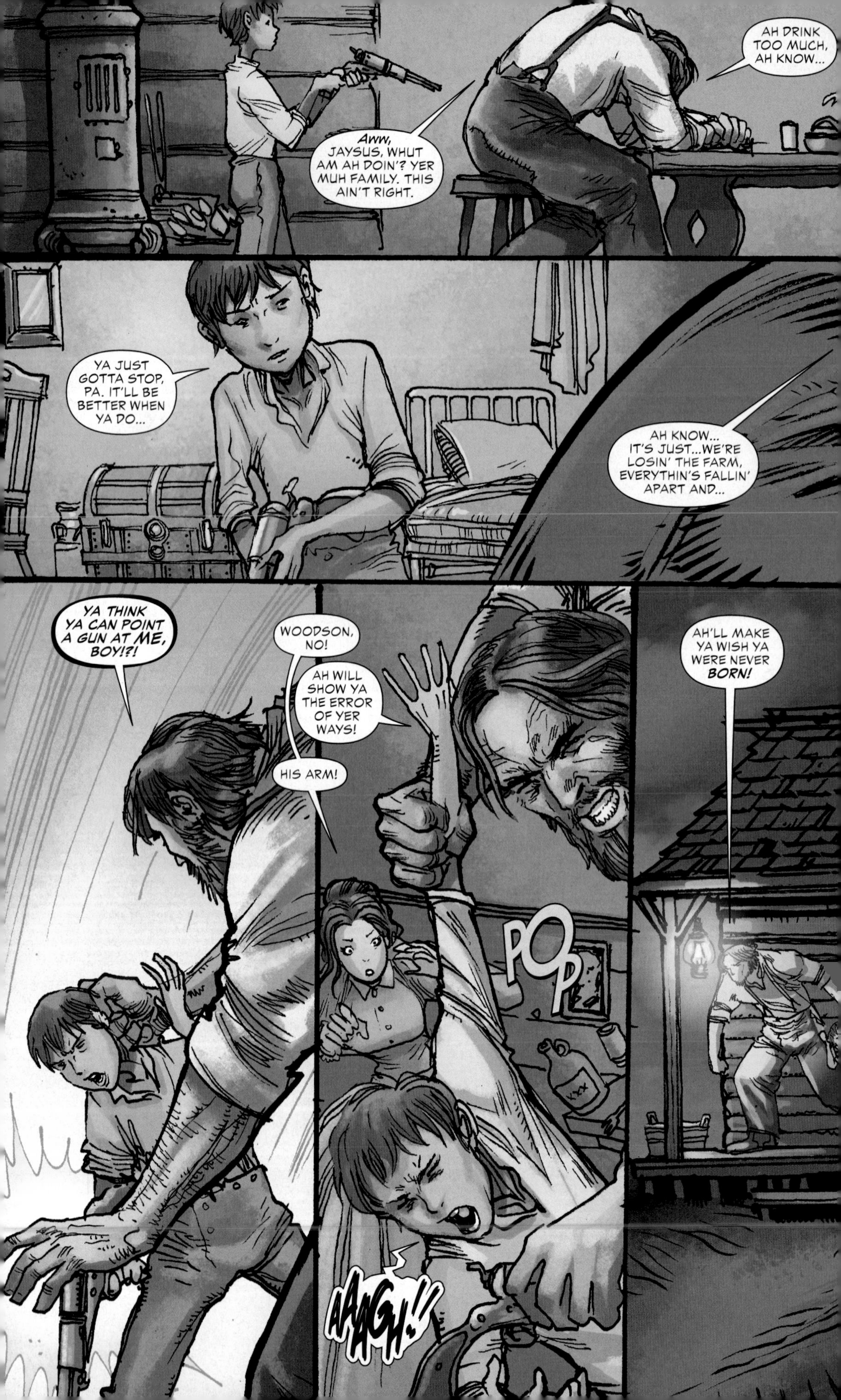

AH DRINK TOO MUCH, AH KNOW...
AWW, JAYSUS, WHUT AM AH DOIN'? YER MUH FAMILY. THIS AIN'T RIGHT.
YA JUST GOTTA STOP, PA. IT'LL BE BETTER WHEN YA DO...
AH KNOW... IT'S JUST...WE'RE LOSIN' THE FARM, EVERYTHIN'S FALLIN' APART AND...
YA THINK YA CAN POINT A GUN AT *ME*, BOY!?!
WOODSON, NO!
AH WILL SHOW YA THE ERROR OF YER WAYS!
HIS ARM!
POP
AAAAGH!!
AH'LL MAKE YA WISH YA WERE NEVER *BORN!*

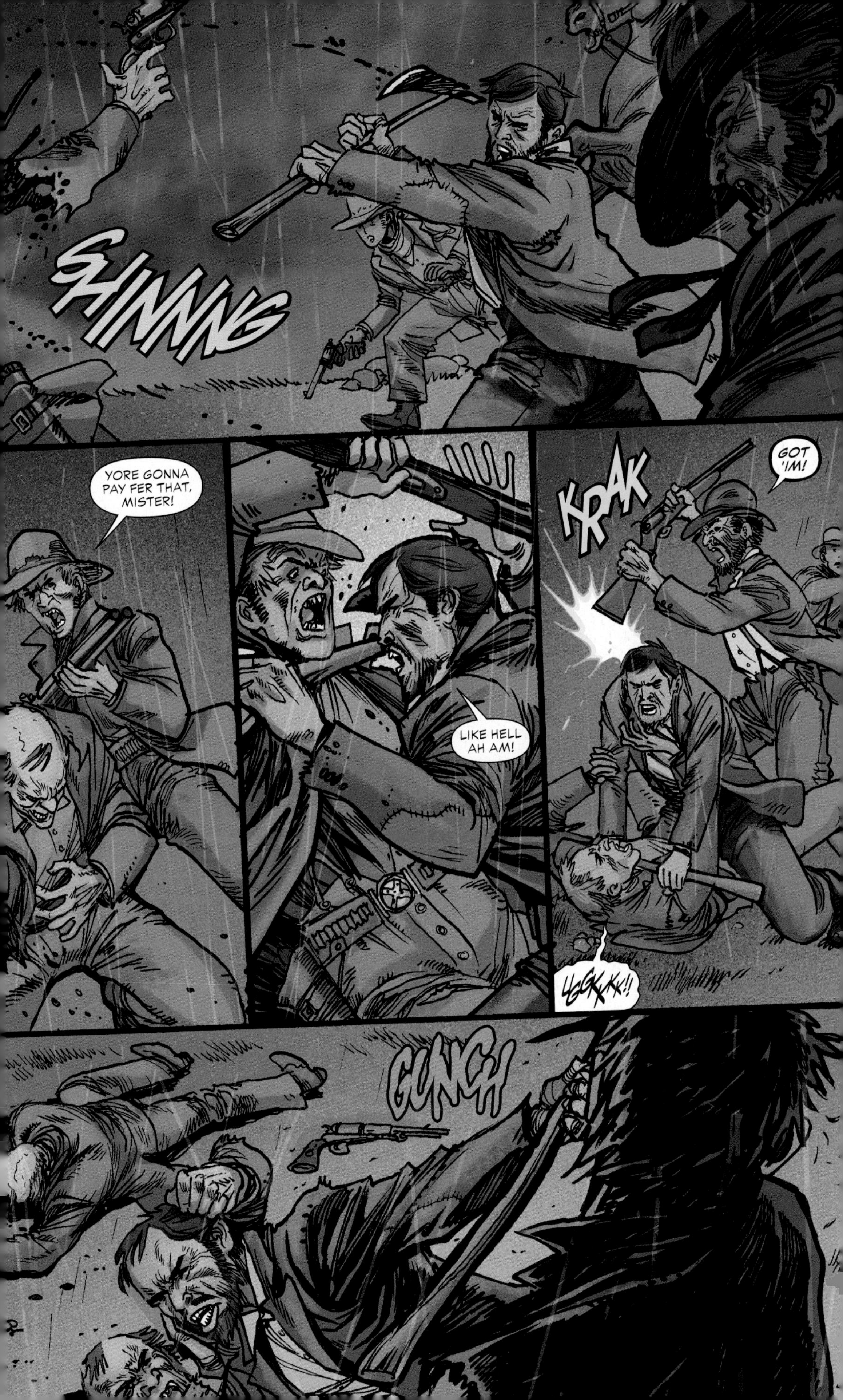
SHINNNG
YORE GONNA PAY FER THAT, MISTER!
LIKE HELL AH AM!
KRAK
GOT 'IM!
UGGKKK!!
GUNCH

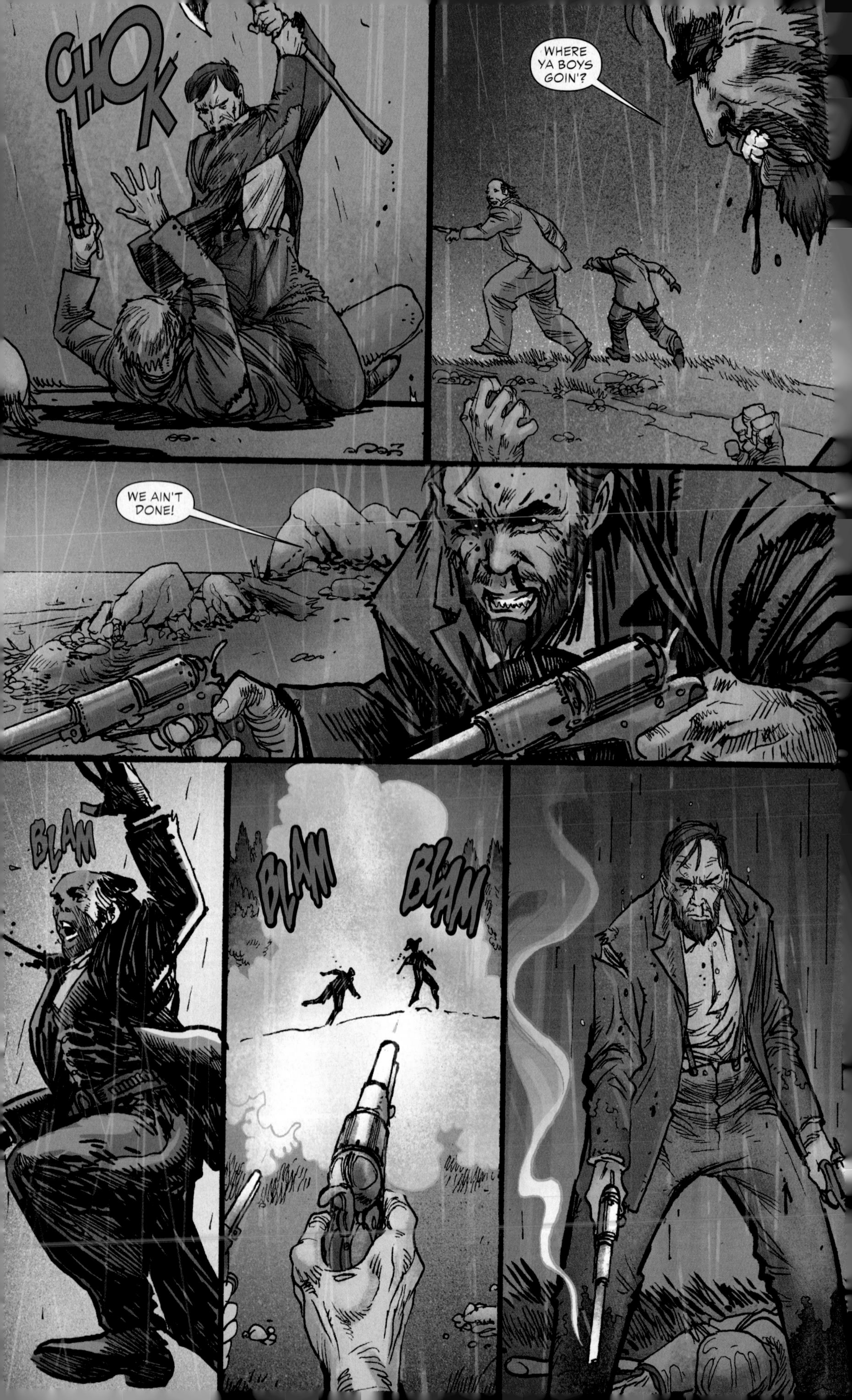
CHOK
WHERE YA BOYS GOIN'?
WE AIN'T DONE!
BLAM
BLAM
BLAM

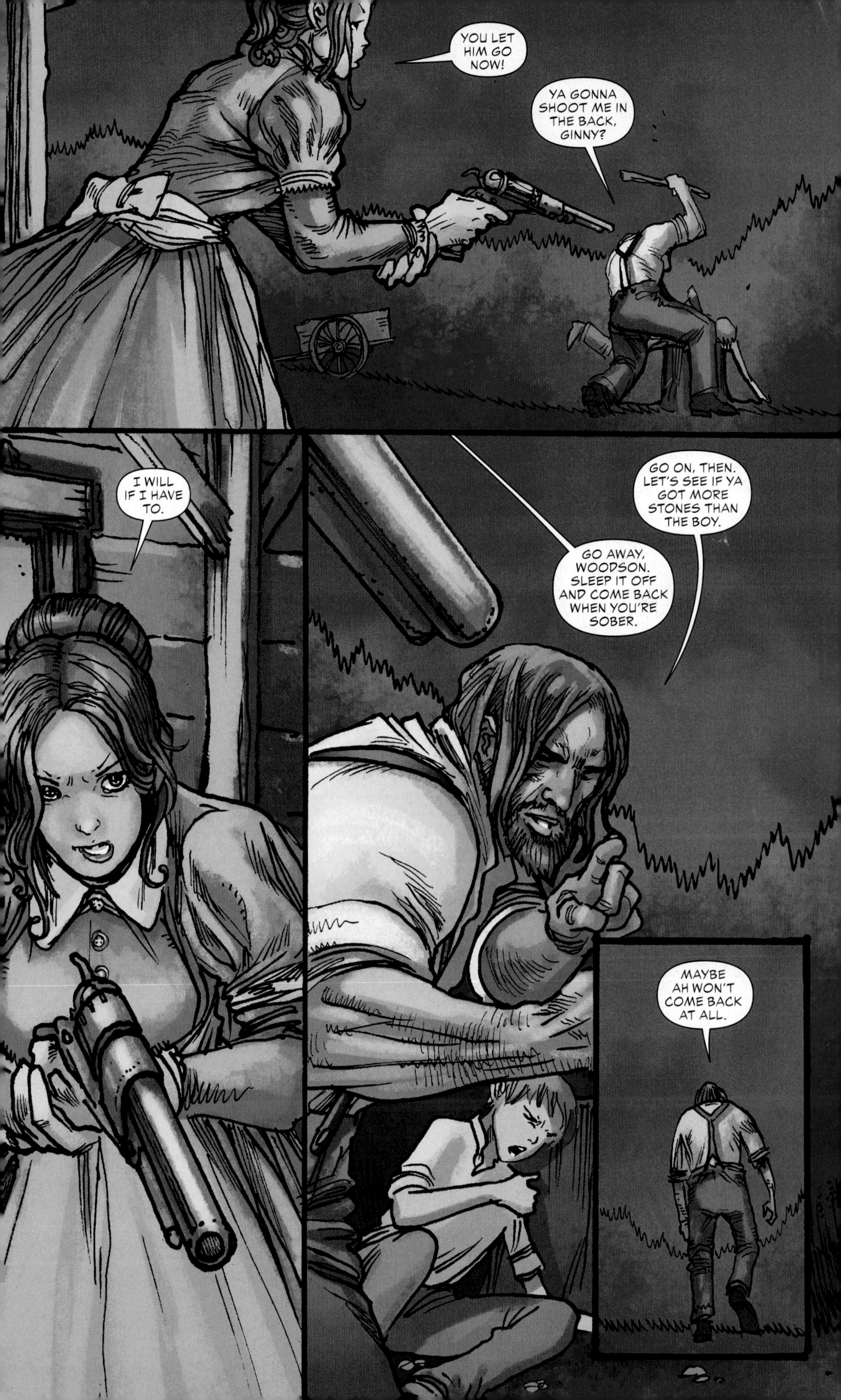
YOU LET HIM GO NOW!
YA GONNA SHOOT ME IN THE BACK, GINNY?
I WILL IF I HAVE TO.
GO ON, THEN. LET'S SEE IF YA GOT MORE STONES THAN THE BOY.
GO AWAY, WOODSON. SLEEP IT OFF AND COME BACK WHEN YOU'RE SOBER.
MAYBE AH WON'T COME BACK AT ALL.

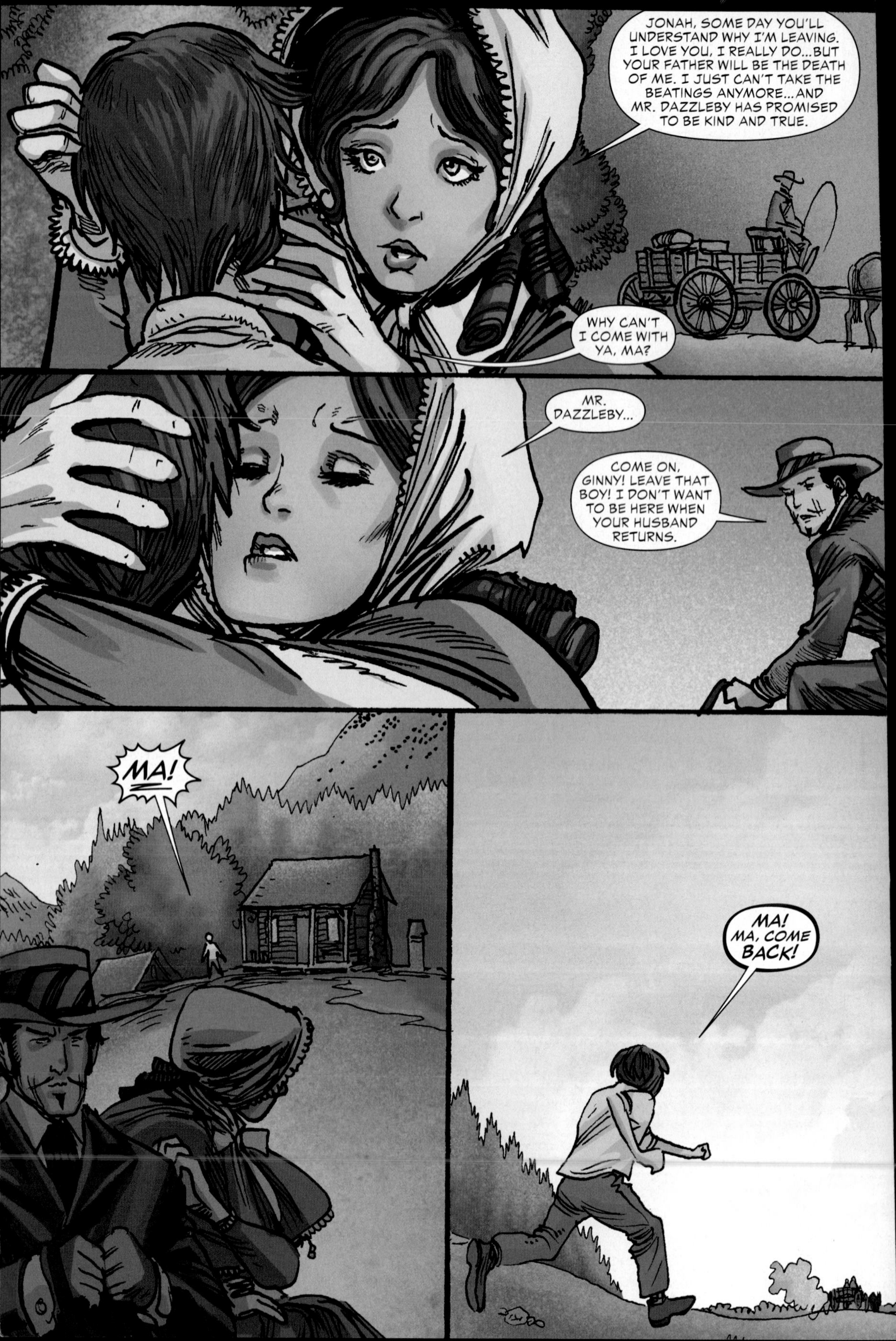
JONAH, SOME DAY YOU'LL UNDERSTAND WHY I'M LEAVING. I LOVE YOU, I REALLY DO...BUT YOUR FATHER WILL BE THE DEATH OF ME. I JUST CAN'T TAKE THE BEATINGS ANYMORE...AND MR. DAZZLEBY HAS PROMISED TO BE KIND AND TRUE.
WHY CAN'T I COME WITH YA, MA?
MR. DAZZLEBY...
COME ON, GINNY! LEAVE THAT BOY! I DON'T WANT TO BE HERE WHEN YOUR HUSBAND RETURNS.
MA!
MA! MA, COME BACK!

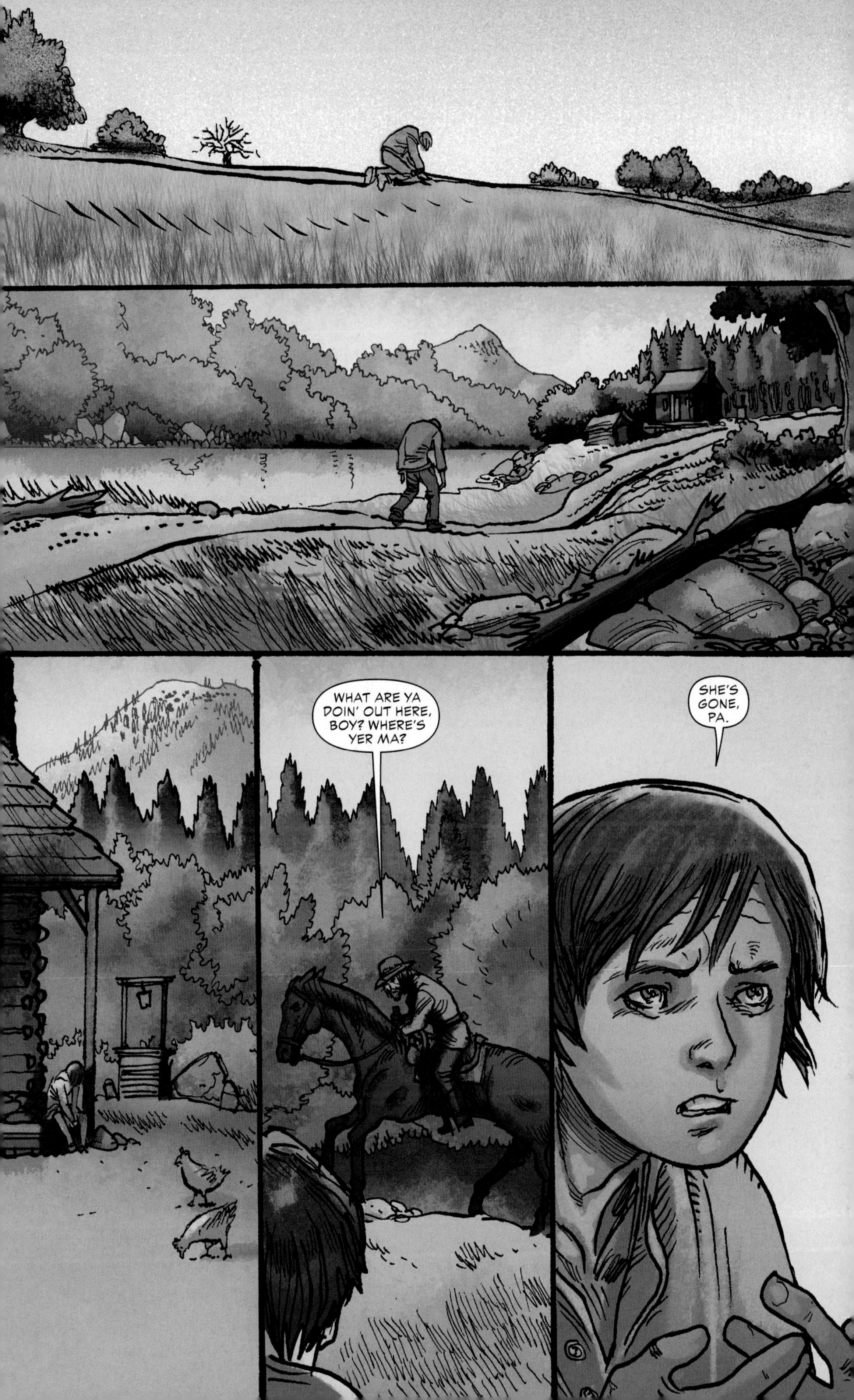
WHAT ARE YA DOIN' OUT HERE, BOY? WHERE'S YER MA?
SHE'S GONE, PA.

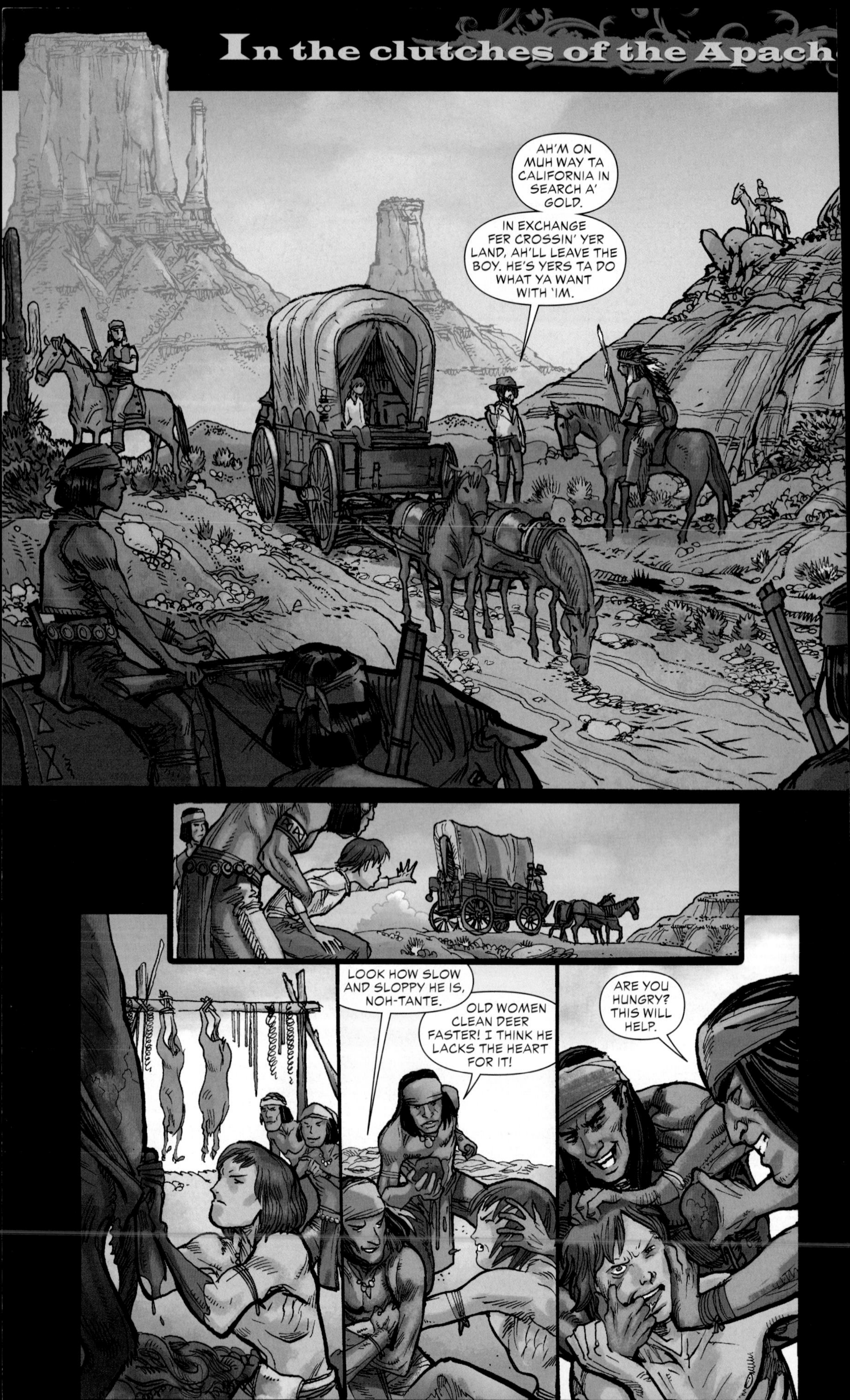
In the clutches of the Apach
AH'M ON MUH WAY TA CALIFORNIA IN SEARCH A' GOLD.
IN EXCHANGE FER CROSSIN' YER LAND, AH'LL LEAVE THE BOY. HE'S YERS TA DO WHAT YA WANT WITH 'IM.
LOOK HOW SLOW AND SLOPPY HE IS, NOH-TANTE.
OLD WOMEN CLEAN DEER FASTER! I THINK HE LACKS THE HEART FOR IT!
ARE YOU HUNGRY? THIS WILL HELP.

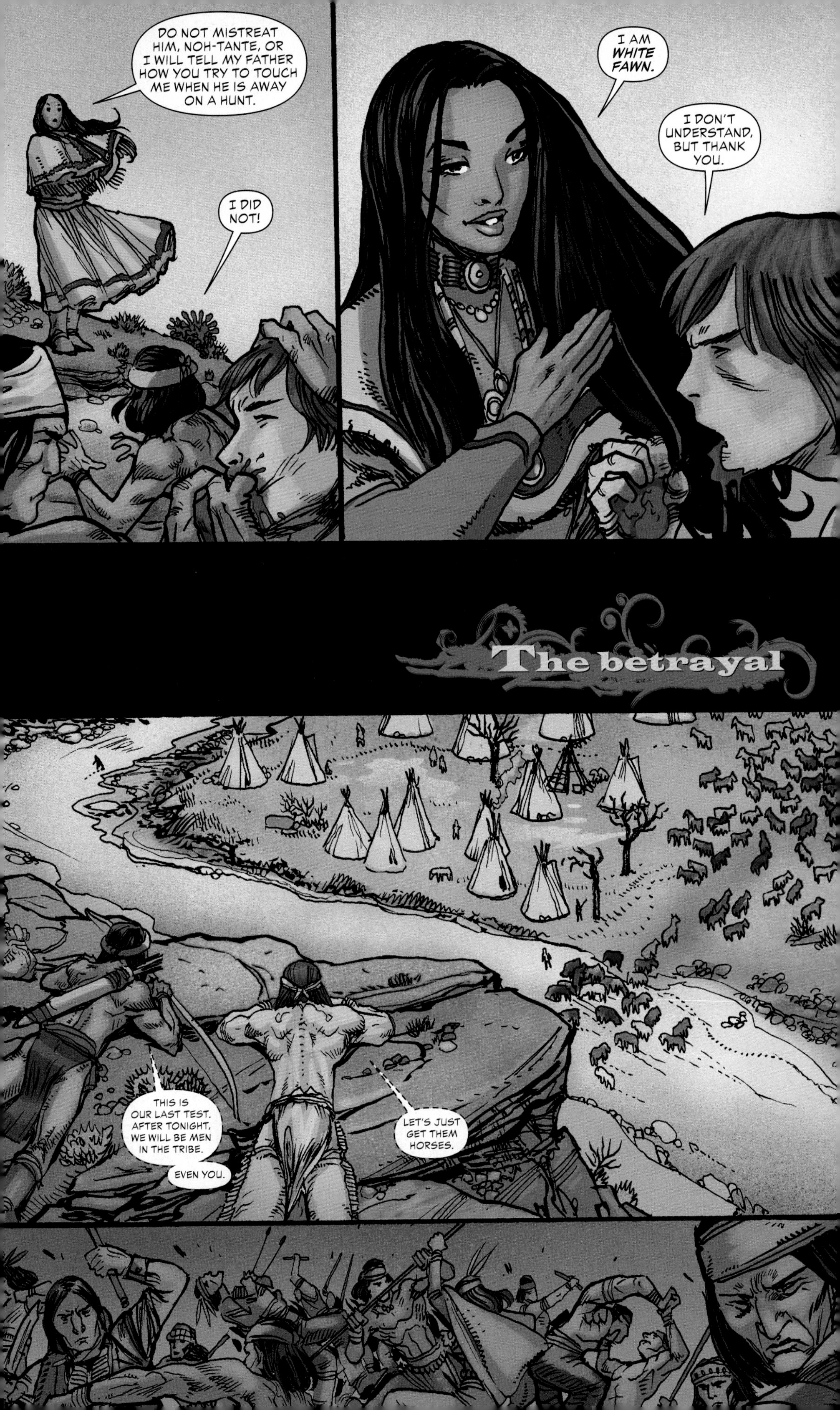
DO NOT MISTREAT HIM, NOH-TANTE, OR I WILL TELL MY FATHER HOW YOU TRY TO TOUCH ME WHEN HE IS AWAY ON A HUNT.
I DID NOT!
I AM WHITE FAWN.
I DON'T UNDERSTAND, BUT THANK YOU.
The betrayal
THIS IS OUR LAST TEST. AFTER TONIGHT, WE WILL BE MEN IN THE TRIBE.
EVEN YOU.
LET'S JUST GET THEM HORSES.

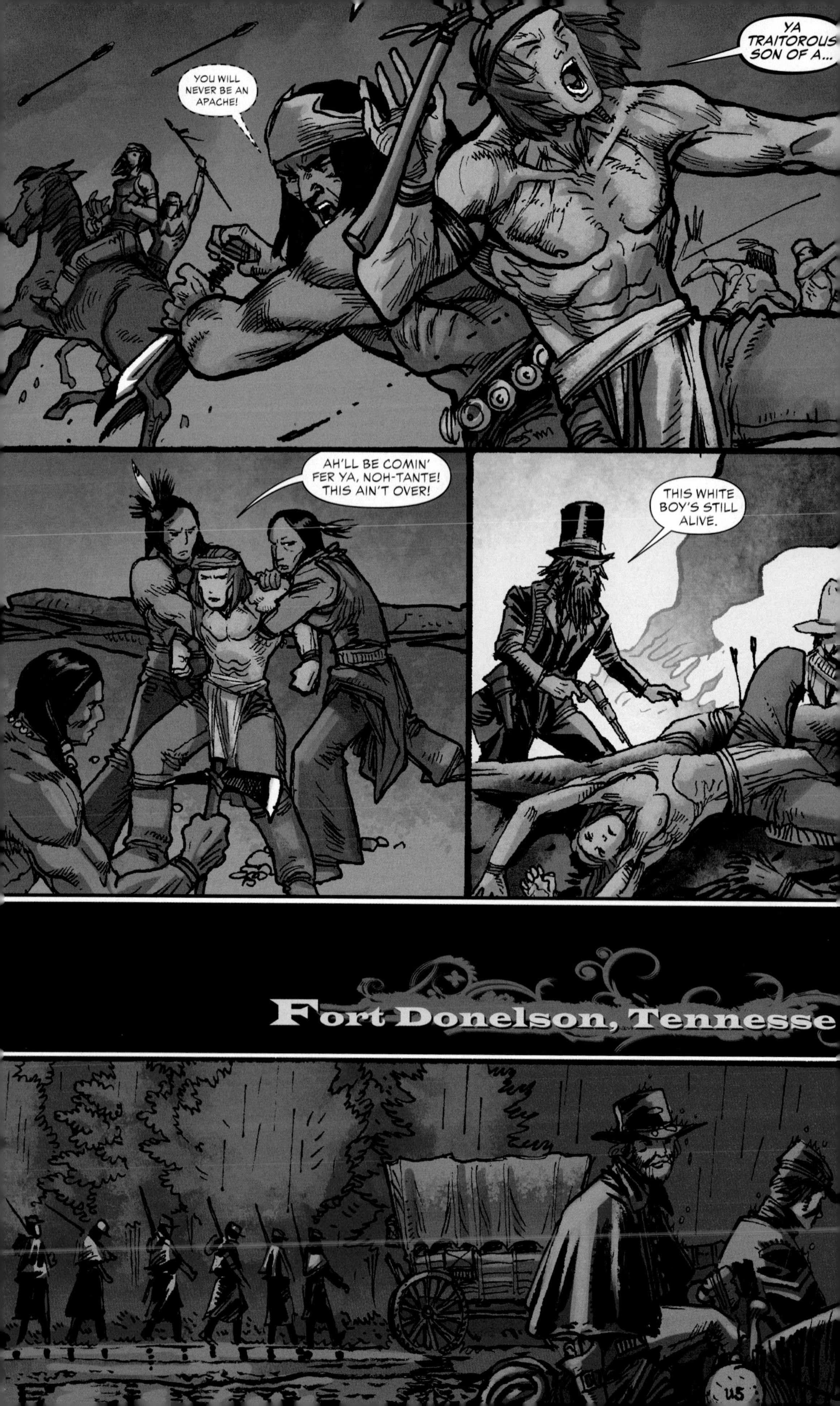
YOU WILL NEVER BE AN APACHE!
YA TRAITOROUS SON OF A...
AH'LL BE COMIN' FER YA, NOH-TANTE! THIS AIN'T OVER!
THIS WHITE BOY'S STILL ALIVE.
Fort Donelson, Tennesse

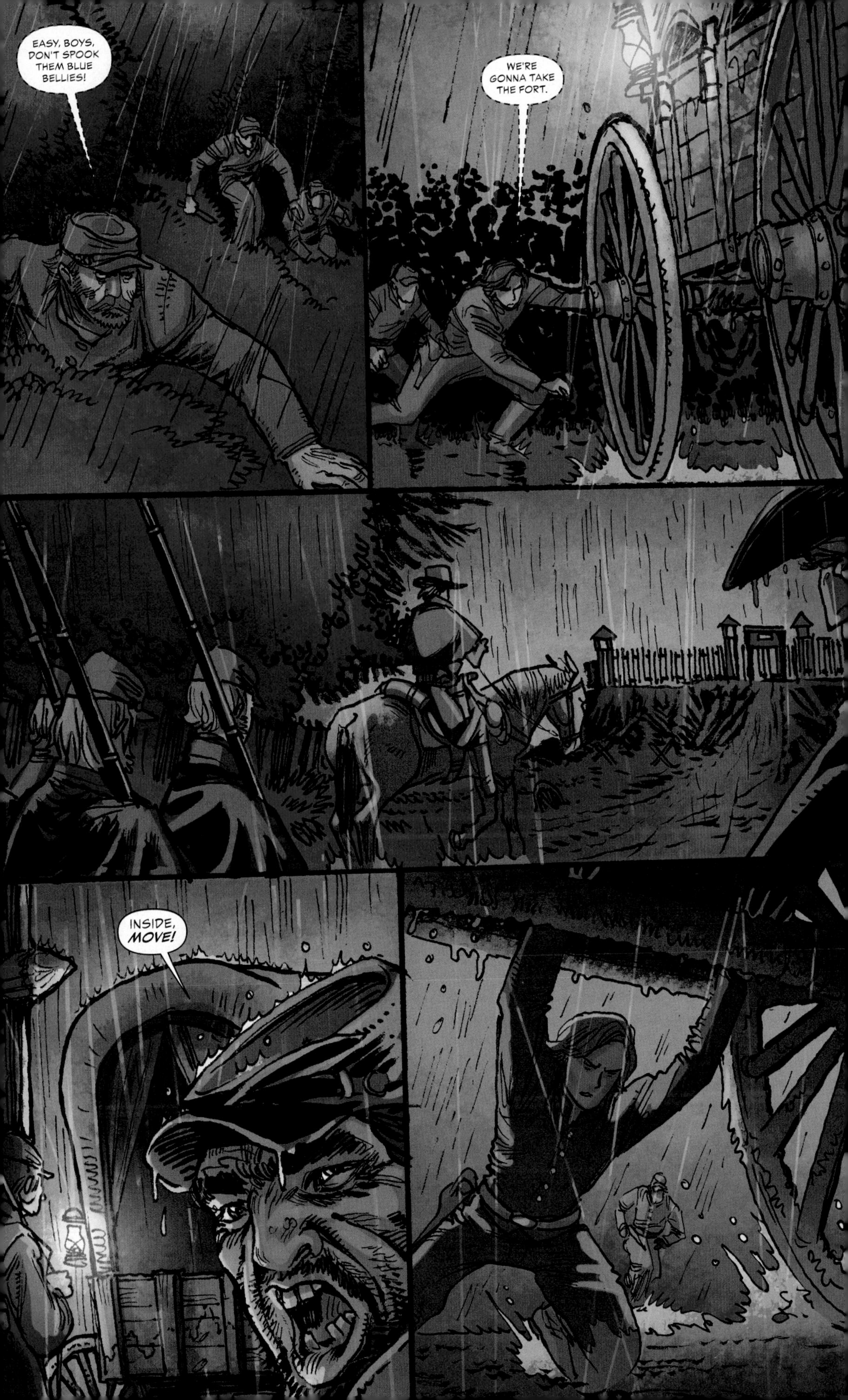
EASY, BOYS, DON'T SPOOK THEM BLUE BELLIES!
WE'RE GONNA TAKE THE FORT.
INSIDE, *MOVE!*

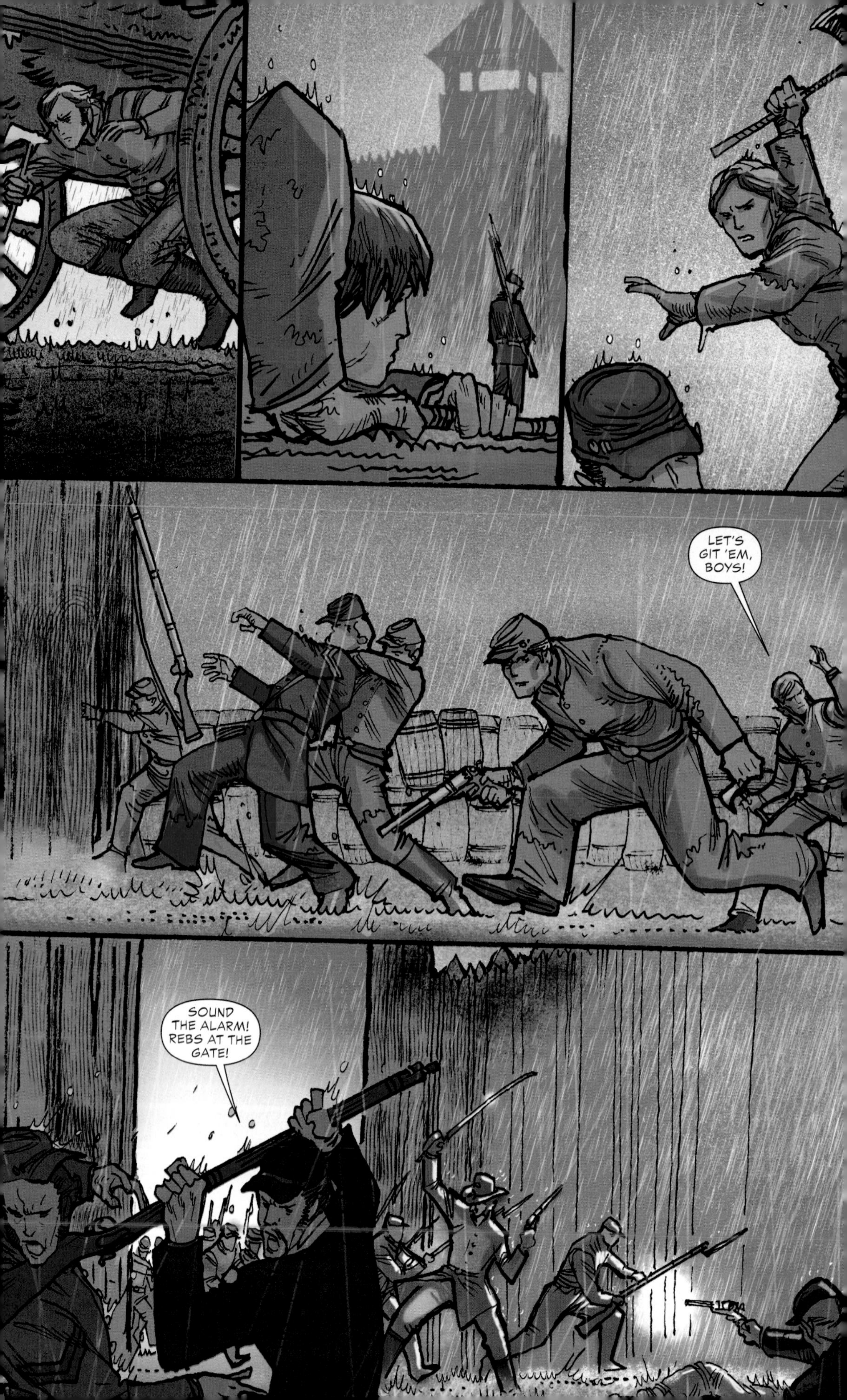
LET'S GIT 'EM, BOYS!
SOUND THE ALARM! REBS AT THE GATE!

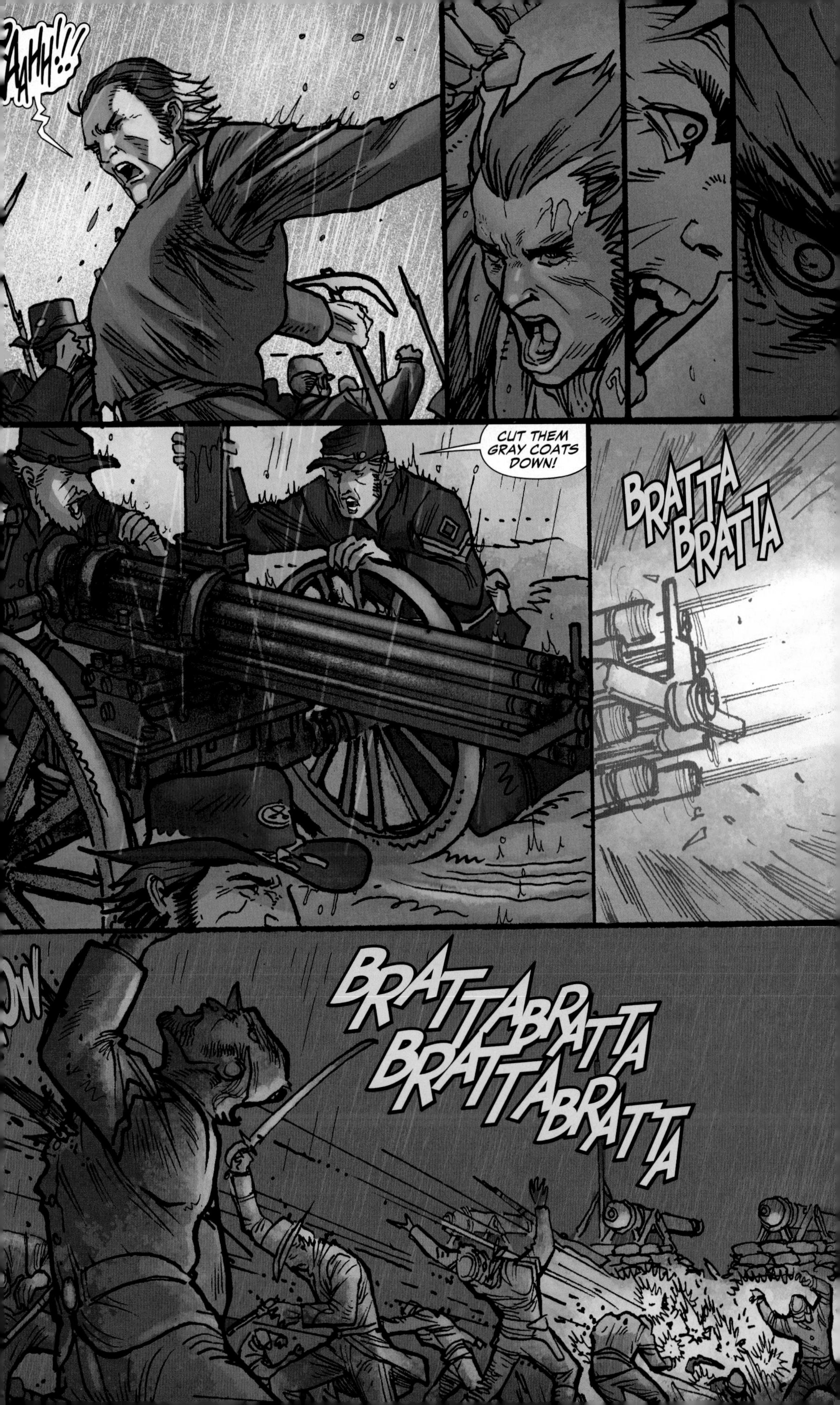
AAHH!!!
CUT THEM GRAY COATS DOWN!
BRATTA BRATTA
OW
BRATTABRATTA BRATTABRATTA

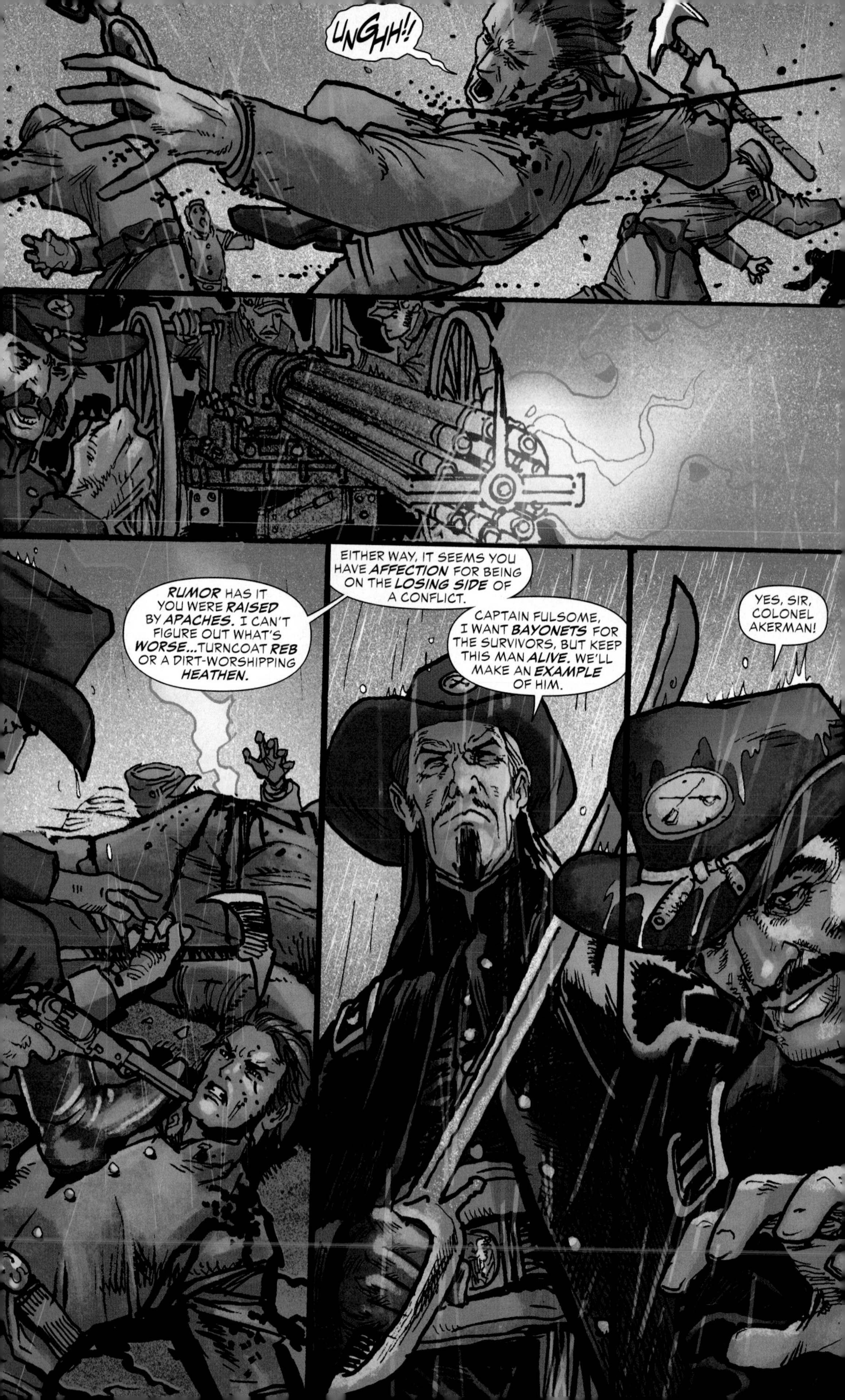
UNGHH!!
RUMOR HAS IT YOU WERE RAISED BY APACHES. I CAN'T FIGURE OUT WHAT'S WORSE...TURNCOAT REB OR A DIRT-WORSHIPPING HEATHEN.
EITHER WAY, IT SEEMS YOU HAVE AFFECTION FOR BEING ON THE LOSING SIDE OF A CONFLICT.
CAPTAIN FULSOME, I WANT BAYONETS FOR THE SURVIVORS, BUT KEEP THIS MAN ALIVE. WE'LL MAKE AN EXAMPLE OF HIM.
YES, SIR, COLONEL AKERMAN!

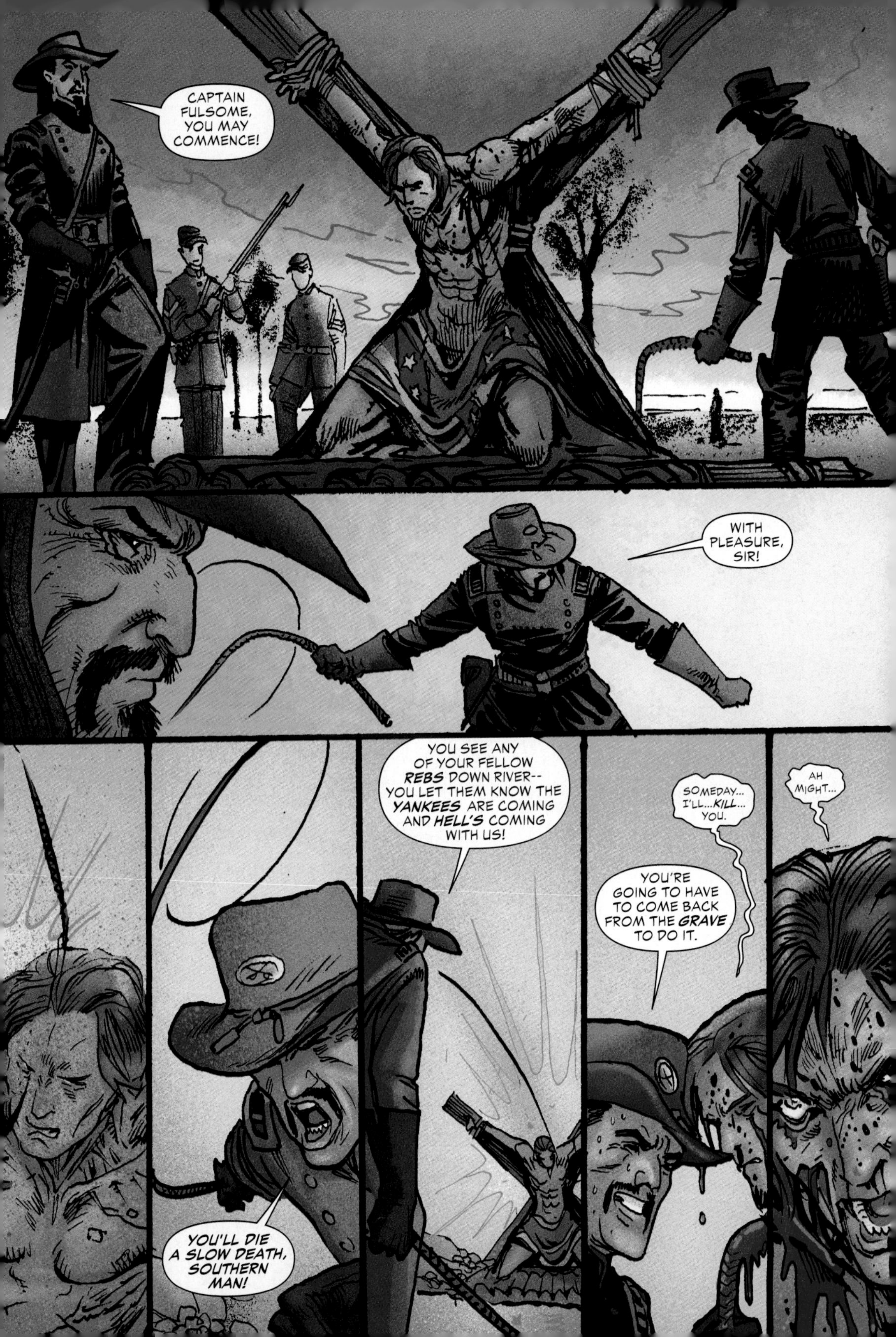
CAPTAIN FULSOME, YOU MAY COMMENCE!
WITH PLEASURE, SIR!
YOU'LL DIE A SLOW DEATH, SOUTHERN MAN!
YOU SEE ANY OF YOUR FELLOW REBS DOWN RIVER-- YOU LET THEM KNOW THE YANKEES ARE COMING AND HELL'S COMING WITH US!
SOMEDAY... I'LL...KILL... YOU.
YOU'RE GOING TO HAVE TO COME BACK FROM THE GRAVE TO DO IT.
AH MIGHT...

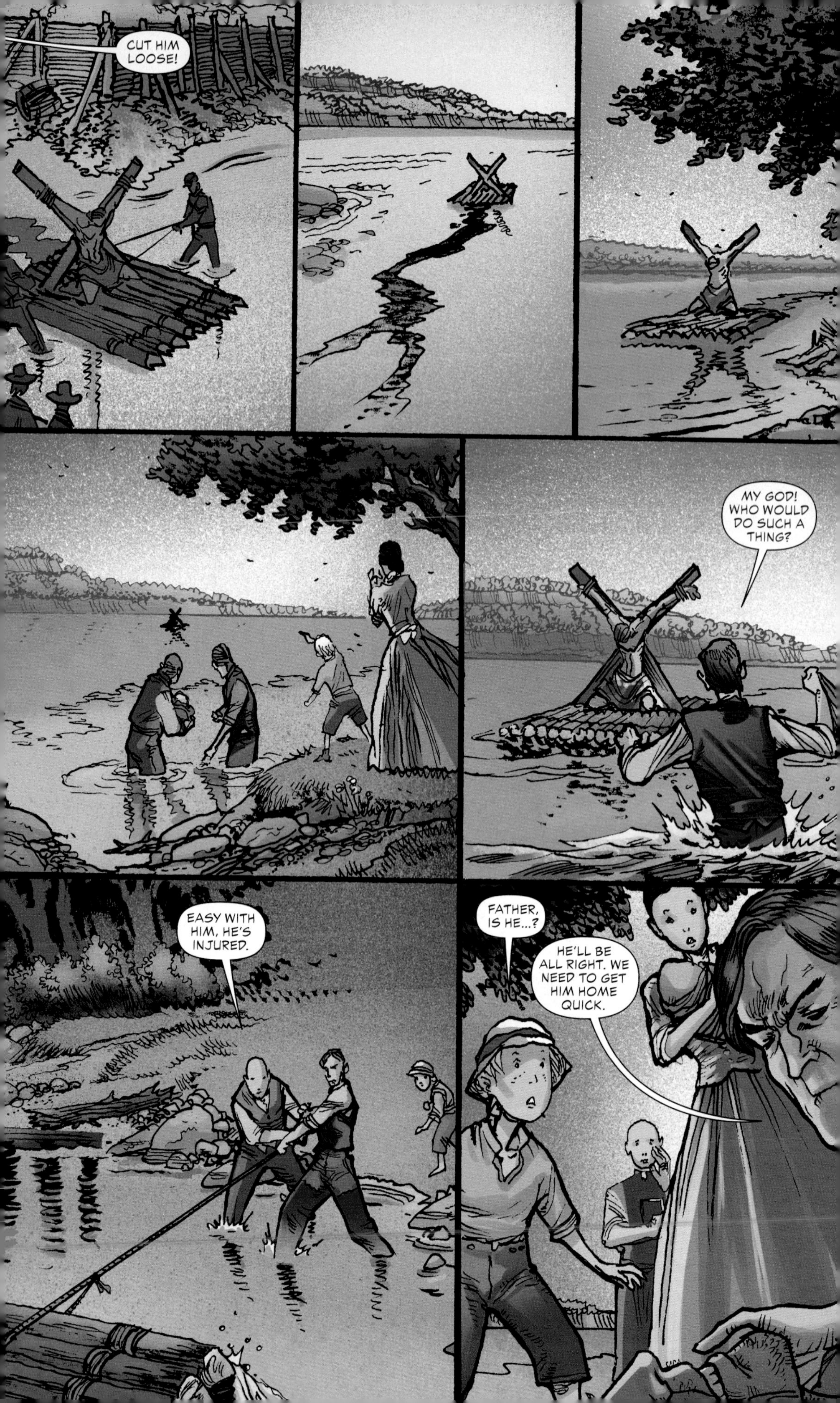
CUT HIM LOOSE!
MY GOD! WHO WOULD DO SUCH A THING?
EASY WITH HIM, HE'S INJURED.
FATHER, IS HE...?
HE'LL BE ALL RIGHT. WE NEED TO GET HIM HOME QUICK.

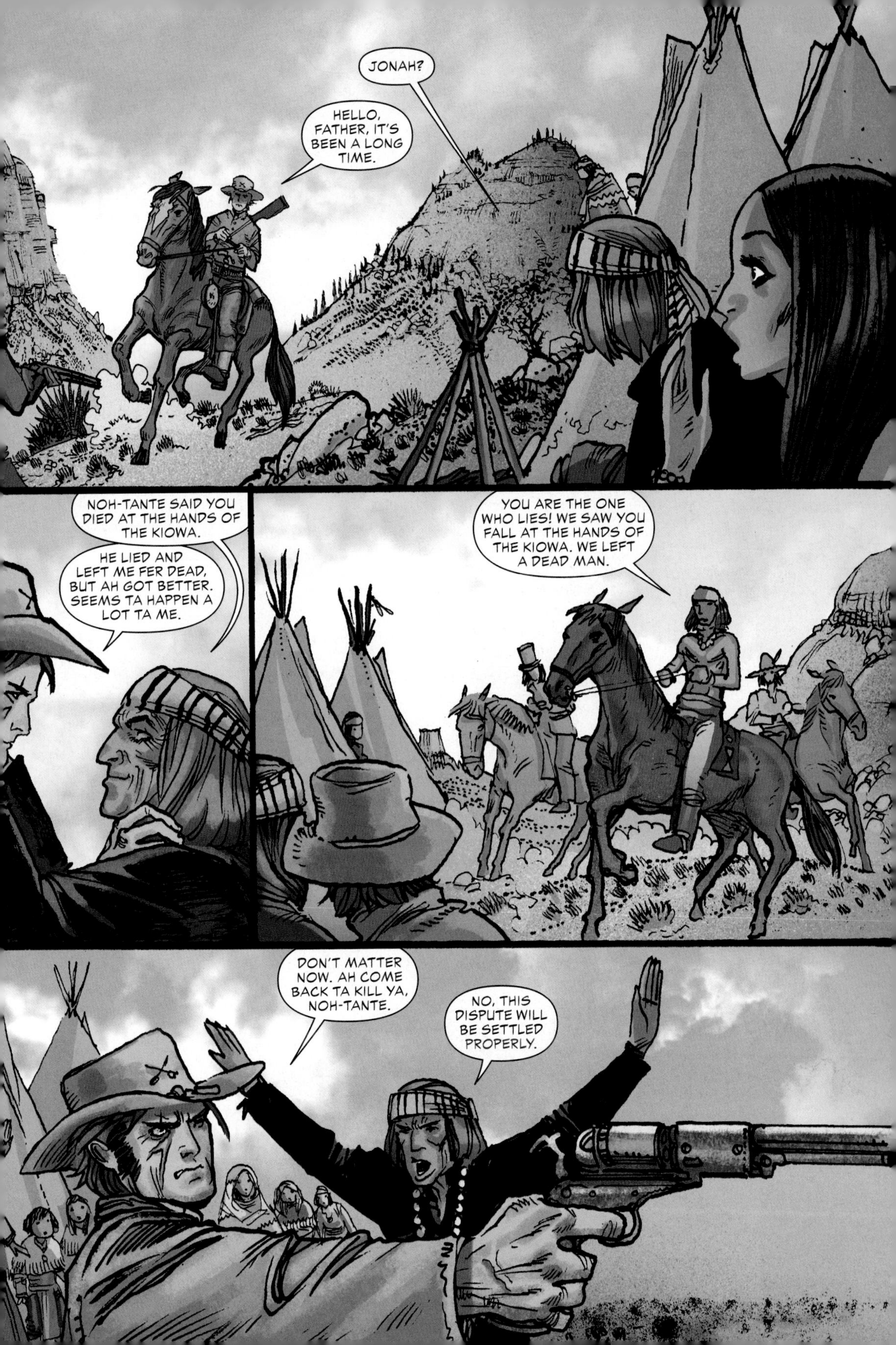
JONAH?
HELLO, FATHER, IT'S BEEN A LONG TIME.
NOH-TANTE SAID YOU DIED AT THE HANDS OF THE KIOWA.
HE LIED AND LEFT ME FER DEAD, BUT AH GOT BETTER. SEEMS TA HAPPEN A LOT TA ME.
YOU ARE THE ONE WHO LIES! WE SAW YOU FALL AT THE HANDS OF THE KIOWA. WE LEFT A DEAD MAN.
DON'T MATTER NOW. AH COME BACK TA KILL YA, NOH-TANTE.
NO, THIS DISPUTE WILL BE SETTLED PROPERLY.

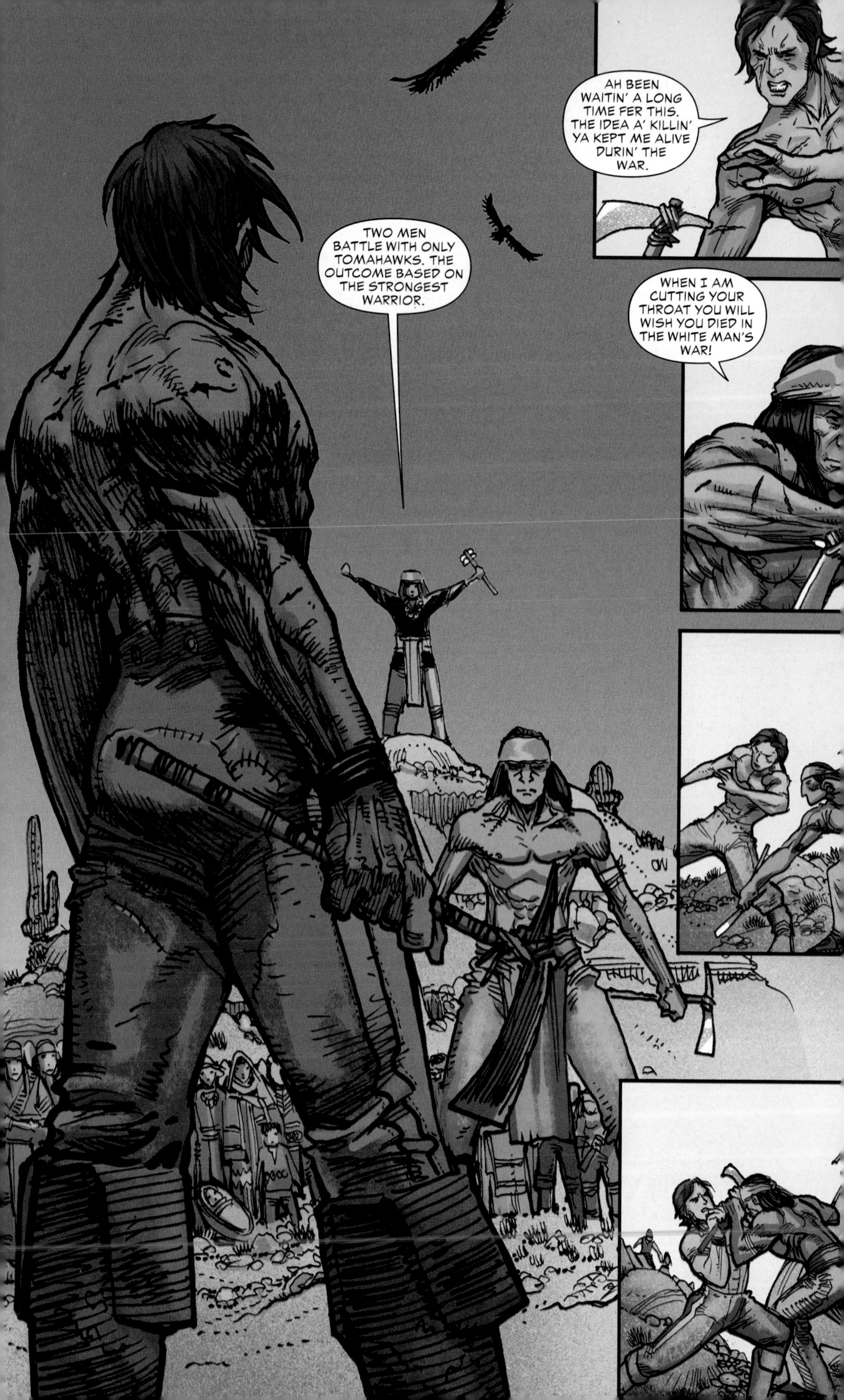
TWO MEN BATTLE WITH ONLY TOMAHAWKS. THE OUTCOME BASED ON THE STRONGEST WARRIOR.
AH BEEN WAITIN' A LONG TIME FER THIS. THE IDEA A' KILLIN' YA KEPT ME ALIVE DURIN' THE WAR.
WHEN I AM CUTTING YOUR THROAT YOU WILL WISH YOU DIED IN THE WHITE MAN'S WAR!

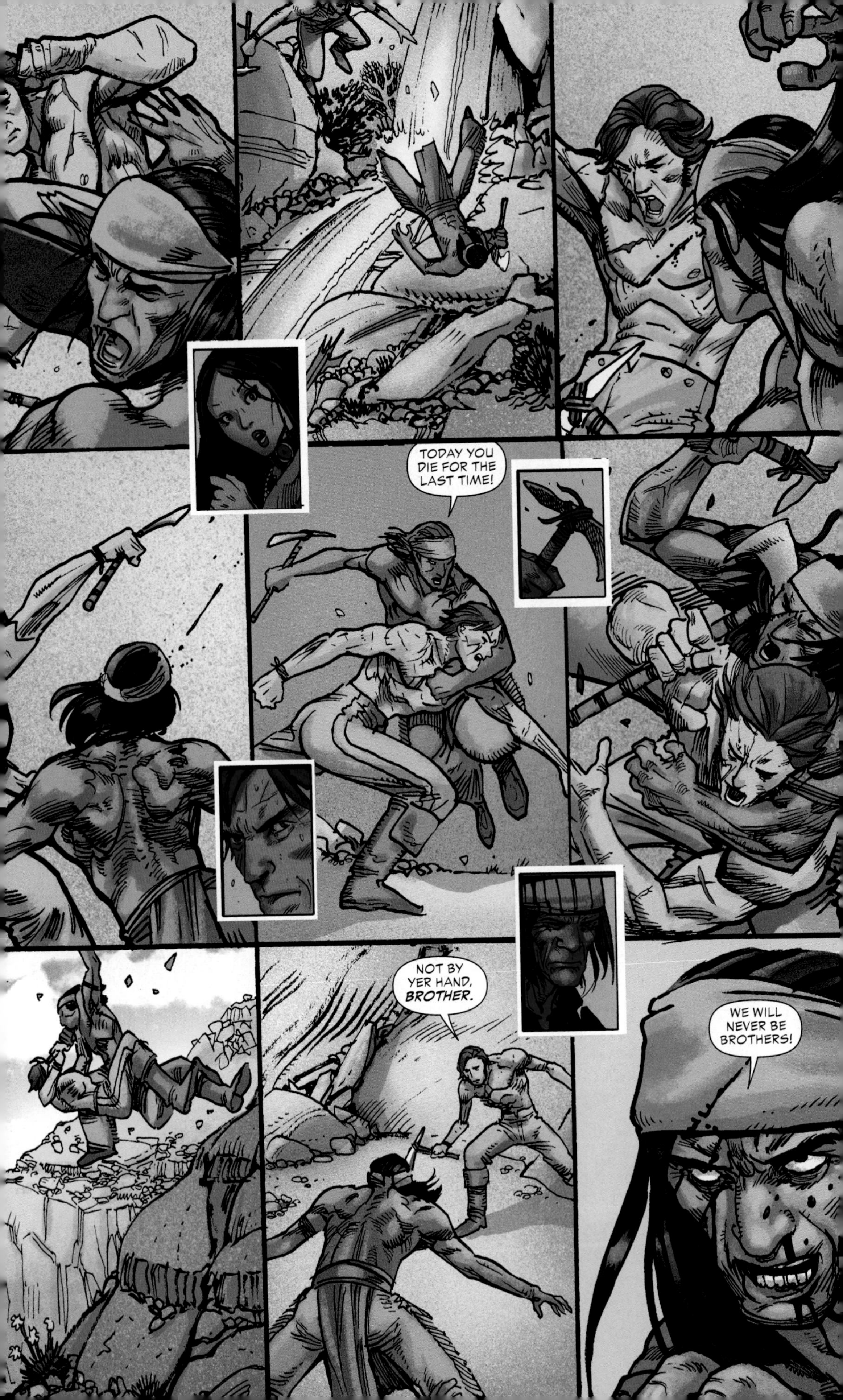
TODAY YOU DIE FOR THE LAST TIME!
NOT BY YER HAND, *BROTHER.*
WE WILL NEVER BE BROTHERS!

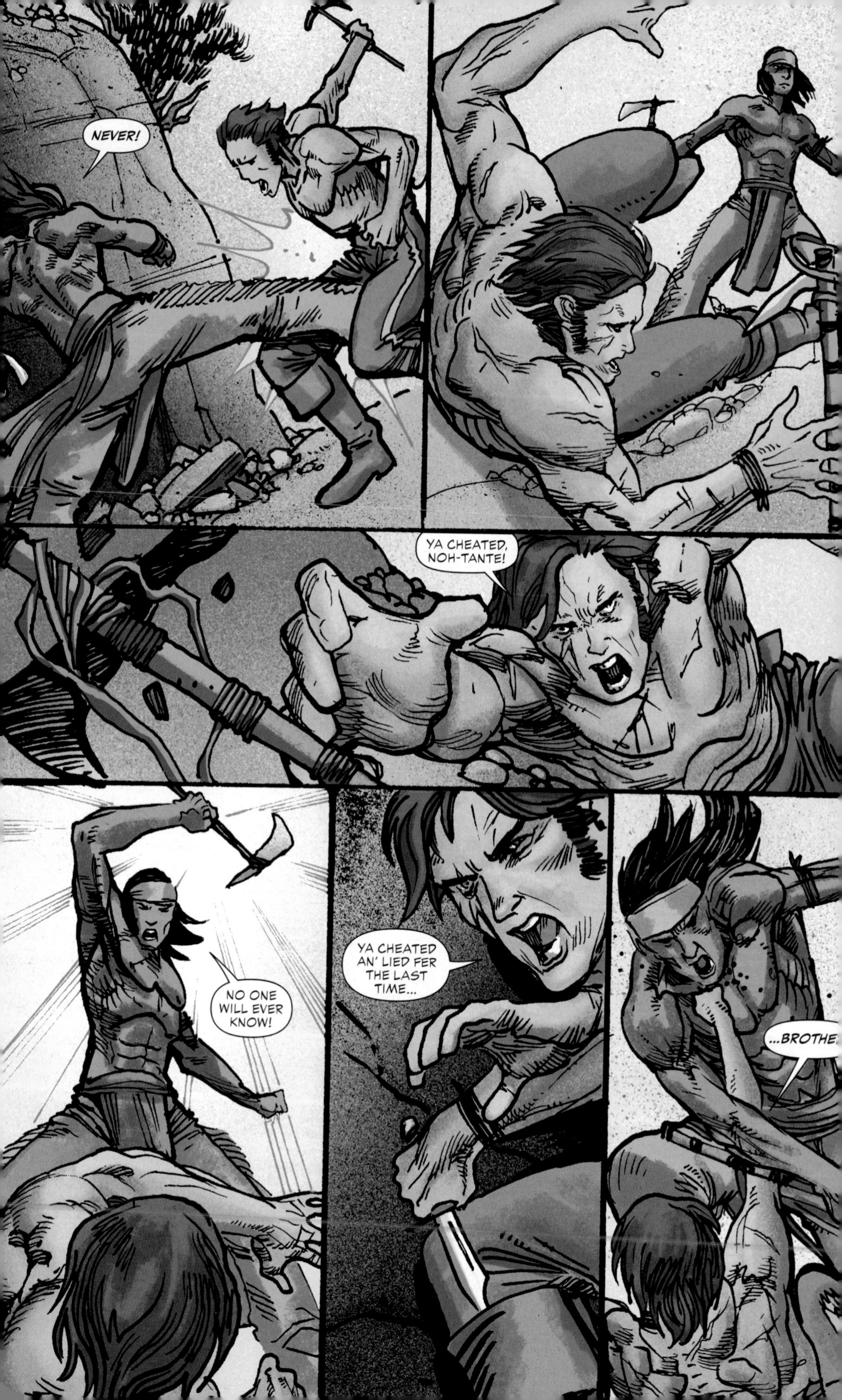
NEVER!
YA CHEATED, NOH-TANTE!
NO ONE WILL EVER KNOW!
YA CHEATED AN' LIED FER THE LAST TIME...
...BROTHE

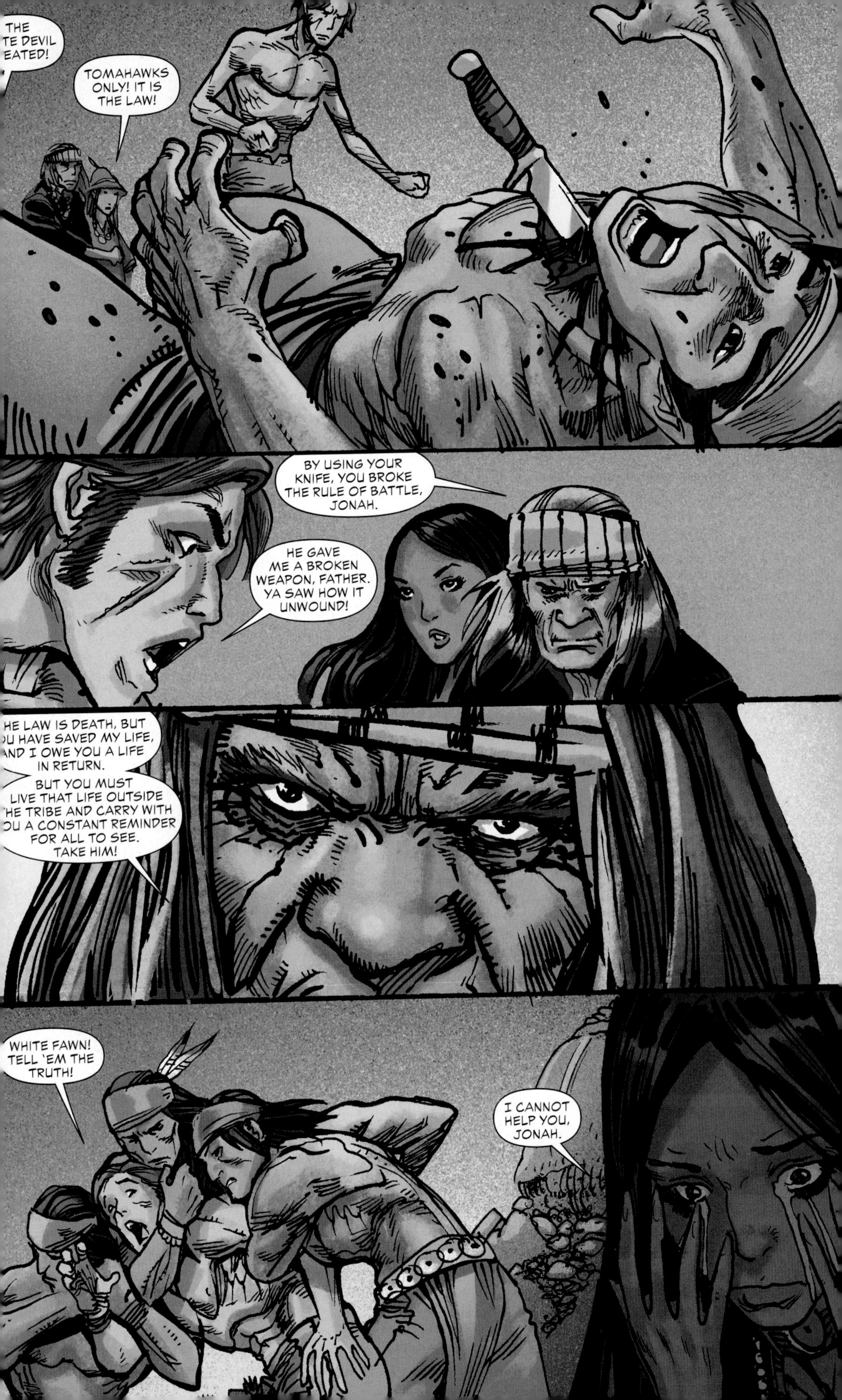
THE
TE DEVIL
EATED!
TOMAHAWKS ONLY! IT IS THE LAW!
BY USING YOUR KNIFE, YOU BROKE THE RULE OF BATTLE, JONAH.
HE GAVE ME A BROKEN WEAPON, FATHER. YA SAW HOW IT UNWOUND!
HE LAW IS DEATH, BUT
U HAVE SAVED MY LIFE,
ND I OWE YOU A LIFE IN RETURN.
BUT YOU MUST LIVE THAT LIFE OUTSIDE
HE TRIBE AND CARRY WITH
U A CONSTANT REMINDER FOR ALL TO SEE.
TAKE HIM!
WHITE FAWN! TELL 'EM THE TRUTH!
I CANNOT HELP YOU, JONAH.

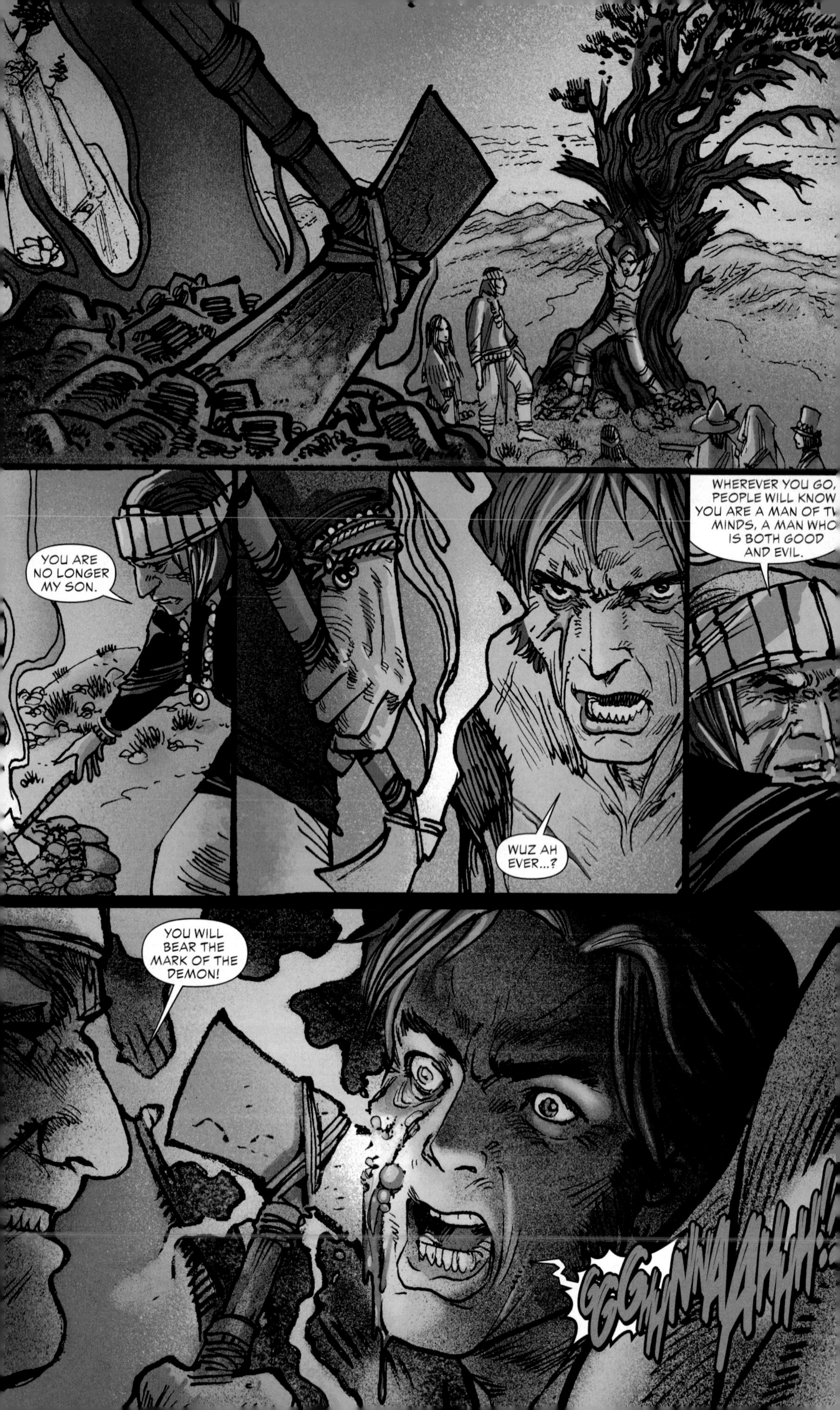

YOU ARE NO LONGER MY SON.
WUZ AH EVER...?
WHEREVER YOU GO, PEOPLE WILL KNOW YOU ARE A MAN OF T' MINDS, A MAN WHO IS BOTH GOOD AND EVIL.
YOU WILL BEAR THE MARK OF THE DEMON!
GGGHNNAAHHH!!

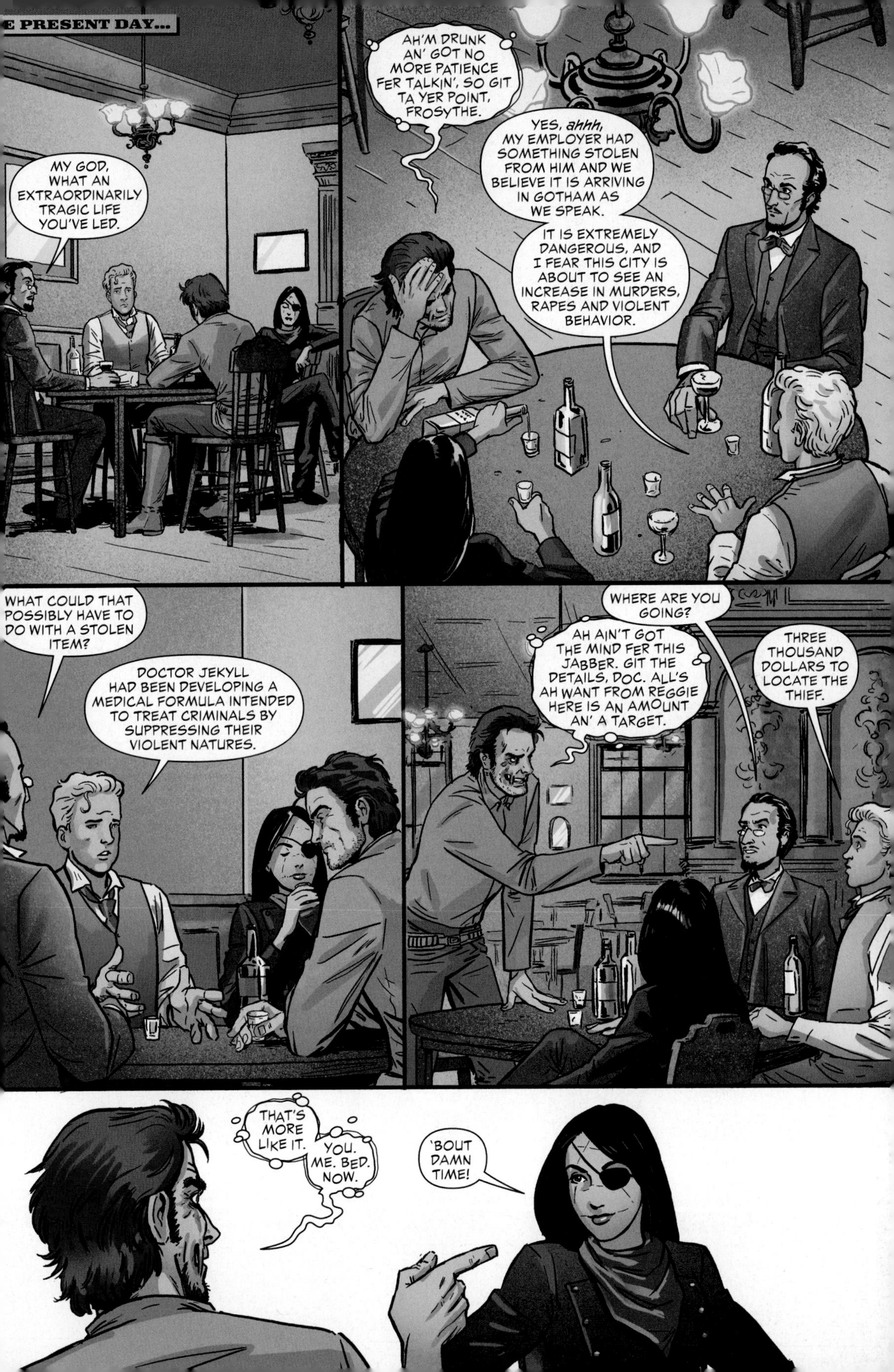

E PRESENT DAY...
MY GOD, WHAT AN EXTRAORDINARILY TRAGIC LIFE YOU'VE LED.
AH'M DRUNK AN' GOT NO MORE PATIENCE FER TALKIN', SO GIT TA YER POINT, FROSYTHE.
YES, *ahhh*, MY EMPLOYER HAD SOMETHING STOLEN FROM HIM AND WE BELIEVE IT IS ARRIVING IN GOTHAM AS WE SPEAK.
IT IS EXTREMELY DANGEROUS, AND I FEAR THIS CITY IS ABOUT TO SEE AN INCREASE IN MURDERS, RAPES AND VIOLENT BEHAVIOR.
WHAT COULD THAT POSSIBLY HAVE TO DO WITH A STOLEN ITEM?
DOCTOR JEKYLL HAD BEEN DEVELOPING A MEDICAL FORMULA INTENDED TO TREAT CRIMINALS BY SUPPRESSING THEIR VIOLENT NATURES.
WHERE ARE YOU GOING?
AH AIN'T GOT THE MIND FER THIS JABBER. GIT THE DETAILS, DOC. ALL'S AH WANT FROM REGGIE HERE IS AN AMOUNT AN' A TARGET.
THREE THOUSAND DOLLARS TO LOCATE THE THIEF.
THAT'S MORE LIKE IT.
YOU. ME. BED. NOW.
'BOUT DAMN TIME!

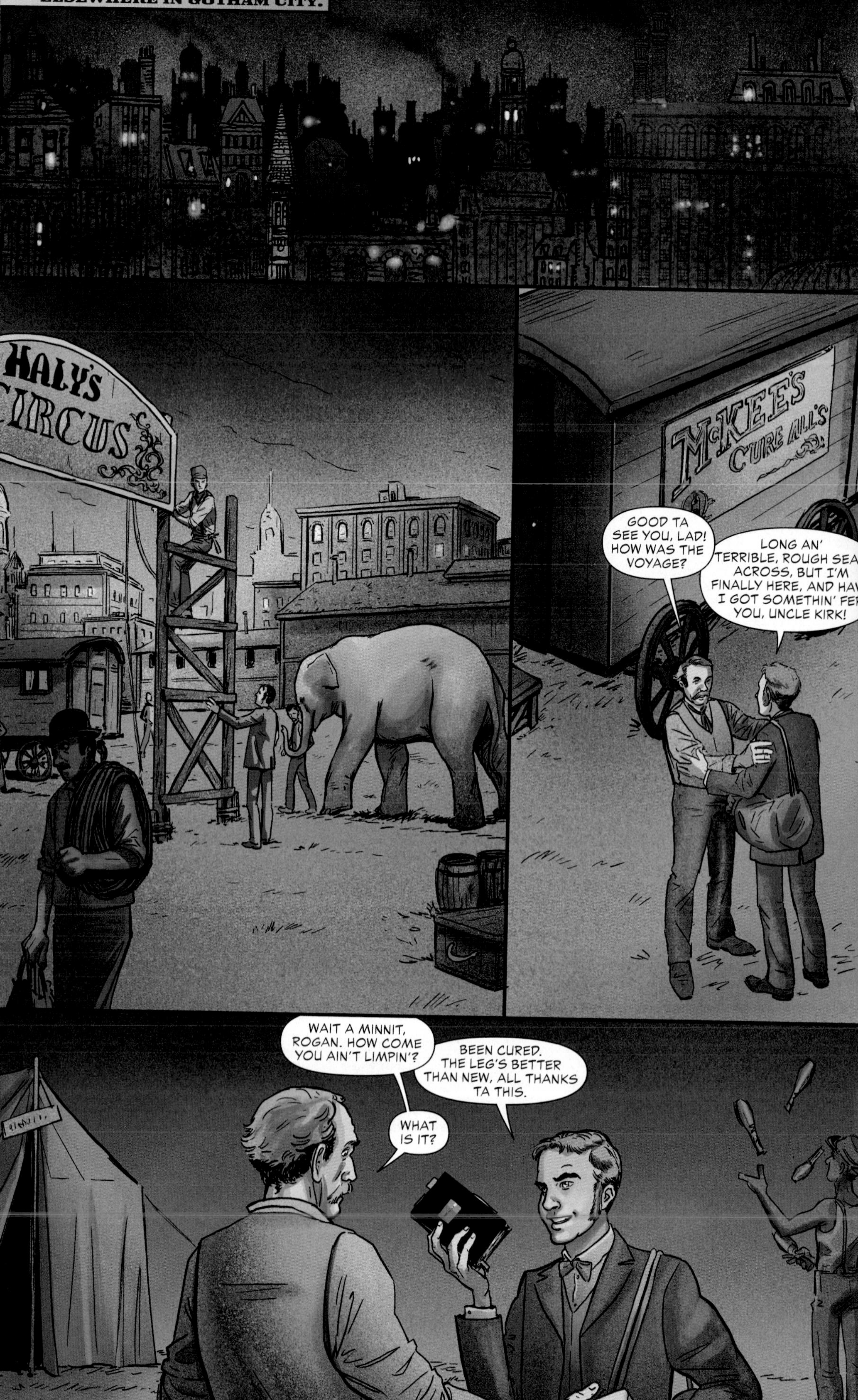
ELSEWHERE IN GOTHAM CITY.
HALY'S CIRCUS
McKEE'S CURE ALL'S
GOOD TA SEE YOU, LAD! HOW WAS THE VOYAGE?
LONG AN' TERRIBLE, ROUGH SEA ACROSS, BUT I'M FINALLY HERE, AND HAV I GOT SOMETHIN' FER YOU, UNCLE KIRK!
WAIT A MINNIT, ROGAN. HOW COME YOU AIN'T LIMPIN'?
BEEN CURED. THE LEG'S BETTER THAN NEW, ALL THANKS TA THIS.
WHAT IS IT?

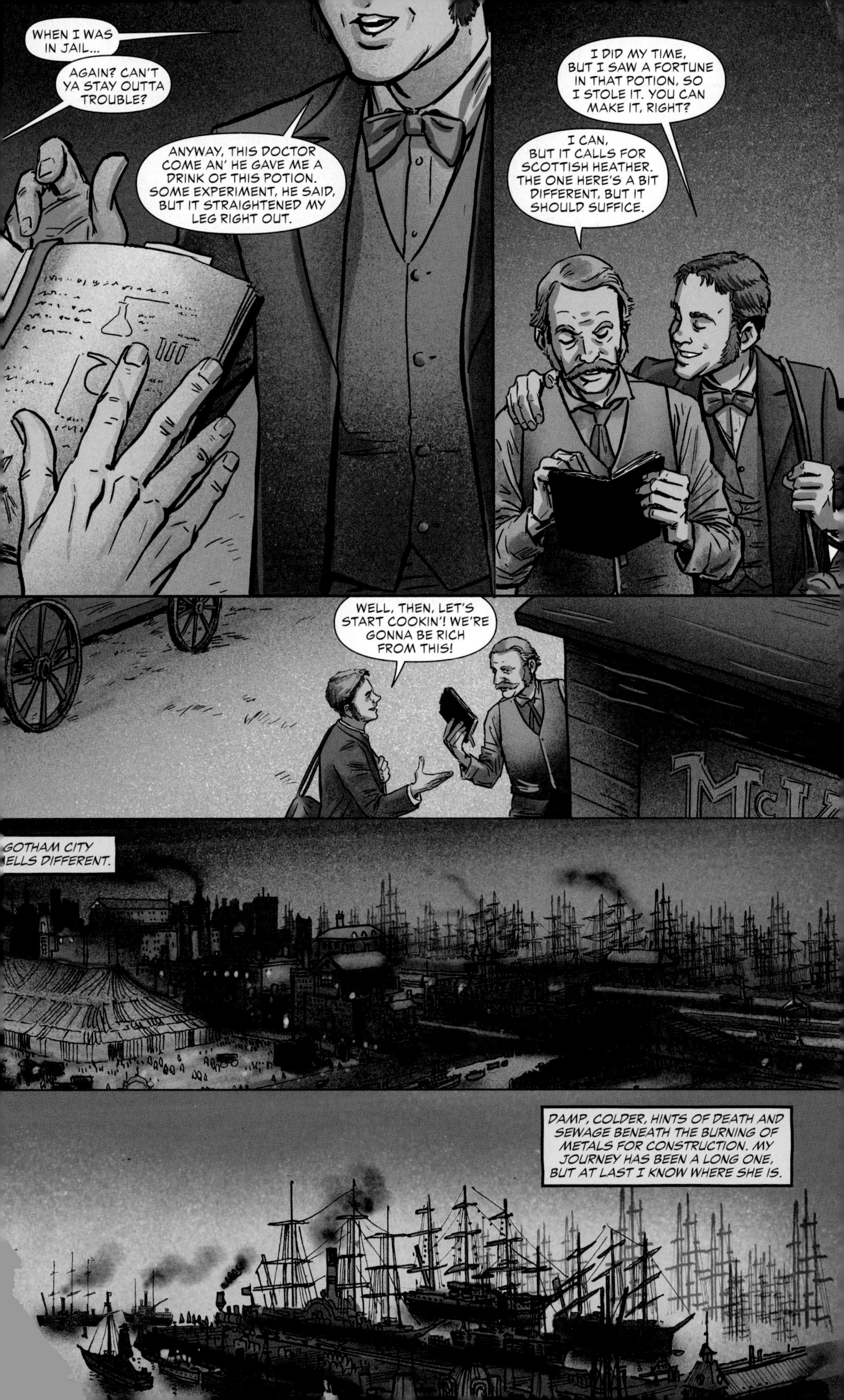

WHEN I WAS IN JAIL...
AGAIN? CAN'T YA STAY OUTTA TROUBLE?
ANYWAY, THIS DOCTOR COME AN' HE GAVE ME A DRINK OF THIS POTION. SOME EXPERIMENT, HE SAID, BUT IT STRAIGHTENED MY LEG RIGHT OUT.
I DID MY TIME, BUT I SAW A FORTUNE IN THAT POTION, SO I STOLE IT. YOU CAN MAKE IT, RIGHT?
I CAN, BUT IT CALLS FOR SCOTTISH HEATHER. THE ONE HERE'S A BIT DIFFERENT, BUT IT SHOULD SUFFICE.
WELL, THEN, LET'S START COOKIN'! WE'RE GONNA BE RICH FROM THIS!
McL
GOTHAM CITY
ELLS DIFFERENT.
DAMP, COLDER, HINTS OF DEATH AND SEWAGE BENEATH THE BURNING OF METALS FOR CONSTRUCTION. MY JOURNEY HAS BEEN A LONG ONE, BUT AT LAST I KNOW WHERE SHE IS.

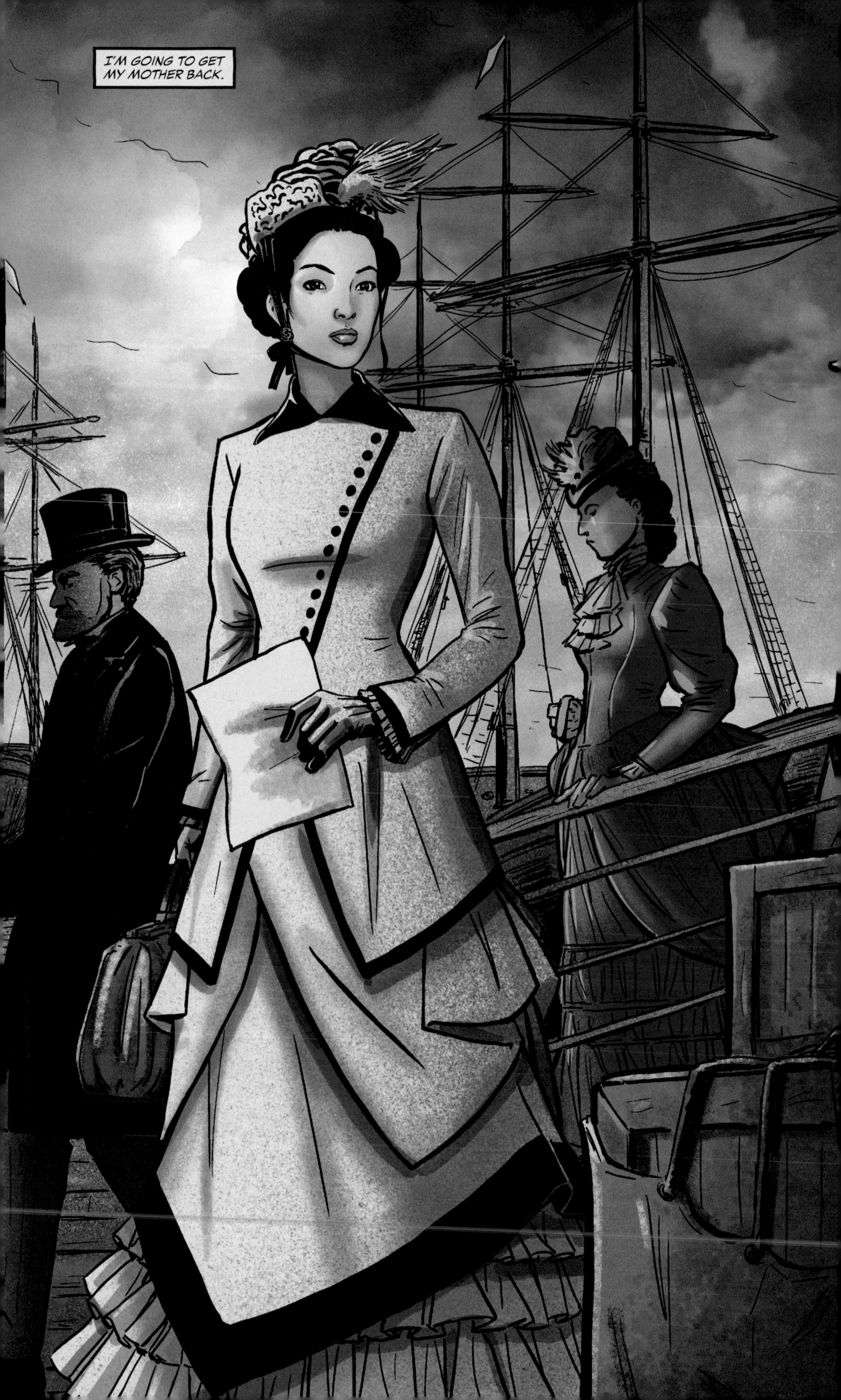
I'M GOING TO GET MY MOTHER BACK.

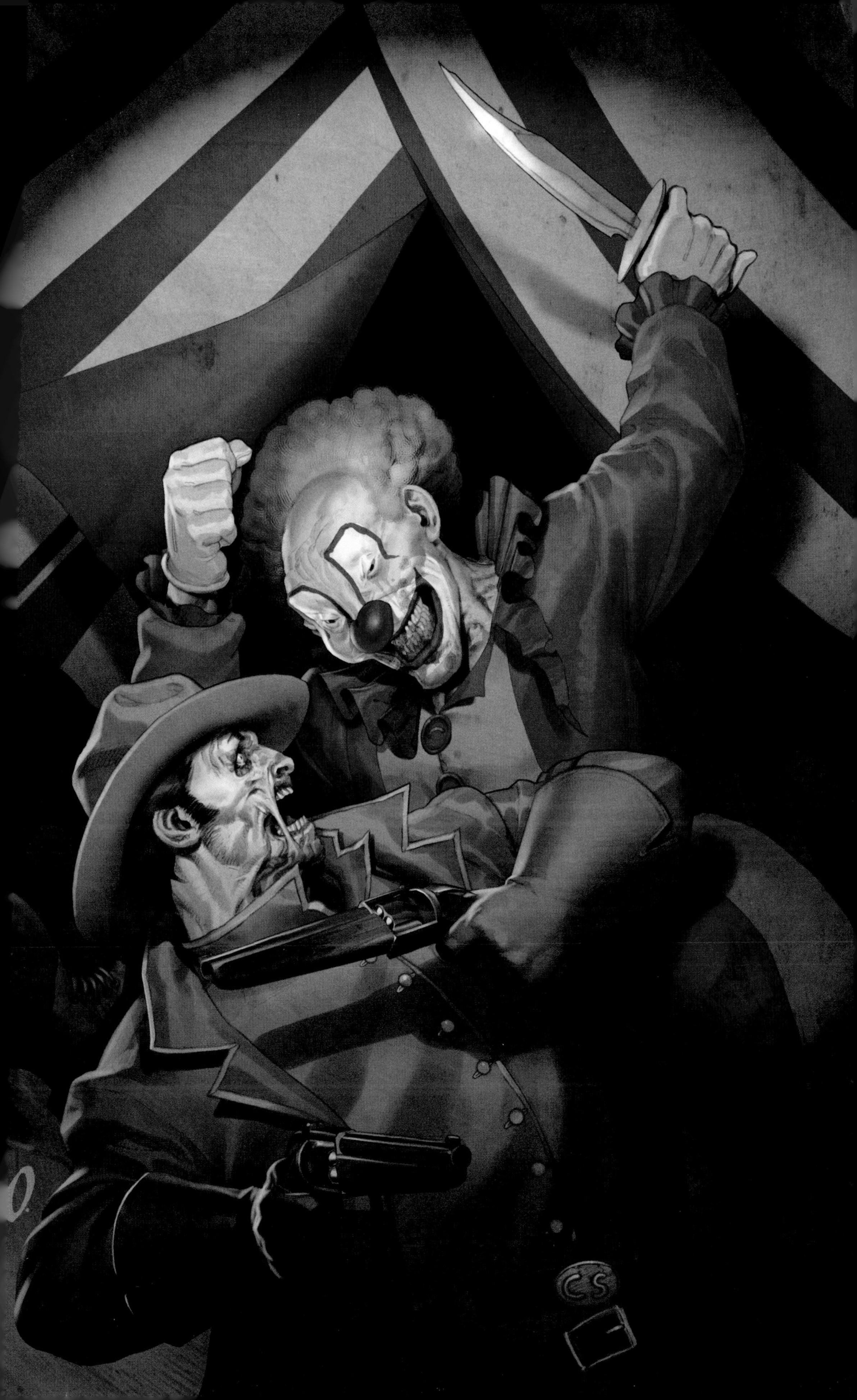

THE STRANGE CASE OF DR. ARKHAM AND MR. HEX

JIMMY PALMIOTTI & JUSTIN GRAY writers **MORITAT** artist cover art by **ARIEL OLIVETTI**

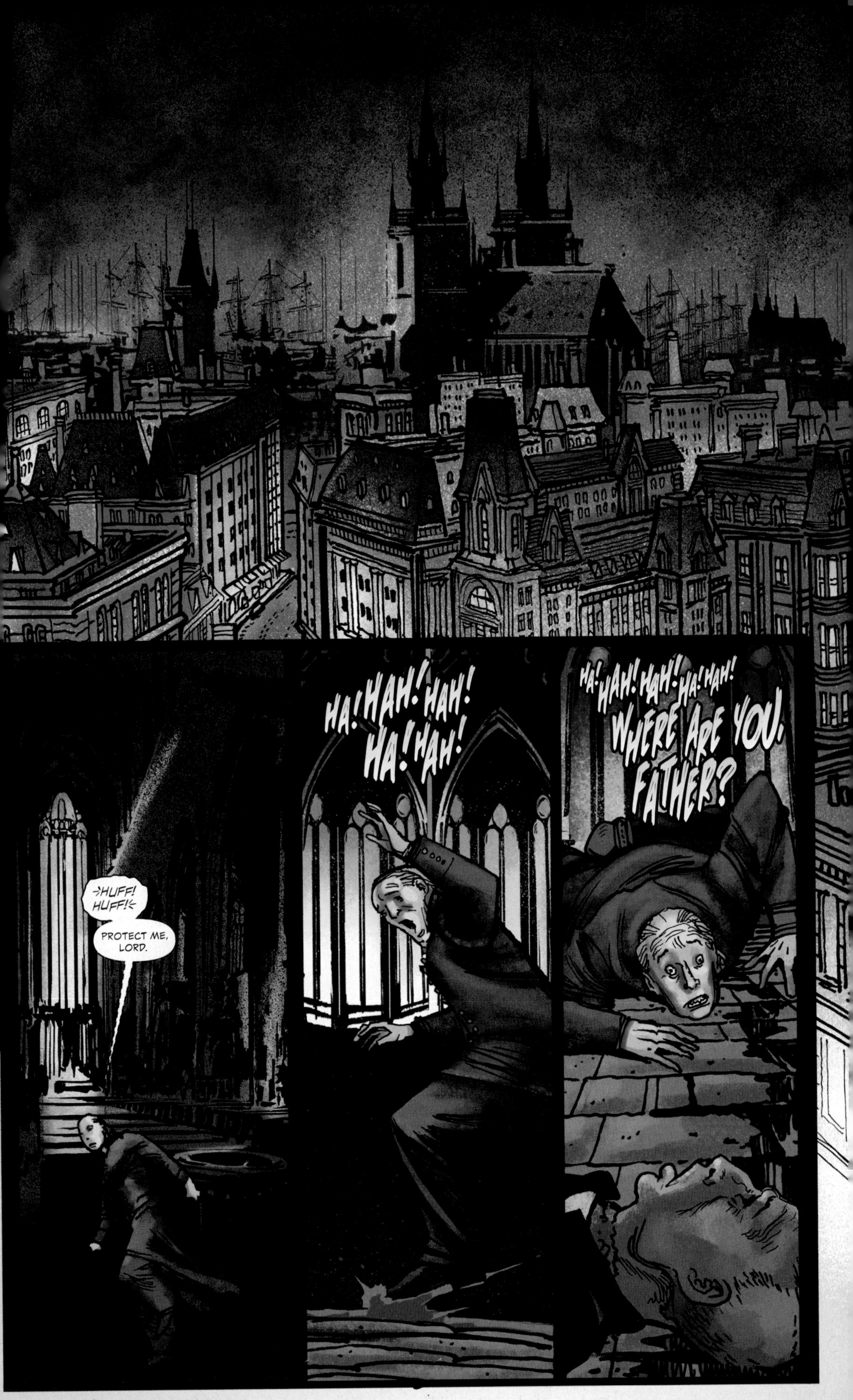

HUFF! HUFF!
PROTECT ME, LORD.
HA! HAH! HAH! HA! HAH!
HA! HAH! HAH! HA! HAH!
WHERE ARE YOU, FATHER?

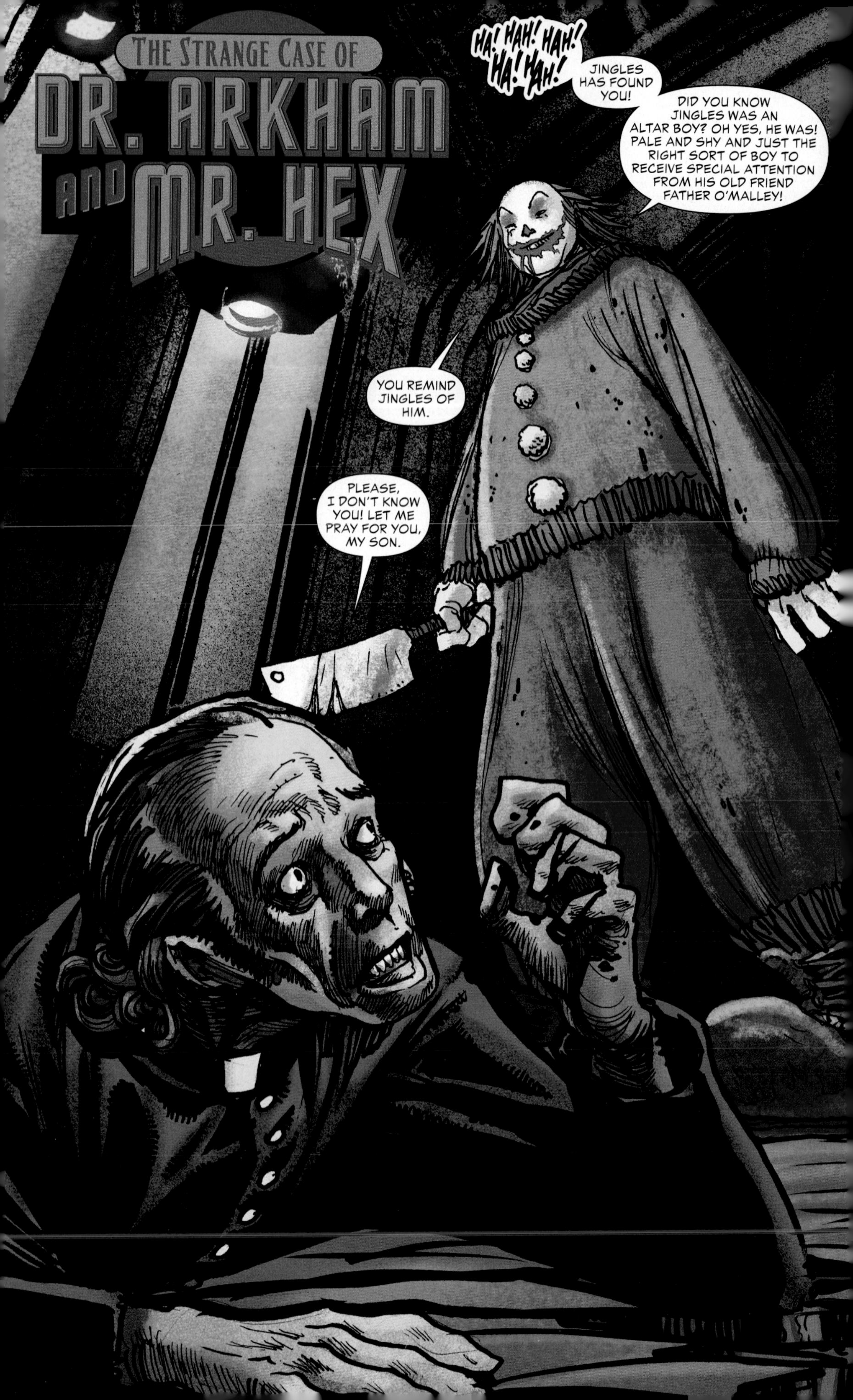
THE STRANGE CASE OF
DR. ARKHAM AND MR. HEX
HA! HAH! HAH! HA! HAH!
JINGLES HAS FOUND YOU!
DID YOU KNOW JINGLES WAS AN ALTAR BOY? OH YES, HE WAS! PALE AND SHY AND JUST THE RIGHT SORT OF BOY TO RECEIVE SPECIAL ATTENTION FROM HIS OLD FRIEND FATHER O'MALLEY!
YOU REMIND JINGLES OF HIM.
PLEASE, I DON'T KNOW YOU! LET ME PRAY FOR YOU, MY SON.

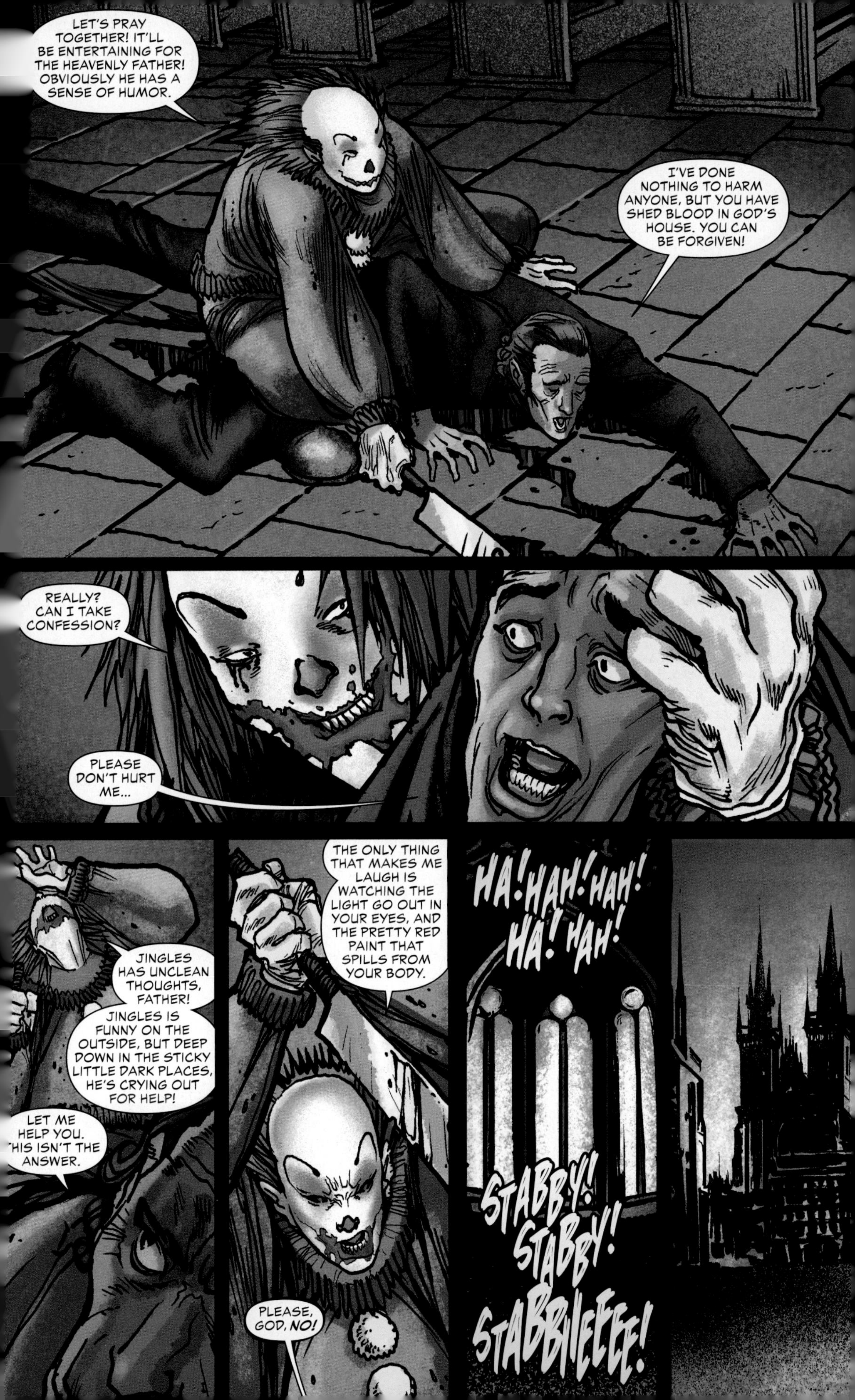
LET'S PRAY TOGETHER! IT'LL BE ENTERTAINING FOR THE HEAVENLY FATHER! OBVIOUSLY HE HAS A SENSE OF HUMOR.
I'VE DONE NOTHING TO HARM ANYONE, BUT YOU HAVE SHED BLOOD IN GOD'S HOUSE. YOU CAN BE FORGIVEN!
REALLY? CAN I TAKE CONFESSION?
PLEASE DON'T HURT ME...
JINGLES HAS UNCLEAN THOUGHTS, FATHER!
JINGLES IS FUNNY ON THE OUTSIDE, BUT DEEP DOWN IN THE STICKY LITTLE DARK PLACES, HE'S CRYING OUT FOR HELP!
LET ME HELP YOU. THIS ISN'T THE ANSWER.
THE ONLY THING THAT MAKES ME LAUGH IS WATCHING THE LIGHT GO OUT IN YOUR EYES, AND THE PRETTY RED PAINT THAT SPILLS FROM YOUR BODY.
PLEASE, GOD, NO!
HA! HAH! HAH! HA! HAH!
STABBY! STABBY! STABBIEEEE!

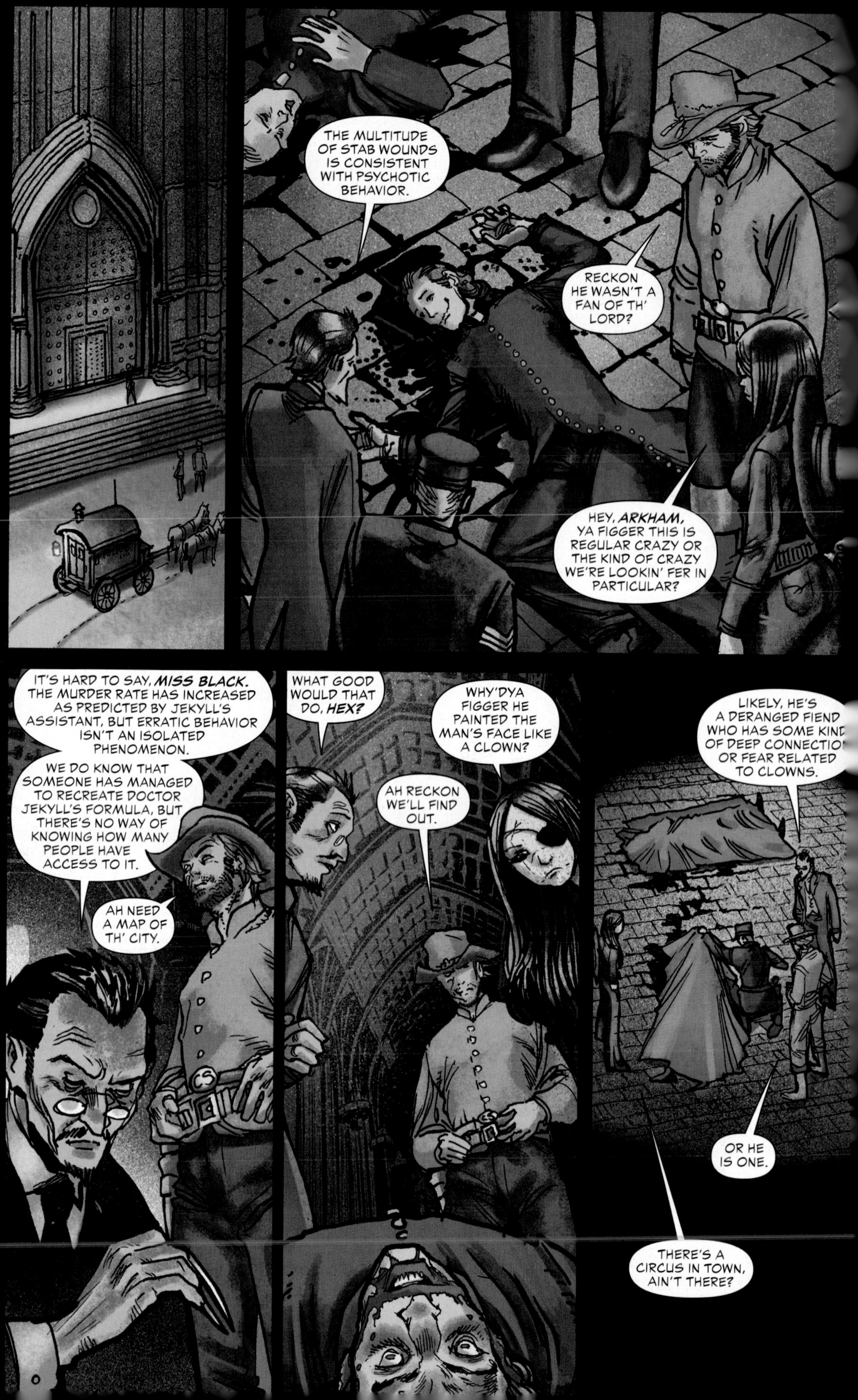
THE MULTITUDE OF STAB WOUNDS IS CONSISTENT WITH PSYCHOTIC BEHAVIOR.
RECKON HE WASN'T A FAN OF TH' LORD?
HEY, ARKHAM, YA FIGGER THIS IS REGULAR CRAZY OR THE KIND OF CRAZY WE'RE LOOKIN' FER IN PARTICULAR?
IT'S HARD TO SAY, MISS BLACK. THE MURDER RATE HAS INCREASED AS PREDICTED BY JEKYLL'S ASSISTANT, BUT ERRATIC BEHAVIOR ISN'T AN ISOLATED PHENOMENON.
WE DO KNOW THAT SOMEONE HAS MANAGED TO RECREATE DOCTOR JEKYLL'S FORMULA, BUT THERE'S NO WAY OF KNOWING HOW MANY PEOPLE HAVE ACCESS TO IT.
AH NEED A MAP OF TH' CITY.
WHAT GOOD WOULD THAT DO, HEX?
WHY'DYA FIGGER HE PAINTED THE MAN'S FACE LIKE A CLOWN?
AH RECKON WE'LL FIND OUT.
LIKELY, HE'S A DERANGED FIEND WHO HAS SOME KIND OF DEEP CONNECTION OR FEAR RELATED TO CLOWNS.
OR HE IS ONE.
THERE'S A CIRCUS IN TOWN, AIN'T THERE?

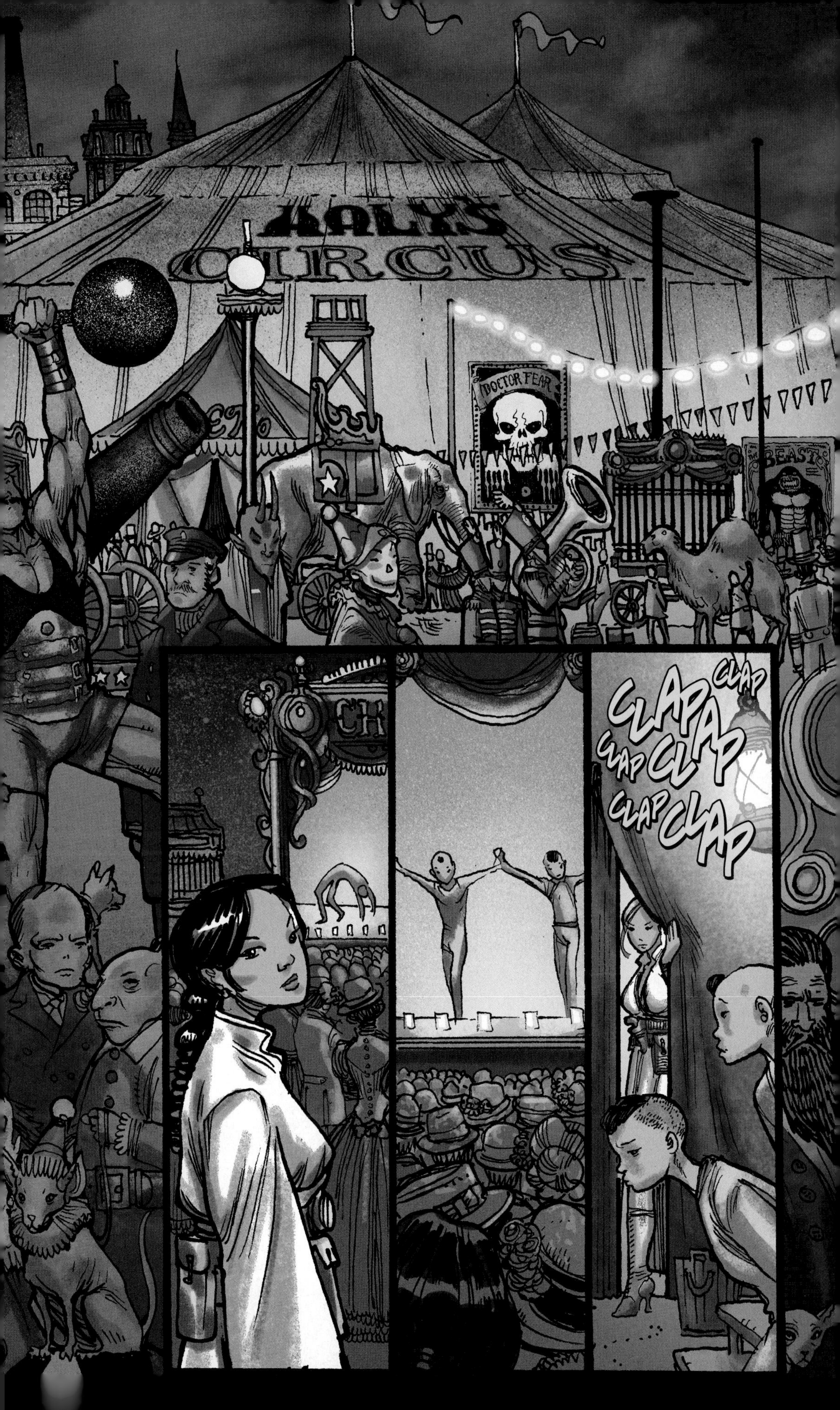

HALY'S
CIRCUS
DOCTOR FEAR
THE BEAST
CLAP
CLAP CLAP
CLAP CLAP
CLAP CLAP

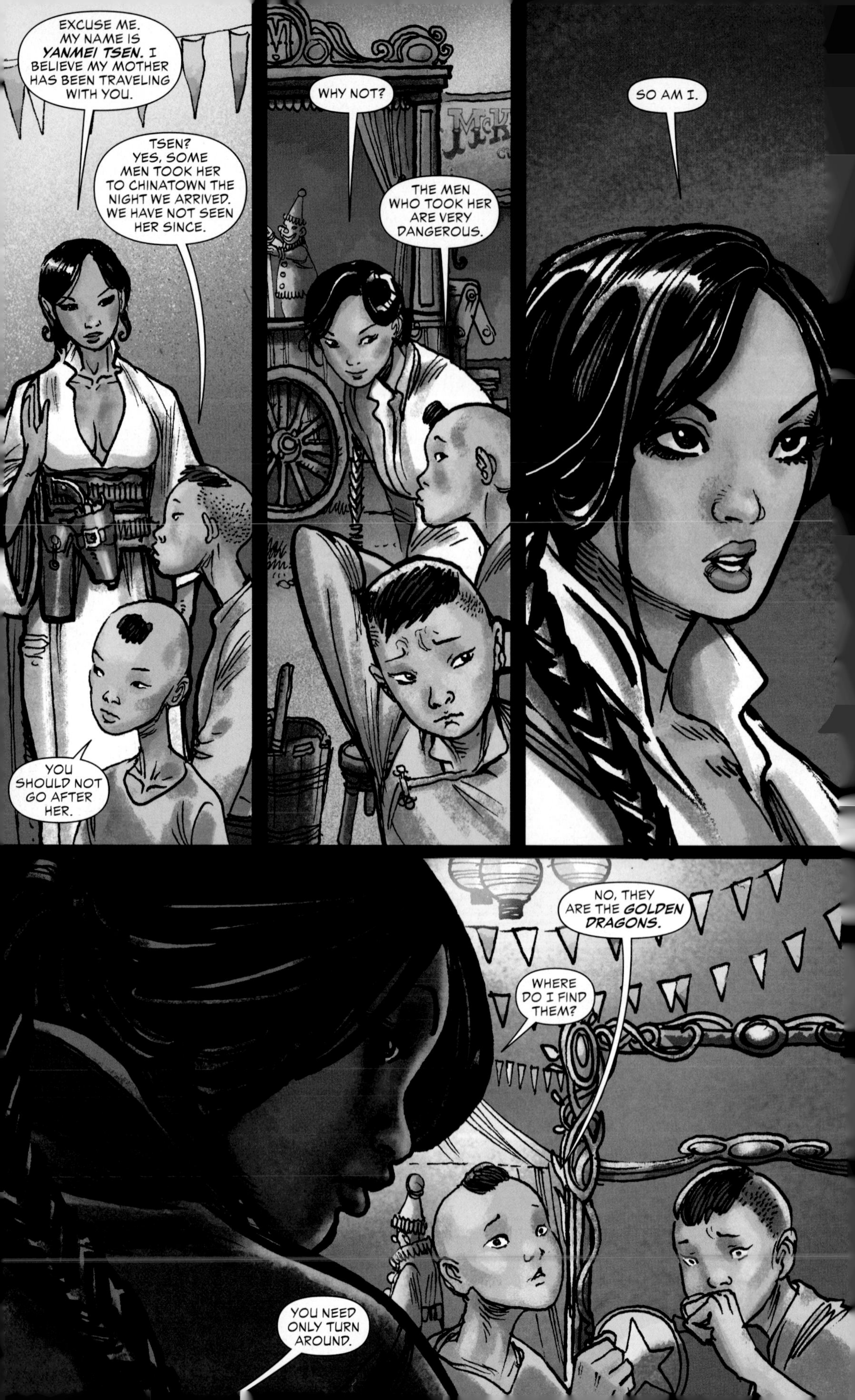
EXCUSE ME. MY NAME IS *YANMEI TSEN.* I BELIEVE MY MOTHER HAS BEEN TRAVELING WITH YOU.
TSEN? YES, SOME MEN TOOK HER TO CHINATOWN THE NIGHT WE ARRIVED. WE HAVE NOT SEEN HER SINCE.
YOU SHOULD NOT GO AFTER HER.
WHY NOT?
THE MEN WHO TOOK HER ARE VERY DANGEROUS.
SO AM I.
WHERE DO I FIND THEM?
NO, THEY ARE THE *GOLDEN DRAGONS.*
YOU NEED ONLY TURN AROUND.

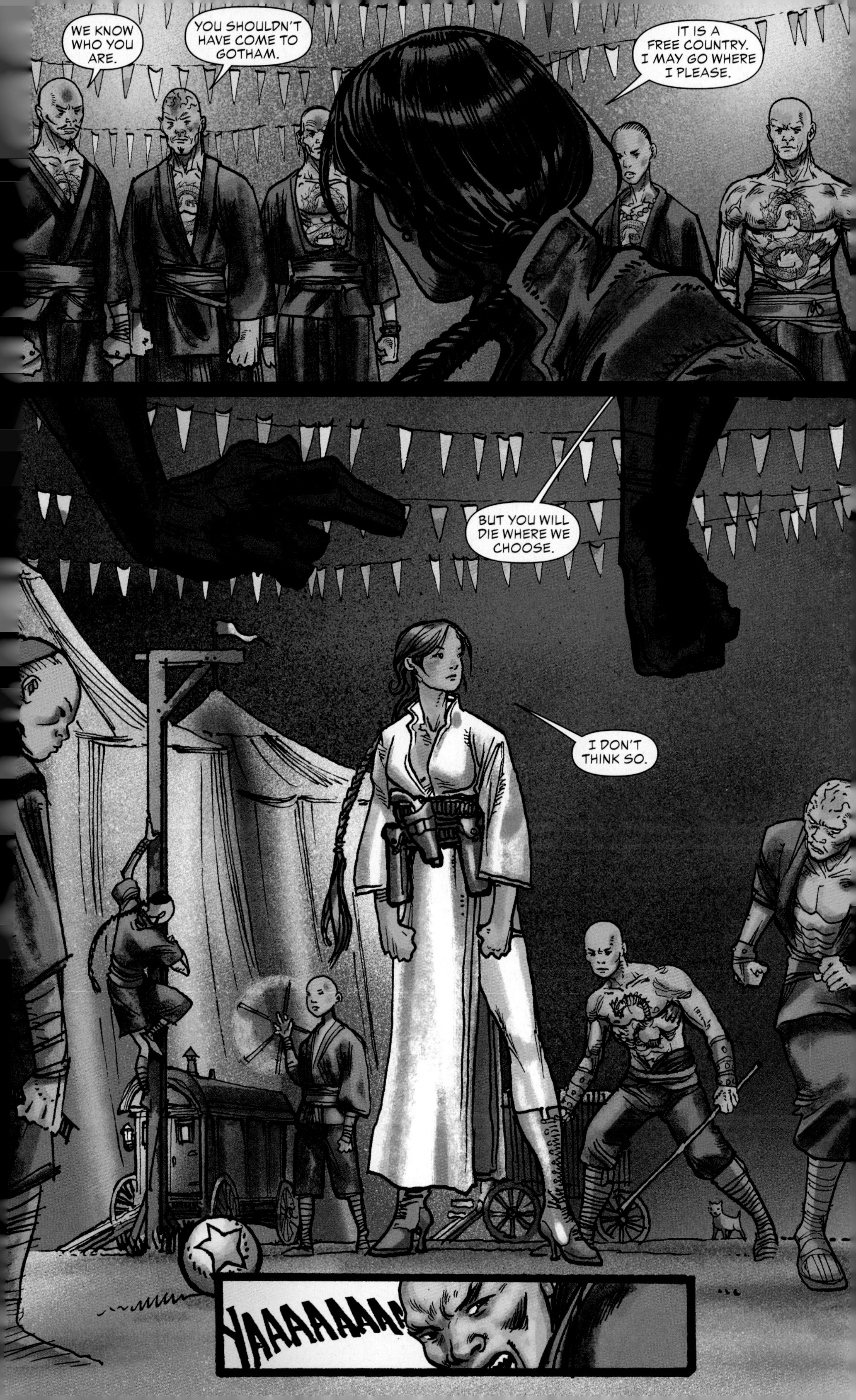
WE KNOW WHO YOU ARE.
YOU SHOULDN'T HAVE COME TO GOTHAM.
IT IS A FREE COUNTRY. I MAY GO WHERE I PLEASE.
BUT YOU WILL DIE WHERE WE CHOOSE.
I DON'T THINK SO.
YAAAAAAA!

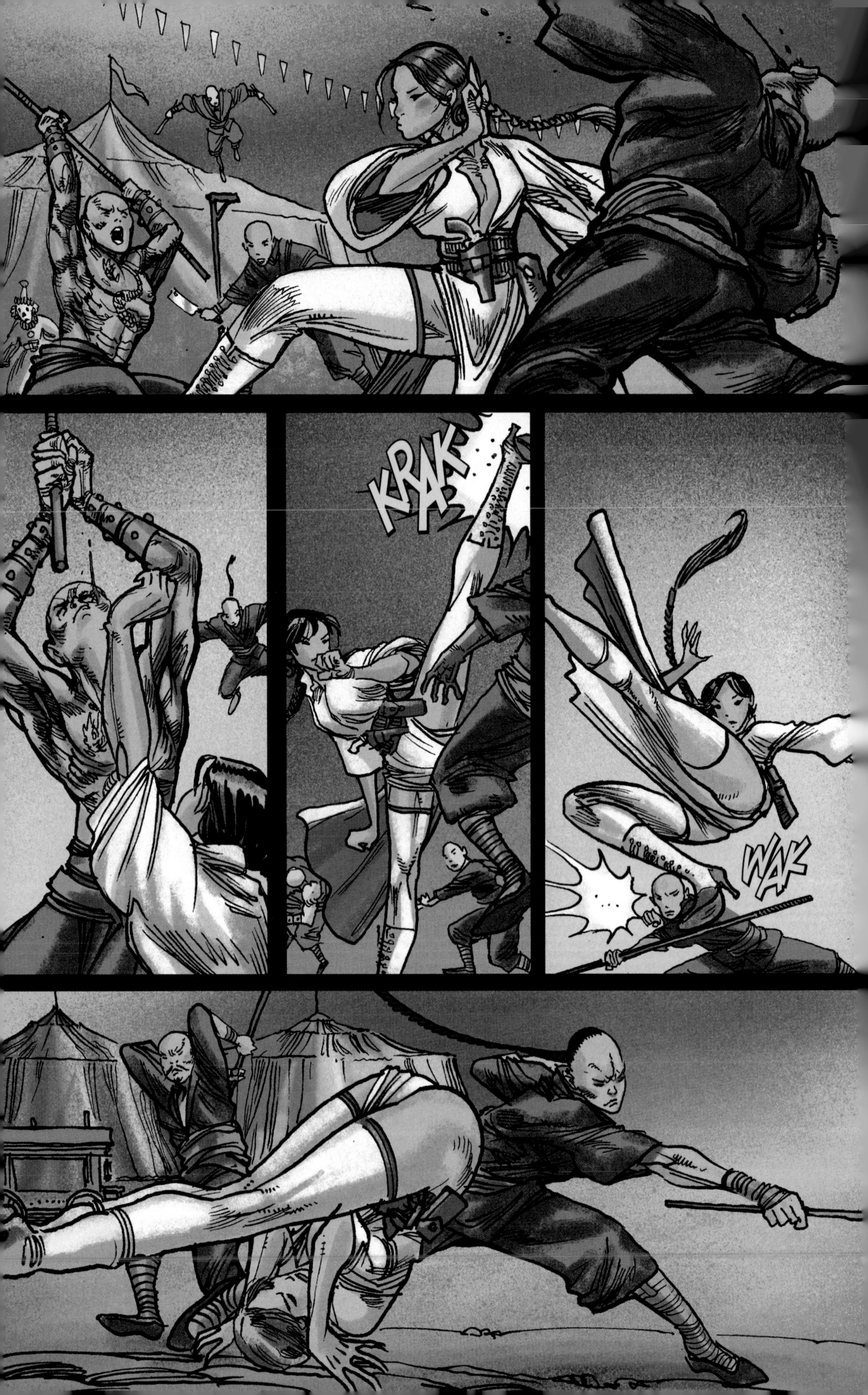
KRAK
WAK

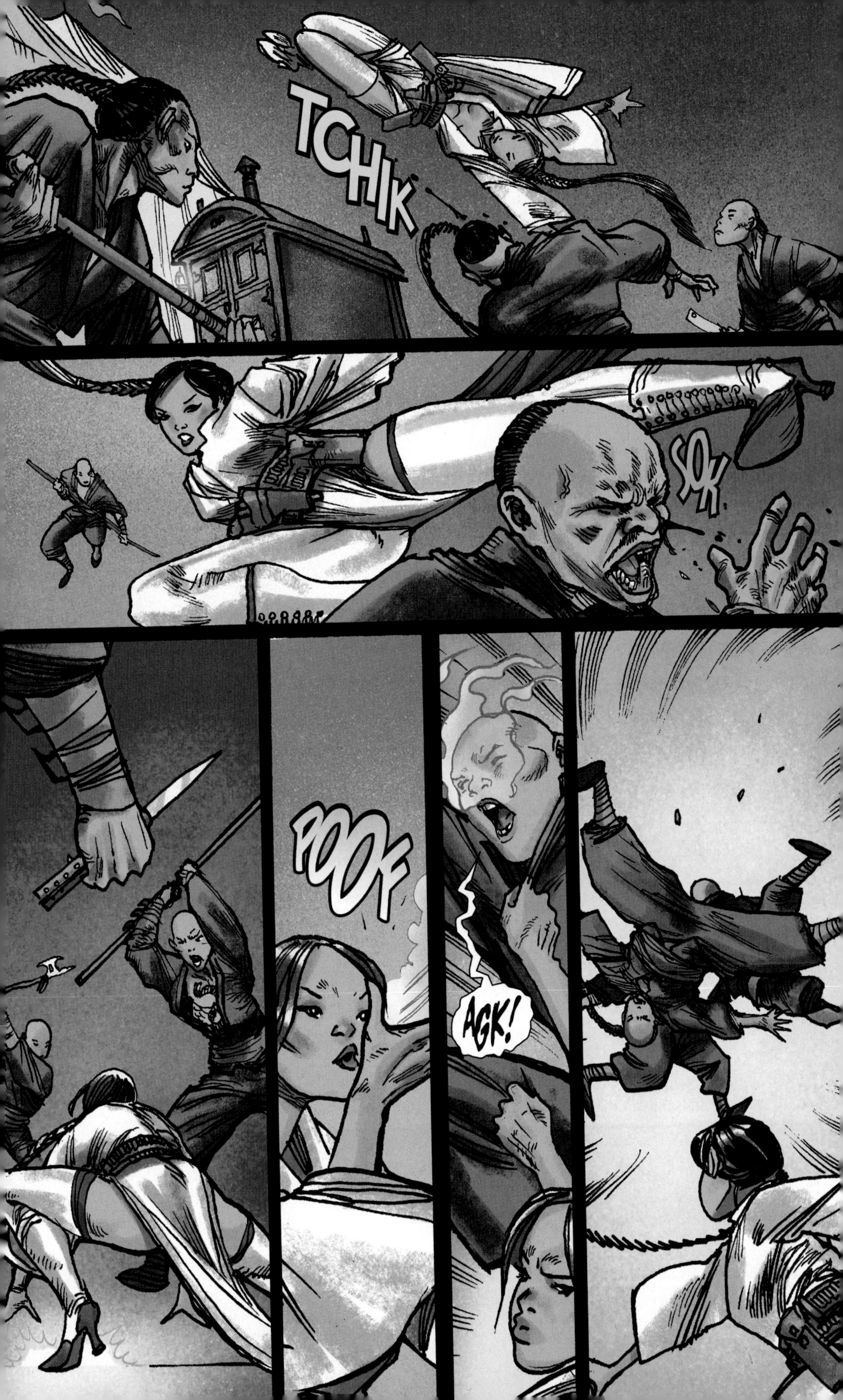
TCHIK
SOK
POOF
AGK!

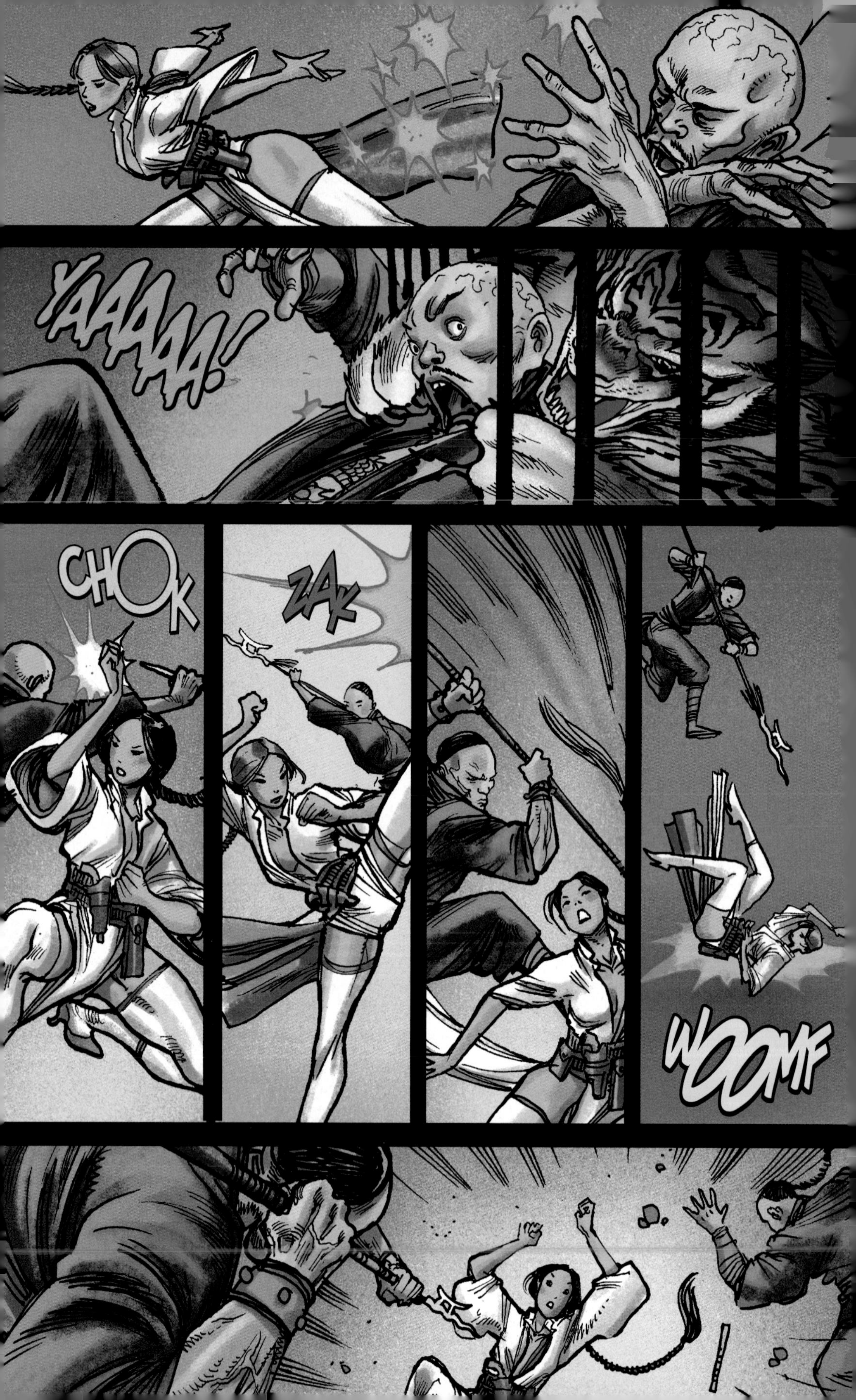
YAAAAA!
CHOK
ZAK
WOOMF

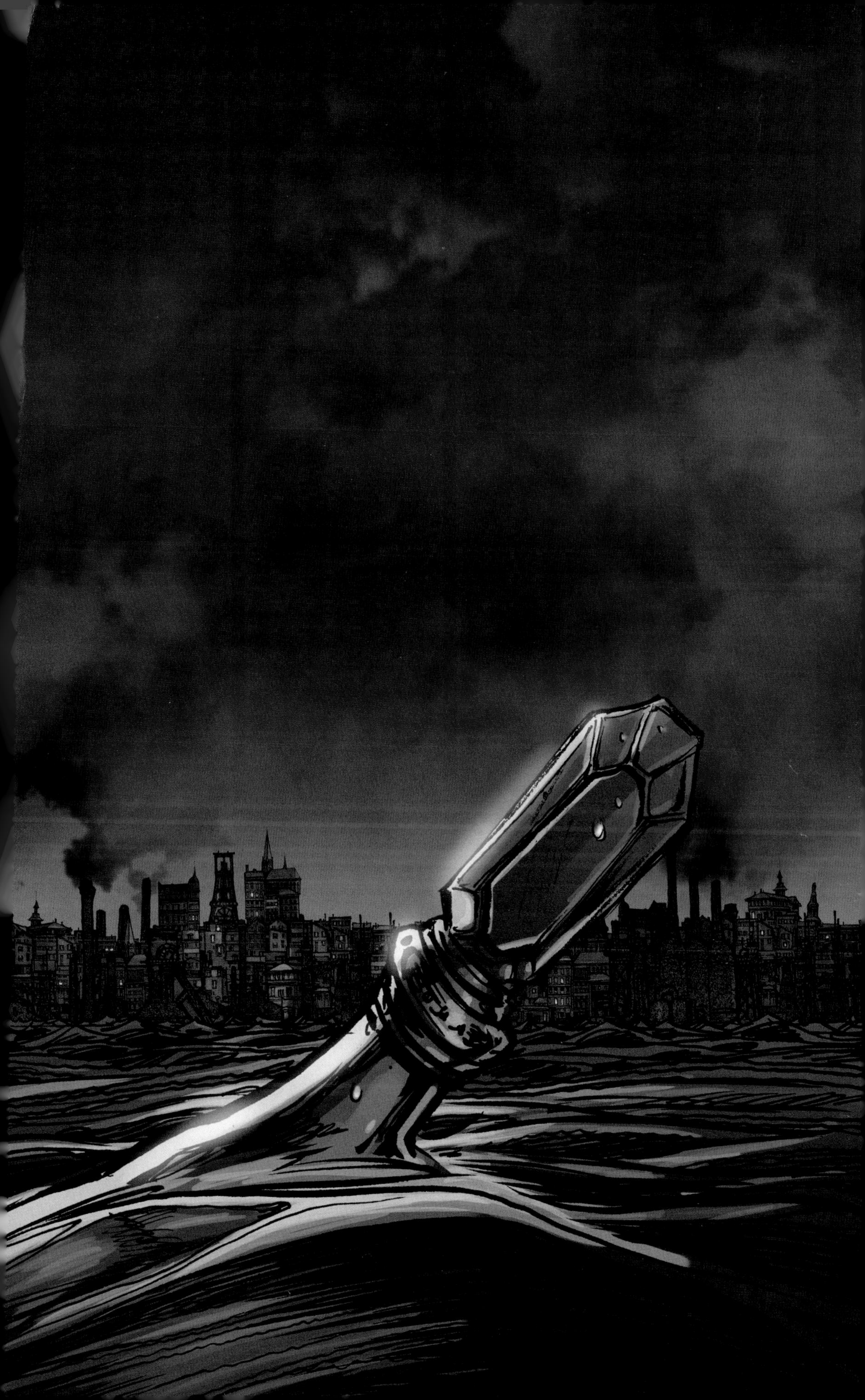

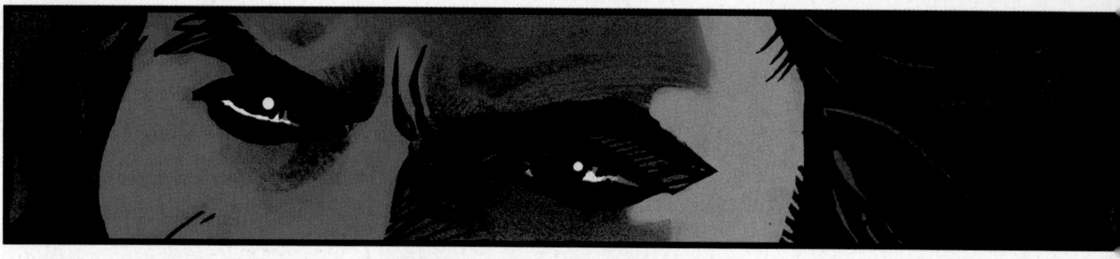

The Englishman

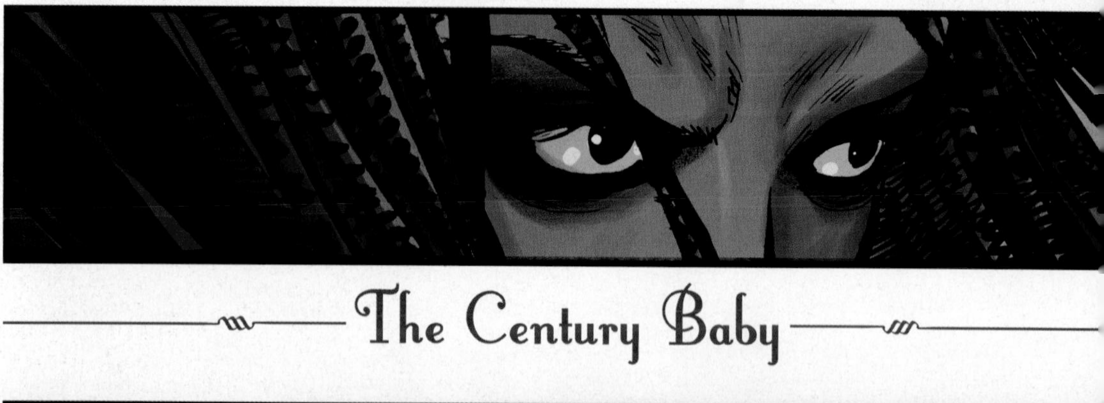

The Century Baby

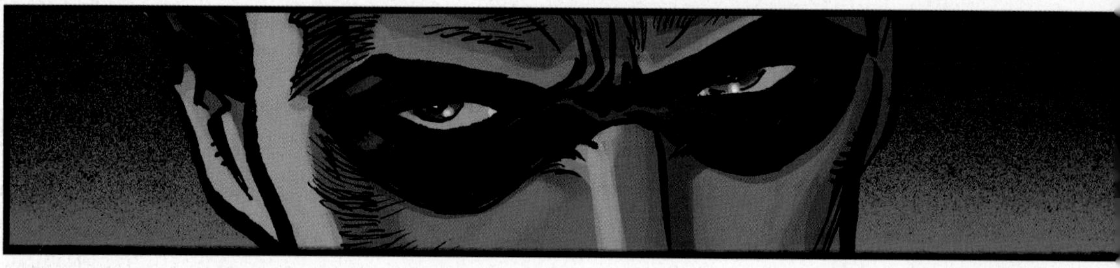

The Lawman

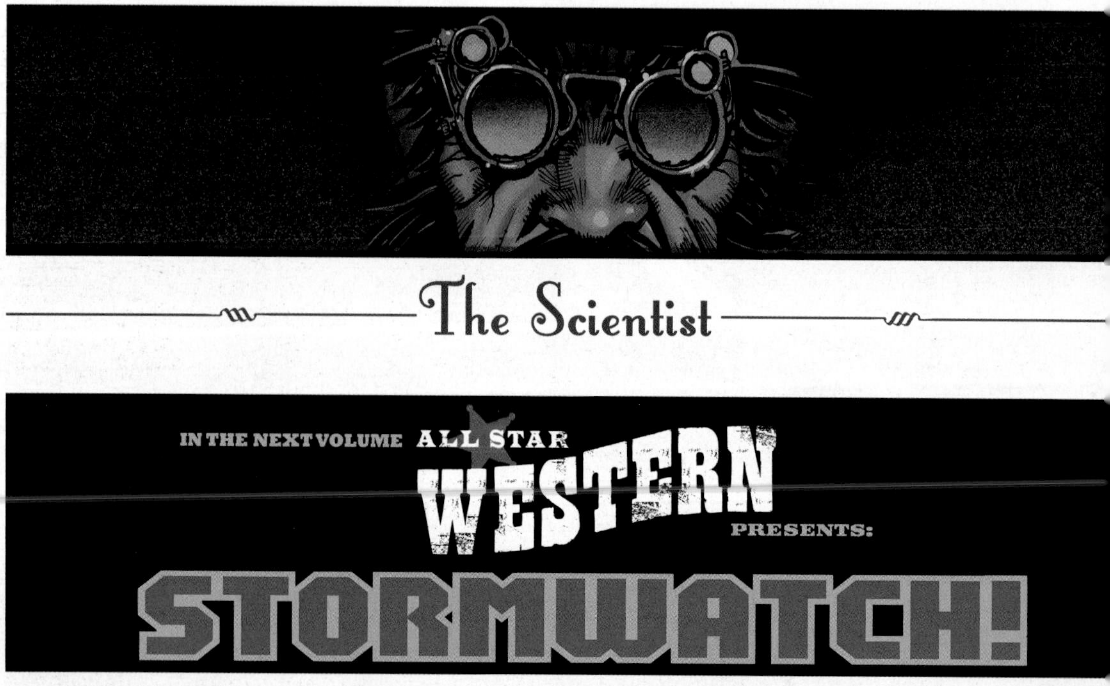

The Scientist

IN THE NEXT VOLUME ALL STAR WESTERN PRESENTS:

STORMWATCH!

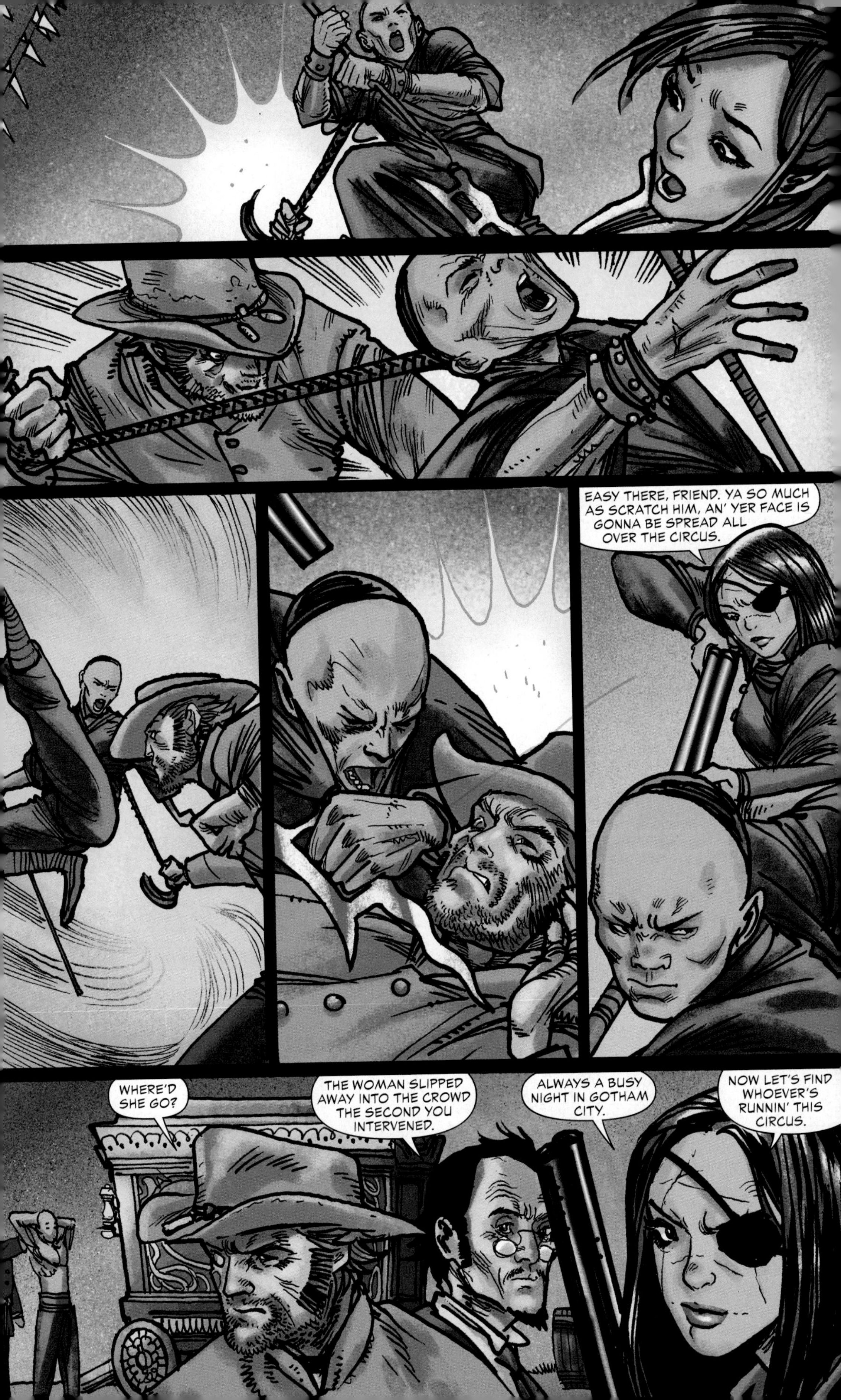
EASY THERE, FRIEND. YA SO MUCH AS SCRATCH HIM, AN' YER FACE IS GONNA BE SPREAD ALL OVER THE CIRCUS.
WHERE'D SHE GO?
THE WOMAN SLIPPED AWAY INTO THE CROWD THE SECOND YOU INTERVENED.
ALWAYS A BUSY NIGHT IN GOTHAM CITY.
NOW LET'S FIND WHOEVER'S RUNNIN' THIS CIRCUS.

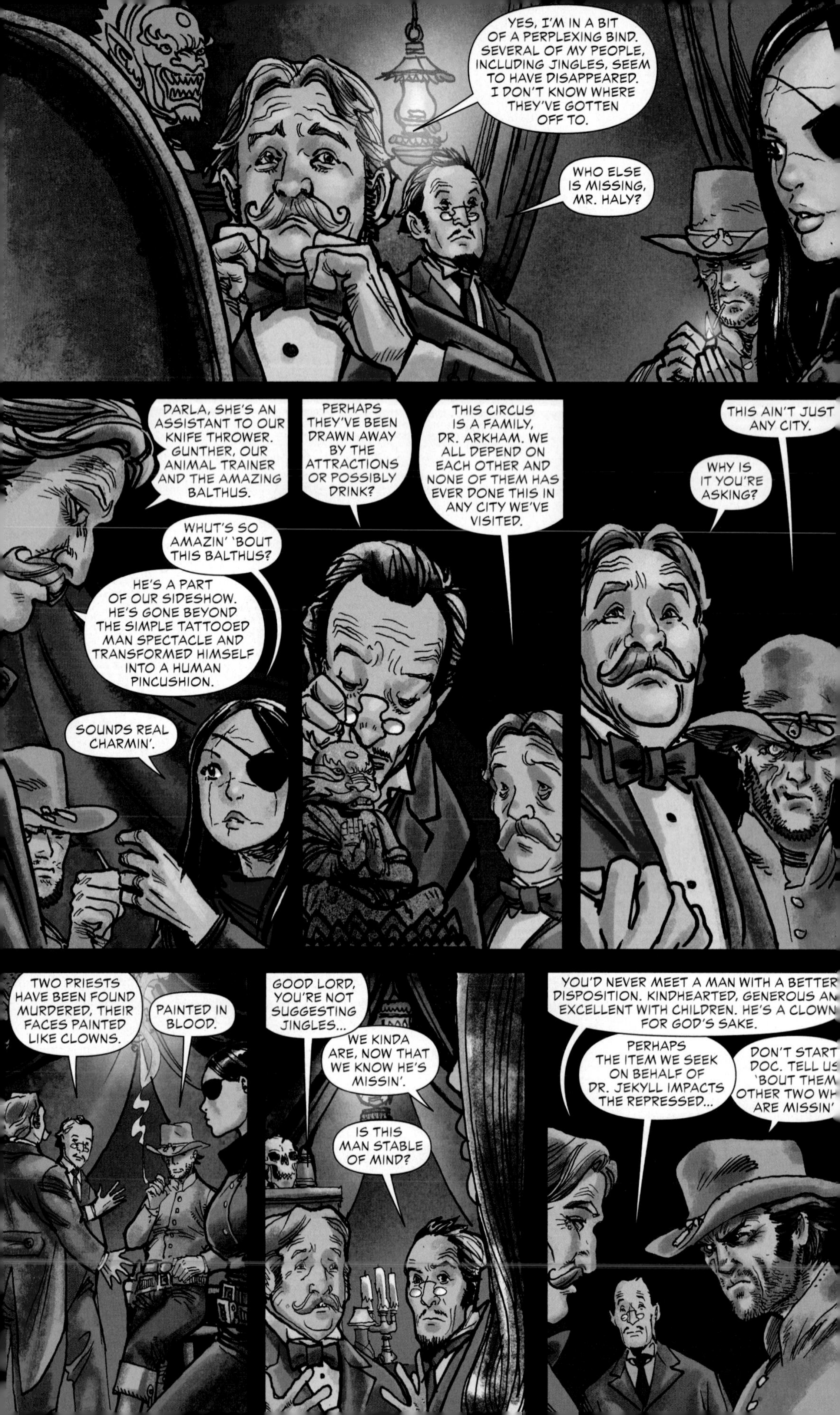
YES, I'M IN A BIT OF A PERPLEXING BIND. SEVERAL OF MY PEOPLE, INCLUDING JINGLES, SEEM TO HAVE DISAPPEARED. I DON'T KNOW WHERE THEY'VE GOTTEN OFF TO.
WHO ELSE IS MISSING, MR. HALY?
DARLA, SHE'S AN ASSISTANT TO OUR KNIFE THROWER. GUNTHER, OUR ANIMAL TRAINER AND THE AMAZING BALTHUS.
WHUT'S SO AMAZIN' 'BOUT THIS BALTHUS?
HE'S A PART OF OUR SIDESHOW. HE'S GONE BEYOND THE SIMPLE TATTOOED MAN SPECTACLE AND TRANSFORMED HIMSELF INTO A HUMAN PINCUSHION.
SOUNDS REAL CHARMIN'.
PERHAPS THEY'VE BEEN DRAWN AWAY BY THE ATTRACTIONS OR POSSIBLY DRINK?
THIS CIRCUS IS A FAMILY, DR. ARKHAM. WE ALL DEPEND ON EACH OTHER AND NONE OF THEM HAS EVER DONE THIS IN ANY CITY WE'VE VISITED.
THIS AIN'T JUST ANY CITY.
WHY IS IT YOU'RE ASKING?
TWO PRIESTS HAVE BEEN FOUND MURDERED, THEIR FACES PAINTED LIKE CLOWNS.
PAINTED IN BLOOD.
GOOD LORD, YOU'RE NOT SUGGESTING JINGLES...
WE KINDA ARE, NOW THAT WE KNOW HE'S MISSIN'.
IS THIS MAN STABLE OF MIND?
YOU'D NEVER MEET A MAN WITH A BETTER DISPOSITION. KINDHEARTED, GENEROUS AN EXCELLENT WITH CHILDREN. HE'S A CLOWN FOR GOD'S SAKE.
PERHAPS THE ITEM WE SEEK ON BEHALF OF DR. JEKYLL IMPACTS THE REPRESSED...
DON'T START DOC. TELL US 'BOUT THEM OTHER TWO WH ARE MISSIN'

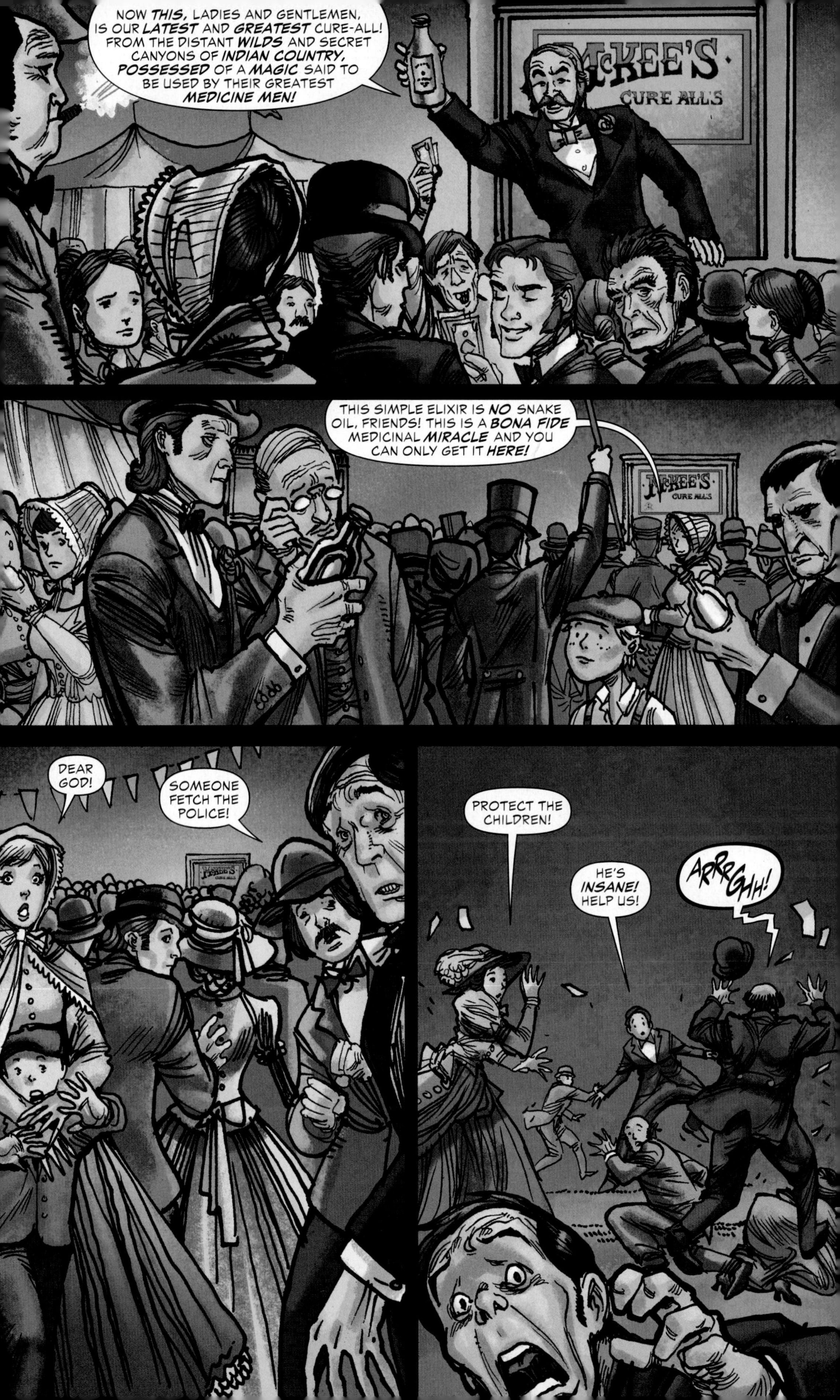
NOW THIS, LADIES AND GENTLEMEN, IS OUR LATEST AND GREATEST CURE-ALL! FROM THE DISTANT WILDS AND SECRET CANYONS OF INDIAN COUNTRY, POSSESSED OF A MAGIC SAID TO BE USED BY THEIR GREATEST MEDICINE MEN!
McKEE'S CURE ALLS
THIS SIMPLE ELIXIR IS NO SNAKE OIL, FRIENDS! THIS IS A BONA FIDE MEDICINAL MIRACLE AND YOU CAN ONLY GET IT HERE!
McKEE'S CURE ALLS
DEAR GOD!
SOMEONE FETCH THE POLICE!
PROTECT THE CHILDREN!
HE'S INSANE! HELP US!
ARRRGHH!

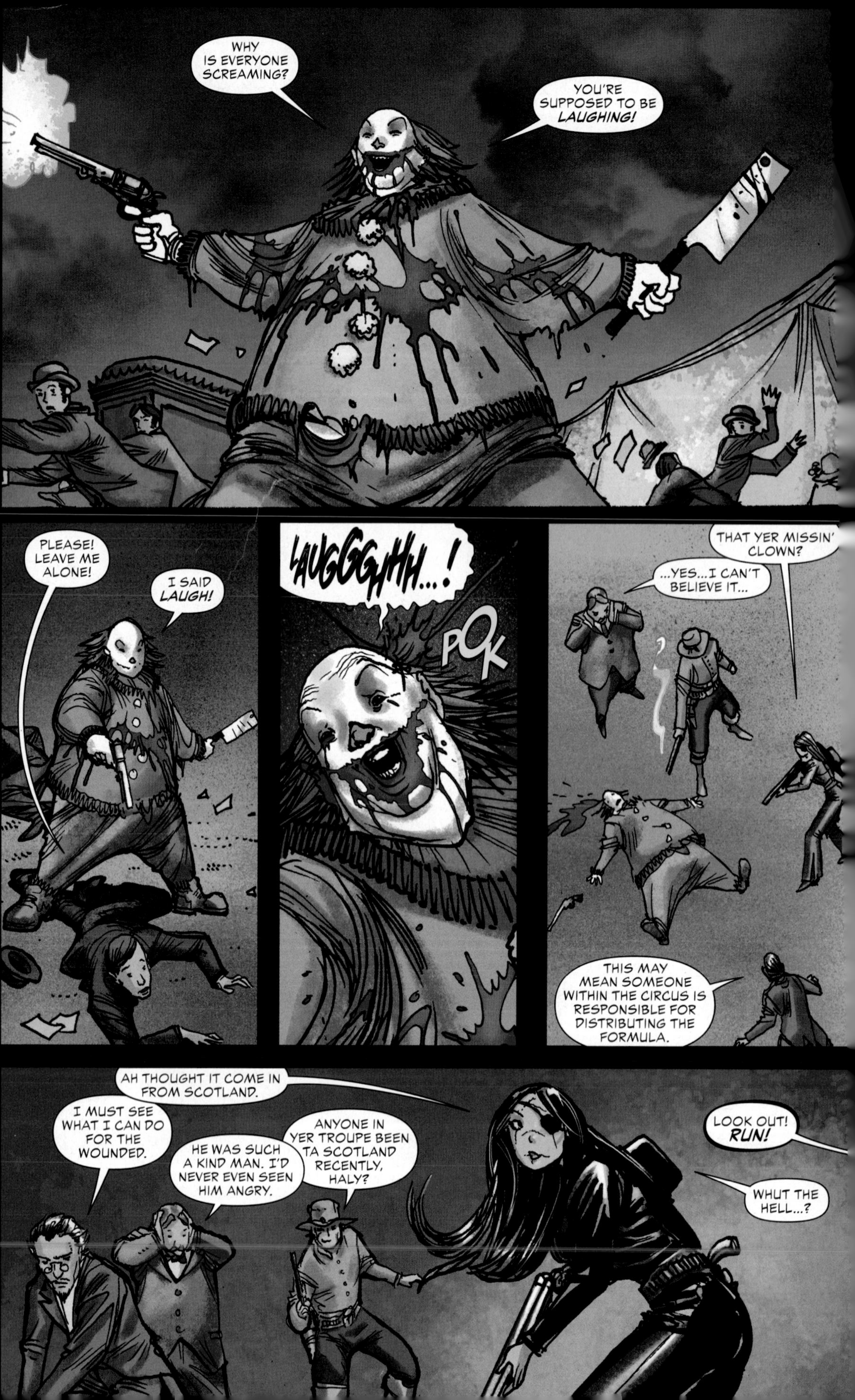

WHY IS EVERYONE SCREAMING?
YOU'RE SUPPOSED TO BE *LAUGHING!*
PLEASE! LEAVE ME ALONE!
I SAID *LAUGH!*
LAUGGGHHH...!
POK
THAT YER MISSIN' CLOWN?
...YES...I CAN'T BELIEVE IT...
THIS MAY MEAN SOMEONE WITHIN THE CIRCUS IS RESPONSIBLE FOR DISTRIBUTING THE FORMULA.
AH THOUGHT IT COME IN FROM SCOTLAND.
I MUST SEE WHAT I CAN DO FOR THE WOUNDED.
HE WAS SUCH A KIND MAN. I'D NEVER EVEN SEEN HIM ANGRY.
ANYONE IN YER TROUPE BEEN TA SCOTLAND RECENTLY, HALY?
LOOK OUT! *RUN!*
WHUT THE HELL...?

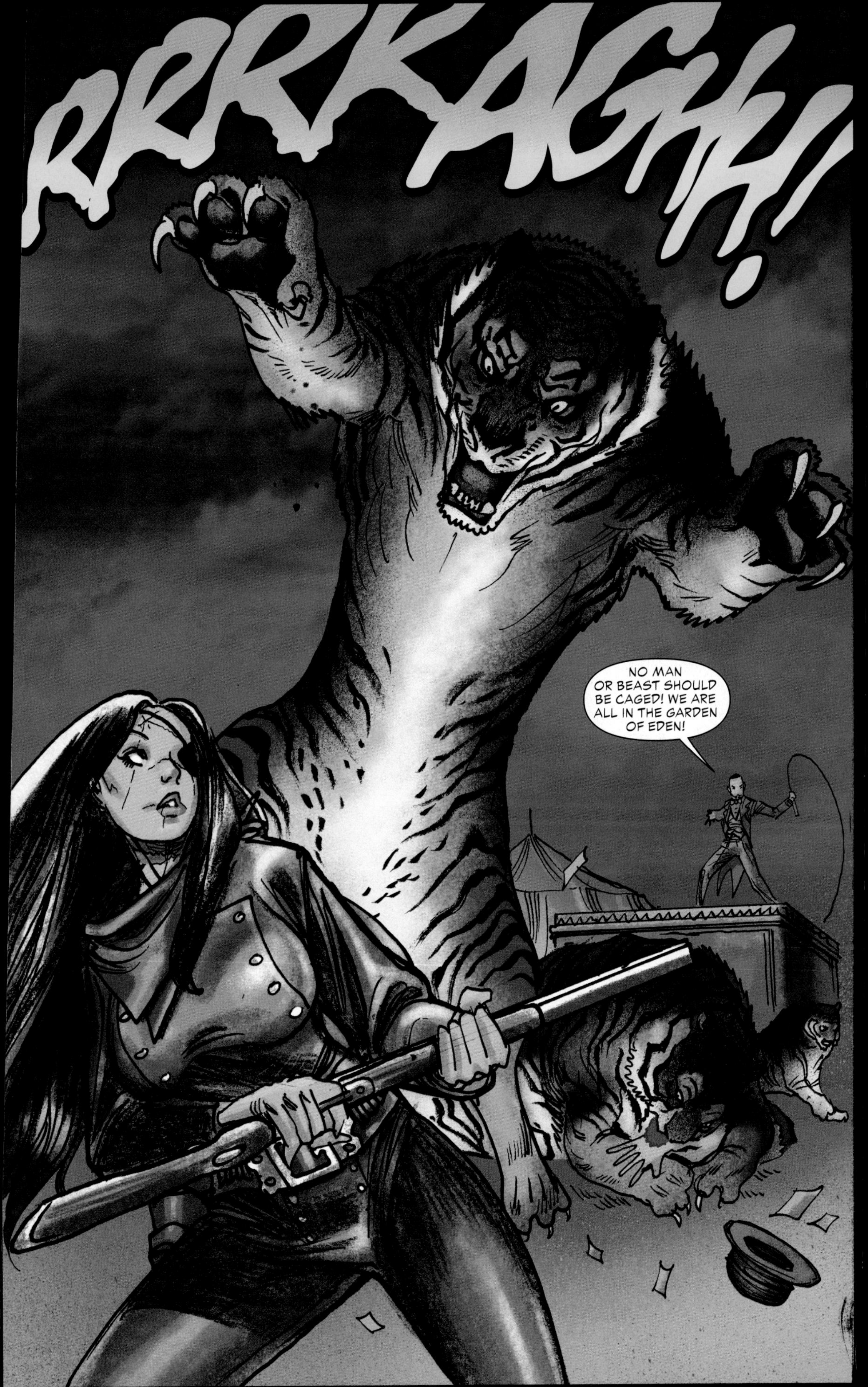
RRRKAGH!
NO MAN OR BEAST SHOULD BE CAGED! WE ARE ALL IN THE GARDEN OF EDEN!

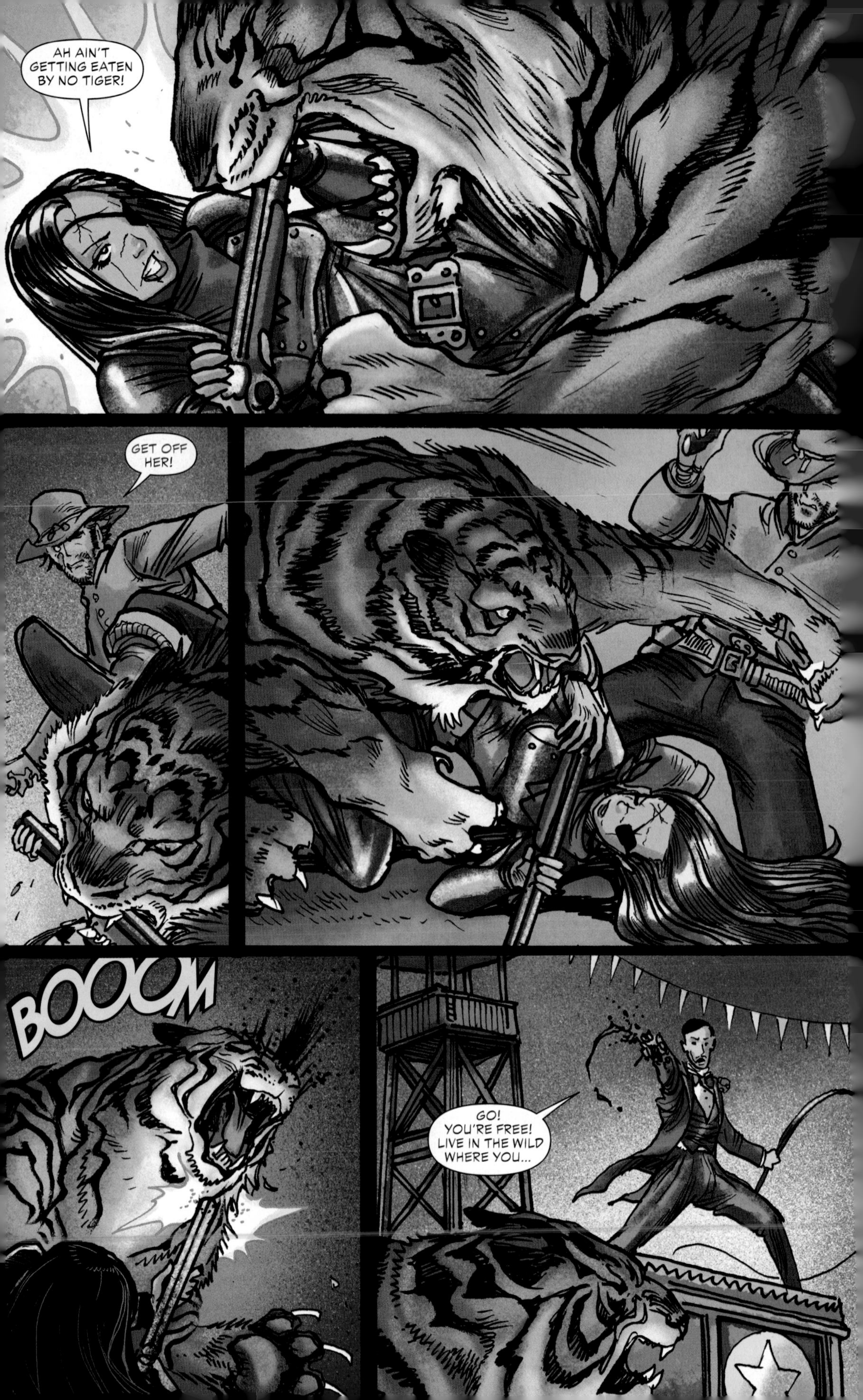
AH AIN'T GETTING EATEN BY NO TIGER!
GET OFF HER!
BOOOM
GO! YOU'RE FREE! LIVE IN THE WILD WHERE YOU...

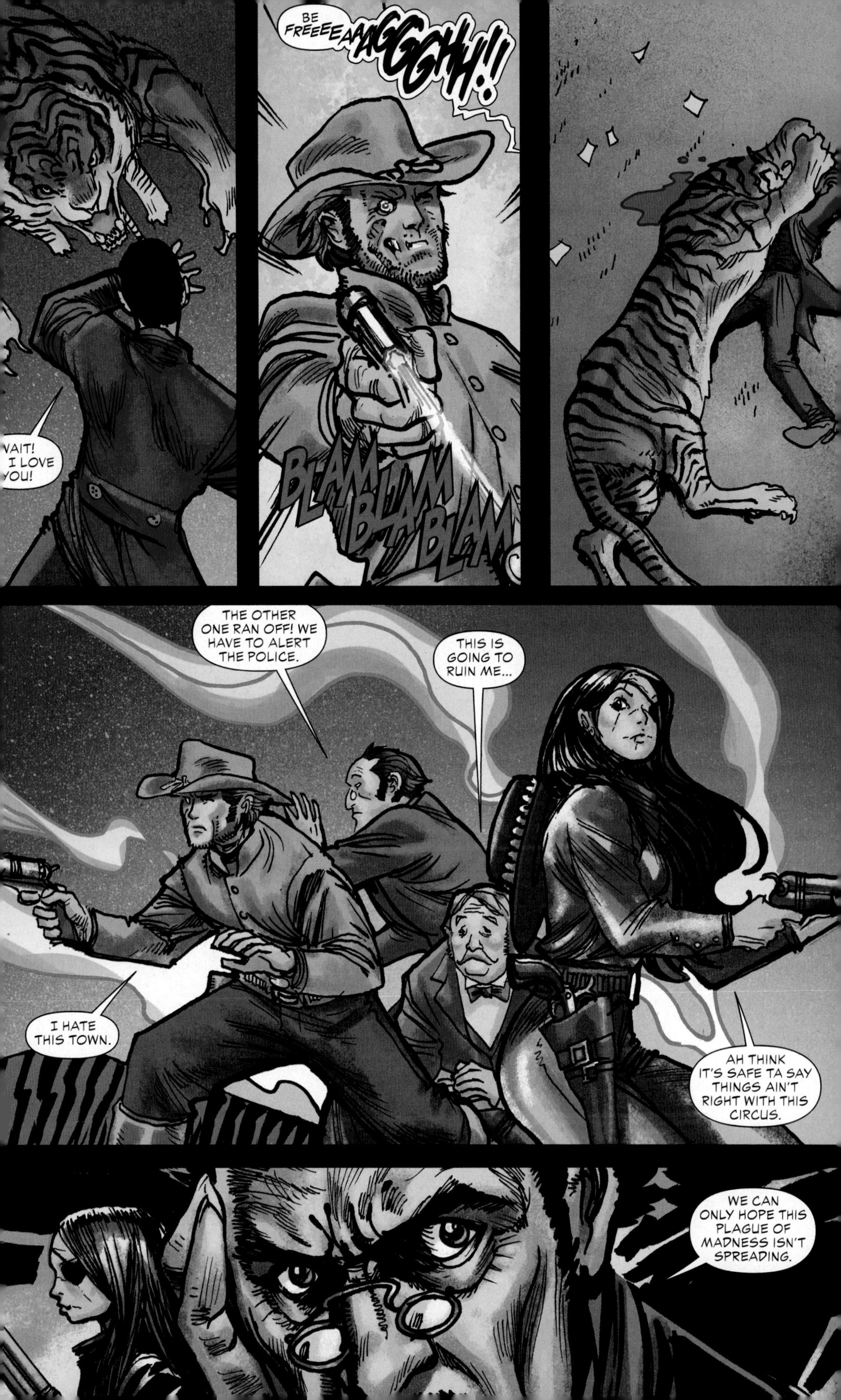
VAIT! I LOVE YOU!
BE FREEEEAAAGGGHH!!
BLAM BLAM BLAM BLAM
THE OTHER ONE RAN OFF! WE HAVE TO ALERT THE POLICE.
THIS IS GOING TO RUIN ME...
I HATE THIS TOWN.
AH THINK IT'S SAFE TA SAY THINGS AIN'T RIGHT WITH THIS CIRCUS.
WE CAN ONLY HOPE THIS PLAGUE OF MADNESS ISN'T SPREADING.

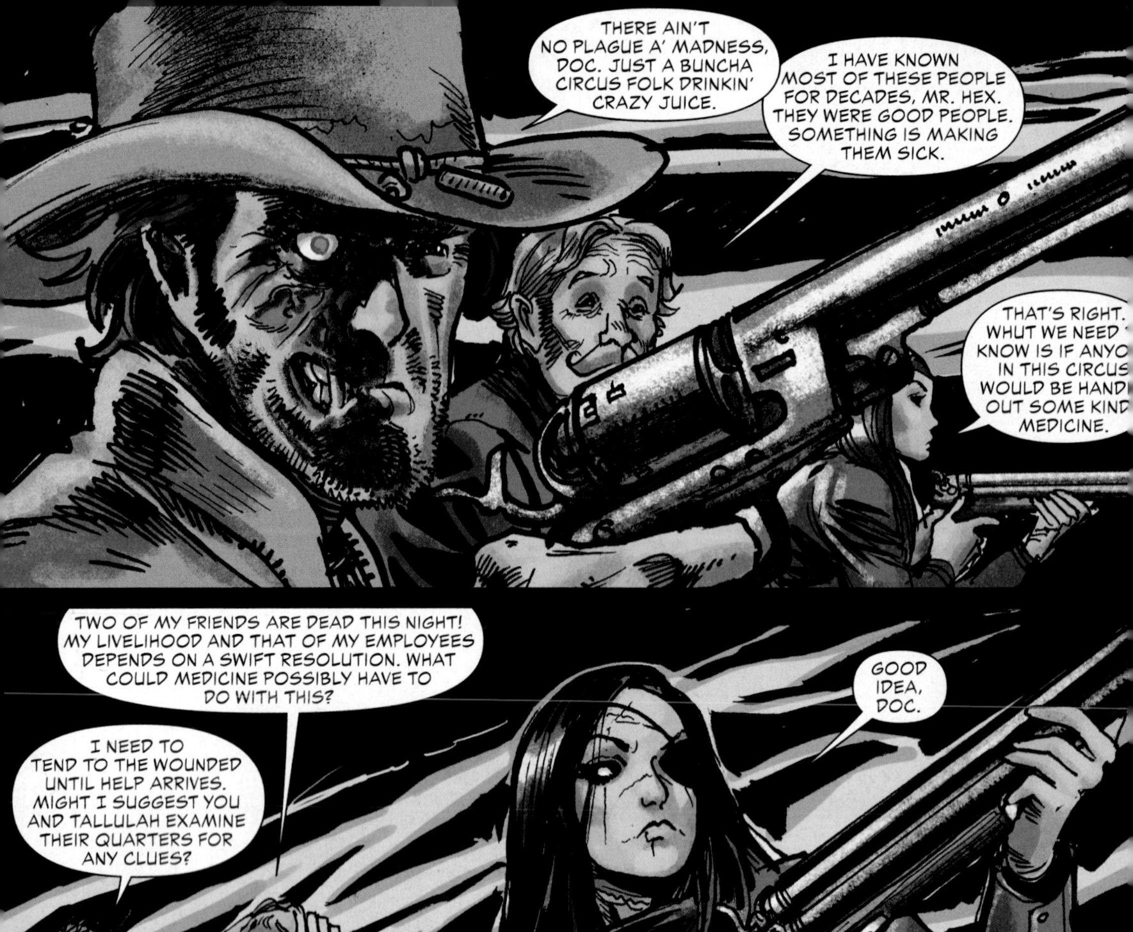
THERE AIN'T NO PLAGUE A' MADNESS, DOC. JUST A BUNCHA CIRCUS FOLK DRINKIN' CRAZY JUICE.
I HAVE KNOWN MOST OF THESE PEOPLE FOR DECADES, MR. HEX. THEY WERE GOOD PEOPLE. SOMETHING IS MAKING THEM SICK.
THAT'S RIGHT. WHUT WE NEED KNOW IS IF ANYO IN THIS CIRCUS WOULD BE HAND OUT SOME KIND MEDICINE.
TWO OF MY FRIENDS ARE DEAD THIS NIGHT! MY LIVELIHOOD AND THAT OF MY EMPLOYEES DEPENDS ON A SWIFT RESOLUTION. WHAT COULD MEDICINE POSSIBLY HAVE TO DO WITH THIS?
I NEED TO TEND TO THE WOUNDED UNTIL HELP ARRIVES. MIGHT I SUGGEST YOU AND TALLULAH EXAMINE THEIR QUARTERS FOR ANY CLUES?
GOOD IDEA, DOC.
YA GOT A SNAKE OIL SALESMAN WITH YA?
AS A MATTER OF FACT WE DO. MR. McKEE FROM SMALLVILLE JOINED WITH US A FEW MONTHS BACK, BUT I STILL DON'T SEE...
I'LL EXPLAIN TO THE AUTHORIT AS BEST I CAN. TA THEM TO McKEE

No place to Hyde in Gotham

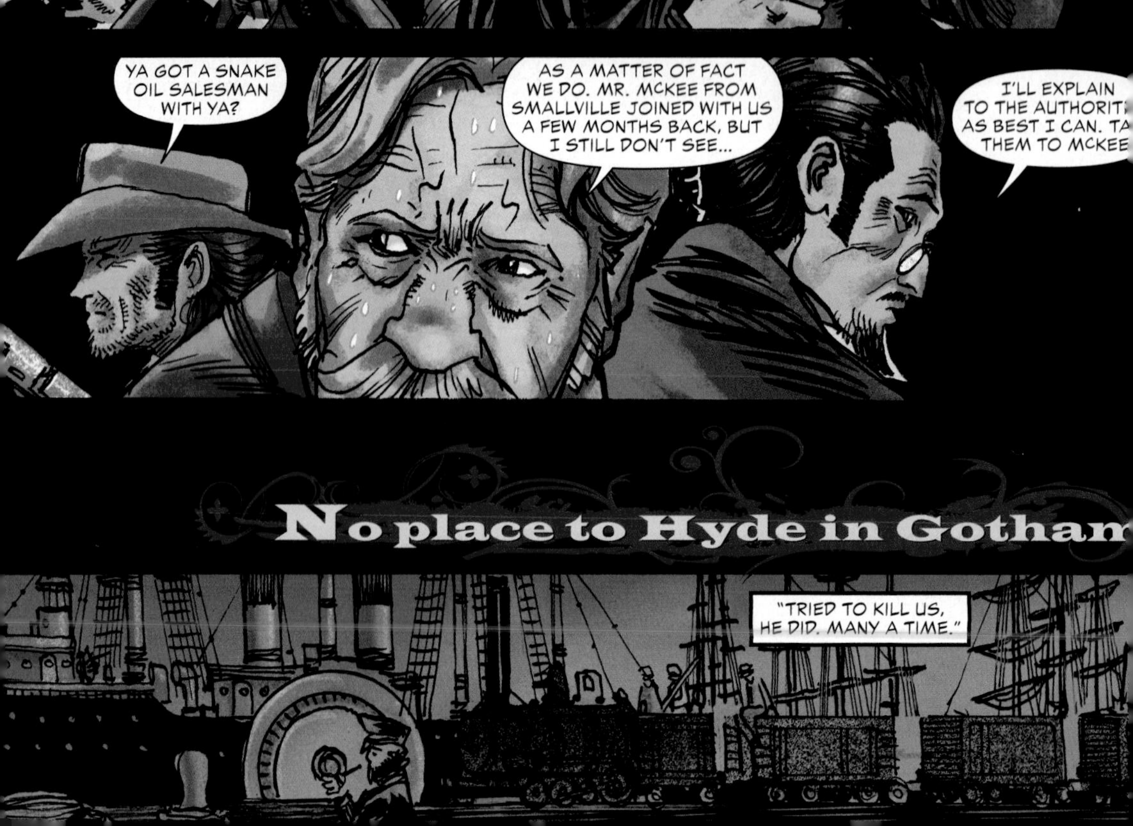
"TRIED TO KILL US, HE DID. MANY A TIME."

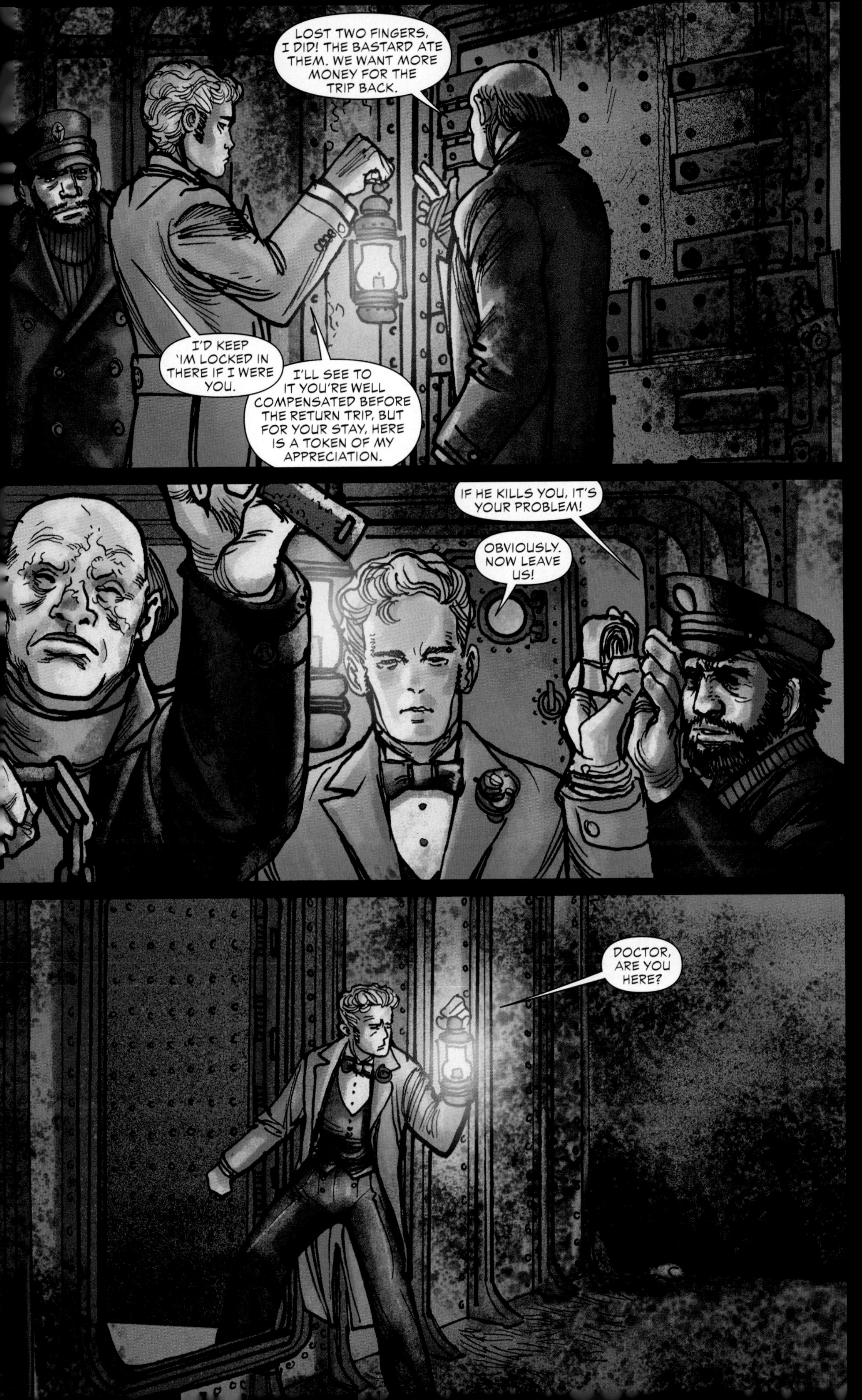
LOST TWO FINGERS, I DID! THE BASTARD ATE THEM. WE WANT MORE MONEY FOR THE TRIP BACK.
I'D KEEP 'IM LOCKED IN THERE IF I WERE YOU.
I'LL SEE TO IT YOU'RE WELL COMPENSATED BEFORE THE RETURN TRIP, BUT FOR YOUR STAY, HERE IS A TOKEN OF MY APPRECIATION.
IF HE KILLS YOU, IT'S YOUR PROBLEM!
OBVIOUSLY. NOW LEAVE US!
DOCTOR, ARE YOU HERE?

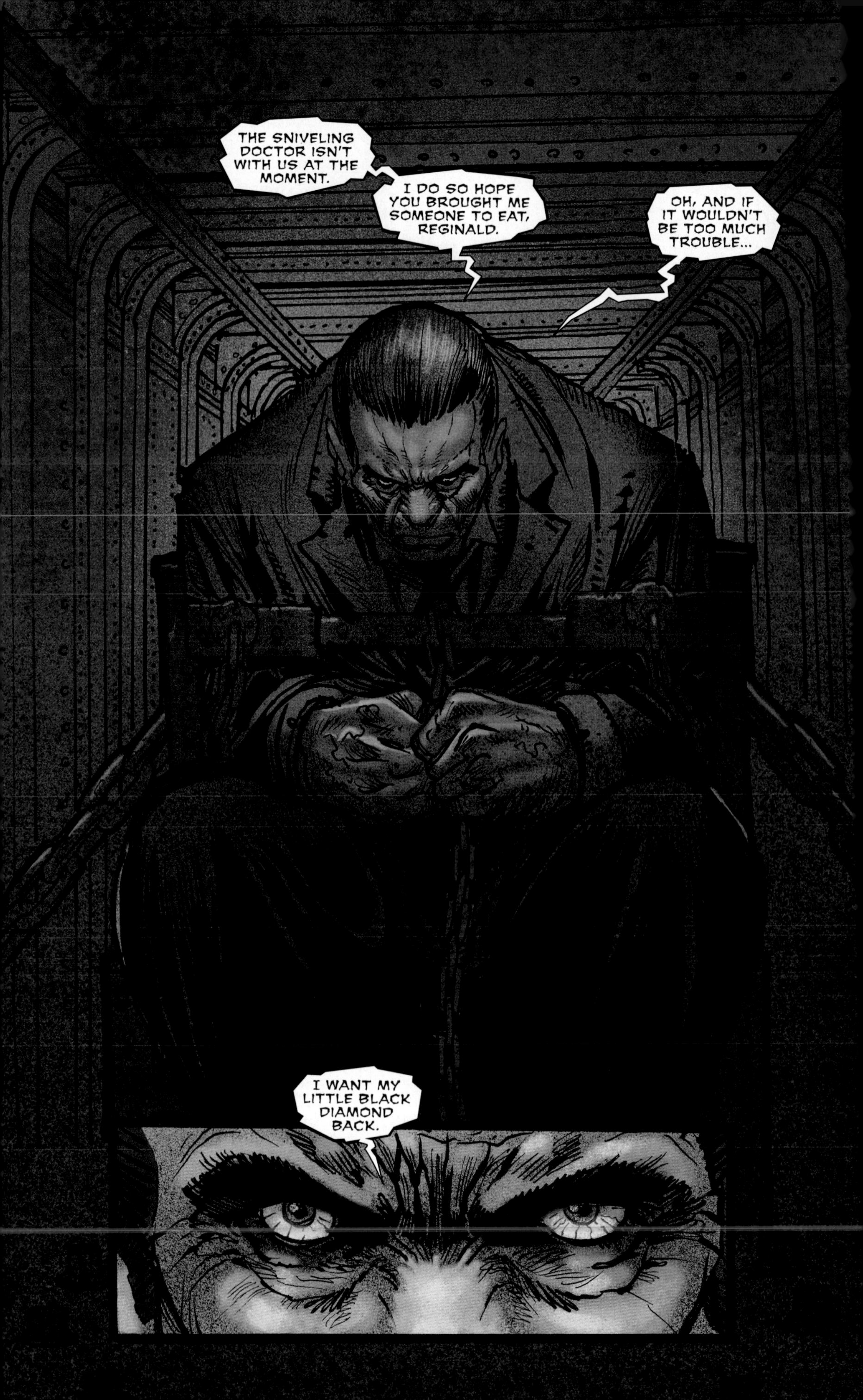
THE SNIVELING DOCTOR ISN'T WITH US AT THE MOMENT.
I DO SO HOPE YOU BROUGHT ME SOMEONE TO EAT, REGINALD.
OH, AND IF IT WOULDN'T BE TOO MUCH TROUBLE...
I WANT MY LITTLE BLACK DIAMOND BACK.

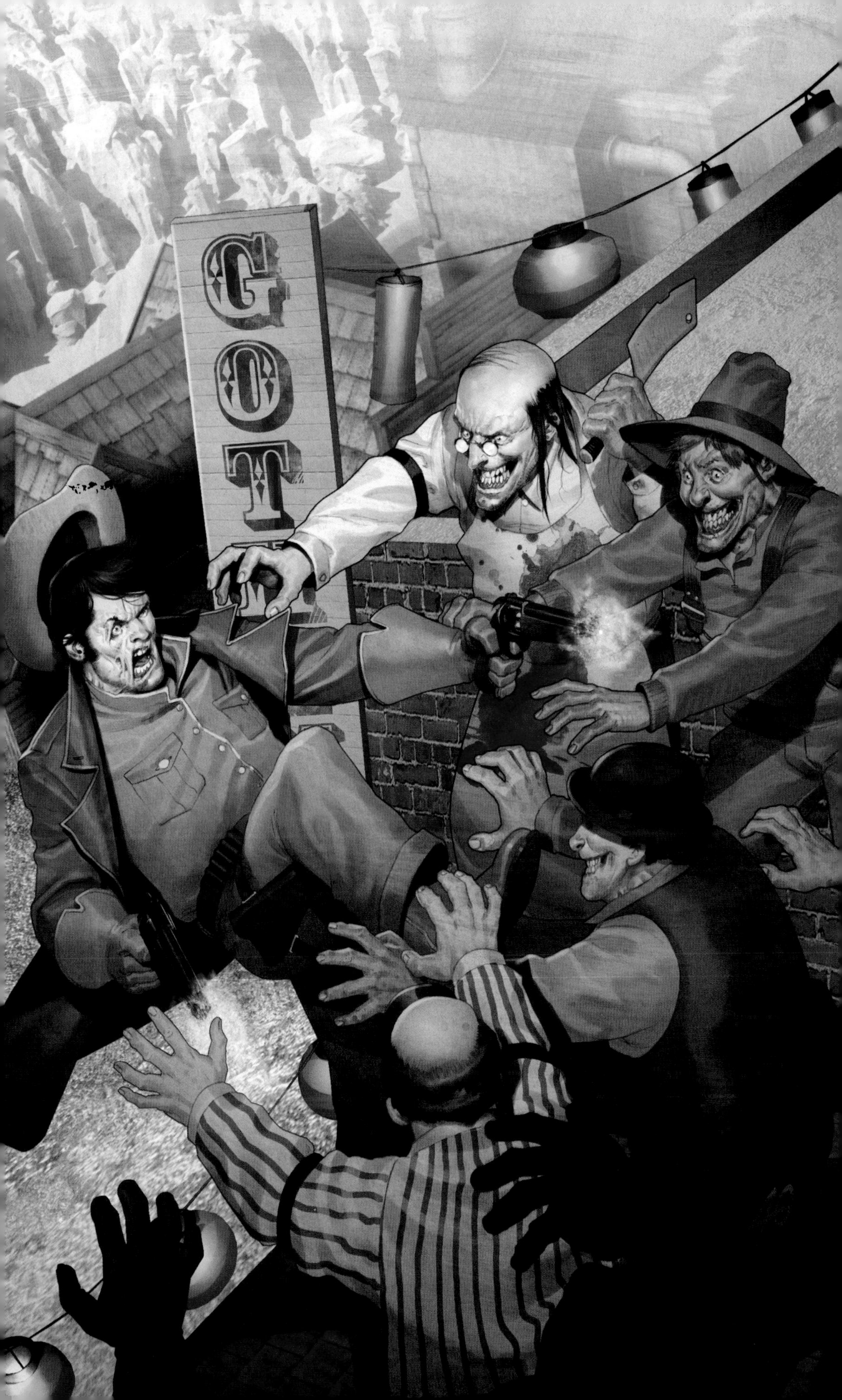

G
O
T

HYDE IN AMERICA

JIMMY PALMIOTTI & JUSTIN GRAY writers MORITAT artist cover art by ARIEL OLIVETTI

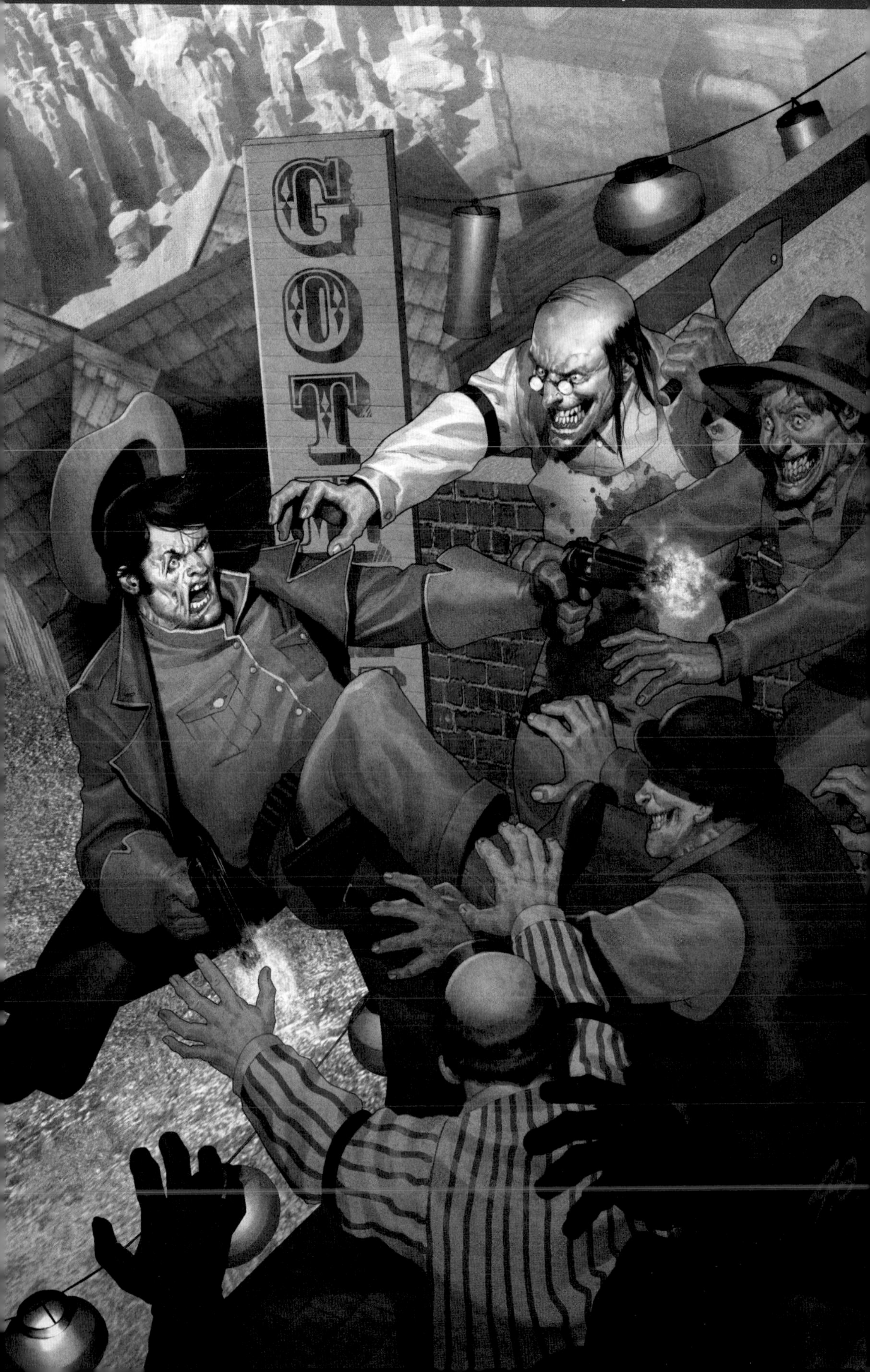
GOT

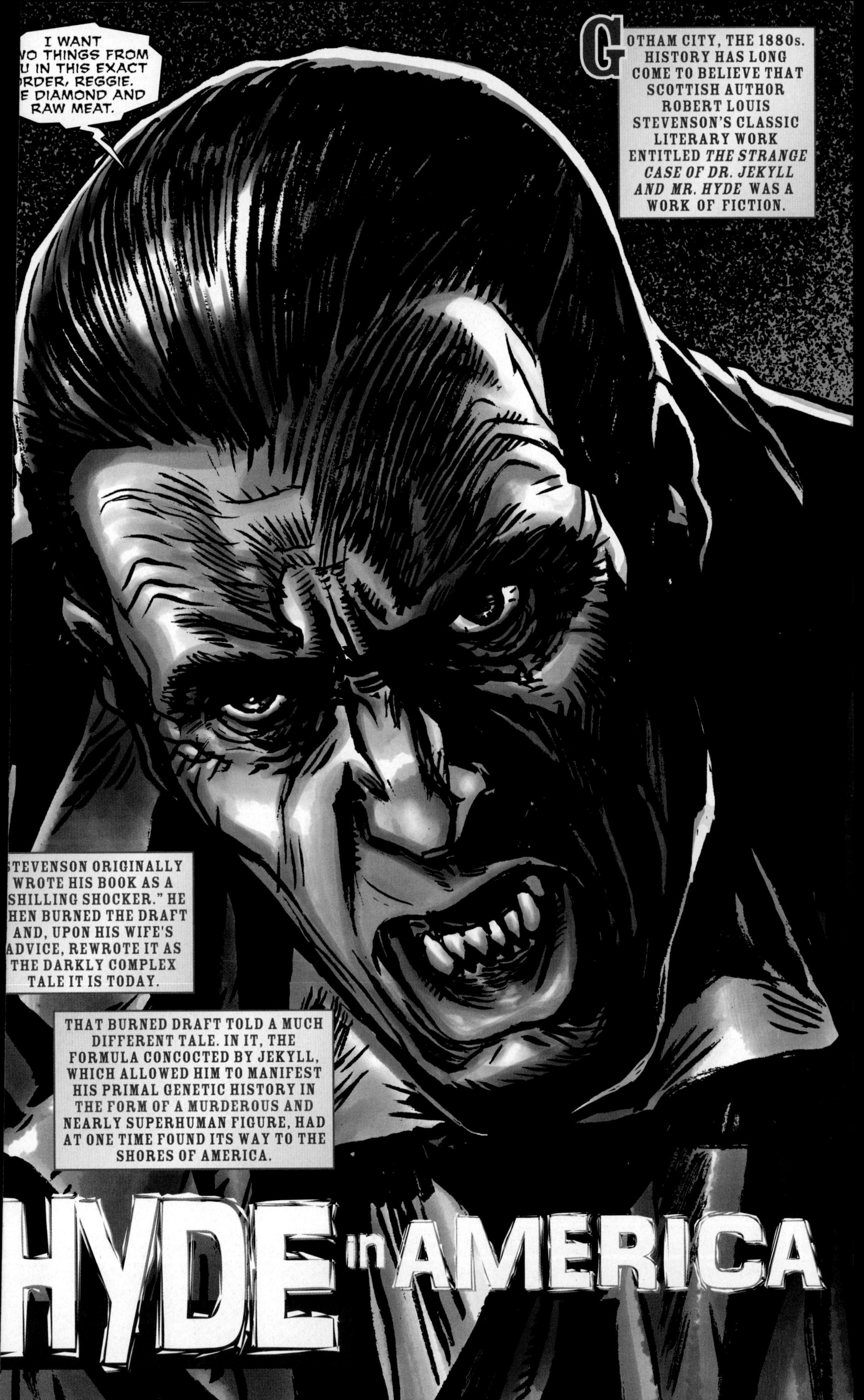
I WANT WO THINGS FROM U IN THIS EXACT RDER, REGGIE. E DIAMOND AND RAW MEAT.
GOTHAM CITY, THE 1880s. HISTORY HAS LONG COME TO BELIEVE THAT SCOTTISH AUTHOR ROBERT LOUIS STEVENSON'S CLASSIC LITERARY WORK ENTITLED *THE STRANGE CASE OF DR. JEKYLL AND MR. HYDE* WAS A WORK OF FICTION.
STEVENSON ORIGINALLY WROTE HIS BOOK AS A SHILLING SHOCKER." HE HEN BURNED THE DRAFT AND, UPON HIS WIFE'S ADVICE, REWROTE IT AS THE DARKLY COMPLEX TALE IT IS TODAY.
THAT BURNED DRAFT TOLD A MUCH DIFFERENT TALE. IN IT, THE FORMULA CONCOCTED BY JEKYLL, WHICH ALLOWED HIM TO MANIFEST HIS PRIMAL GENETIC HISTORY IN THE FORM OF A MURDEROUS AND NEARLY SUPERHUMAN FIGURE, HAD AT ONE TIME FOUND ITS WAY TO THE SHORES OF AMERICA.
HYDE in AMERICA

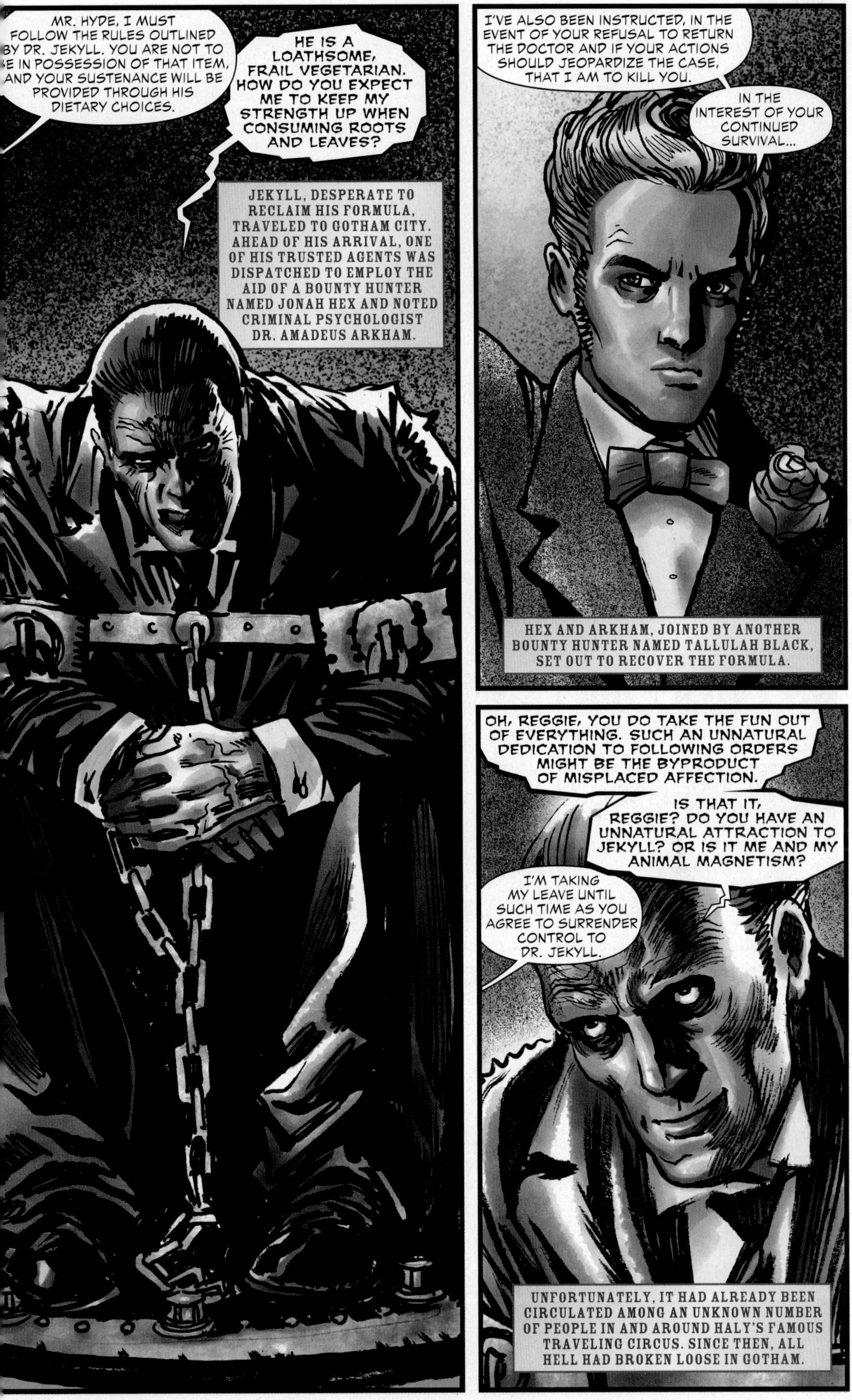
MR. HYDE, I MUST FOLLOW THE RULES OUTLINED BY DR. JEKYLL. YOU ARE NOT TO BE IN POSSESSION OF THAT ITEM, AND YOUR SUSTENANCE WILL BE PROVIDED THROUGH HIS DIETARY CHOICES.
HE IS A LOATHSOME, FRAIL VEGETARIAN. HOW DO YOU EXPECT ME TO KEEP MY STRENGTH UP WHEN CONSUMING ROOTS AND LEAVES?
JEKYLL, DESPERATE TO RECLAIM HIS FORMULA, TRAVELED TO GOTHAM CITY. AHEAD OF HIS ARRIVAL, ONE OF HIS TRUSTED AGENTS WAS DISPATCHED TO EMPLOY THE AID OF A BOUNTY HUNTER NAMED JONAH HEX AND NOTED CRIMINAL PSYCHOLOGIST DR. AMADEUS ARKHAM.
I'VE ALSO BEEN INSTRUCTED, IN THE EVENT OF YOUR REFUSAL TO RETURN THE DOCTOR AND IF YOUR ACTIONS SHOULD JEOPARDIZE THE CASE, THAT I AM TO KILL YOU.
IN THE INTEREST OF YOUR CONTINUED SURVIVAL...
HEX AND ARKHAM, JOINED BY ANOTHER BOUNTY HUNTER NAMED TALLULAH BLACK, SET OUT TO RECOVER THE FORMULA.
OH, REGGIE, YOU DO TAKE THE FUN OUT OF EVERYTHING. SUCH AN UNNATURAL DEDICATION TO FOLLOWING ORDERS MIGHT BE THE BYPRODUCT OF MISPLACED AFFECTION.
IS THAT IT, REGGIE? DO YOU HAVE AN UNNATURAL ATTRACTION TO JEKYLL? OR IS IT ME AND MY ANIMAL MAGNETISM?
I'M TAKING MY LEAVE UNTIL SUCH TIME AS YOU AGREE TO SURRENDER CONTROL TO DR. JEKYLL.
UNFORTUNATELY, IT HAD ALREADY BEEN CIRCULATED AMONG AN UNKNOWN NUMBER OF PEOPLE IN AND AROUND HALY'S FAMOUS TRAVELING CIRCUS. SINCE THEN, ALL HELL HAD BROKEN LOOSE IN GOTHAM.

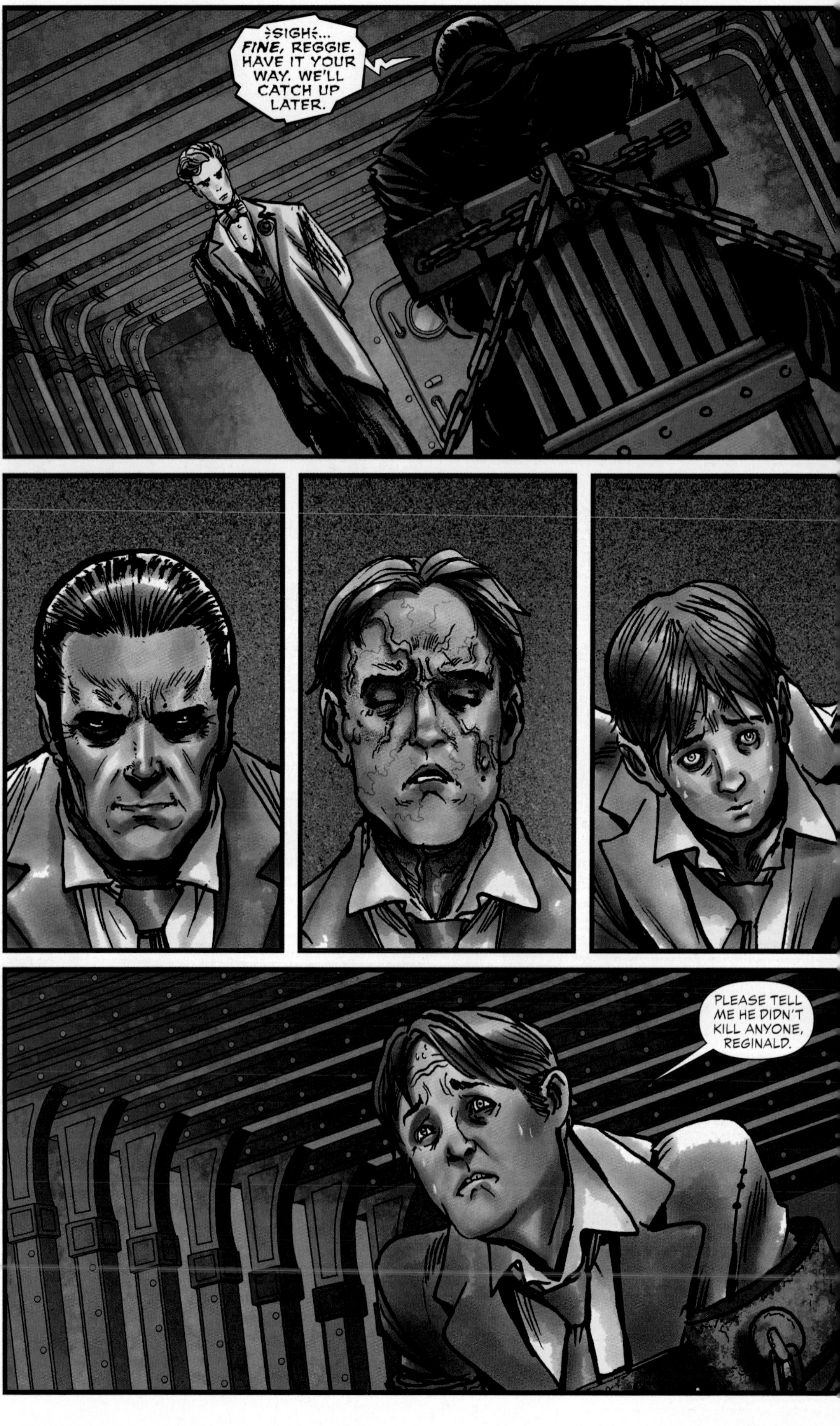

SIGH... FINE, REGGIE. HAVE IT YOUR WAY. WE'LL CATCH UP LATER.
PLEASE TELL ME HE DIDN'T KILL ANYONE, REGINALD.

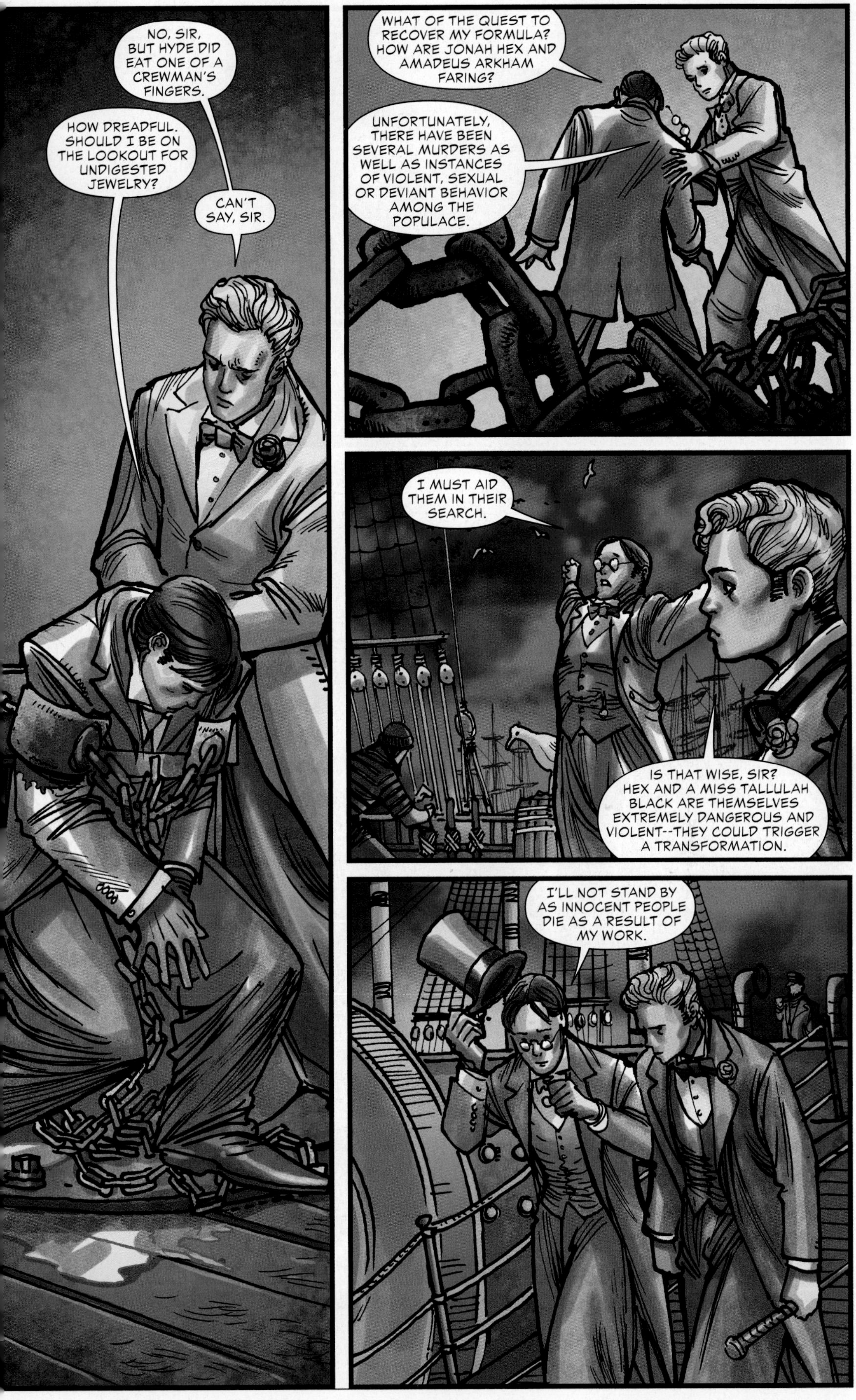
NO, SIR, BUT HYDE DID EAT ONE OF A CREWMAN'S FINGERS.
HOW DREADFUL. SHOULD I BE ON THE LOOKOUT FOR UNDIGESTED JEWELRY?
CAN'T SAY, SIR.
WHAT OF THE QUEST TO RECOVER MY FORMULA? HOW ARE JONAH HEX AND AMADEUS ARKHAM FARING?
UNFORTUNATELY, THERE HAVE BEEN SEVERAL MURDERS AS WELL AS INSTANCES OF VIOLENT, SEXUAL OR DEVIANT BEHAVIOR AMONG THE POPULACE.
I MUST AID THEM IN THEIR SEARCH.
IS THAT WISE, SIR? HEX AND A MISS TALLULAH BLACK ARE THEMSELVES EXTREMELY DANGEROUS AND VIOLENT--THEY COULD TRIGGER A TRANSFORMATION.
I'LL NOT STAND BY AS INNOCENT PEOPLE DIE AS A RESULT OF MY WORK.

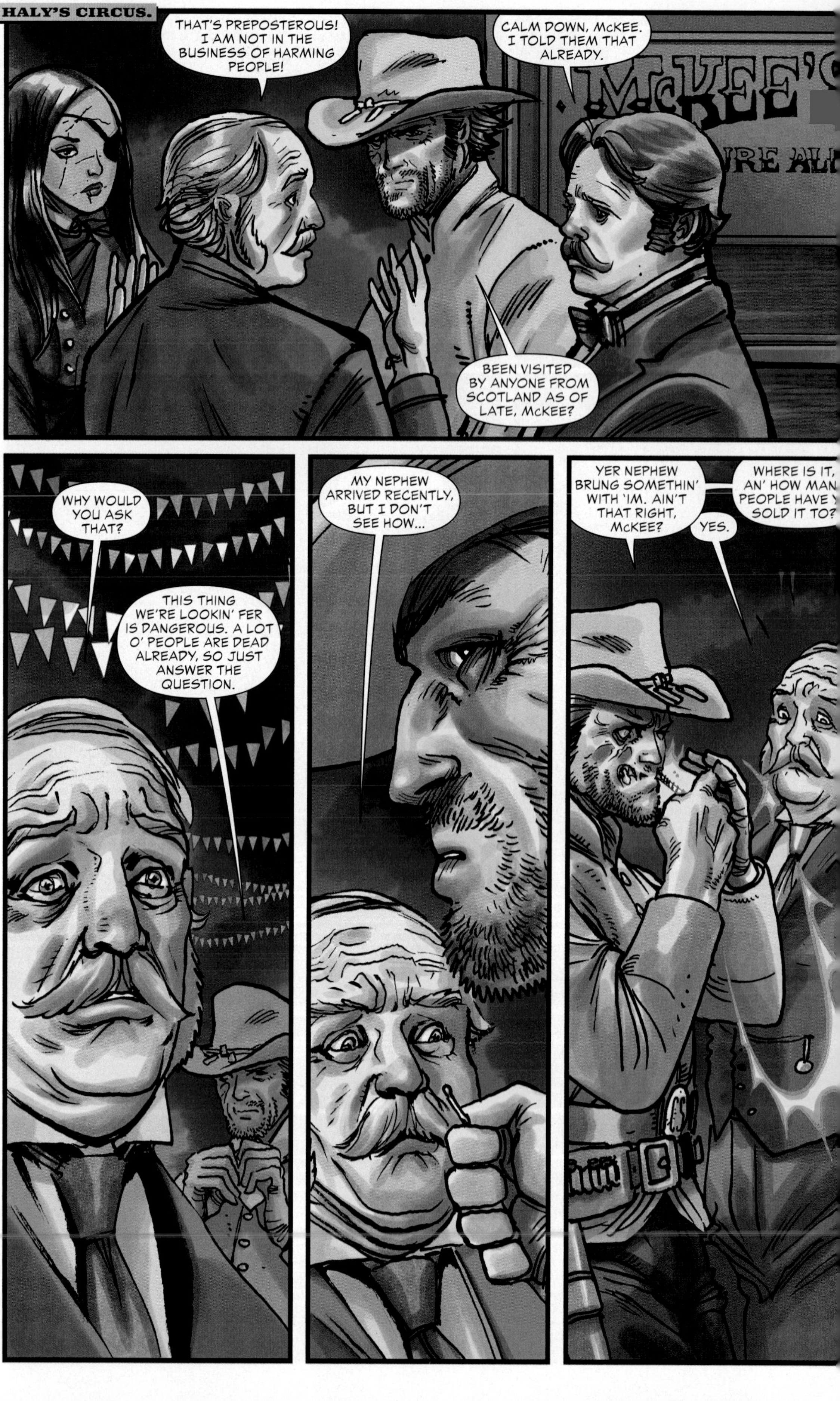
THAT'S PREPOSTEROUS! I AM NOT IN THE BUSINESS OF HARMING PEOPLE!
CALM DOWN, McKEE. I TOLD THEM THAT ALREADY.
McKEE'S
URE AL
BEEN VISITED BY ANYONE FROM SCOTLAND AS OF LATE, McKEE?
WHY WOULD YOU ASK THAT?
THIS THING WE'RE LOOKIN' FER IS DANGEROUS. A LOT O' PEOPLE ARE DEAD ALREADY, SO JUST ANSWER THE QUESTION.
MY NEPHEW ARRIVED RECENTLY, BUT I DON'T SEE HOW...
YER NEPHEW BRUNG SOMETHIN' WITH 'IM. AIN'T THAT RIGHT, McKEE?
YES.
WHERE IS IT, AN' HOW MAN PEOPLE HAVE Y SOLD IT TO?

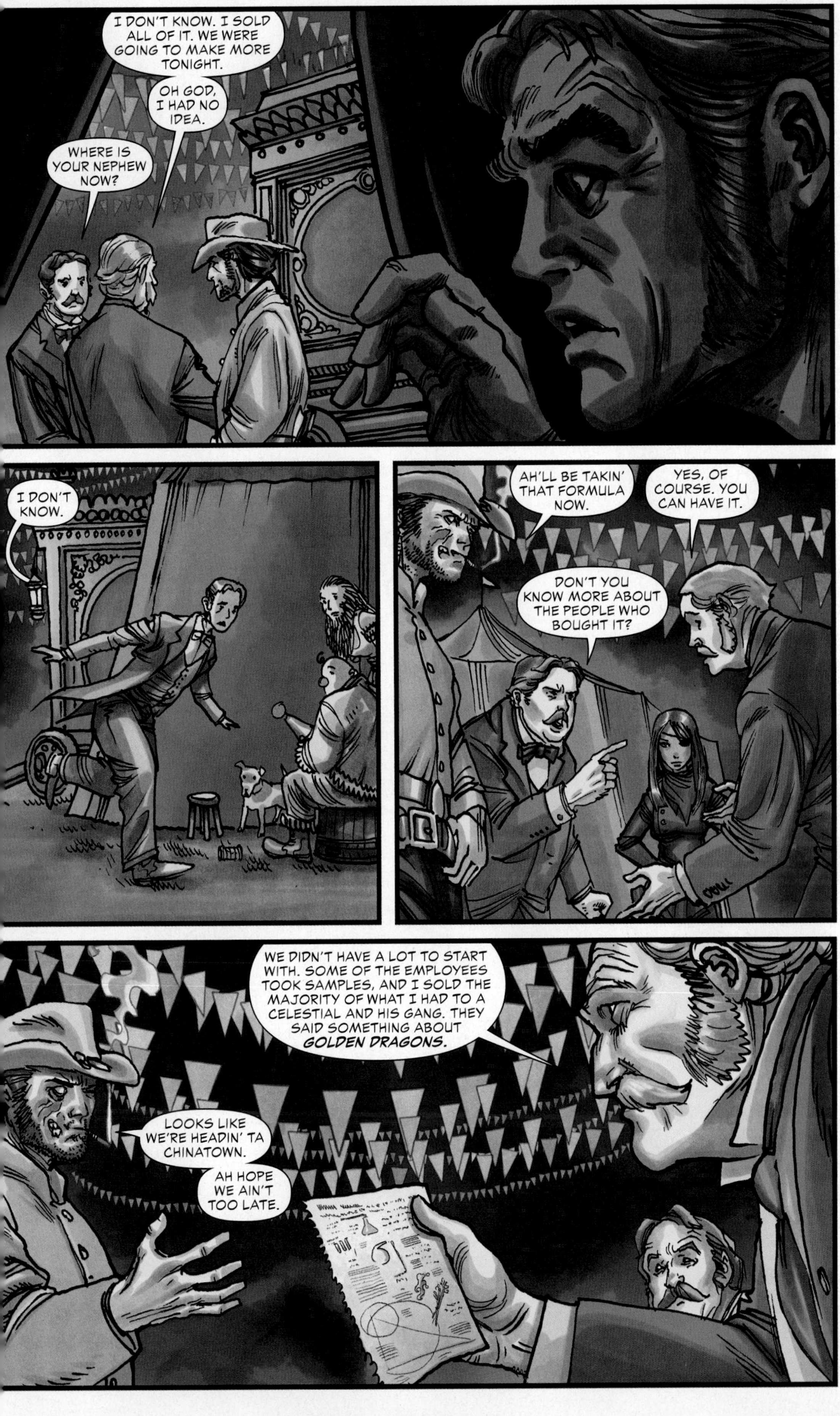

I DON'T KNOW. I SOLD ALL OF IT. WE WERE GOING TO MAKE MORE TONIGHT.
OH GOD, I HAD NO IDEA.
WHERE IS YOUR NEPHEW NOW?
I DON'T KNOW.
AH'LL BE TAKIN' THAT FORMULA NOW.
YES, OF COURSE. YOU CAN HAVE IT.
DON'T YOU KNOW MORE ABOUT THE PEOPLE WHO BOUGHT IT?
WE DIDN'T HAVE A LOT TO START WITH. SOME OF THE EMPLOYEES TOOK SAMPLES, AND I SOLD THE MAJORITY OF WHAT I HAD TO A CELESTIAL AND HIS GANG. THEY SAID SOMETHING ABOUT *GOLDEN DRAGONS.*
LOOKS LIKE WE'RE HEADIN' TA CHINATOWN.
AH HOPE WE AIN'T TOO LATE.

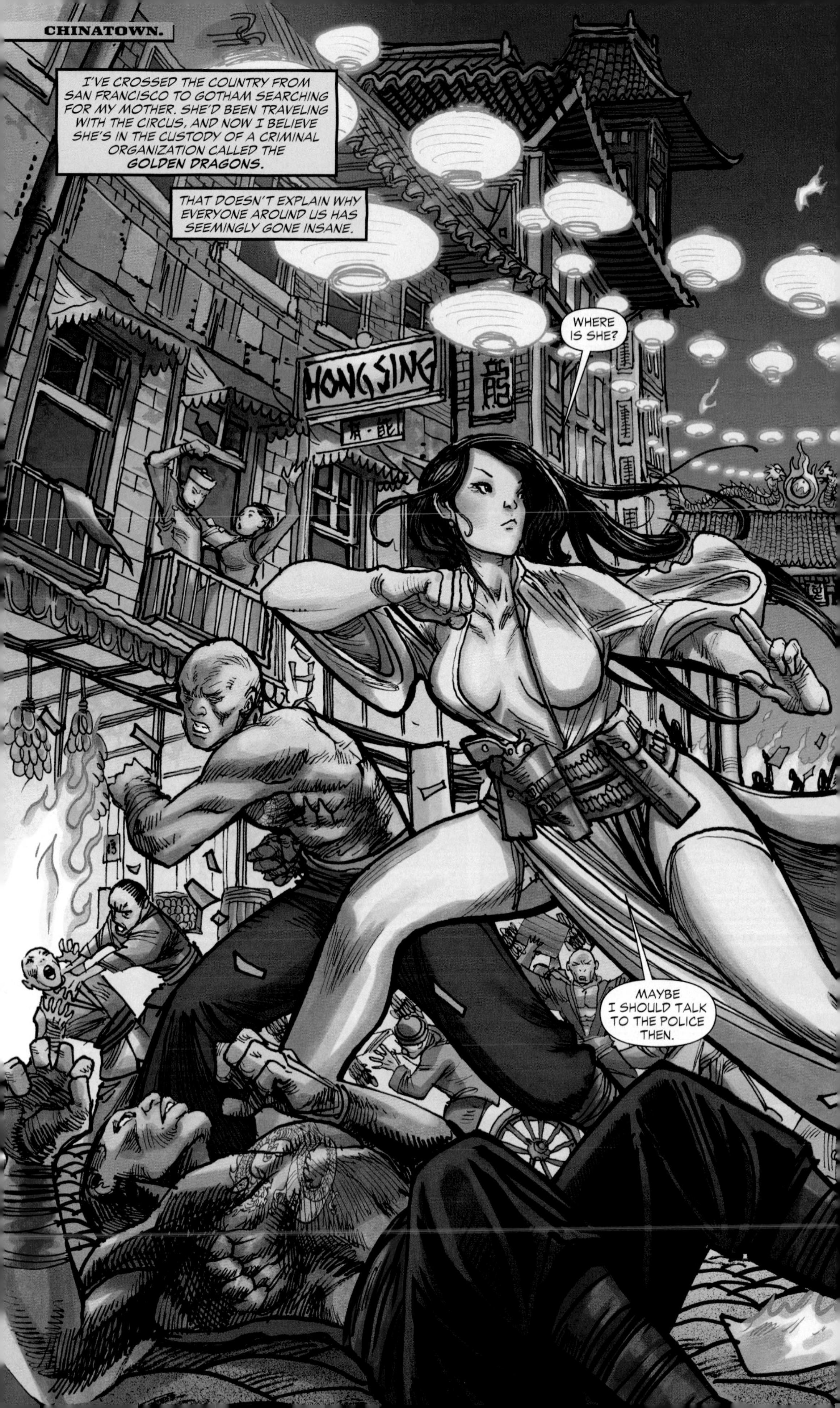
CHINATOWN.
I'VE CROSSED THE COUNTRY FROM SAN FRANCISCO TO GOTHAM SEARCHING FOR MY MOTHER. SHE'D BEEN TRAVELING WITH THE CIRCUS, AND NOW I BELIEVE SHE'S IN THE CUSTODY OF A CRIMINAL ORGANIZATION CALLED THE GOLDEN DRAGONS.
THAT DOESN'T EXPLAIN WHY EVERYONE AROUND US HAS SEEMINGLY GONE INSANE.
HONG SING
WHERE IS SHE?
MAYBE I SHOULD TALK TO THE POLICE THEN.

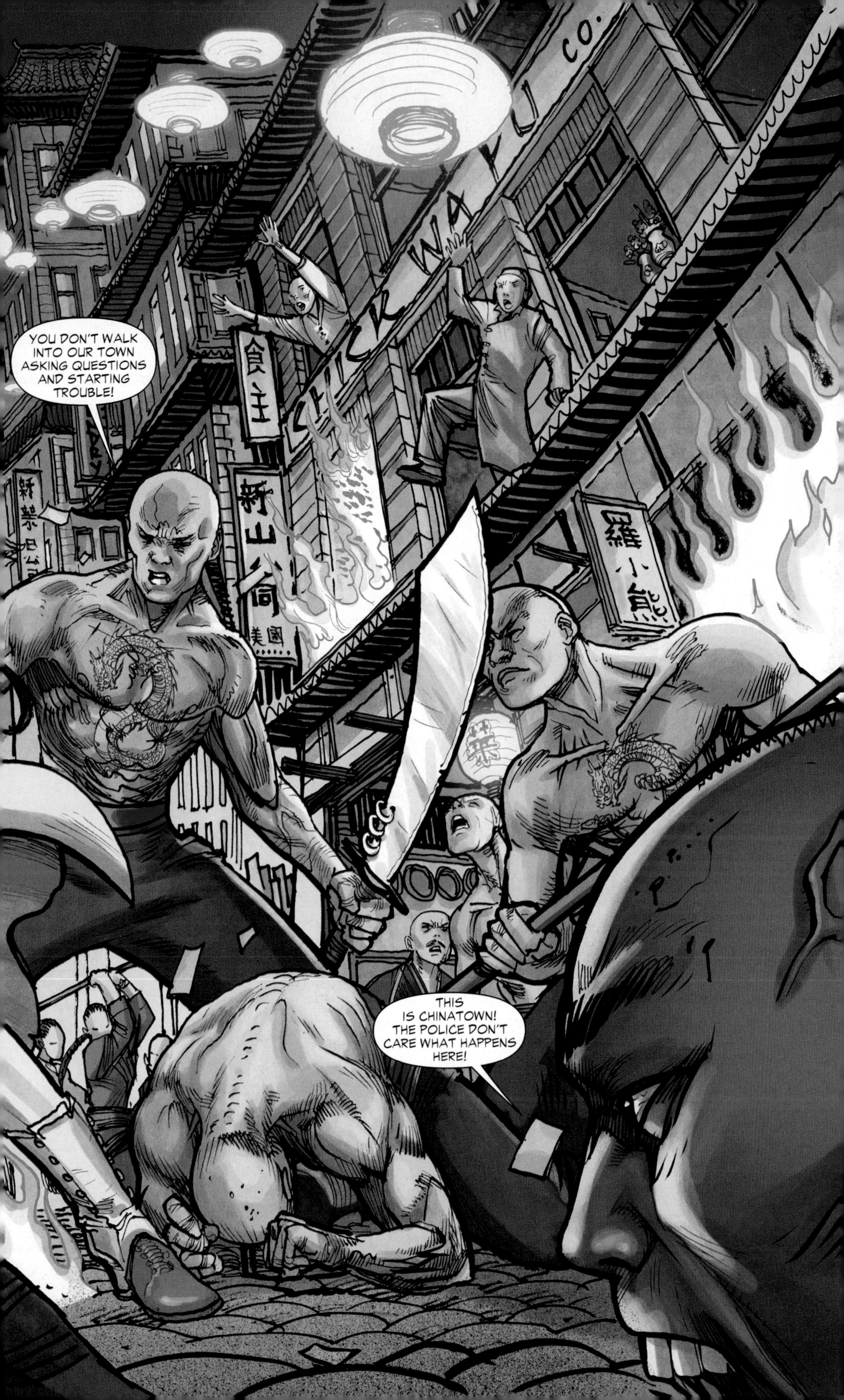
YOU DON'T WALK INTO OUR TOWN ASKING QUESTIONS AND STARTING TROUBLE!
THIS IS CHINATOWN! THE POLICE DON'T CARE WHAT HAPPENS HERE!

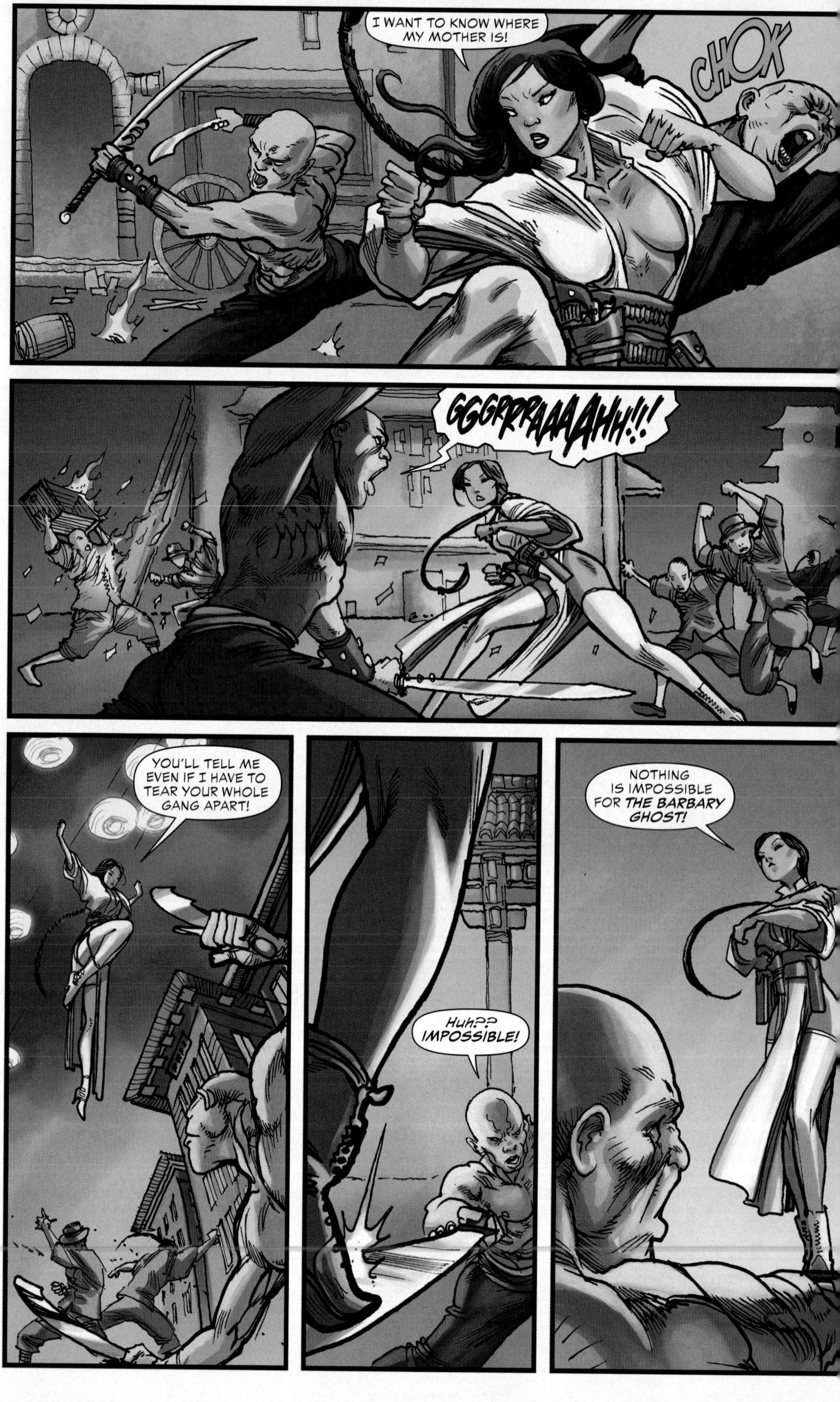
I WANT TO KNOW WHERE MY MOTHER IS!
CHOK
GGGRRRAAAAHH!!!
YOU'LL TELL ME EVEN IF I HAVE TO TEAR YOUR WHOLE GANG APART!
Huh?? IMPOSSIBLE!
NOTHING IS IMPOSSIBLE FOR THE BARBARY GHOST!

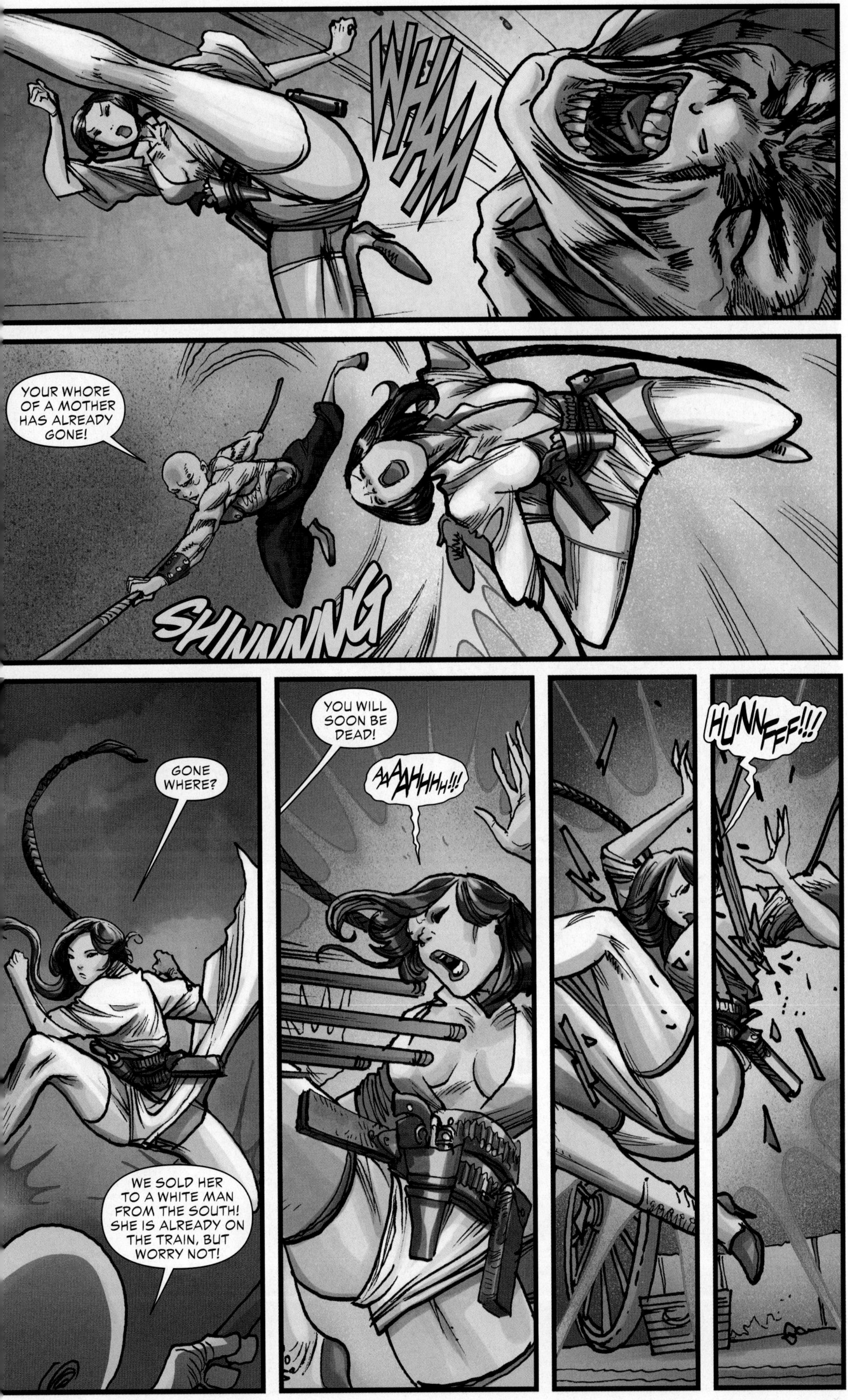
WHAM
YOUR WHORE OF A MOTHER HAS ALREADY GONE!
SHINNNNG
GONE WHERE?
WE SOLD HER TO A WHITE MAN FROM THE SOUTH! SHE IS ALREADY ON THE TRAIN, BUT WORRY NOT!
YOU WILL SOON BE DEAD!
AAAAHHHH!!!
HUNNFFF!!!

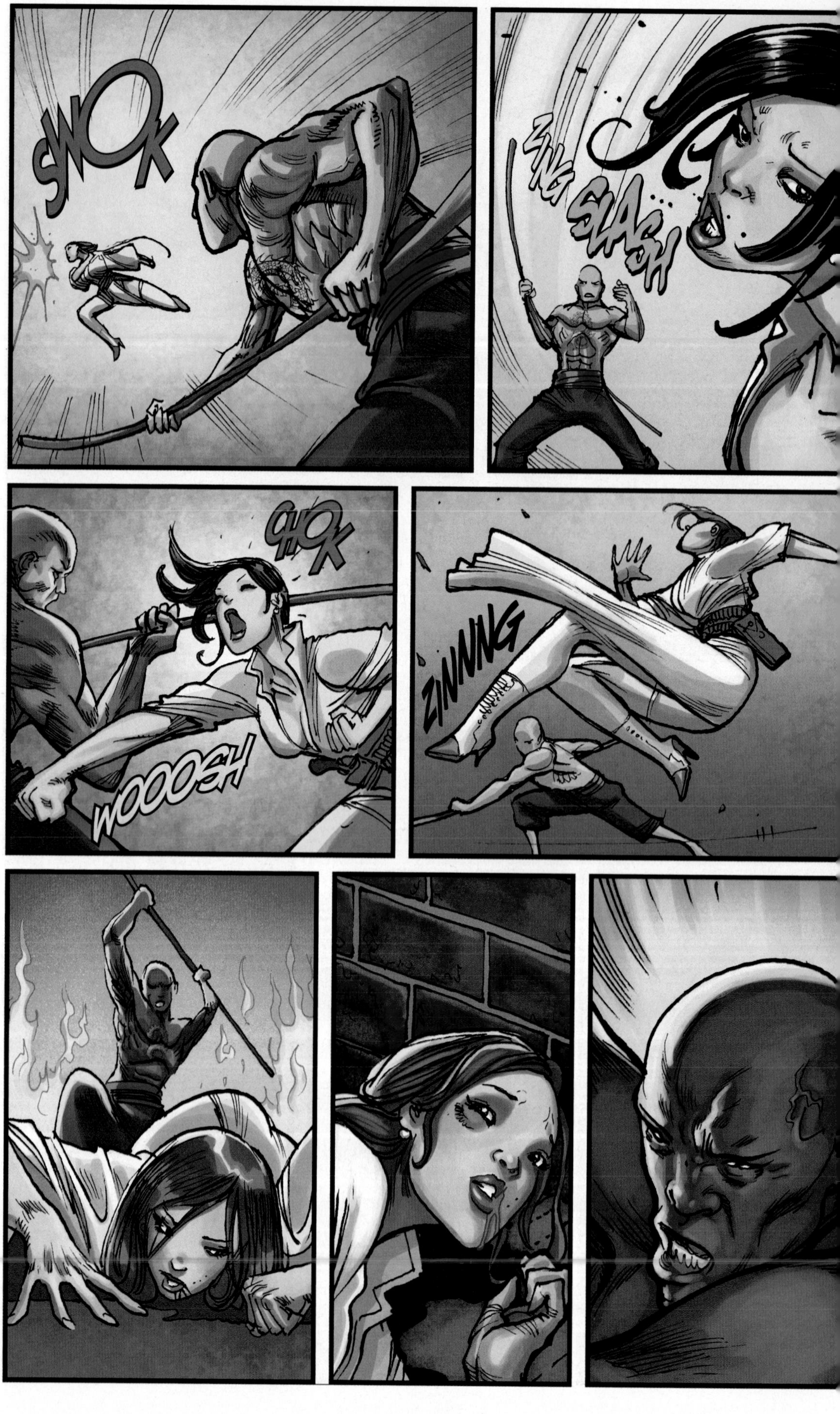
SNOK
ZING
SLASH
CHOK
WOOOSH
ZINNNG

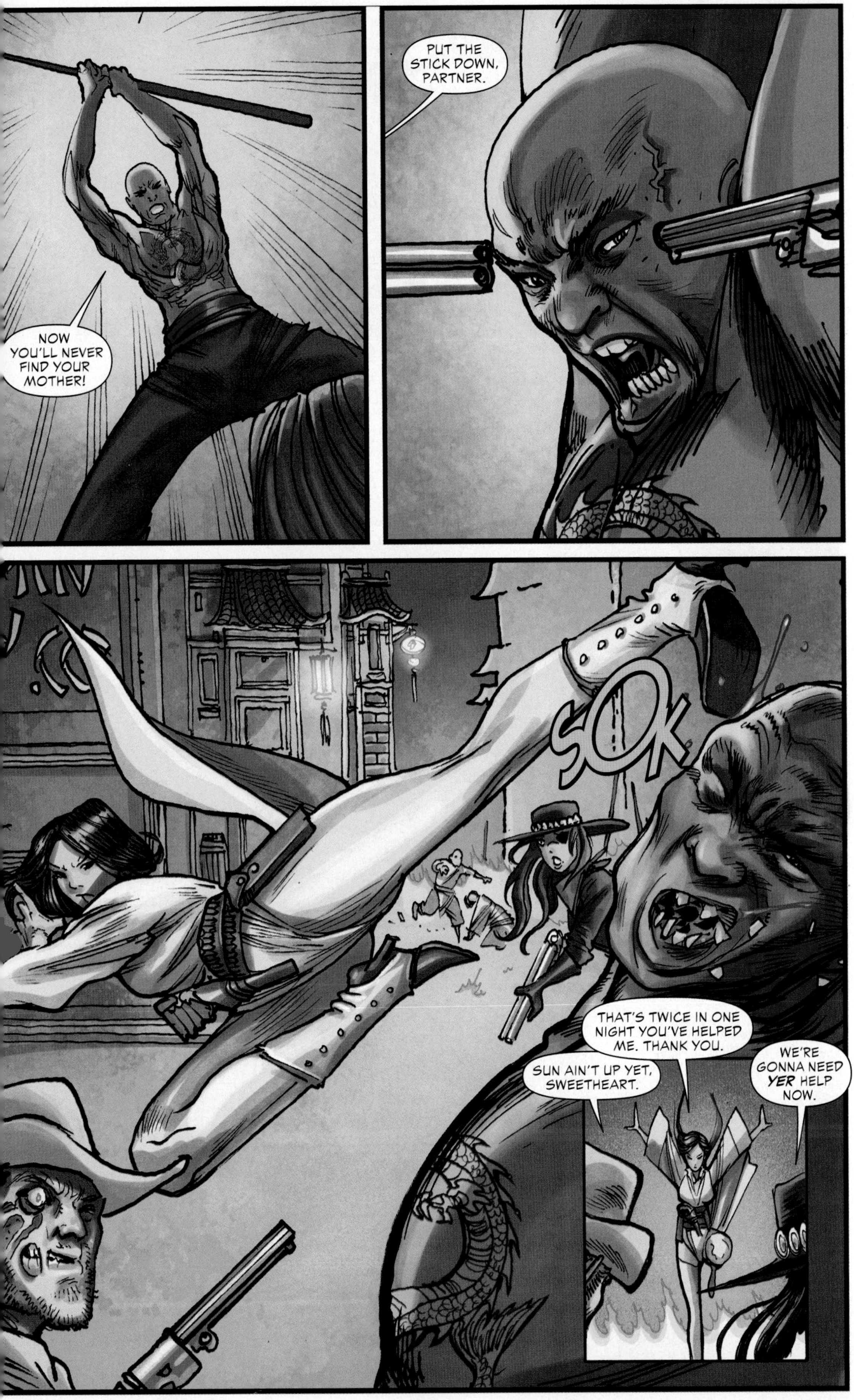
NOW YOU'LL NEVER FIND YOUR MOTHER!
PUT THE STICK DOWN, PARTNER.
SOK
THAT'S TWICE IN ONE NIGHT YOU'VE HELPED ME. THANK YOU.
SUN AIN'T UP YET, SWEETHEART.
WE'RE GONNA NEED YER HELP NOW.

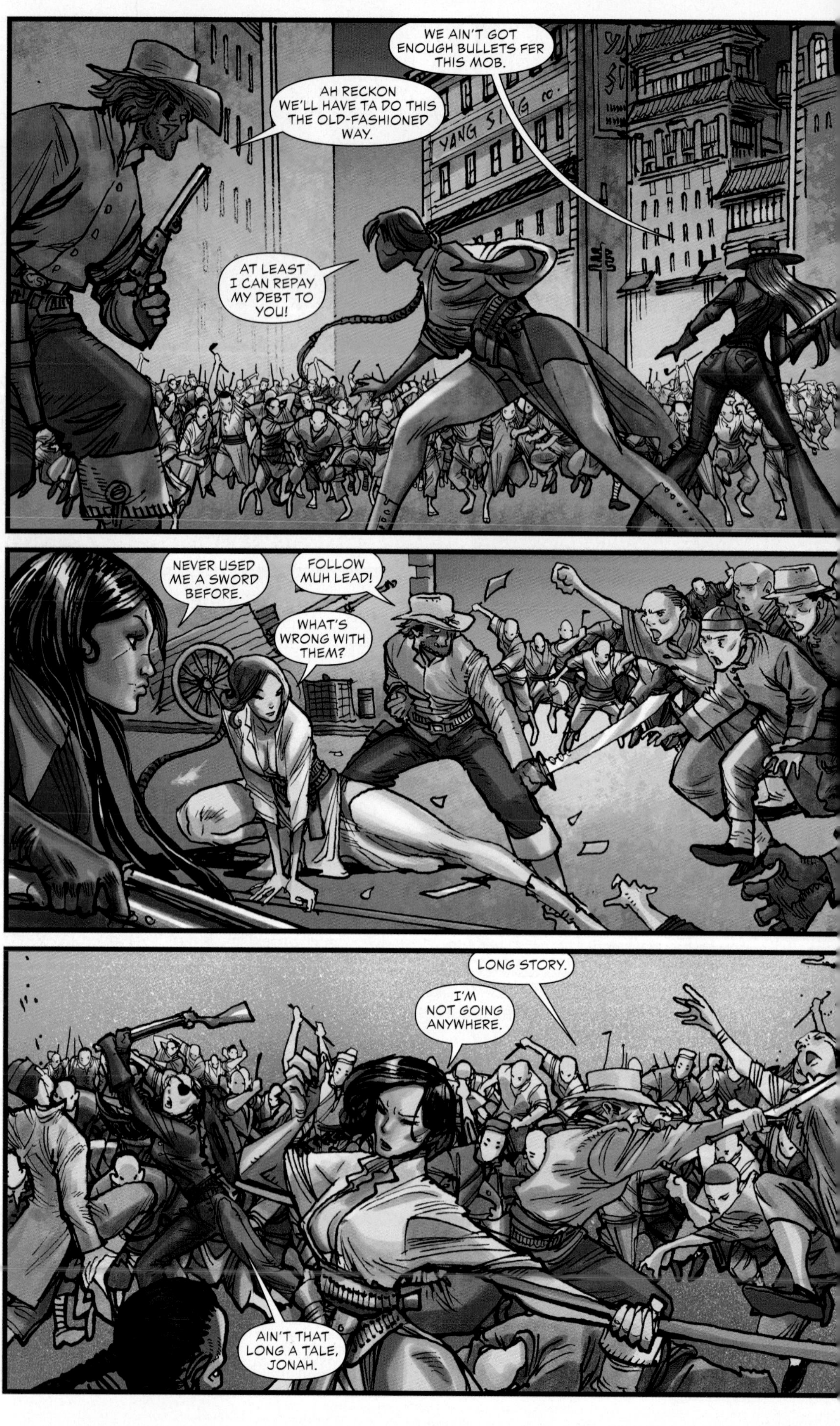
AH RECKON WE'LL HAVE TA DO THIS THE OLD-FASHIONED WAY.
WE AIN'T GOT ENOUGH BULLETS FER THIS MOB.
YANG SING CO.
AT LEAST I CAN REPAY MY DEBT TO YOU!
NEVER USED ME A SWORD BEFORE.
FOLLOW MUH LEAD!
WHAT'S WRONG WITH THEM?
LONG STORY.
I'M NOT GOING ANYWHERE.
AIN'T THAT LONG A TALE, JONAH.

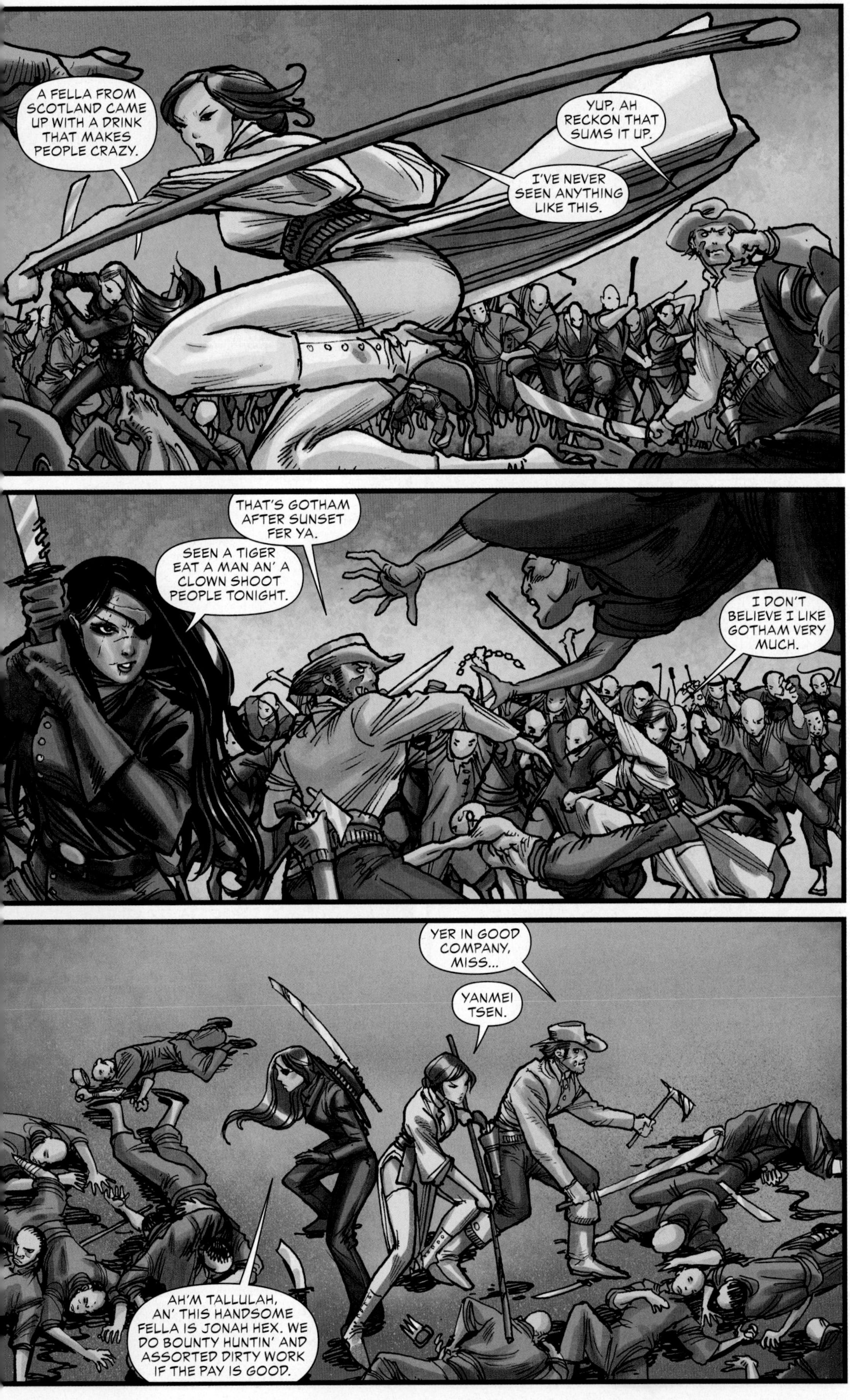
A FELLA FROM SCOTLAND CAME UP WITH A DRINK THAT MAKES PEOPLE CRAZY.
I'VE NEVER SEEN ANYTHING LIKE THIS.
YUP, AH RECKON THAT SUMS IT UP.
SEEN A TIGER EAT A MAN AN' A CLOWN SHOOT PEOPLE TONIGHT.
THAT'S GOTHAM AFTER SUNSET FER YA.
I DON'T BELIEVE I LIKE GOTHAM VERY MUCH.
YER IN GOOD COMPANY, MISS...
YANMEI TSEN.
AH'M TALLULAH, AN' THIS HANDSOME FELLA IS JONAH HEX. WE DO BOUNTY HUNTIN' AND ASSORTED DIRTY WORK IF THE PAY IS GOOD.

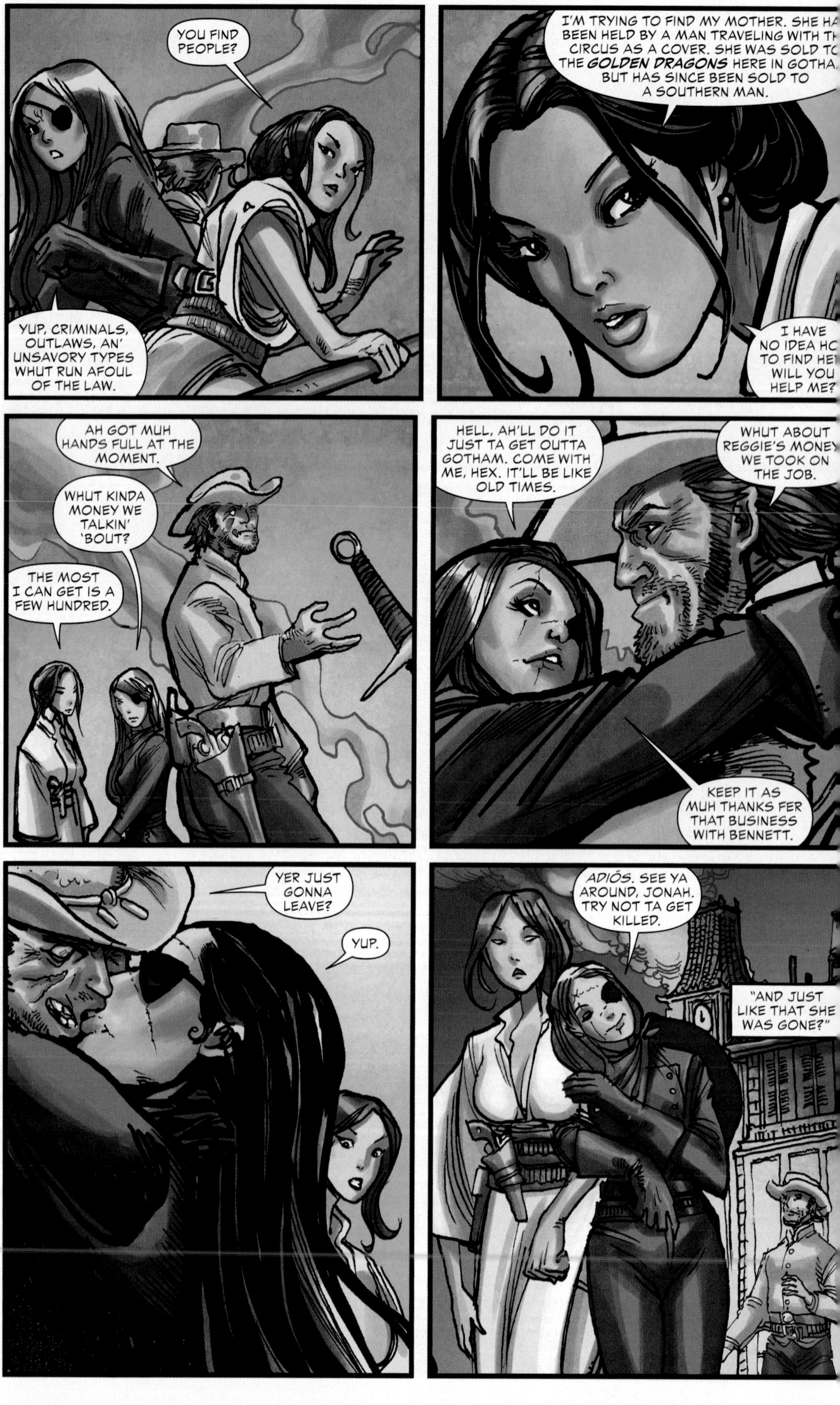

YOU FIND PEOPLE?
YUP, CRIMINALS, OUTLAWS, AN' UNSAVORY TYPES WHUT RUN AFOUL OF THE LAW.
I'M TRYING TO FIND MY MOTHER. SHE HA BEEN HELD BY A MAN TRAVELING WITH TH CIRCUS AS A COVER. SHE WAS SOLD TO THE GOLDEN DRAGONS HERE IN GOTHA BUT HAS SINCE BEEN SOLD TO A SOUTHERN MAN.
I HAVE NO IDEA HO TO FIND HE WILL YOU HELP ME?
AH GOT MUH HANDS FULL AT THE MOMENT.
WHUT KINDA MONEY WE TALKIN' 'BOUT?
THE MOST I CAN GET IS A FEW HUNDRED.
HELL, AH'LL DO IT JUST TA GET OUTTA GOTHAM. COME WITH ME, HEX. IT'LL BE LIKE OLD TIMES.
WHUT ABOUT REGGIE'S MONE WE TOOK ON THE JOB.
KEEP IT AS MUH THANKS FER THAT BUSINESS WITH BENNETT.
YER JUST GONNA LEAVE?
YUP.
ADIÓS. SEE YA AROUND, JONAH. TRY NOT TA GET KILLED.
"AND JUST LIKE THAT SHE WAS GONE?"

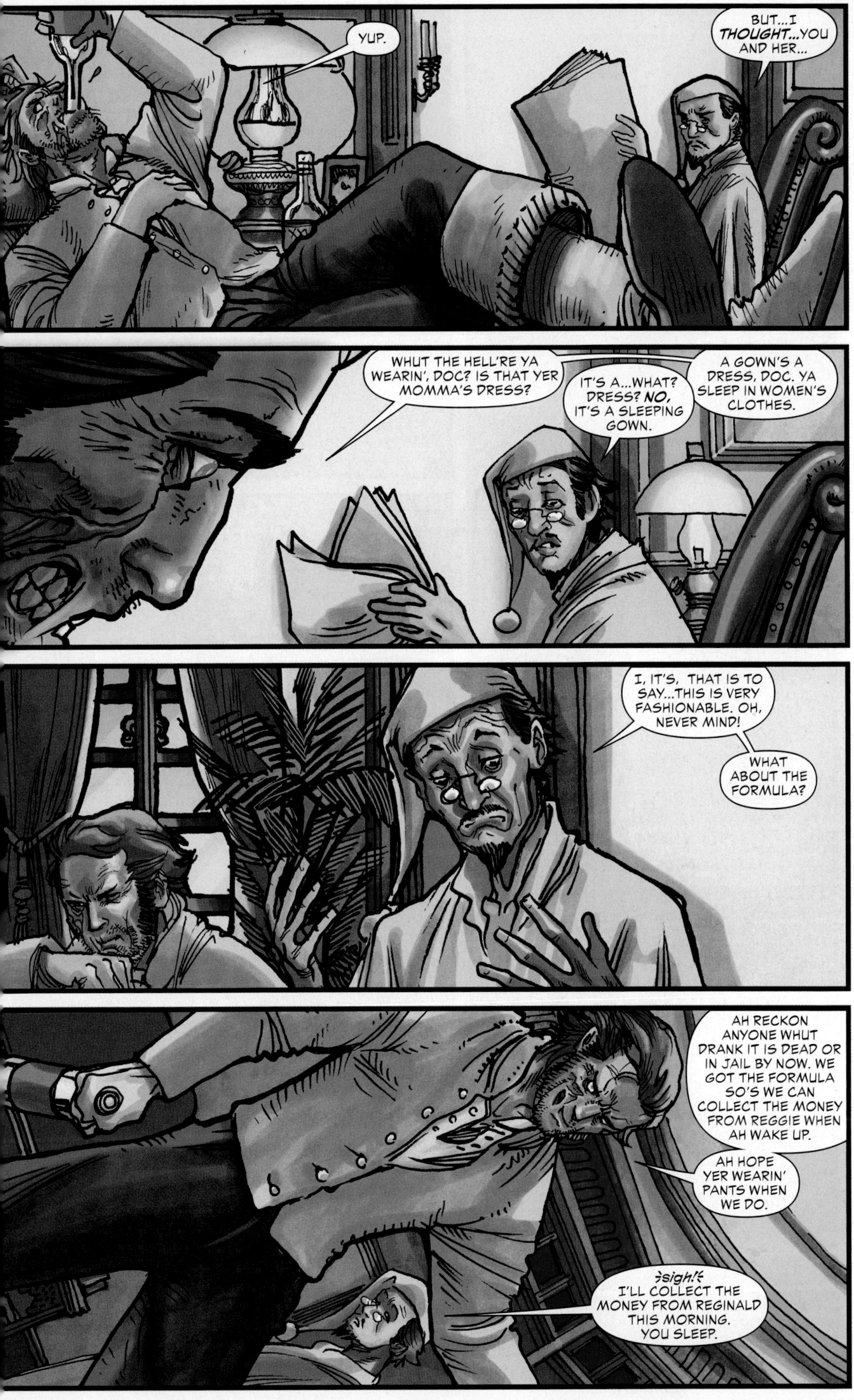

YUP.
BUT...I THOUGHT...YOU AND HER...
WHUT THE HELL'RE YA WEARIN', DOC? IS THAT YER MOMMA'S DRESS?
IT'S A...WHAT? DRESS? NO, IT'S A SLEEPING GOWN.
A GOWN'S A DRESS, DOC. YA SLEEP IN WOMEN'S CLOTHES.
I, IT'S, THAT IS TO SAY...THIS IS VERY FASHIONABLE. OH, NEVER MIND!
WHAT ABOUT THE FORMULA?
AH RECKON ANYONE WHUT DRANK IT IS DEAD OR IN JAIL BY NOW. WE GOT THE FORMULA SO'S WE CAN COLLECT THE MONEY FROM REGGIE WHEN AH WAKE UP.
AH HOPE YER WEARIN' PANTS WHEN WE DO.
sigh!
I'LL COLLECT THE MONEY FROM REGINALD THIS MORNING. YOU SLEEP.

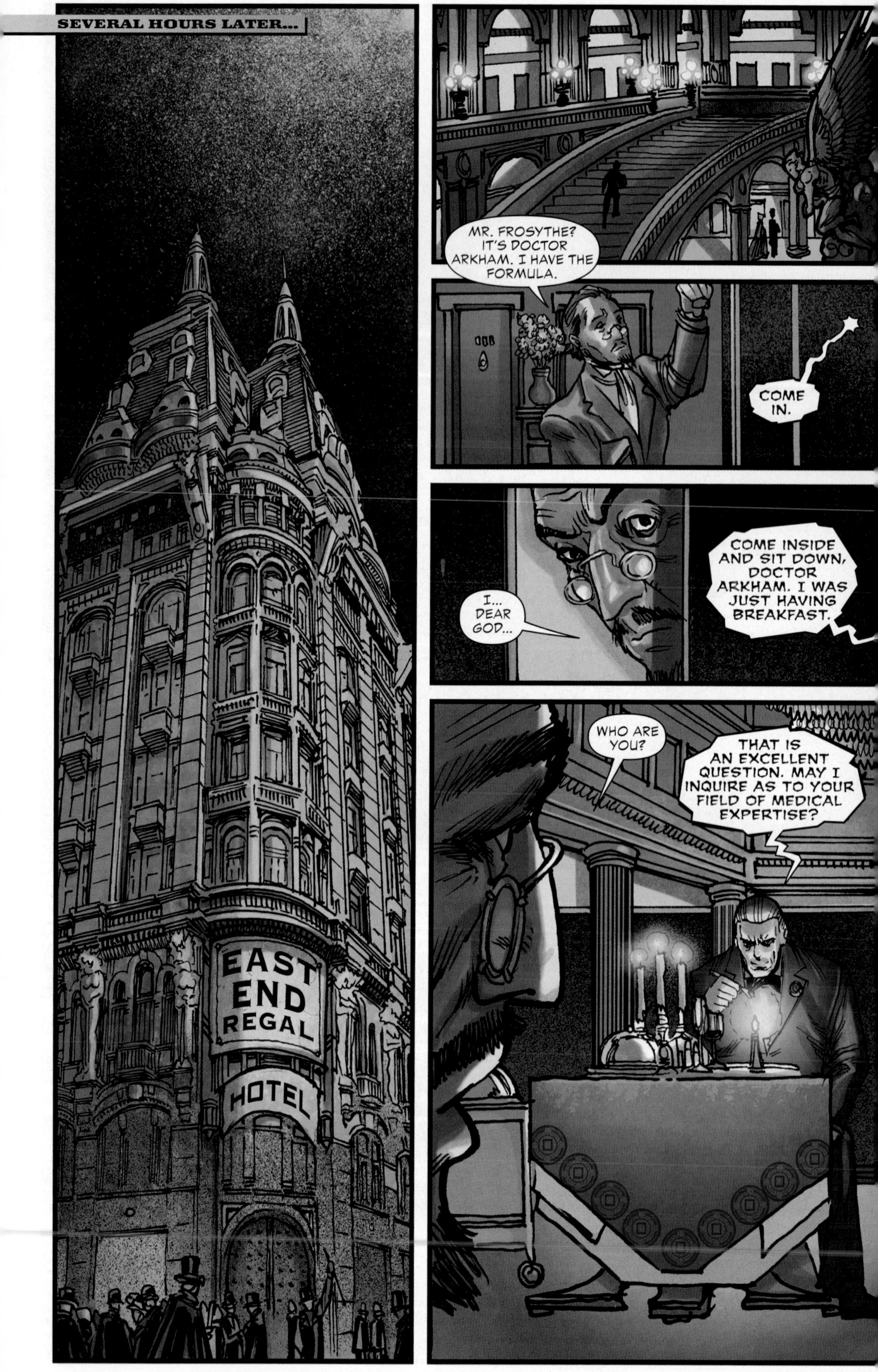
SEVERAL HOURS LATER...
EAST END REGAL
HOTEL
MR. FROSYTHE? IT'S DOCTOR ARKHAM. I HAVE THE FORMULA.
COME IN.
I... DEAR GOD...
COME INSIDE AND SIT DOWN, DOCTOR ARKHAM. I WAS JUST HAVING BREAKFAST.
WHO ARE YOU?
THAT IS AN EXCELLENT QUESTION. MAY I INQUIRE AS TO YOUR FIELD OF MEDICAL EXPERTISE?

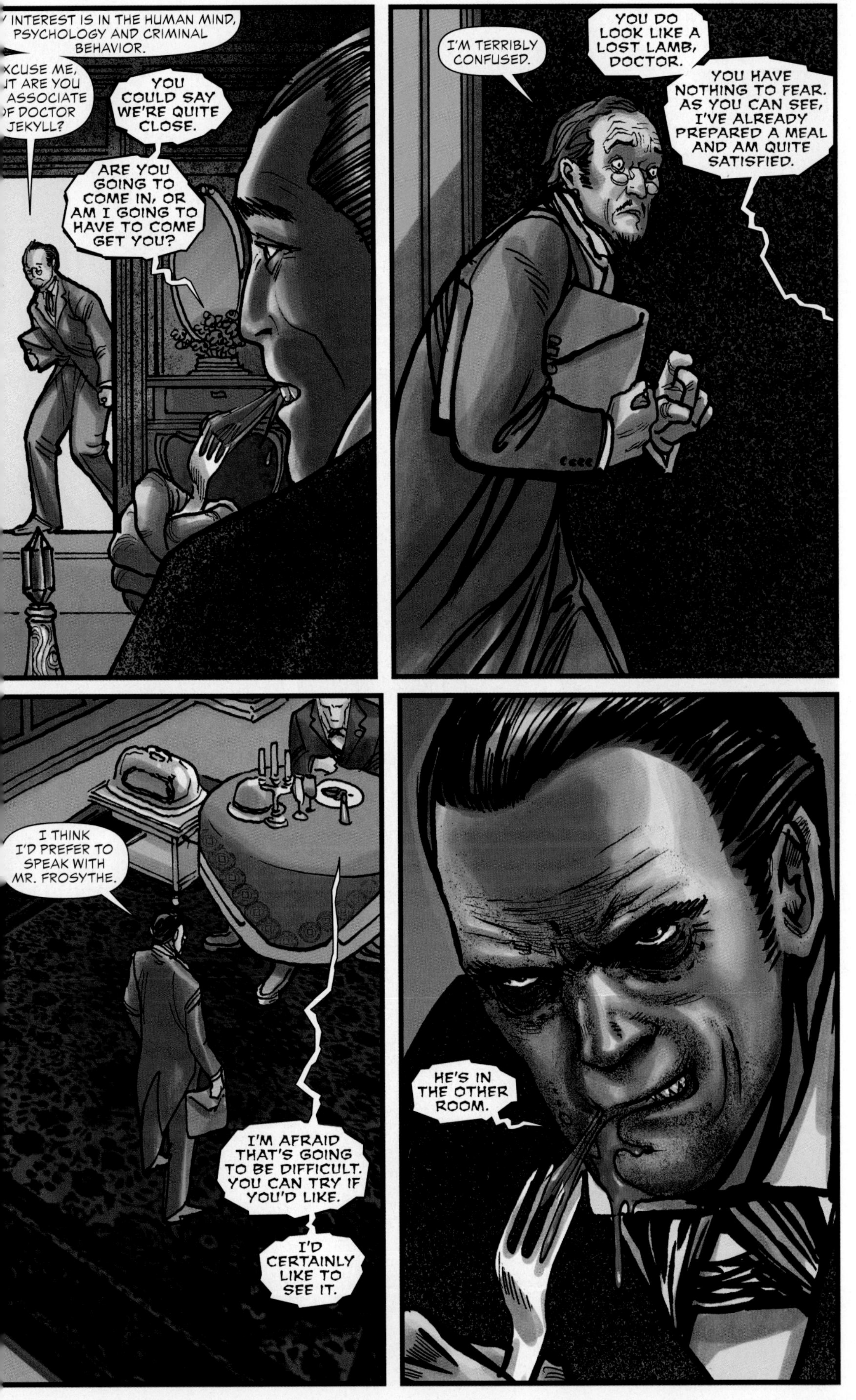

INTEREST IS IN THE HUMAN MIND, PSYCHOLOGY AND CRIMINAL BEHAVIOR.
XCUSE ME, T ARE YOU ASSOCIATE F DOCTOR JEKYLL?
YOU COULD SAY WE'RE QUITE CLOSE.
ARE YOU GOING TO COME IN, OR AM I GOING TO HAVE TO COME GET YOU?
I'M TERRIBLY CONFUSED.
YOU DO LOOK LIKE A LOST LAMB, DOCTOR.
YOU HAVE NOTHING TO FEAR. AS YOU CAN SEE, I'VE ALREADY PREPARED A MEAL AND AM QUITE SATISFIED.
I THINK I'D PREFER TO SPEAK WITH MR. FROSYTHE.
I'M AFRAID THAT'S GOING TO BE DIFFICULT. YOU CAN TRY IF YOU'D LIKE.
I'D CERTAINLY LIKE TO SEE IT.
HE'S IN THE OTHER ROOM.

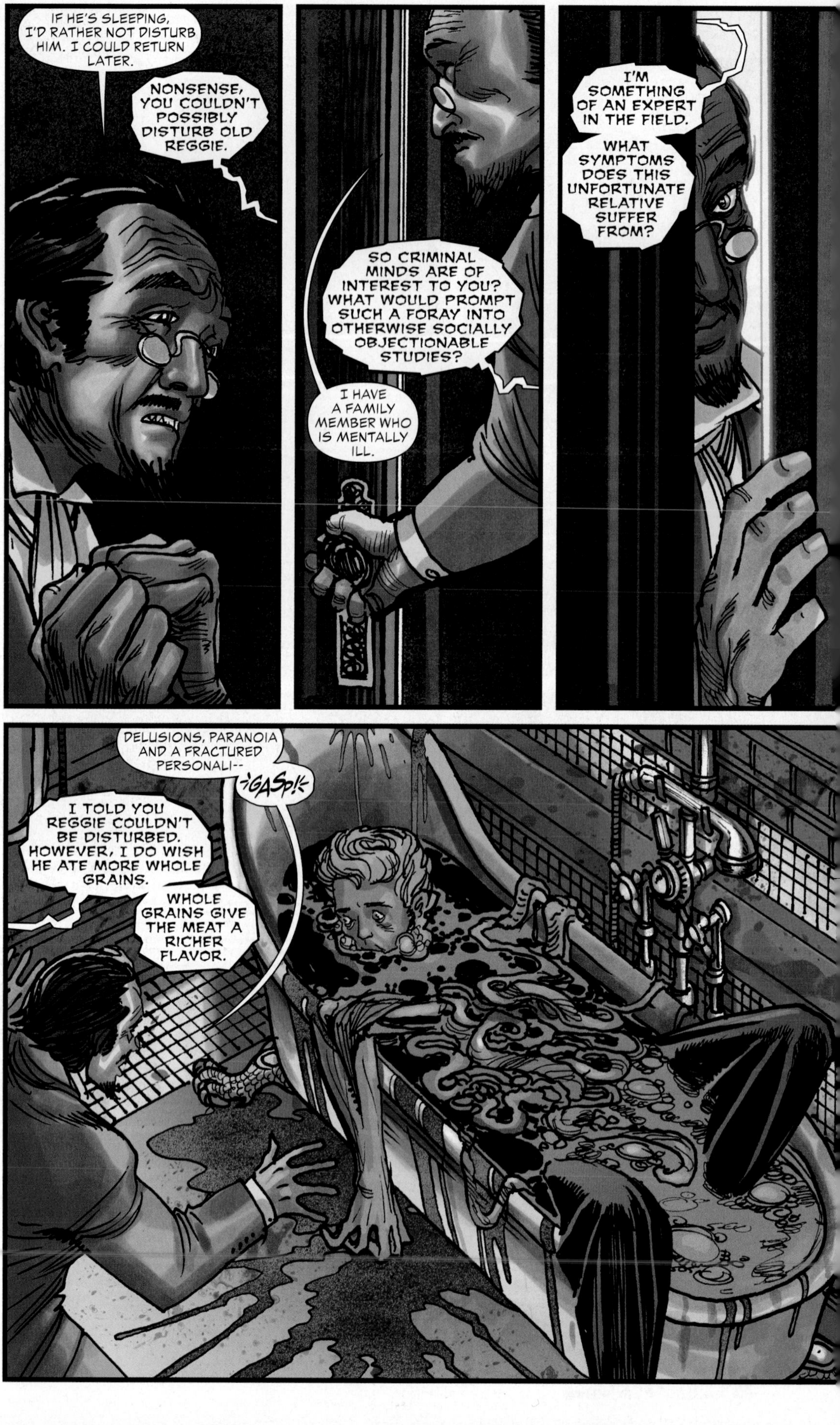
IF HE'S SLEEPING, I'D RATHER NOT DISTURB HIM. I COULD RETURN LATER.
NONSENSE, YOU COULDN'T POSSIBLY DISTURB OLD REGGIE.
SO CRIMINAL MINDS ARE OF INTEREST TO YOU? WHAT WOULD PROMPT SUCH A FORAY INTO OTHERWISE SOCIALLY OBJECTIONABLE STUDIES?
I HAVE A FAMILY MEMBER WHO IS MENTALLY ILL.
I'M SOMETHING OF AN EXPERT IN THE FIELD.
WHAT SYMPTOMS DOES THIS UNFORTUNATE RELATIVE SUFFER FROM?
DELUSIONS, PARANOIA AND A FRACTURED PERSONALI--
GASP!
I TOLD YOU REGGIE COULDN'T BE DISTURBED. HOWEVER, I DO WISH HE ATE MORE WHOLE GRAINS.
WHOLE GRAINS GIVE THE MEAT A RICHER FLAVOR.

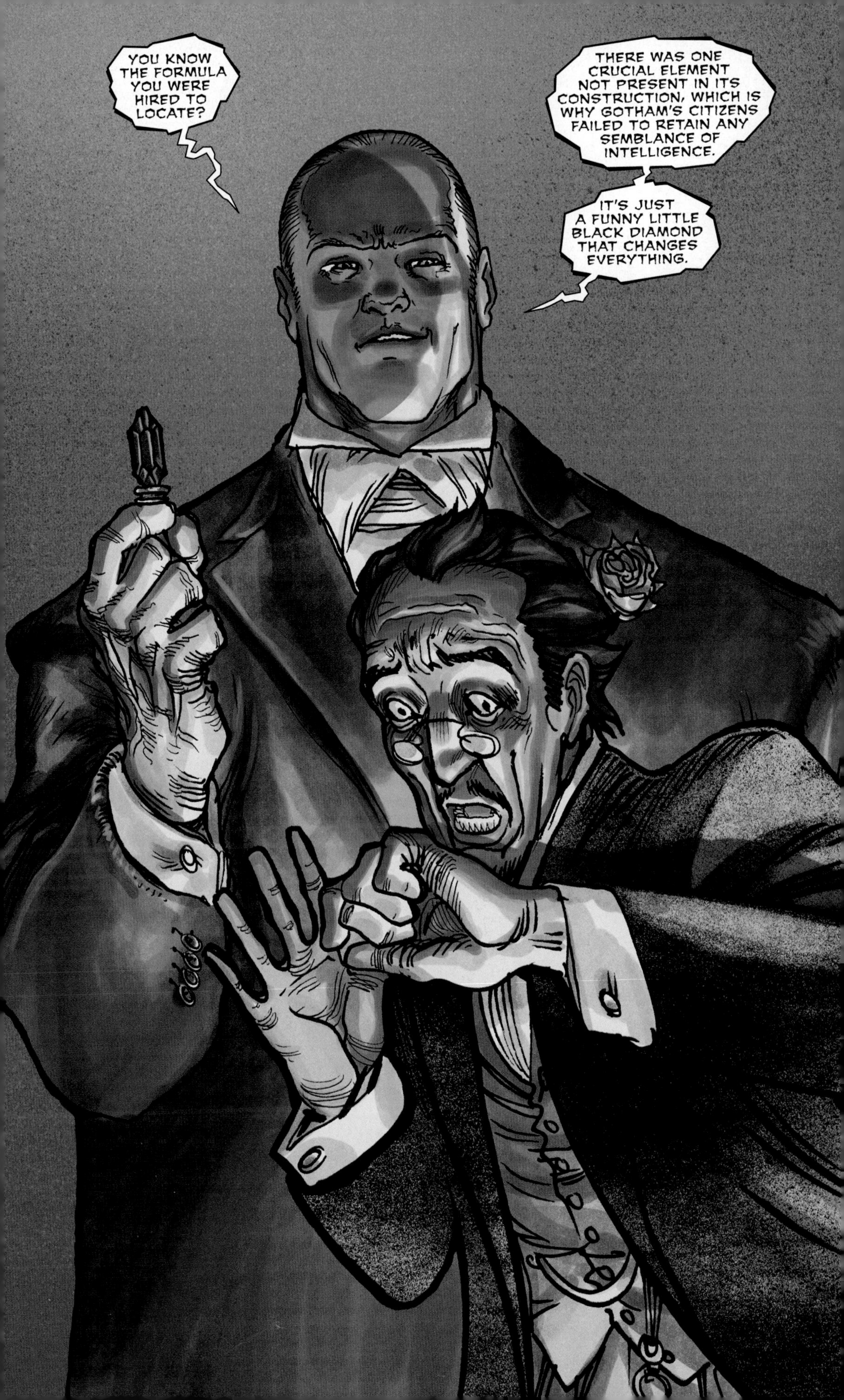
YOU KNOW THE FORMULA YOU WERE HIRED TO LOCATE?
THERE WAS ONE CRUCIAL ELEMENT NOT PRESENT IN ITS CONSTRUCTION, WHICH IS WHY GOTHAM'S CITIZENS FAILED TO RETAIN ANY SEMBLANCE OF INTELLIGENCE.
IT'S JUST A FUNNY LITTLE BLACK DIAMOND THAT CHANGES EVERYTHING.

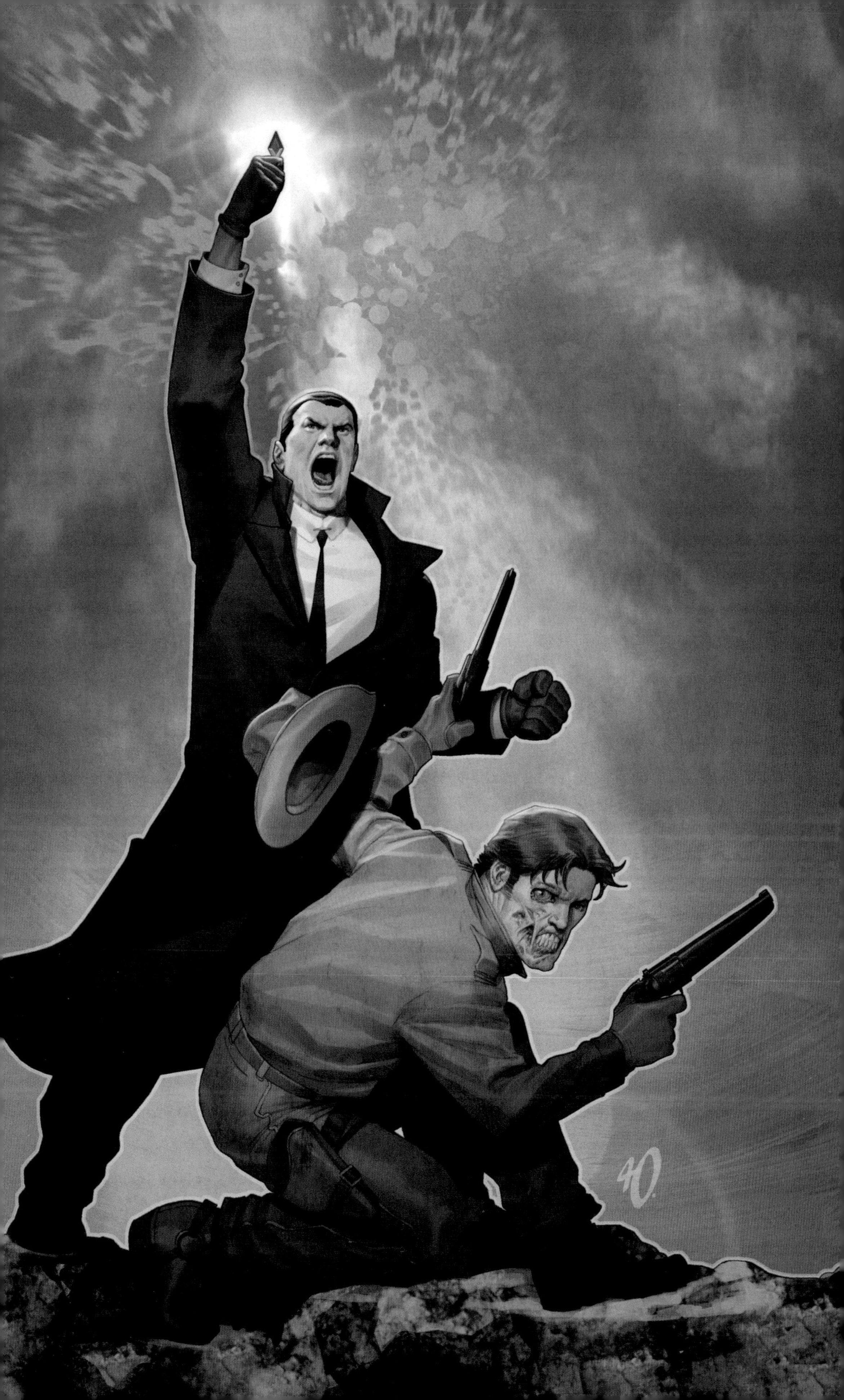

STRANGE MEDICINE

JIMMY PALMIOTTI & JUSTIN GRAY writers **MORITAT** artist cover art by **ARIEL OLIVETTI**

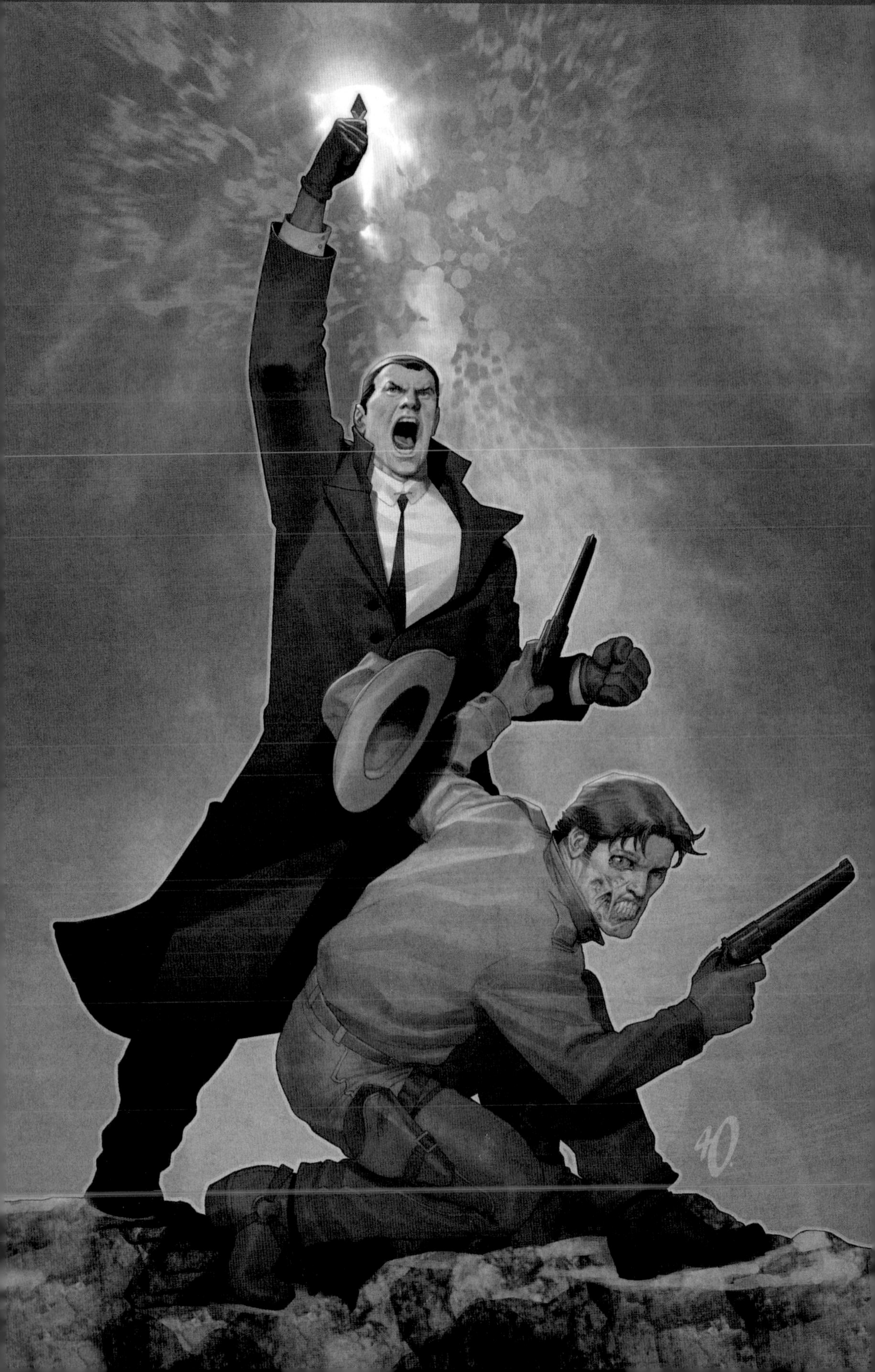

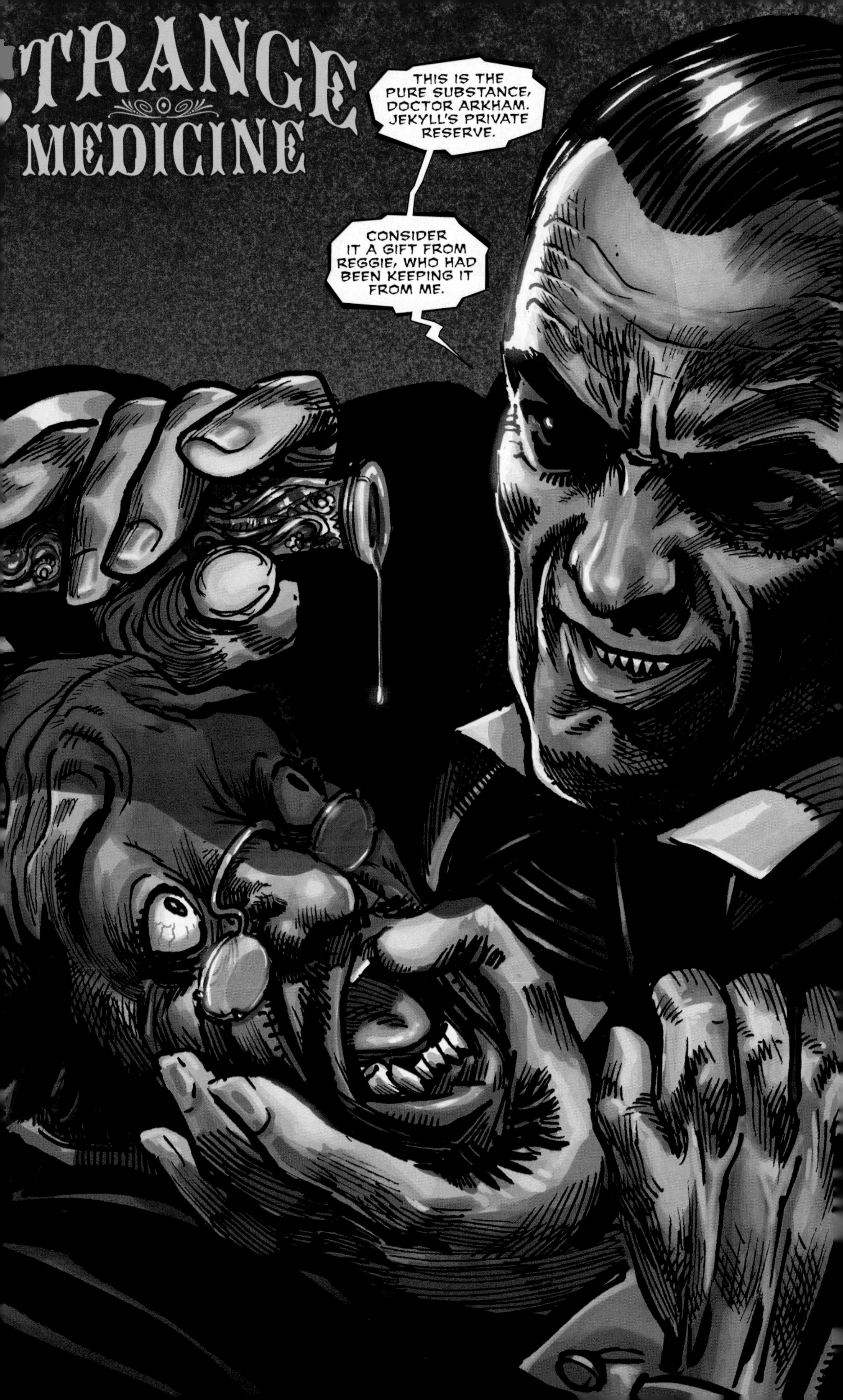
STRANGE MEDICINE
THIS IS THE PURE SUBSTANCE, DOCTOR ARKHAM. JEKYLL'S PRIVATE RESERVE.
CONSIDER IT A GIFT FROM REGGIE, WHO HAD BEEN KEEPING IT FROM ME.

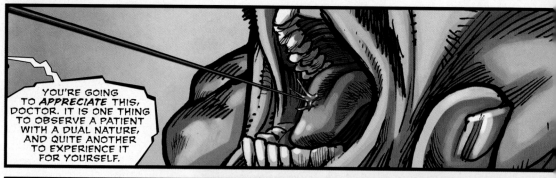

YOU'RE GOING TO *APPRECIATE* THIS, DOCTOR. IT IS ONE THING TO OBSERVE A PATIENT WITH A DUAL NATURE, AND QUITE ANOTHER TO EXPERIENCE IT FOR YOURSELF.

I MUST ADMIT I'M *CURIOUS* TO SEE WHAT VULGARITY AND POTENTIAL FOR VIOLENCE LURKS INSIDE THAT *TREMBLING* FRAME OF YOURS.

WHAT CURIOUS BEHAVIORS HAVE YOU BEEN *REPRESSING* IN YOUR DAILY LIFE?

WHAT SECRET *DESIRES* OF YOUR *TRUE SELF* WILL BE REVEALED?

GGHAAAAKK!!!

IT DOES TAKE TIME TO CULTIVATE YOUR INNER PERSON, SO I SUSPECT YOU'L BE A BIT SAVAGE AT THE START.

I WAS POSITIVEL *BESTIAL.*

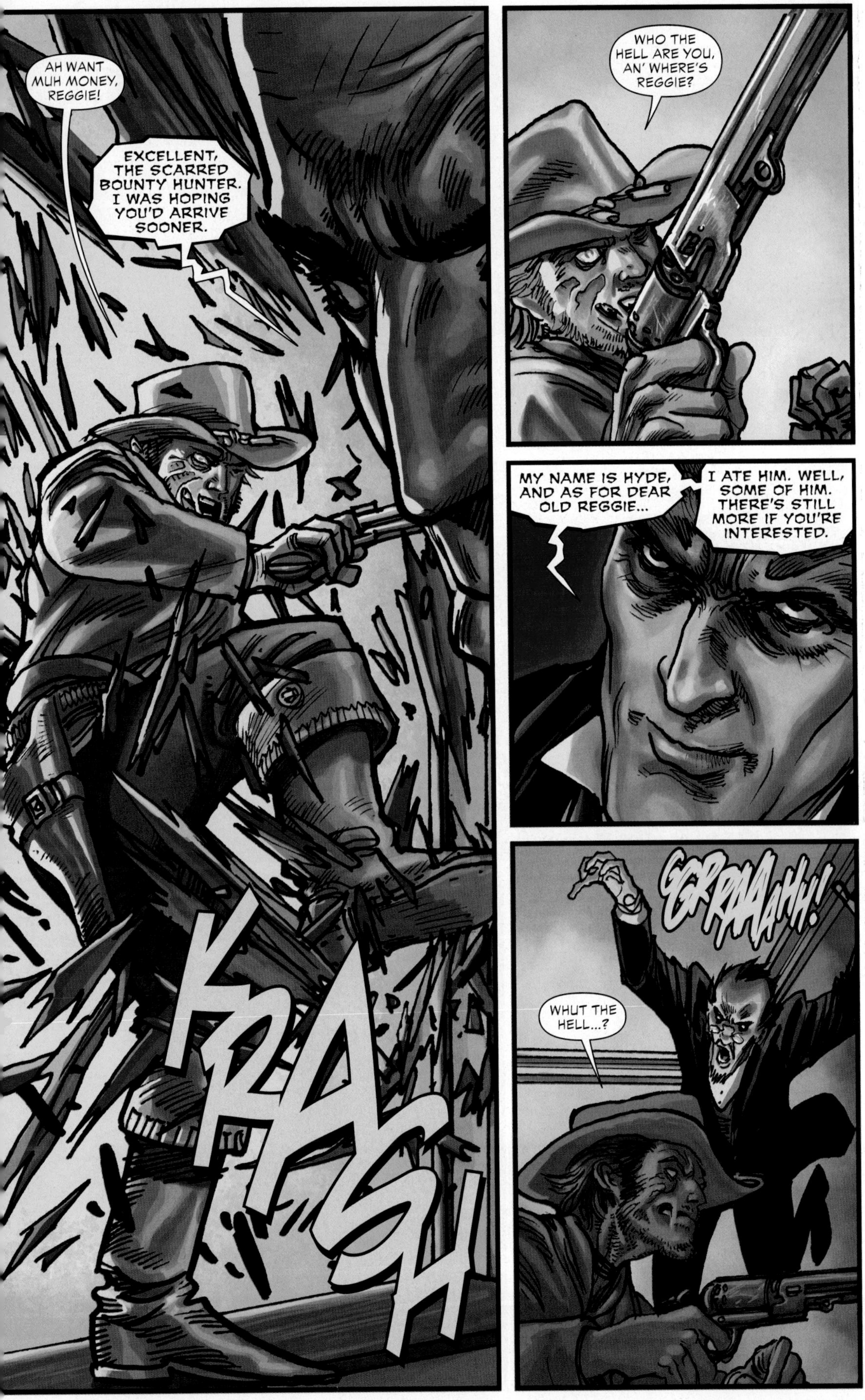
AH WANT MUH MONEY, REGGIE!
EXCELLENT, THE SCARRED BOUNTY HUNTER. I WAS HOPING YOU'D ARRIVE SOONER.
KRASH
WHO THE HELL ARE YOU, AN' WHERE'S REGGIE?
MY NAME IS HYDE, AND AS FOR DEAR OLD REGGIE...
I ATE HIM. WELL, SOME OF HIM. THERE'S STILL MORE IF YOU'RE INTERESTED.
GGRRAAAAHH!
WHUT THE HELL...?

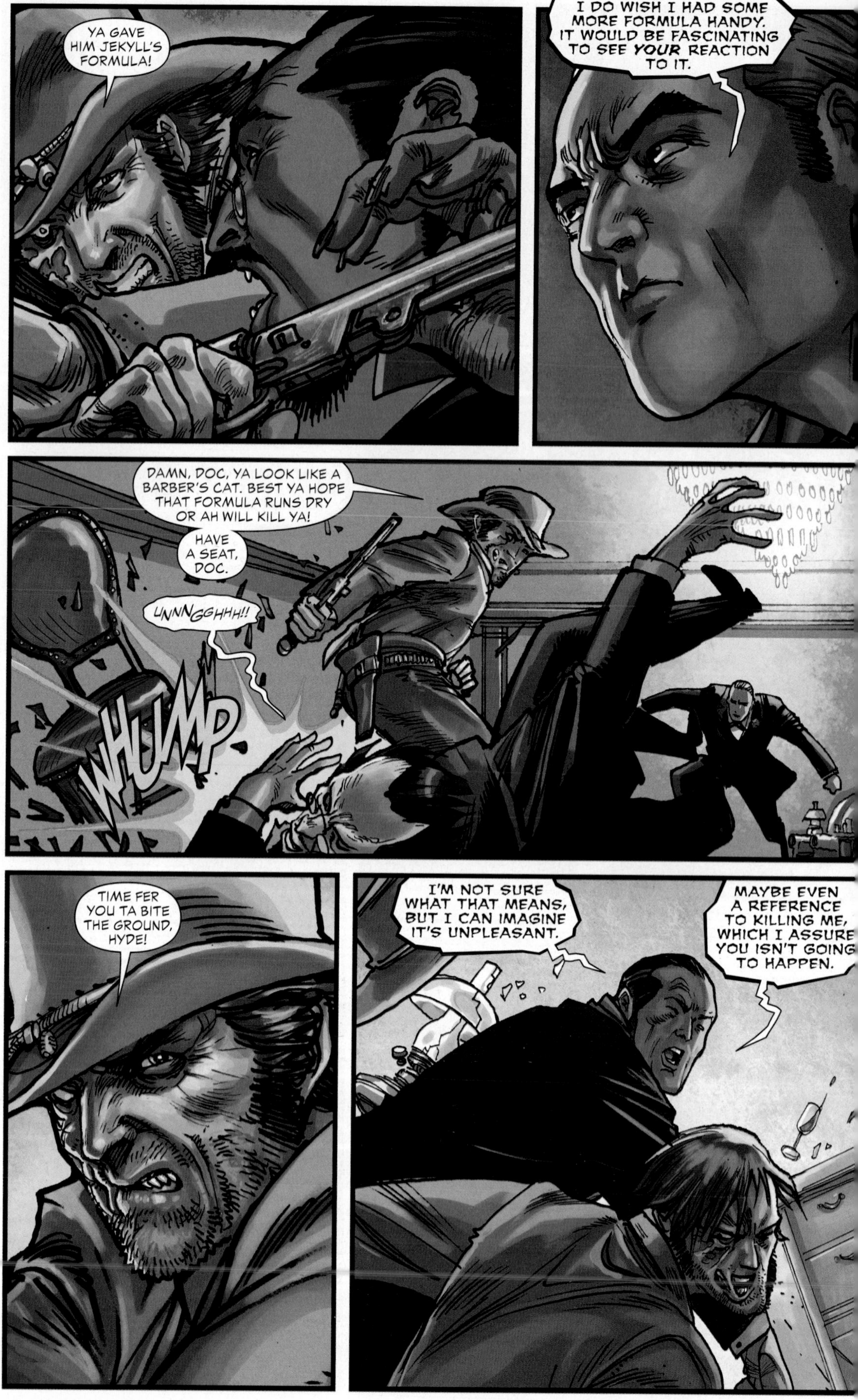
YA GAVE HIM JEKYLL'S FORMULA!
HOW ASTUTE OF YOU. I DO WISH I HAD SOME MORE FORMULA HANDY. IT WOULD BE FASCINATING TO SEE YOUR REACTION TO IT.
DAMN, DOC, YA LOOK LIKE A BARBER'S CAT. BEST YA HOPE THAT FORMULA RUNS DRY OR AH WILL KILL YA!
HAVE A SEAT, DOC.
UNNNGGHHH!!
WHUMP
TIME FER YOU TA BITE THE GROUND, HYDE!
I'M NOT SURE WHAT THAT MEANS, BUT I CAN IMAGINE IT'S UNPLEASANT.
MAYBE EVEN A REFERENCE TO KILLING ME, WHICH I ASSURE YOU ISN'T GOING TO HAPPEN.

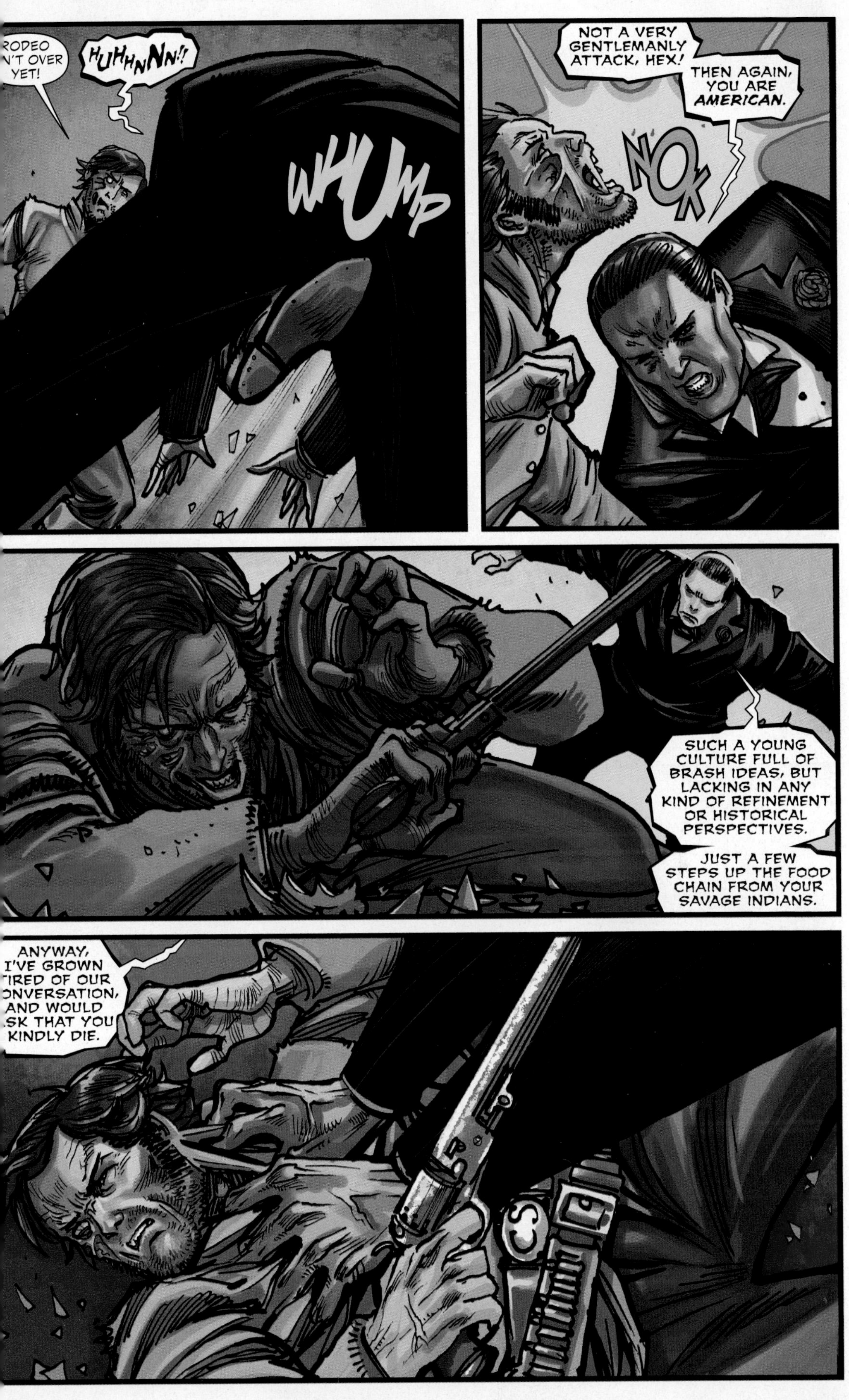

RODEO N'T OVER YET!
HUHHNNN!!
WHUMP
NOT A VERY GENTLEMANLY ATTACK, HEX!
THEN AGAIN, YOU ARE AMERICAN.
NOK
SUCH A YOUNG CULTURE FULL OF BRASH IDEAS, BUT LACKING IN ANY KIND OF REFINEMENT OR HISTORICAL PERSPECTIVES.
JUST A FEW STEPS UP THE FOOD CHAIN FROM YOUR SAVAGE INDIANS.
ANYWAY, I'VE GROWN IRED OF OUR ONVERSATION, AND WOULD SK THAT YOU KINDLY DIE.

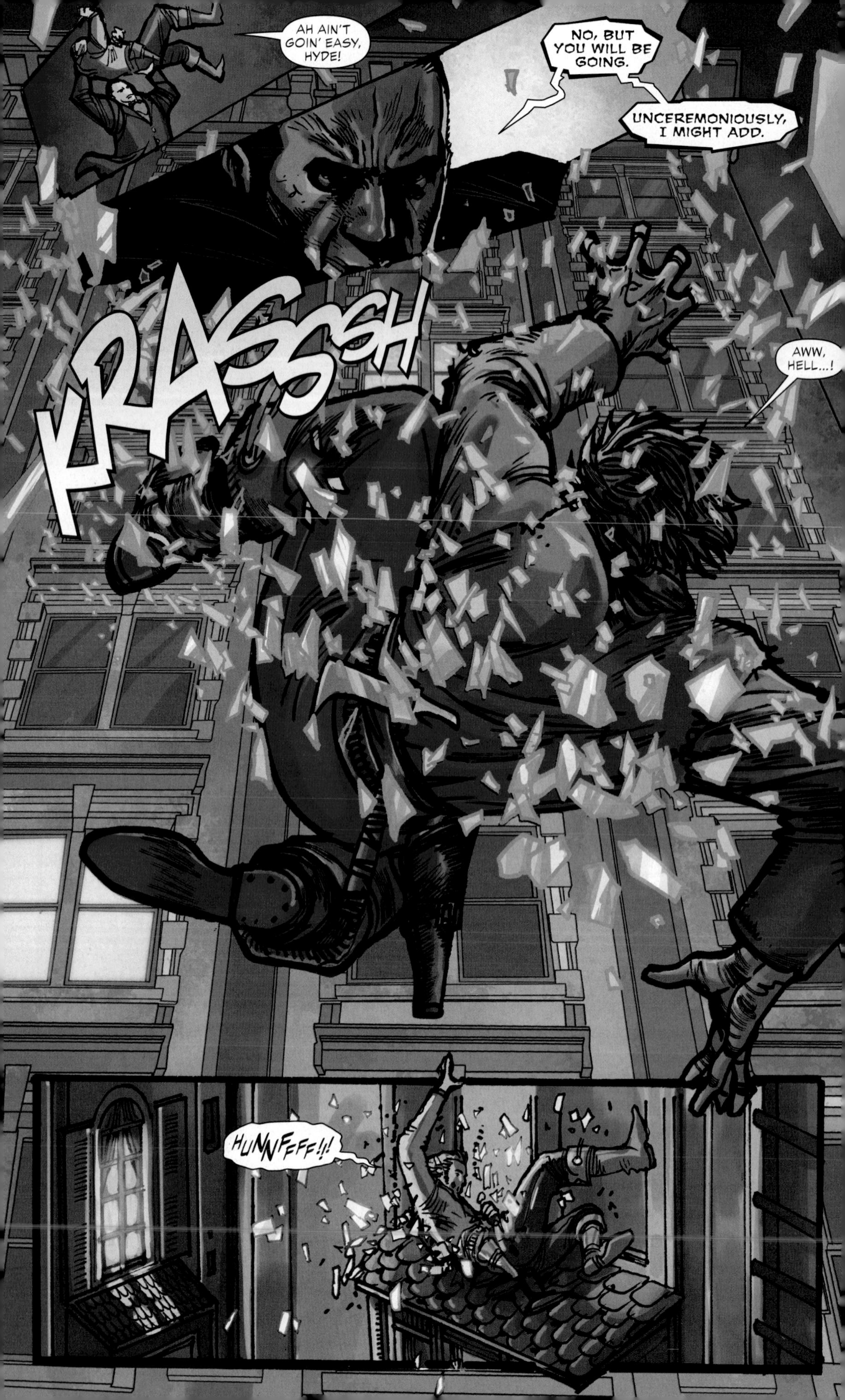
AH AIN'T GOIN' EASY, HYDE!
NO, BUT YOU WILL BE GOING.
UNCEREMONIOUSLY, I MIGHT ADD.
KRASSSH
AWW, HELL...!
HUNNFFFF!!!

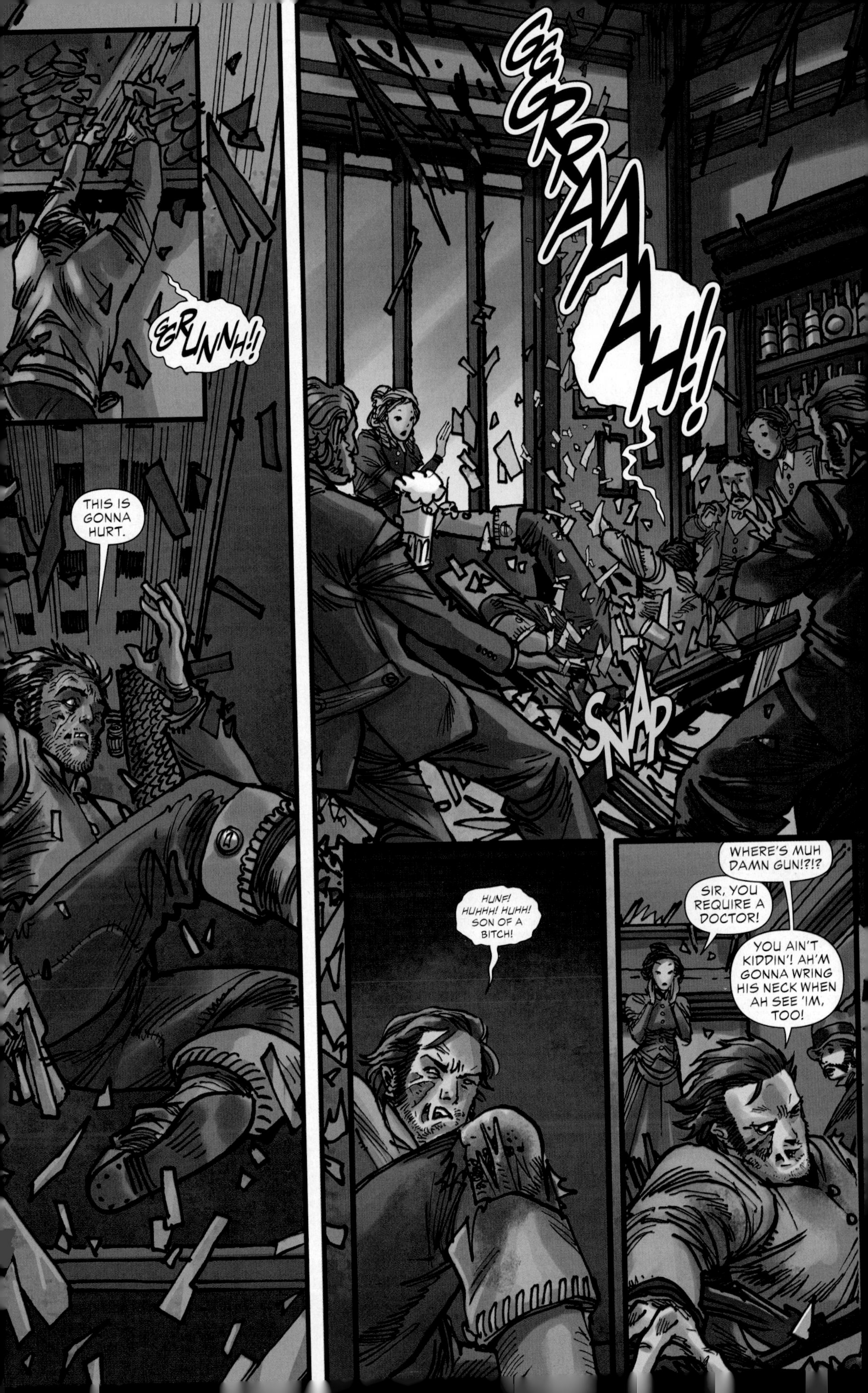

EGRUNNH!!
THIS IS GONNA HURT.
GGRAAAAHH!!
SNAP
HUNF! HUHHH! HUHH! SON OF A BITCH!
WHERE'S MUH DAMN GUN!?!?
SIR, YOU REQUIRE A DOCTOR!
YOU AIN'T KIDDIN'! AH'M GONNA WRING HIS NECK WHEN AH SEE 'IM, TOO!

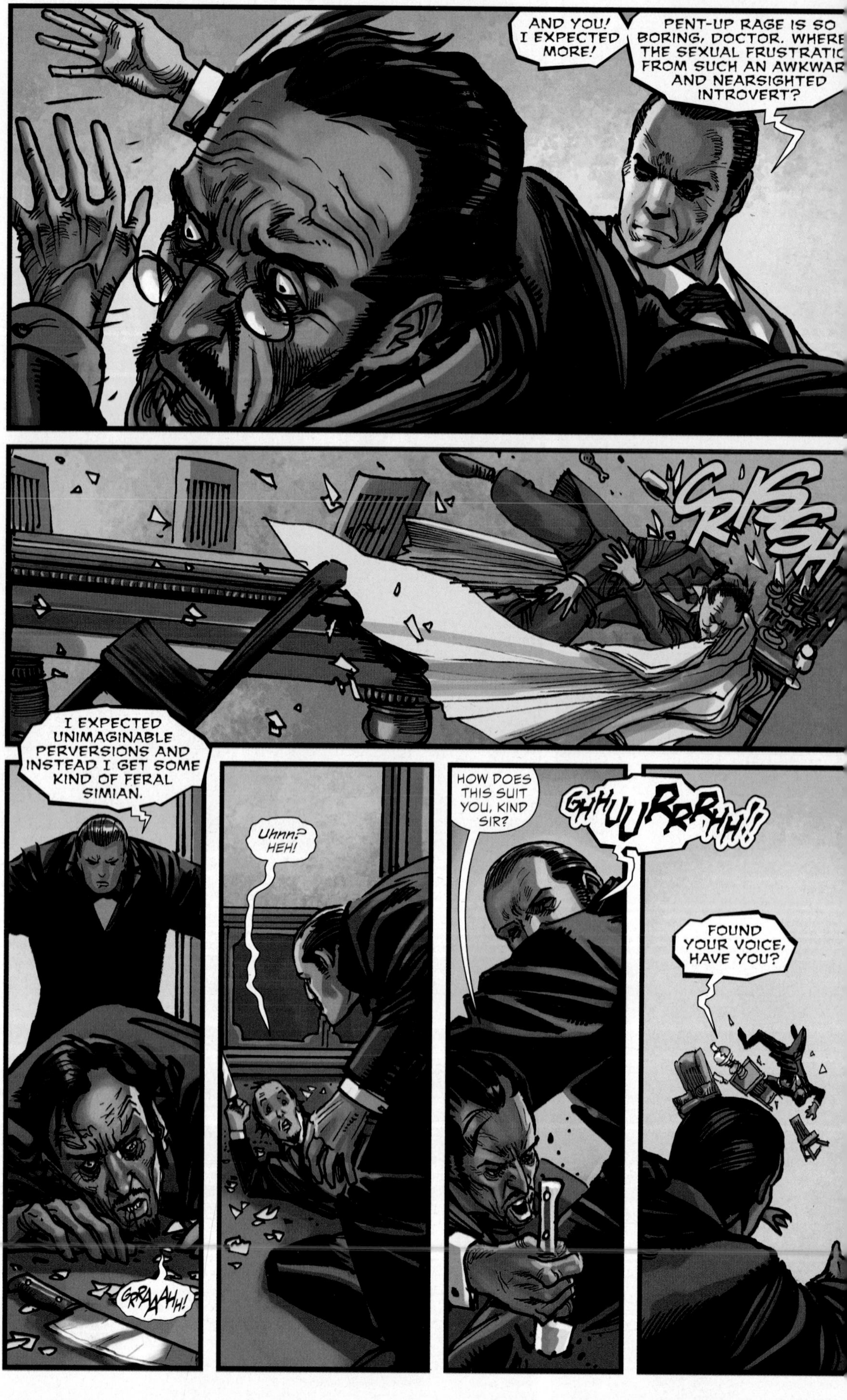

AND YOU! I EXPECTED MORE!
PENT-UP RAGE IS SO BORING, DOCTOR. WHERE THE SEXUAL FRUSTRATIC FROM SUCH AN AWKWAR AND NEARSIGHTED INTROVERT?
CRISSH
I EXPECTED UNIMAGINABLE PERVERSIONS AND INSTEAD I GET SOME KIND OF FERAL SIMIAN.
GRRAAAHH!
Uhnn? HEH!
HOW DOES THIS SUIT YOU, KIND SIR?
GHHUURRRHH!!
FOUND YOUR VOICE, HAVE YOU?

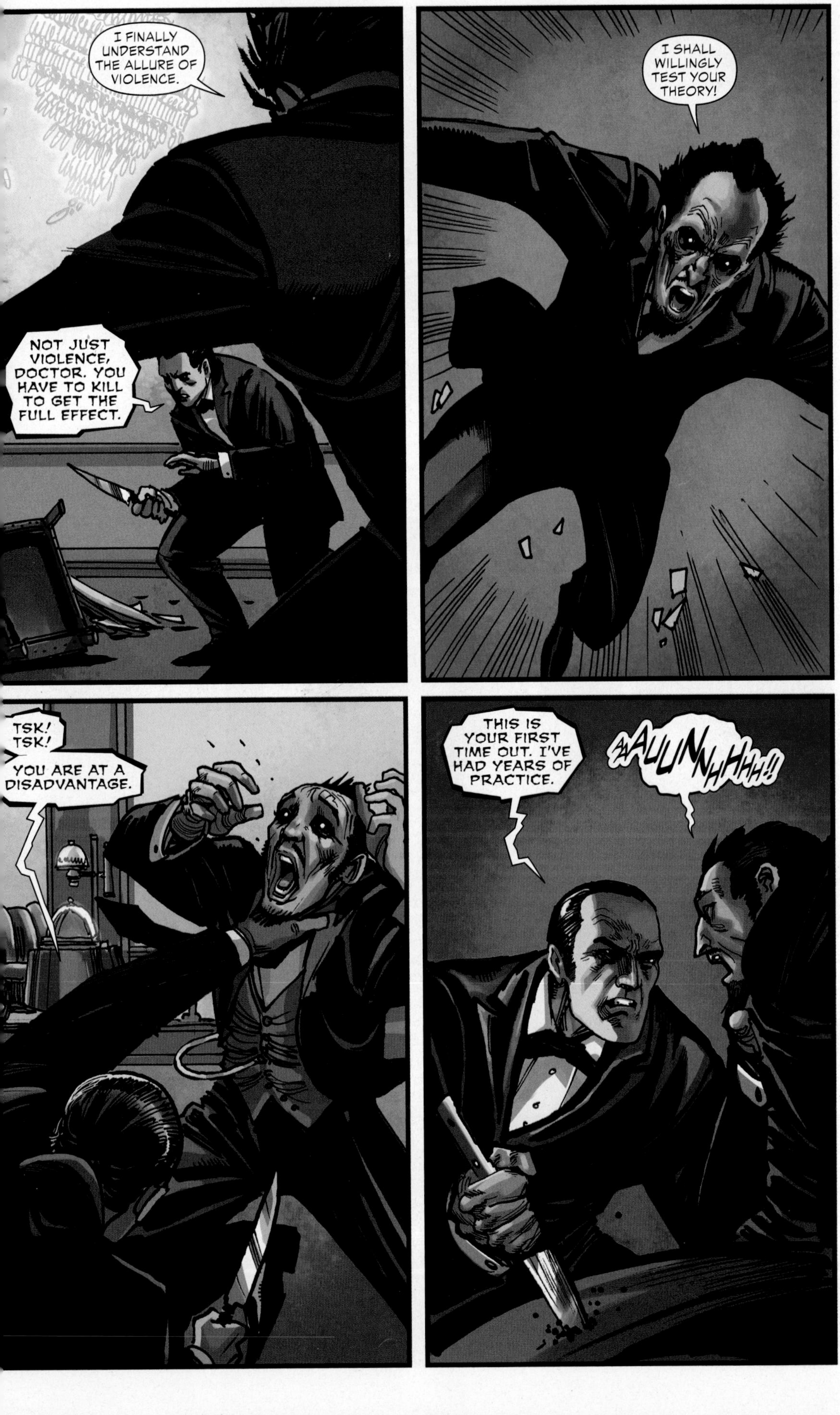
I FINALLY UNDERSTAND THE ALLURE OF VIOLENCE.
NOT JUST VIOLENCE, DOCTOR. YOU HAVE TO KILL TO GET THE FULL EFFECT.
I SHALL WILLINGLY TEST YOUR THEORY!
TSK! TSK!
YOU ARE AT A DISADVANTAGE.
THIS IS YOUR FIRST TIME OUT. I'VE HAD YEARS OF PRACTICE.
AAUUNNHHHH!!

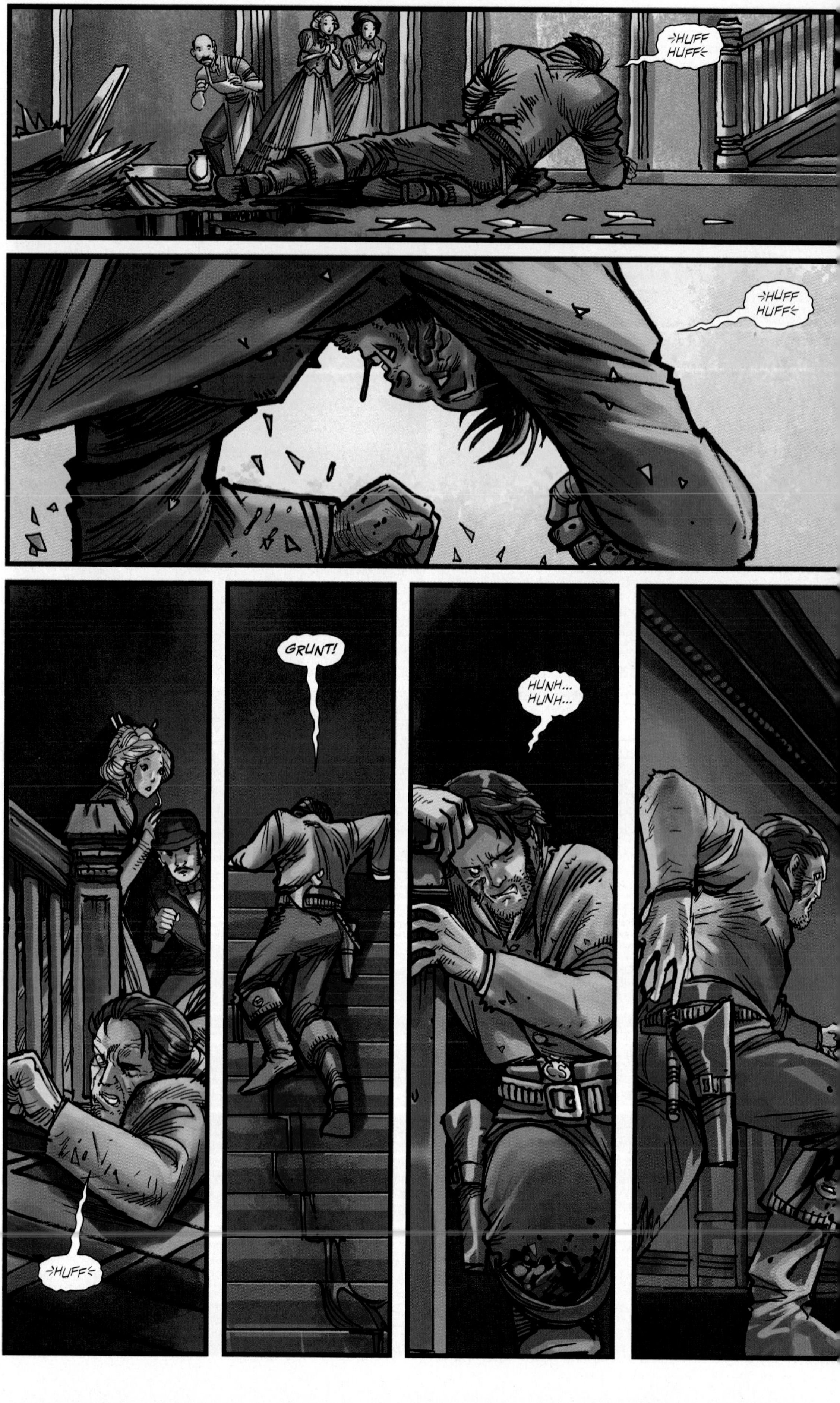
HUFF HUFF
HUFF HUFF
HUFF
GRUNT!
HUNH... HUNH...

CRASH

THEN THERE'S THE INEQUALITY OF PHYSICAL STRENGTH, WHICH PLACES YOU AT A FURTHER DISADVANTAGE.

YOU'D BE SURPRISED AT THE NUTRITIONAL VALUE OF EATING A MAN'S STILL-BEATING HEART.

GUURRGGLE!!!

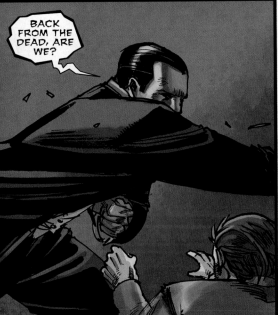

BACK FROM THE DEAD, ARE WE?

FIGGERED AH'D COME AN' GIT YA. WE CAN GO TA HELL TOGETHER.

DAMMIT, ARKHAM! WHUT THE HELL ARE YA' DOIN'?

SPREADING MY WINGS! ENJOY YOUR TIME WITH HYDE!

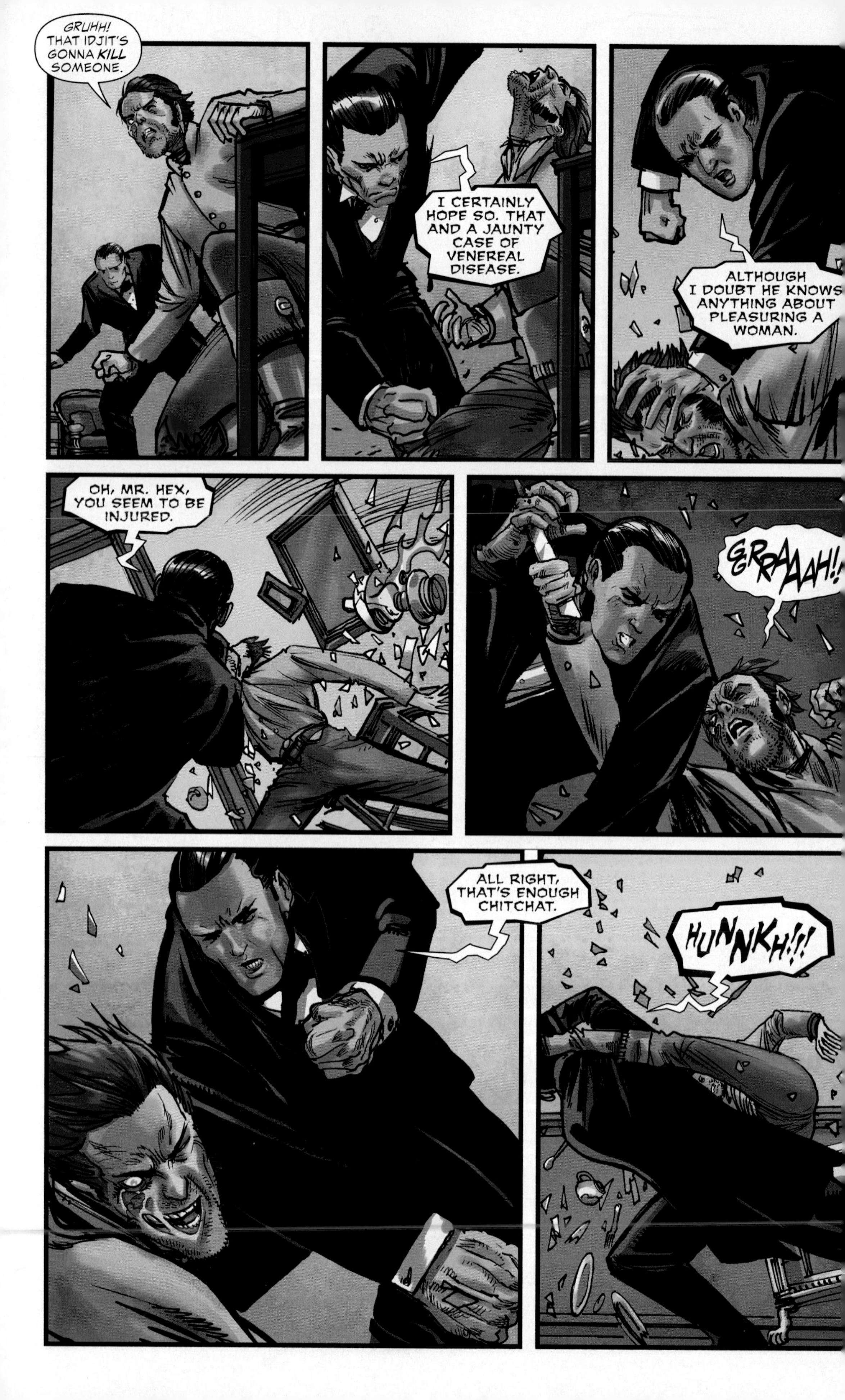
GRUHH! THAT IDJIT'S GONNA KILL SOMEONE.
I CERTAINLY HOPE SO. THAT AND A JAUNTY CASE OF VENEREAL DISEASE.
ALTHOUGH I DOUBT HE KNOWS ANYTHING ABOUT PLEASURING A WOMAN.
OH, MR. HEX, YOU SEEM TO BE INJURED.
GGRRAAAH!!
ALL RIGHT, THAT'S ENOUGH CHITCHAT.
HUNNKH!!!

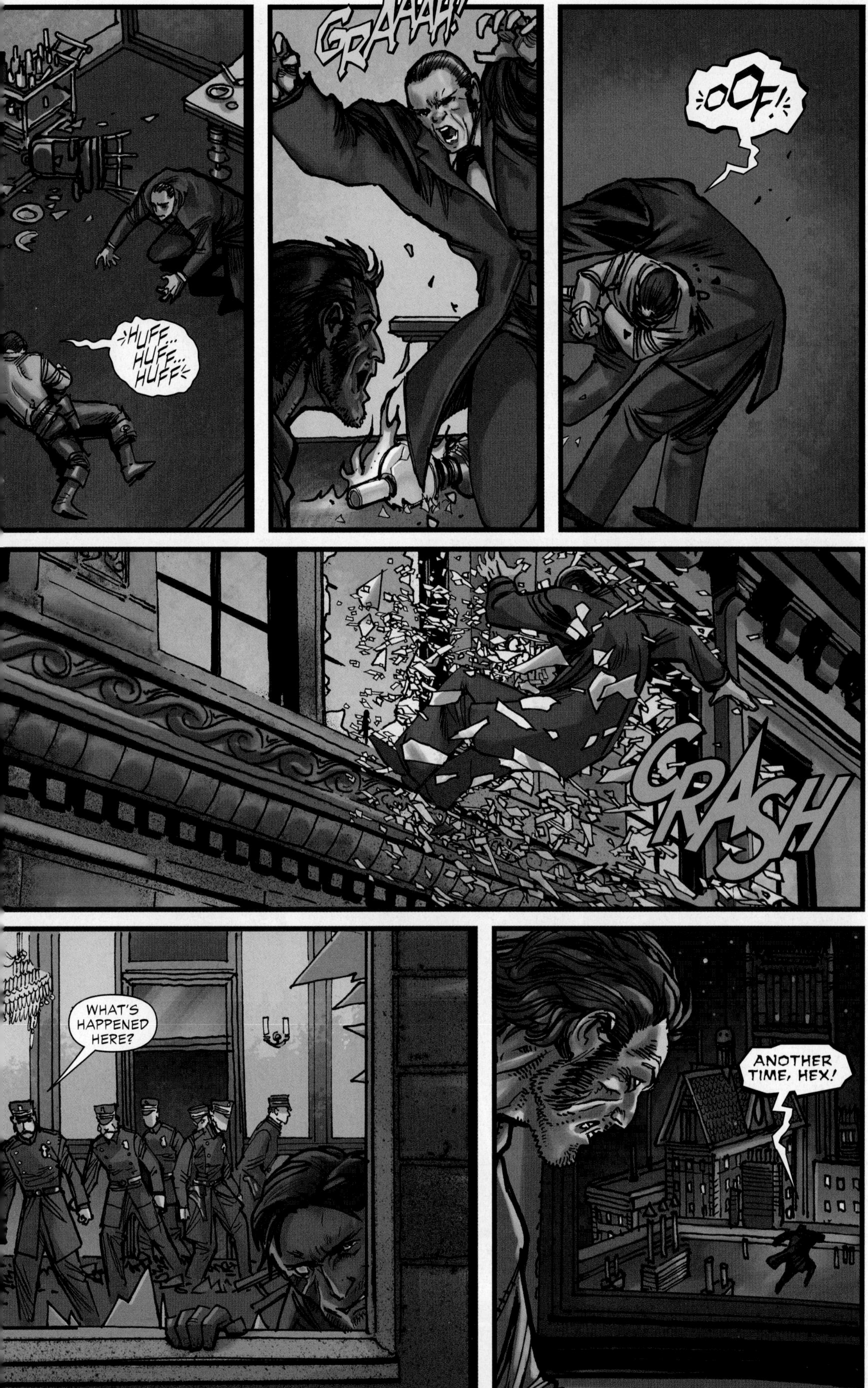
HUFF... HUFF... HUFF
GRAAAH!
OOF!
CRASH
WHAT'S HAPPENED HERE?
ANOTHER TIME, HEX!

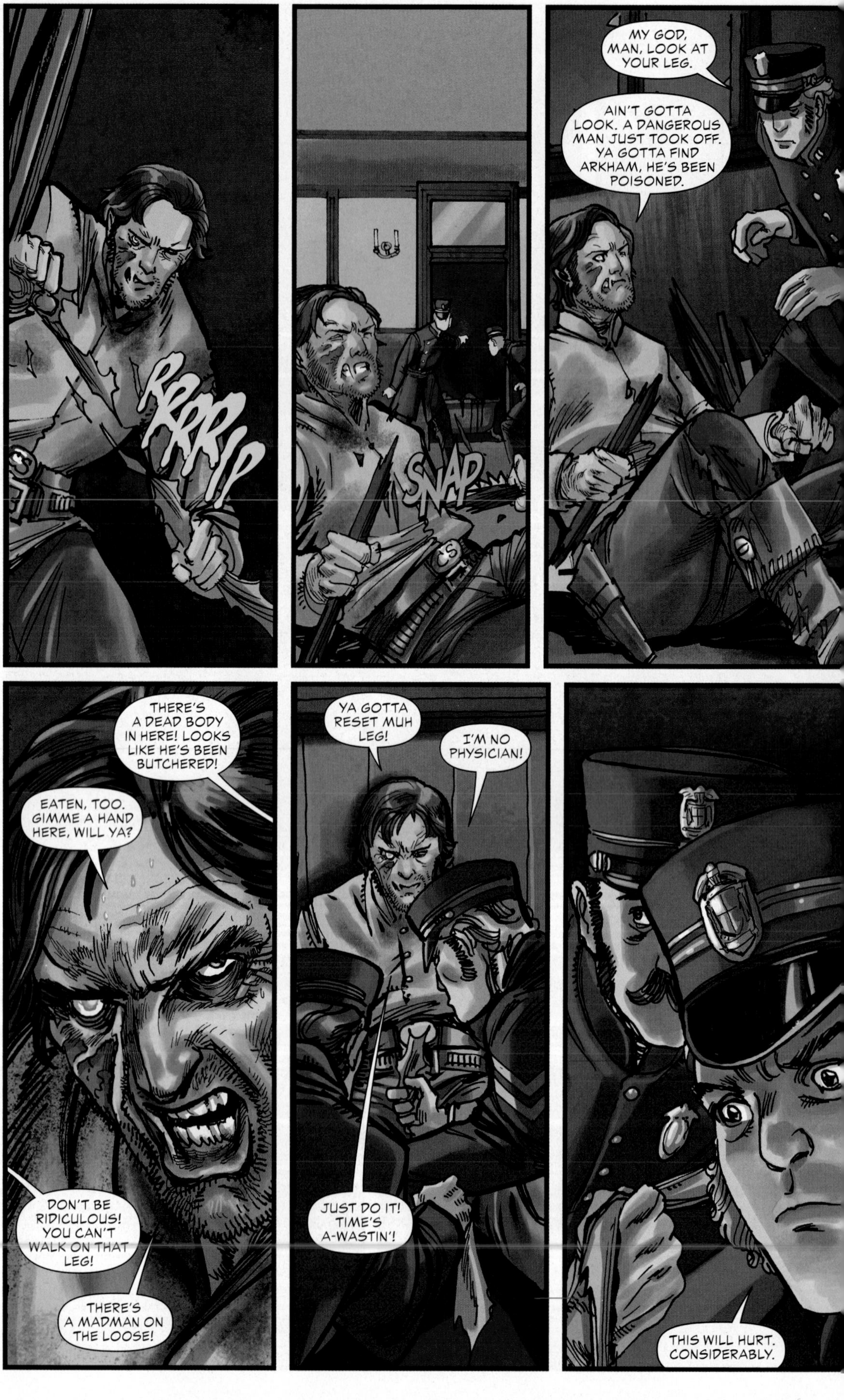
RRRIP!
SNAP
MY GOD, MAN, LOOK AT YOUR LEG.
AIN'T GOTTA LOOK. A DANGEROUS MAN JUST TOOK OFF. YA GOTTA FIND ARKHAM, HE'S BEEN POISONED.
THERE'S A DEAD BODY IN HERE! LOOKS LIKE HE'S BEEN BUTCHERED!
EATEN, TOO. GIMME A HAND HERE, WILL YA?
DON'T BE RIDICULOUS! YOU CAN'T WALK ON THAT LEG!
THERE'S A MADMAN ON THE LOOSE!
YA GOTTA RESET MUH LEG!
I'M NO PHYSICIAN!
JUST DO IT! TIME'S A-WASTIN'!
THIS WILL HURT. CONSIDERABLY.

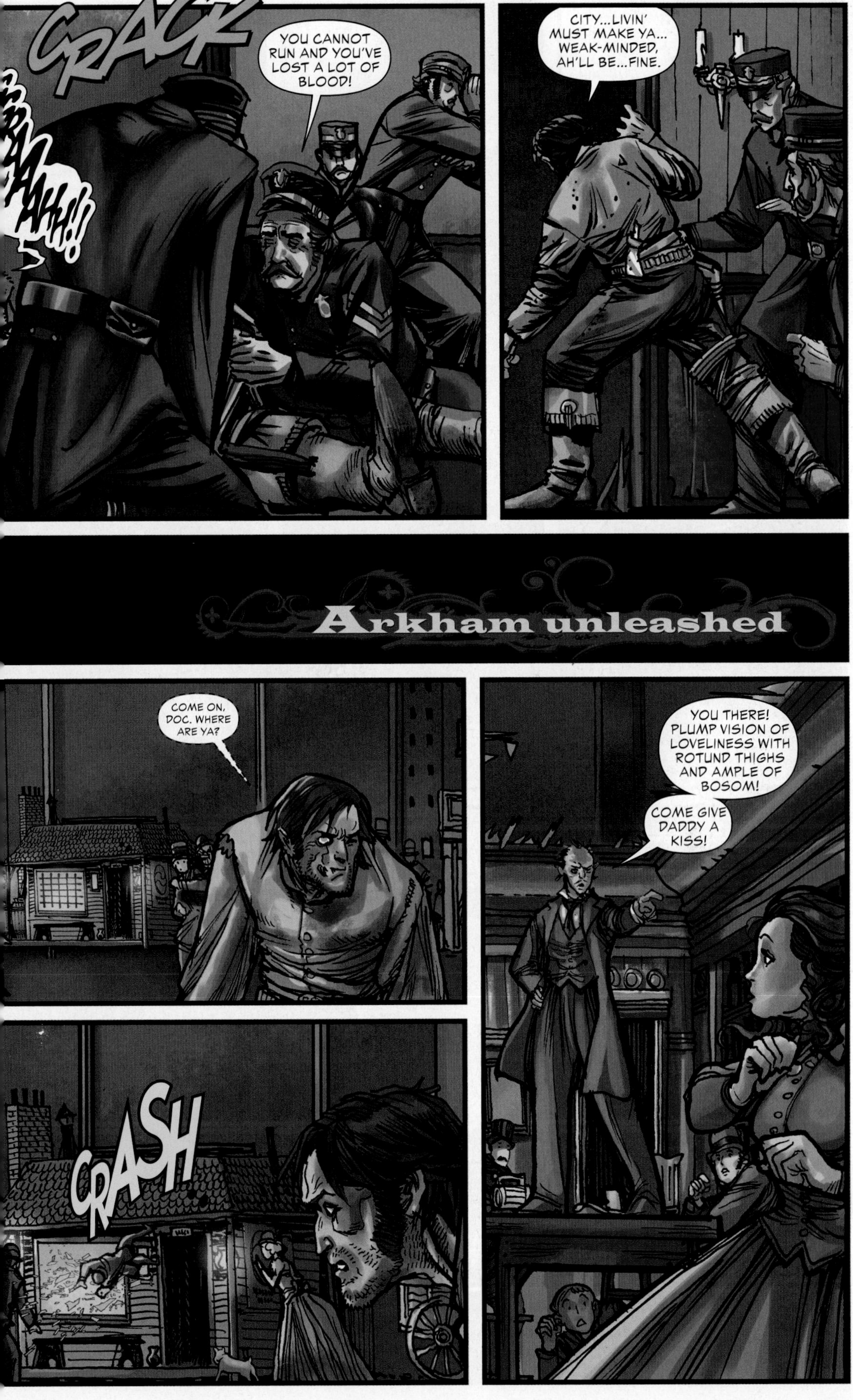
CRACK
YOU CANNOT RUN AND YOU'VE LOST A LOT OF BLOOD!
CITY...LIVIN' MUST MAKE YA... WEAK-MINDED, AH'LL BE...FINE.
Arkham unleashed
COME ON, DOC. WHERE ARE YA?
CRASH
YOU THERE! PLUMP VISION OF LOVELINESS WITH ROTUND THIGHS AND AMPLE OF BOSOM!
COME GIVE DADDY A KISS!

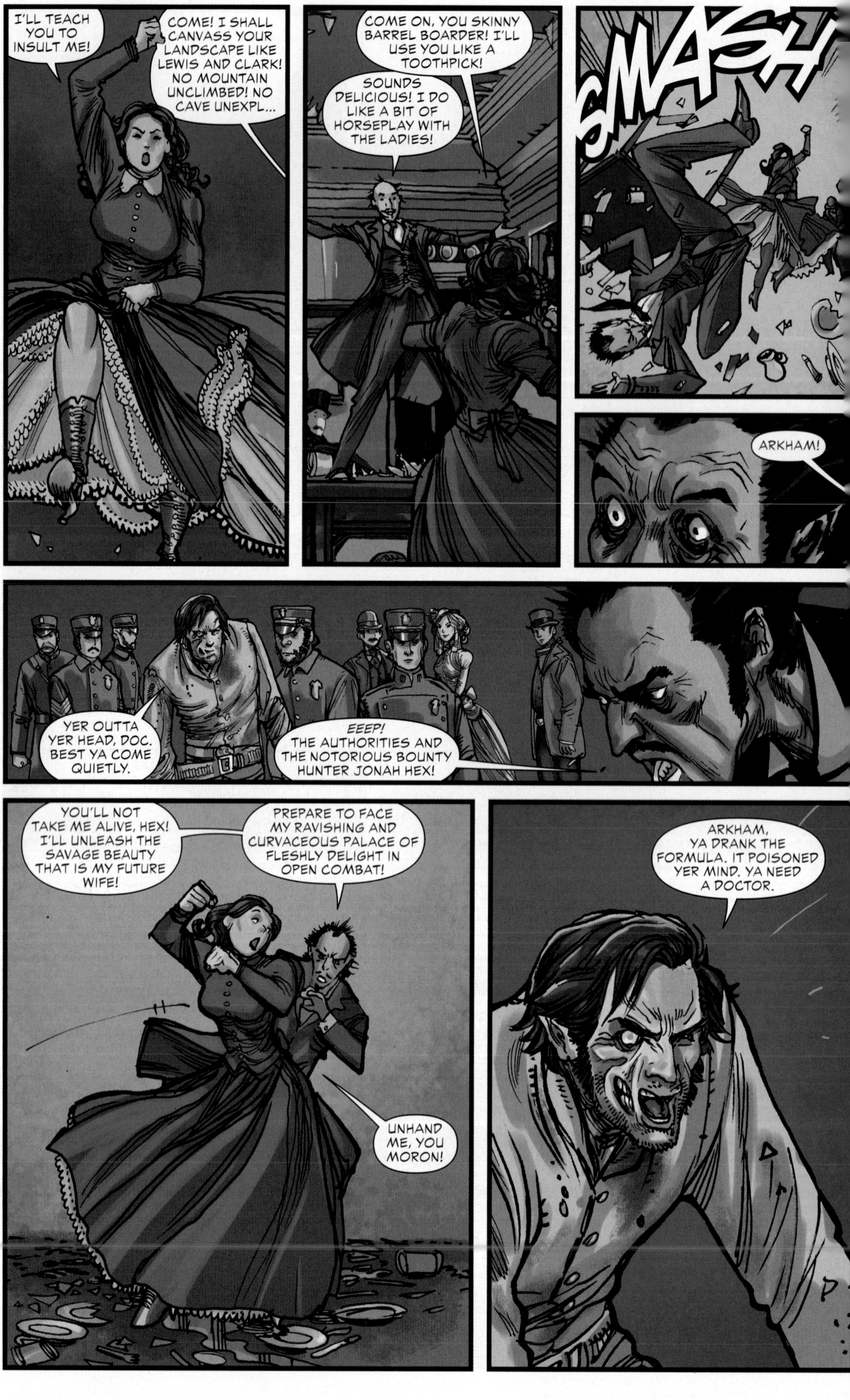
I'LL TEACH YOU TO INSULT ME!
COME! I SHALL CANVASS YOUR LANDSCAPE LIKE LEWIS AND CLARK! NO MOUNTAIN UNCLIMBED! NO CAVE UNEXPL...
COME ON, YOU SKINNY BARREL BOARDER! I'LL USE YOU LIKE A TOOTHPICK!
SOUNDS DELICIOUS! I DO LIKE A BIT OF HORSEPLAY WITH THE LADIES!
SMASH
ARKHAM!
YER OUTTA YER HEAD, DOC. BEST YA COME QUIETLY.
EEEP! THE AUTHORITIES AND THE NOTORIOUS BOUNTY HUNTER JONAH HEX!
YOU'LL NOT TAKE ME ALIVE, HEX! I'LL UNLEASH THE SAVAGE BEAUTY THAT IS MY FUTURE WIFE!
PREPARE TO FACE MY RAVISHING AND CURVACEOUS PALACE OF FLESHLY DELIGHT IN OPEN COMBAT!
UNHAND ME, YOU MORON!
ARKHAM, YA DRANK THE FORMULA. IT POISONED YER MIND. YA NEED A DOCTOR.

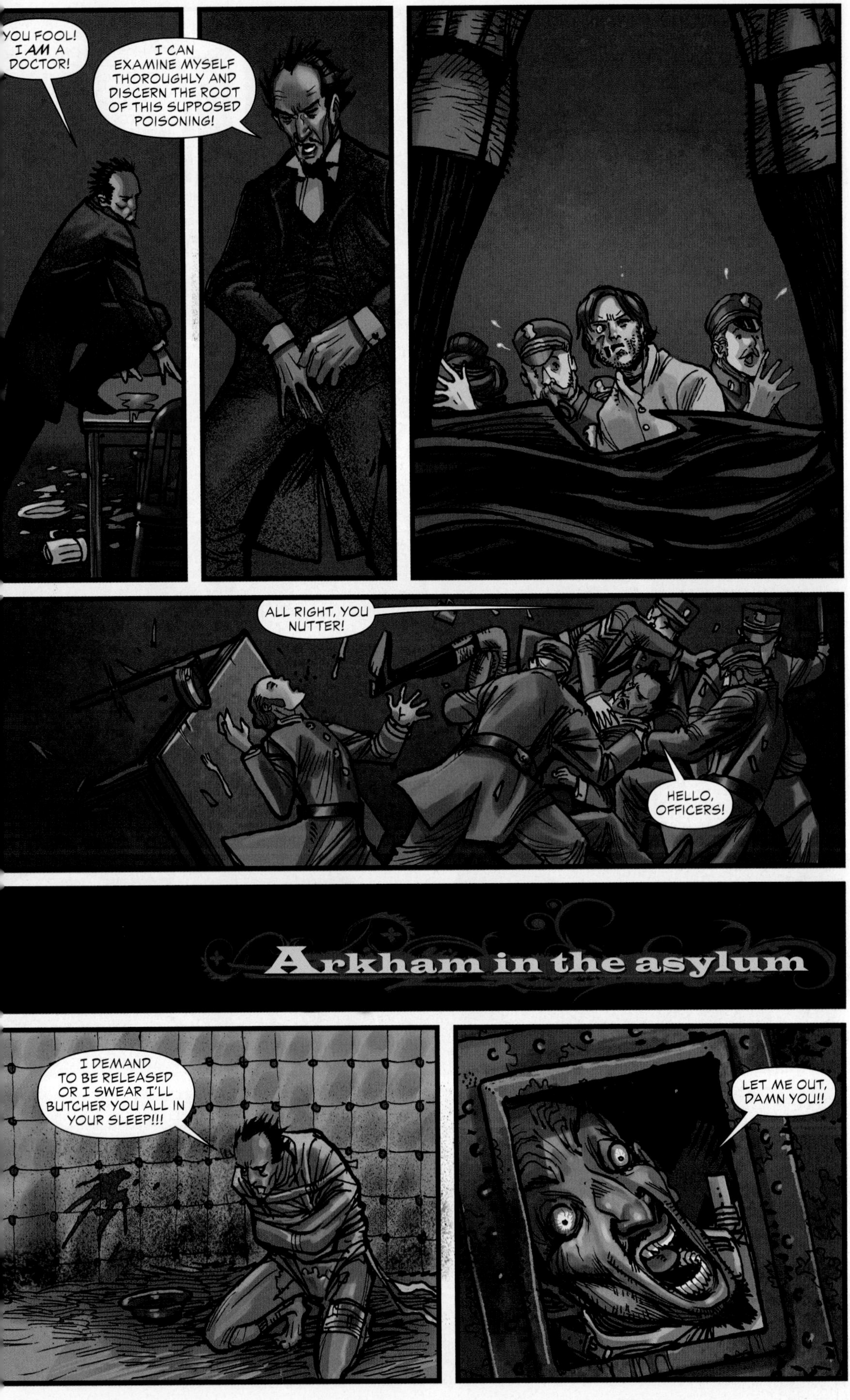
YOU FOOL! I AM A DOCTOR!
I CAN EXAMINE MYSELF THOROUGHLY AND DISCERN THE ROOT OF THIS SUPPOSED POISONING!
ALL RIGHT, YOU NUTTER!
HELLO, OFFICERS!
Arkham in the asylum
I DEMAND TO BE RELEASED OR I SWEAR I'LL BUTCHER YOU ALL IN YOUR SLEEP!!!
LET ME OUT, DAMN YOU!!

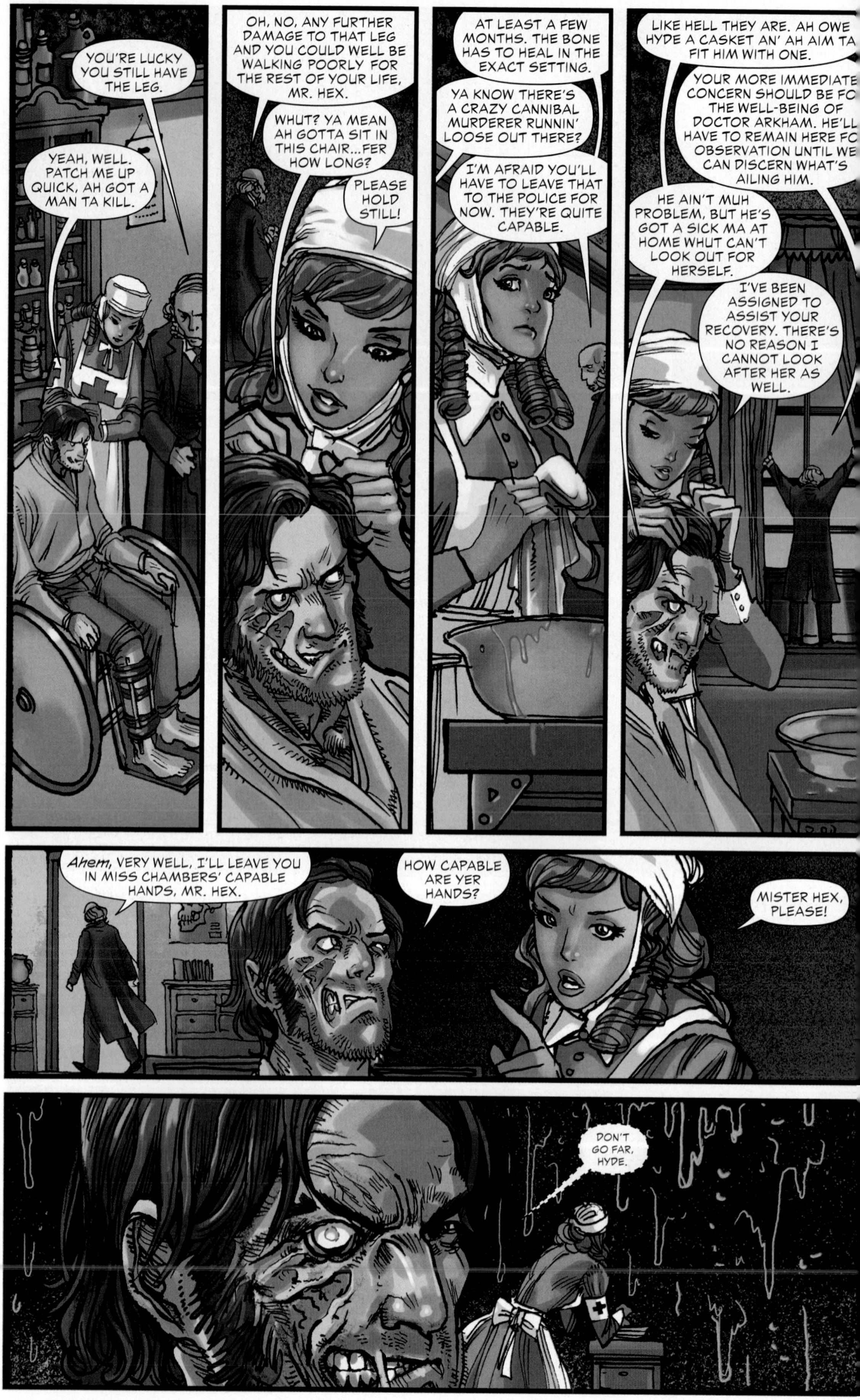

YOU'RE LUCKY YOU STILL HAVE THE LEG.
YEAH, WELL. PATCH ME UP QUICK, AH GOT A MAN TA KILL.
OH, NO, ANY FURTHER DAMAGE TO THAT LEG AND YOU COULD WELL BE WALKING POORLY FOR THE REST OF YOUR LIFE, MR. HEX.
WHUT? YA MEAN AH GOTTA SIT IN THIS CHAIR...FER HOW LONG?
PLEASE HOLD STILL!
AT LEAST A FEW MONTHS. THE BONE HAS TO HEAL IN THE EXACT SETTING.
YA KNOW THERE'S A CRAZY CANNIBAL MURDERER RUNNIN' LOOSE OUT THERE?
I'M AFRAID YOU'LL HAVE TO LEAVE THAT TO THE POLICE FOR NOW. THEY'RE QUITE CAPABLE.
LIKE HELL THEY ARE. AH OWE HYDE A CASKET AN' AH AIM TA FIT HIM WITH ONE.
YOUR MORE IMMEDIATE CONCERN SHOULD BE FO THE WELL-BEING OF DOCTOR ARKHAM. HE'LL HAVE TO REMAIN HERE FO OBSERVATION UNTIL WE CAN DISCERN WHAT'S AILING HIM.
HE AIN'T MUH PROBLEM, BUT HE'S GOT A SICK MA AT HOME WHUT CAN'T LOOK OUT FOR HERSELF.
I'VE BEEN ASSIGNED TO ASSIST YOUR RECOVERY. THERE'S NO REASON I CANNOT LOOK AFTER HER AS WELL.
Ahem, VERY WELL, I'LL LEAVE YOU IN MISS CHAMBERS' CAPABLE HANDS, MR. HEX.
HOW CAPABLE ARE YER HANDS?
MISTER HEX, PLEASE!
DON'T GO FAR, HYDE.

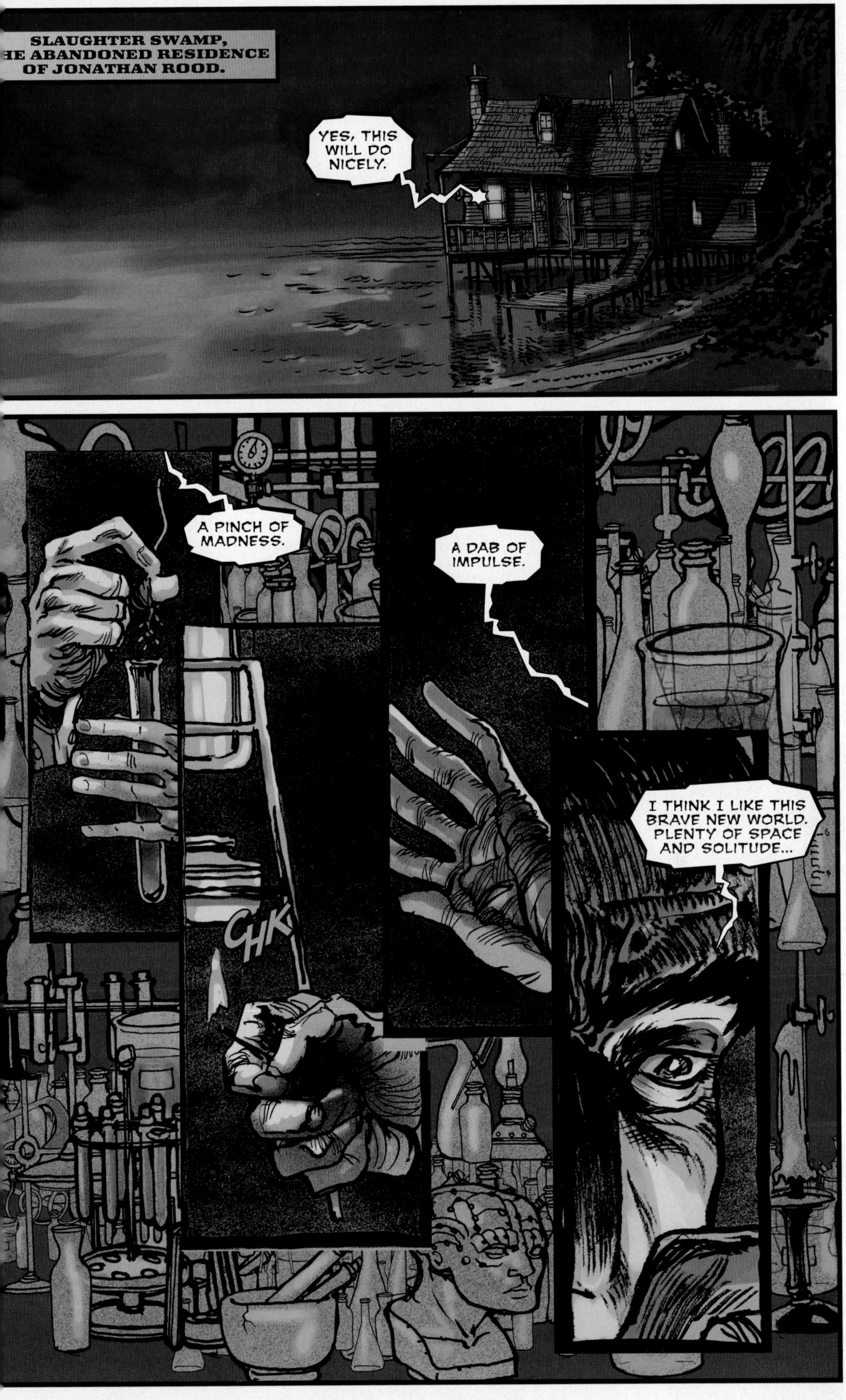
SLAUGHTER SWAMP,
HE ABANDONED RESIDENCE
OF JONATHAN ROOD.
YES, THIS WILL DO NICELY.
A PINCH OF MADNESS.
A DAB OF IMPULSE.
CHK
I THINK I LIKE THIS BRAVE NEW WORLD. PLENTY OF SPACE AND SOLITUDE...

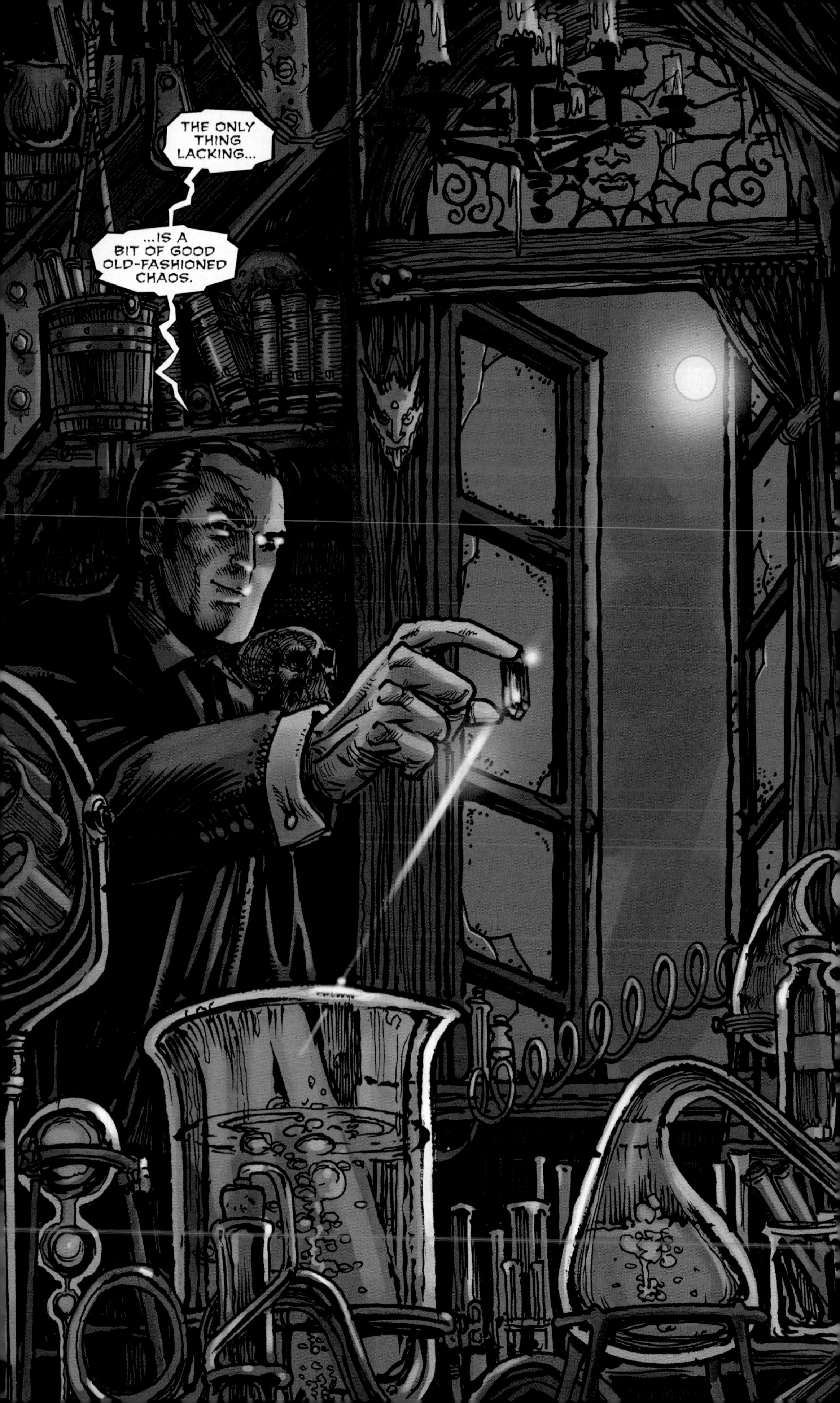
THE ONLY THING LACKING...
...IS A BIT OF GOOD OLD-FASHIONED CHAOS.

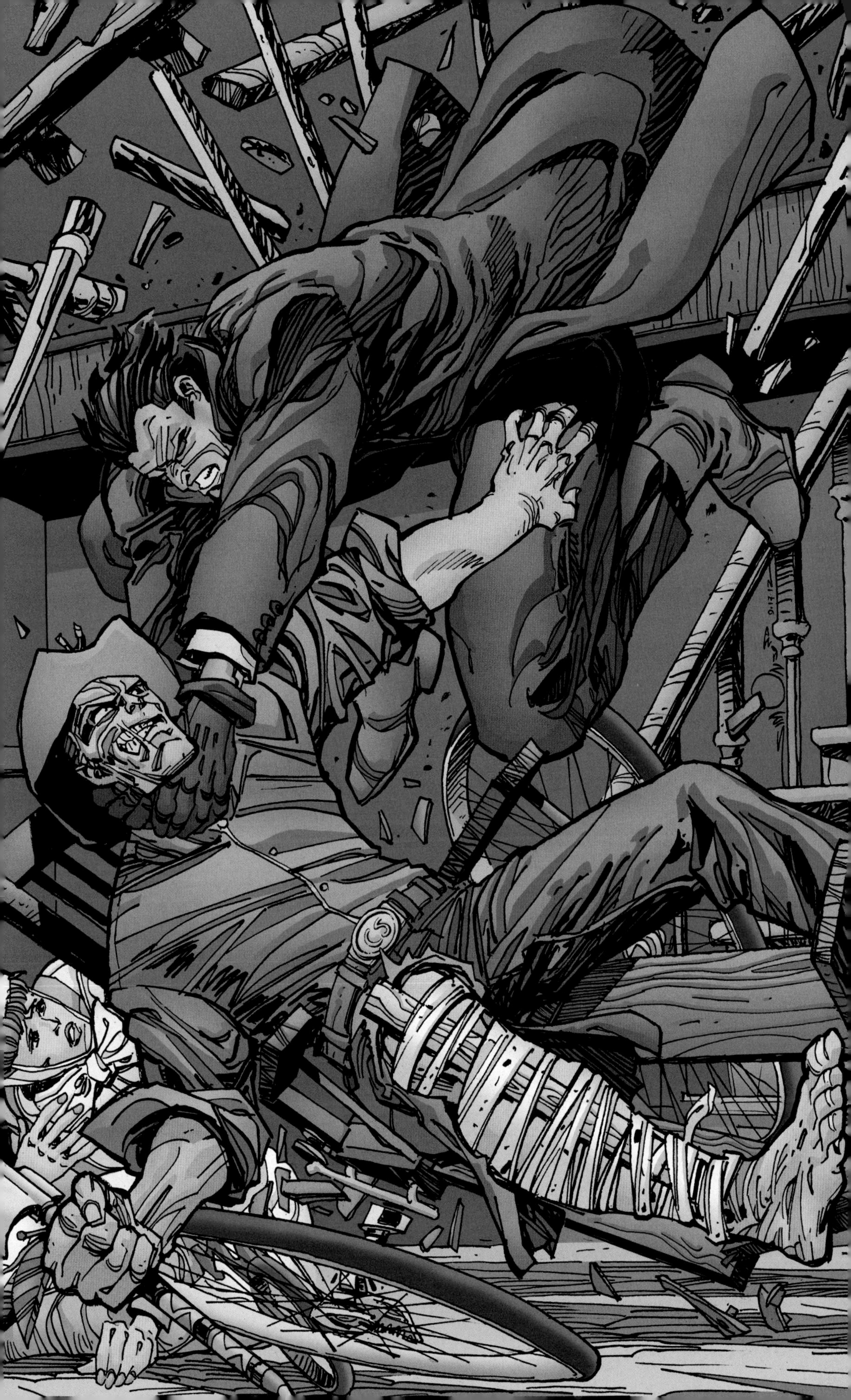

IT'S A MADHOUSE

JIMMY PALMIOTTI & JUSTIN GRAY writers **MORITAT** artist cover art by **WALTER SIMONSON & LOVERN KINDZIERSKI**

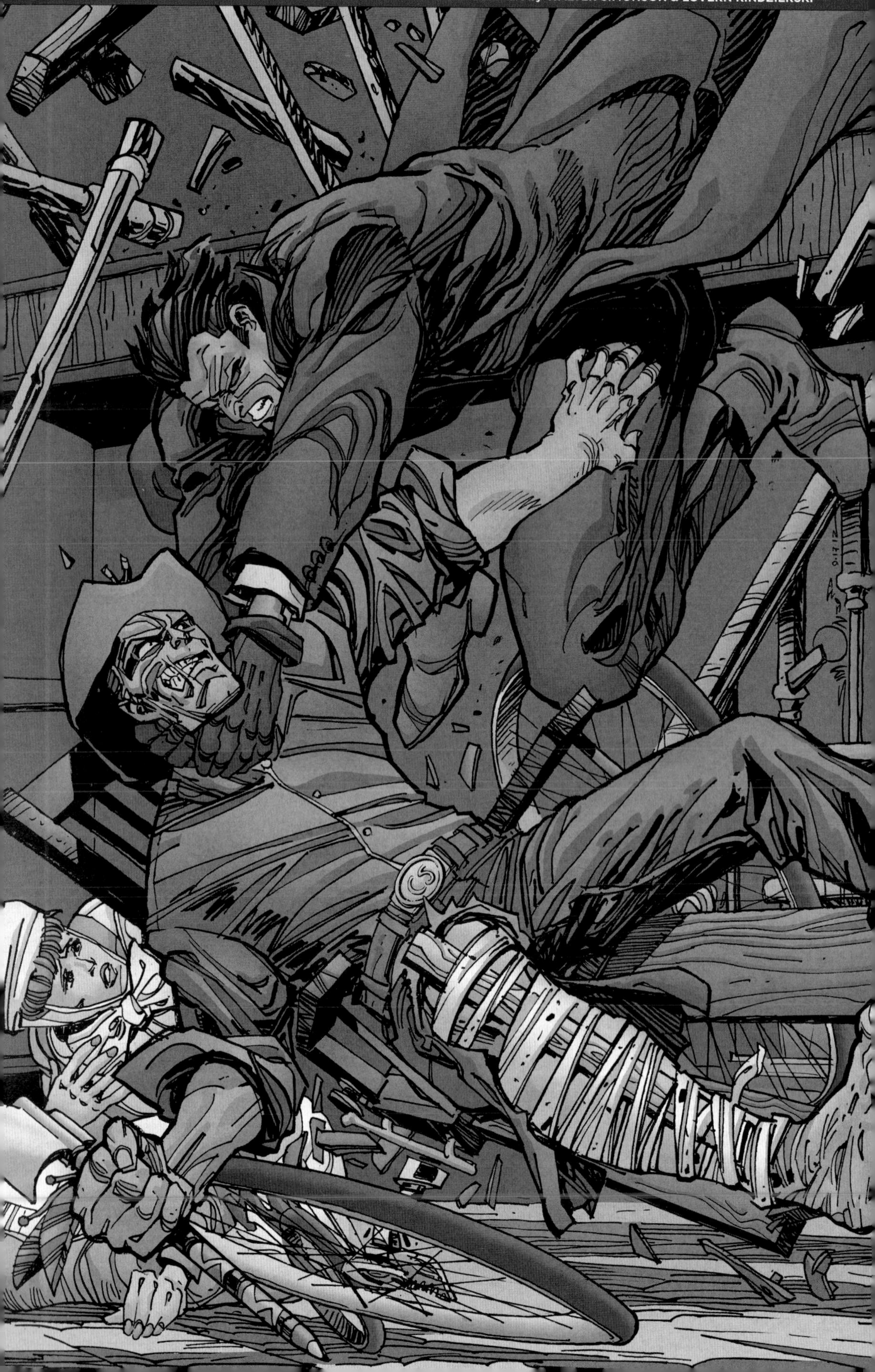

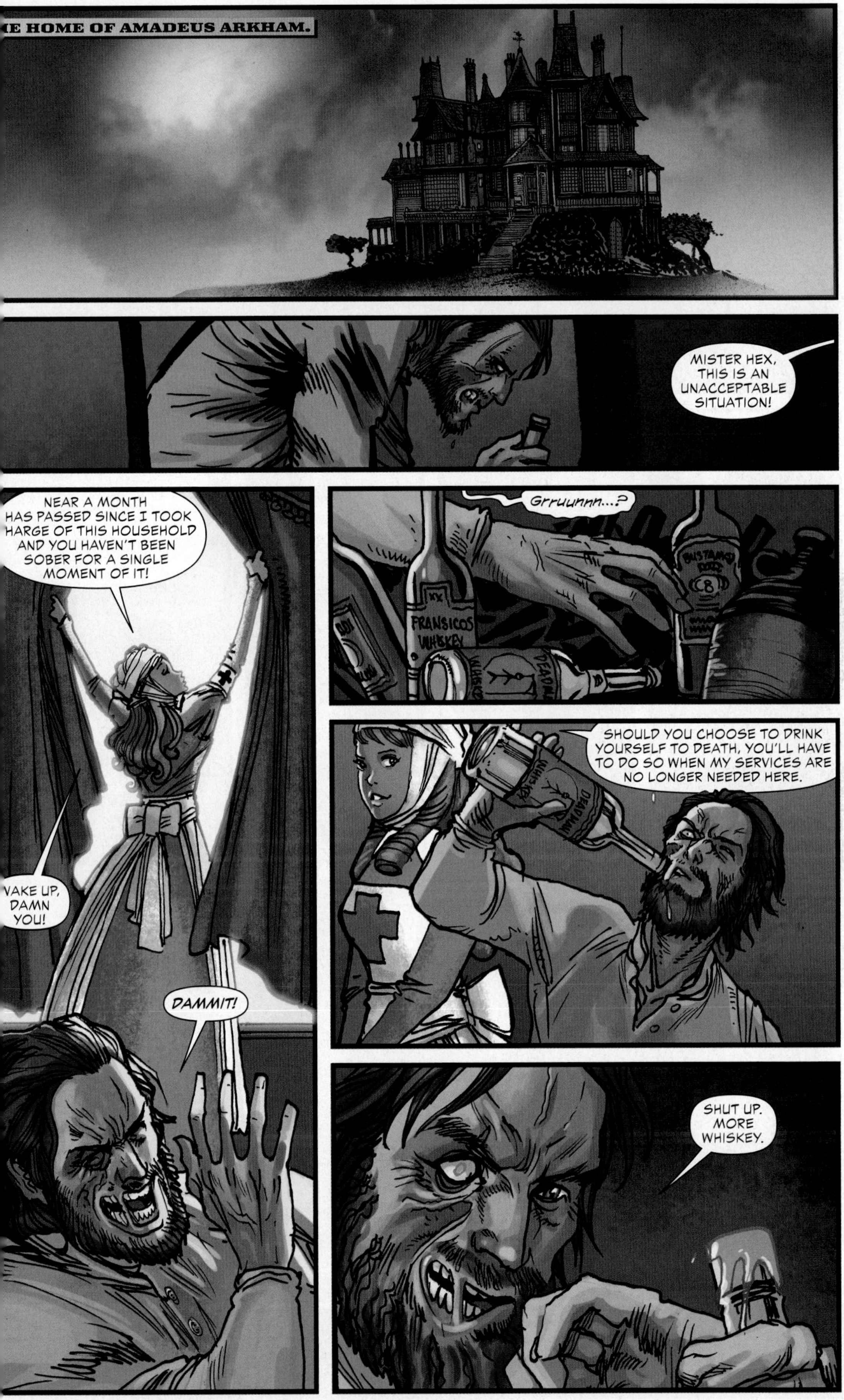

E HOME OF AMADEUS ARKHAM.
MISTER HEX, THIS IS AN UNACCEPTABLE SITUATION!
NEAR A MONTH HAS PASSED SINCE I TOOK HARGE OF THIS HOUSEHOLD AND YOU HAVEN'T BEEN SOBER FOR A SINGLE MOMENT OF IT!
VAKE UP, DAMN YOU!
DAMMIT!
Grruunnn...?
FRANSICOS WHISKEY
SHOULD YOU CHOOSE TO DRINK YOURSELF TO DEATH, YOU'LL HAVE TO DO SO WHEN MY SERVICES ARE NO LONGER NEEDED HERE.
SHUT UP. MORE WHISKEY.

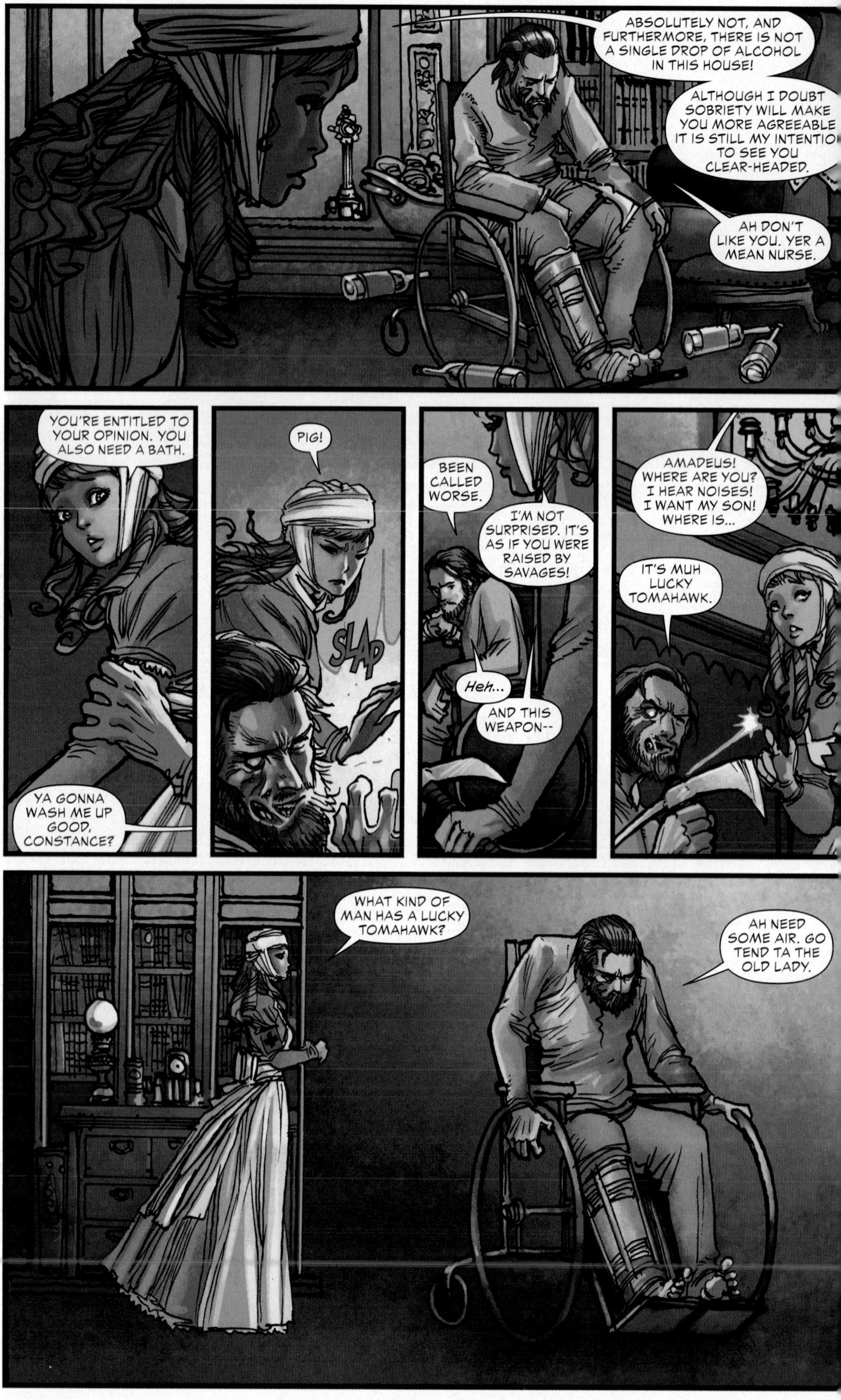
ABSOLUTELY NOT, AND FURTHERMORE, THERE IS NOT A SINGLE DROP OF ALCOHOL IN THIS HOUSE!
ALTHOUGH I DOUBT SOBRIETY WILL MAKE YOU MORE AGREEABLE IT IS STILL MY INTENTIO TO SEE YOU CLEAR-HEADED.
AH DON'T LIKE YOU. YER A MEAN NURSE.
YOU'RE ENTITLED TO YOUR OPINION. YOU ALSO NEED A BATH.
YA GONNA WASH ME UP GOOD, CONSTANCE?
PIG!
SLAP
BEEN CALLED WORSE.
I'M NOT SURPRISED. IT'S AS IF YOU WERE RAISED BY SAVAGES!
Heh...
AND THIS WEAPON--
AMADEUS! WHERE ARE YOU? I HEAR NOISES! I WANT MY SON! WHERE IS...
IT'S MUH LUCKY TOMAHAWK.
WHAT KIND OF MAN HAS A LUCKY TOMAHAWK?
AH NEED SOME AIR. GO TEND TA THE OLD LADY.

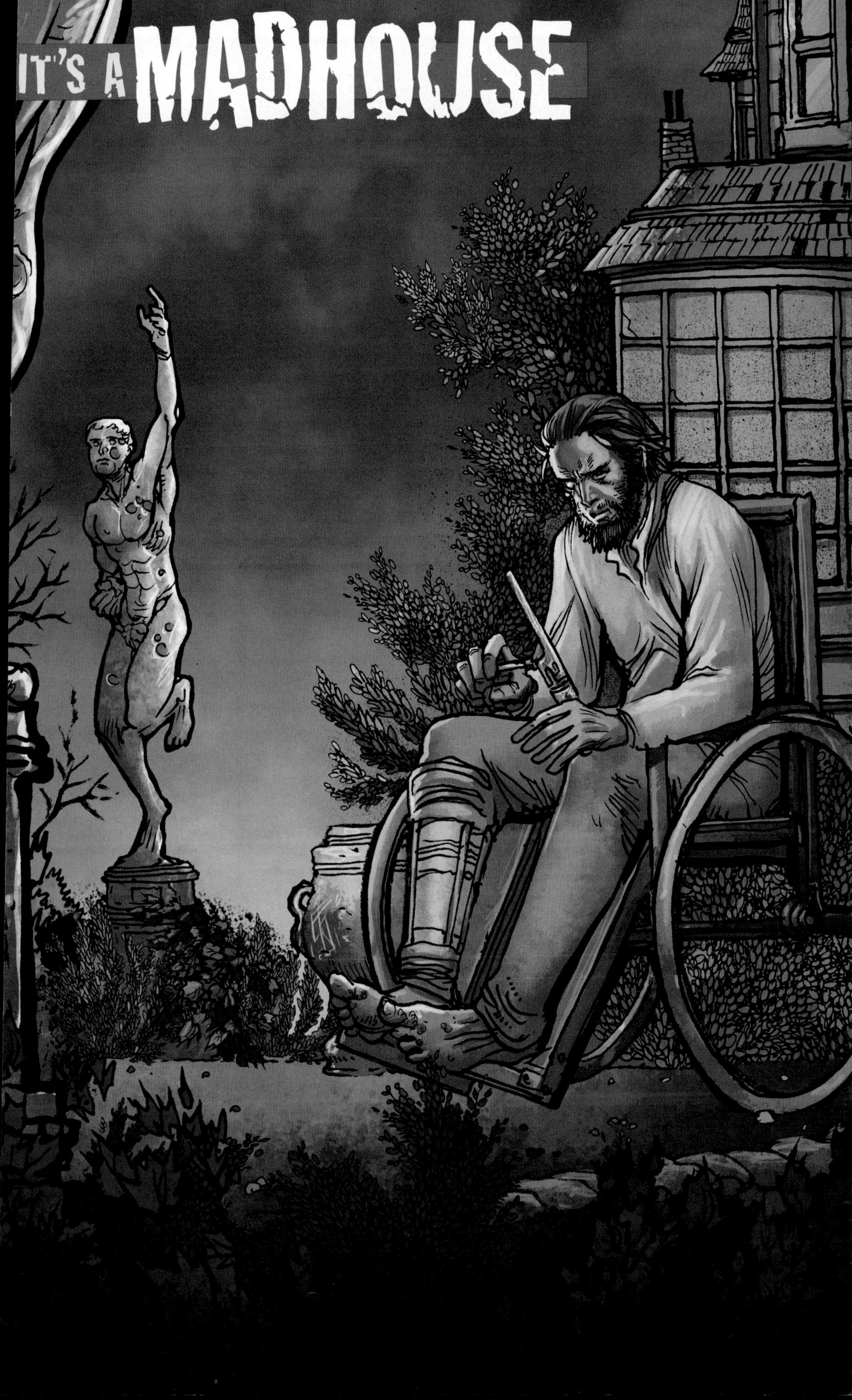
IT'S A MADHOUSE

NO DOUBT SOME WOULD BE PLEASED WITH THAT OUTCOME.

IF'N YA AIN'T GONNA BRING ME WHISKEY, THEN LEAVE ME THE HELL ALONE, WOMAN.

I'VE COME TO ASK WHAT YOU'D LIKE TO DINE ON THIS EVENING. IS THERE A PARTICULAR FOOD YOU FAVOR ABOVE ALL OTHERS?

YOU'RE GOING TO BE CHILDLIKE AND IGNORE ME? VERY WELL, THEN.

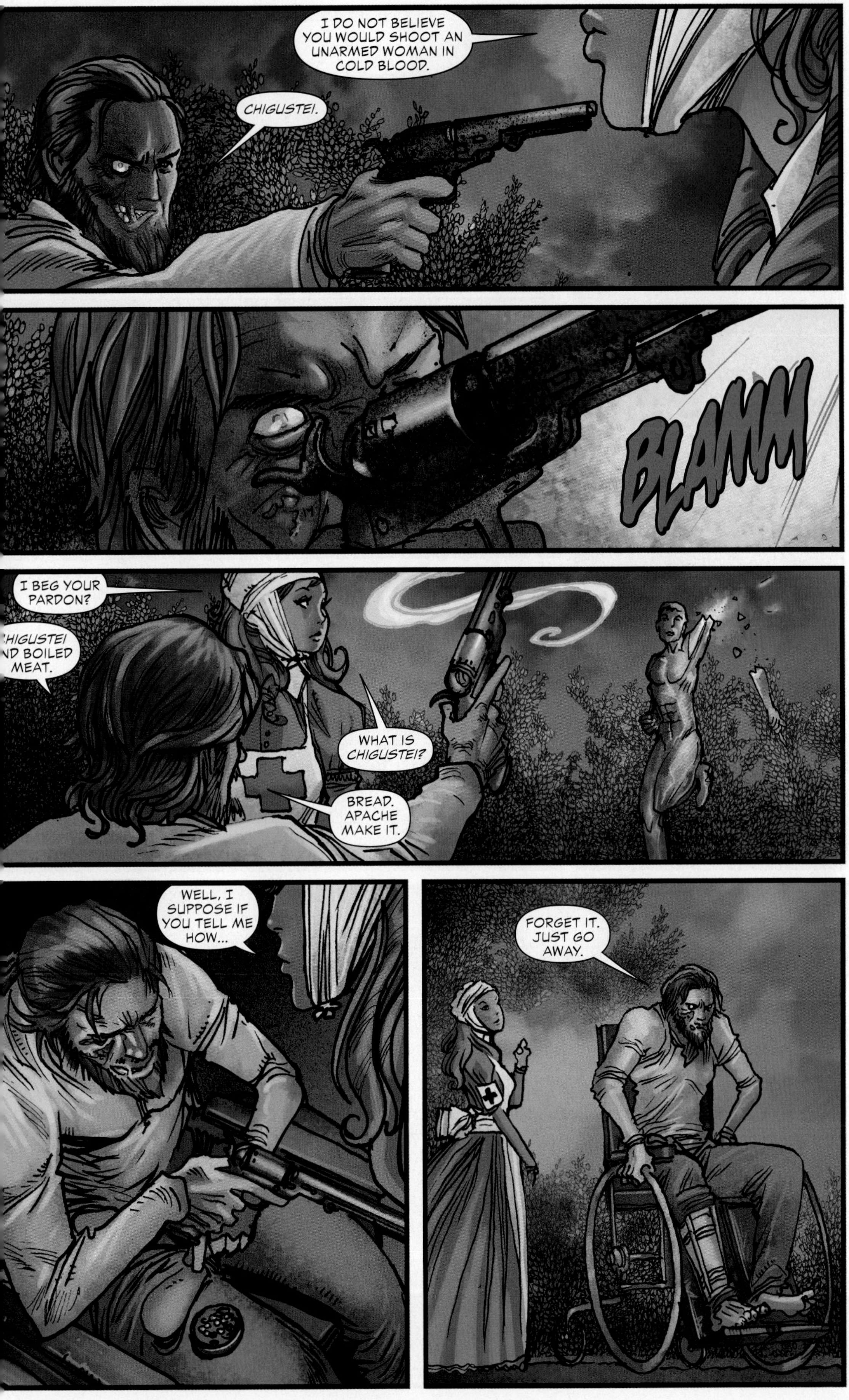
I DO NOT BELIEVE YOU WOULD SHOOT AN UNARMED WOMAN IN COLD BLOOD.
CHIGUSTEI.
BLAMM
I BEG YOUR PARDON?
CHIGUSTEI AND BOILED MEAT.
WHAT IS CHIGUSTEI?
BREAD. APACHE MAKE IT.
WELL, I SUPPOSE IF YOU TELL ME HOW...
FORGET IT. JUST GO AWAY.

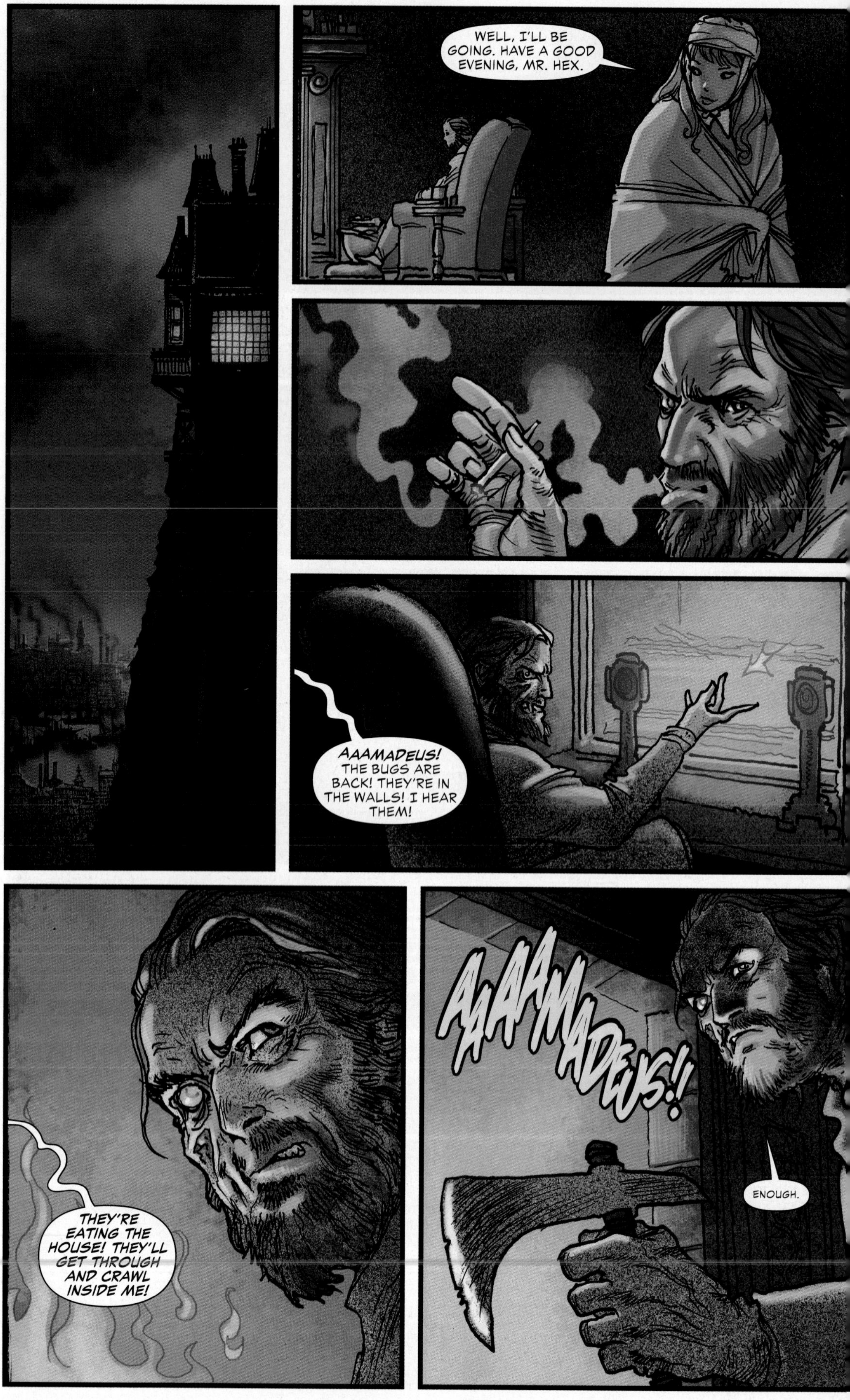
WELL, I'LL BE GOING. HAVE A GOOD EVENING, MR. HEX.
AAAMADEUS! THE BUGS ARE BACK! THEY'RE IN THE WALLS! I HEAR THEM!
THEY'RE EATING THE HOUSE! THEY'LL GET THROUGH AND CRAWL INSIDE ME!
AAAAMADEUS!!
ENOUGH.

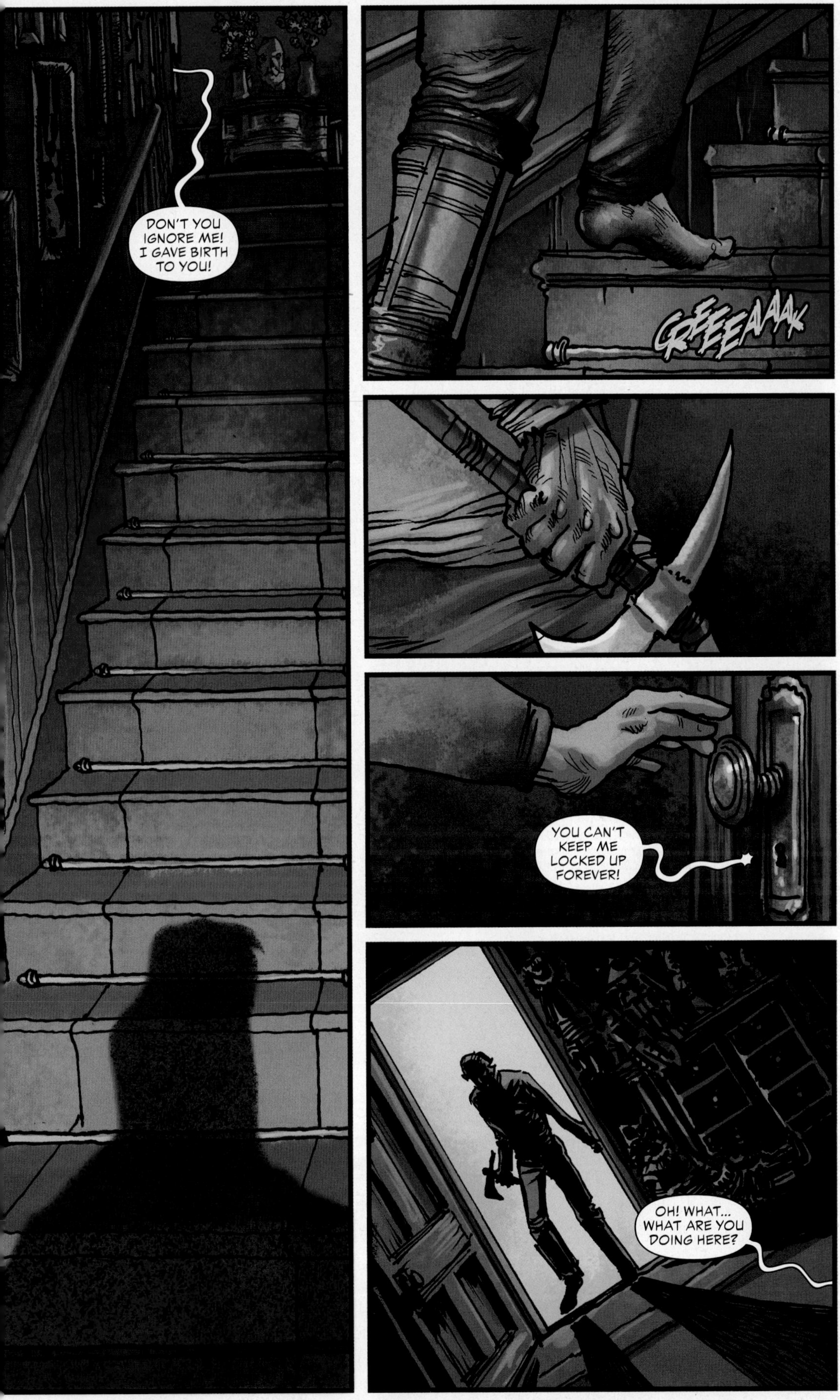
DON'T YOU IGNORE ME! I GAVE BIRTH TO YOU!
CREEEAAAK
YOU CAN'T KEEP ME LOCKED UP FOREVER!
OH! WHAT... WHAT ARE YOU DOING HERE?

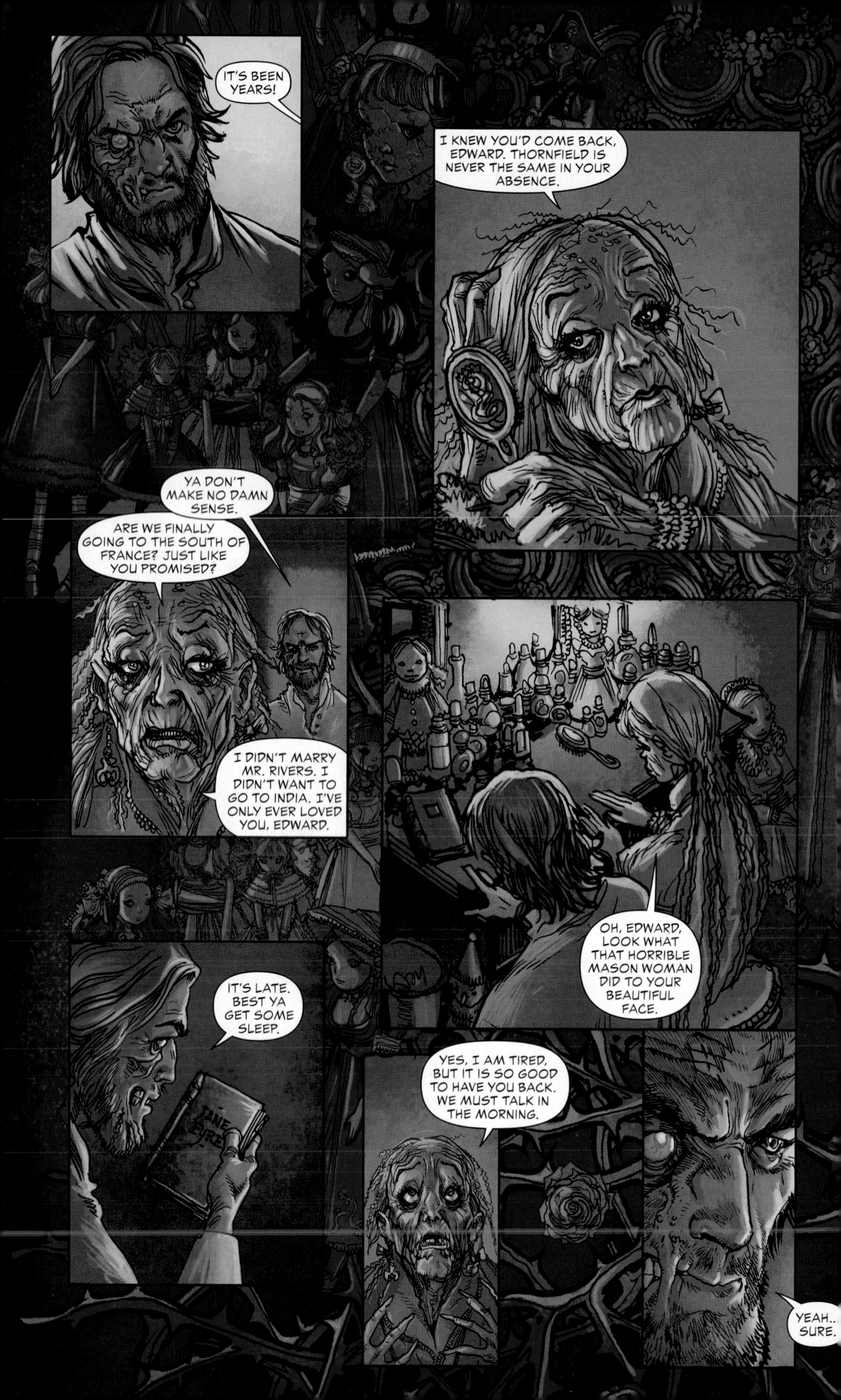
IT'S BEEN YEARS!
I KNEW YOU'D COME BACK, EDWARD. THORNFIELD IS NEVER THE SAME IN YOUR ABSENCE.
YA DON'T MAKE NO DAMN SENSE.
ARE WE FINALLY GOING TO THE SOUTH OF FRANCE? JUST LIKE YOU PROMISED?
I DIDN'T MARRY MR. RIVERS. I DIDN'T WANT TO GO TO INDIA. I'VE ONLY EVER LOVED YOU, EDWARD.
OH, EDWARD, LOOK WHAT THAT HORRIBLE MASON WOMAN DID TO YOUR BEAUTIFUL FACE.
IT'S LATE. BEST YA GET SOME SLEEP.
JANE EYRE
YES, I AM TIRED, BUT IT IS SO GOOD TO HAVE YOU BACK. WE MUST TALK IN THE MORNING.
YEAH.. SURE.

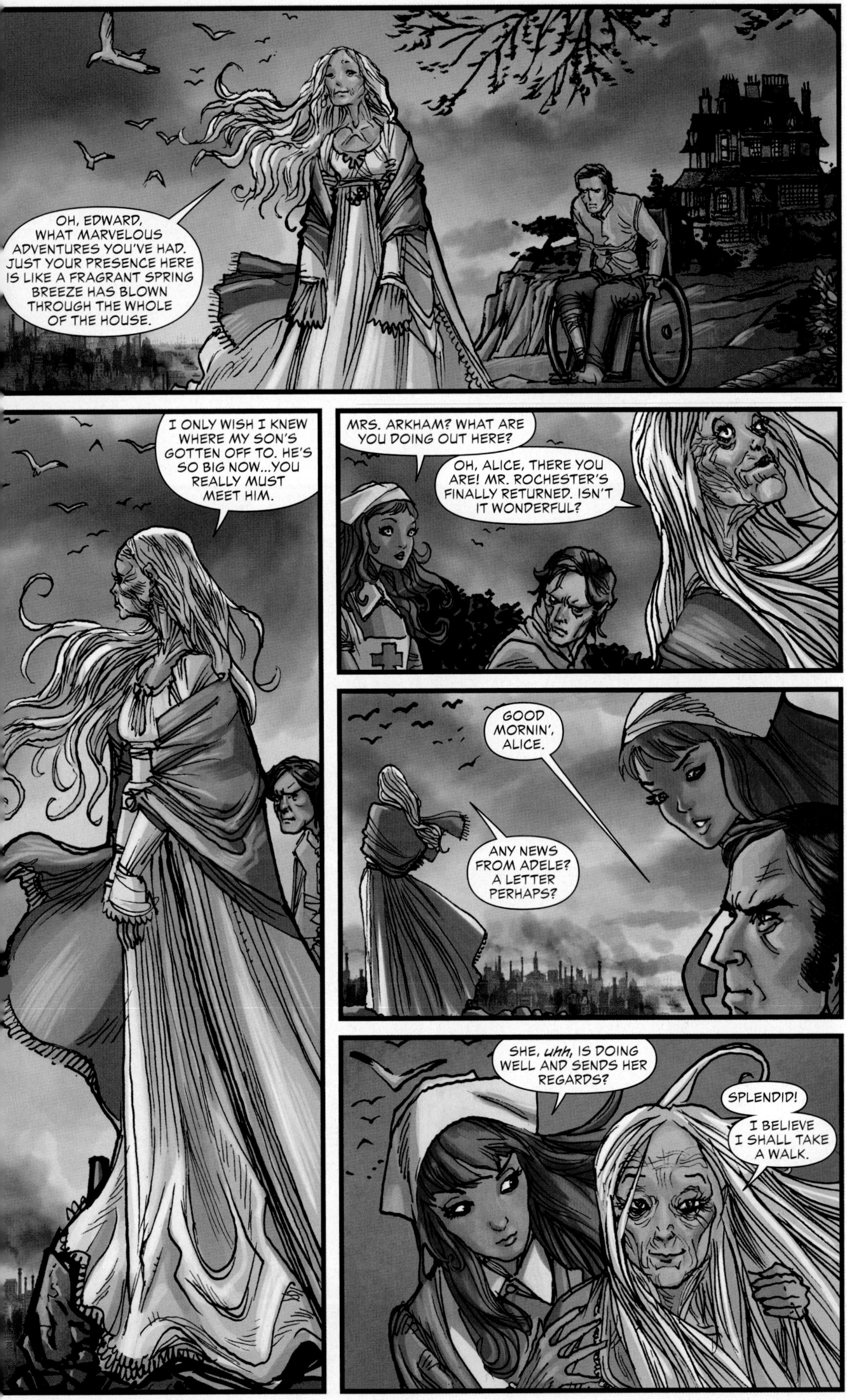

OH, EDWARD, WHAT MARVELOUS ADVENTURES YOU'VE HAD. JUST YOUR PRESENCE HERE IS LIKE A FRAGRANT SPRING BREEZE HAS BLOWN THROUGH THE WHOLE OF THE HOUSE.
I ONLY WISH I KNEW WHERE MY SON'S GOTTEN OFF TO. HE'S SO BIG NOW...YOU REALLY MUST MEET HIM.
MRS. ARKHAM? WHAT ARE YOU DOING OUT HERE?
OH, ALICE, THERE YOU ARE! MR. ROCHESTER'S FINALLY RETURNED. ISN'T IT WONDERFUL?
GOOD MORNIN', ALICE.
ANY NEWS FROM ADELE? A LETTER PERHAPS?
SHE, *uhh*, IS DOING WELL AND SENDS HER REGARDS?
SPLENDID!
I BELIEVE I SHALL TAKE A WALK.

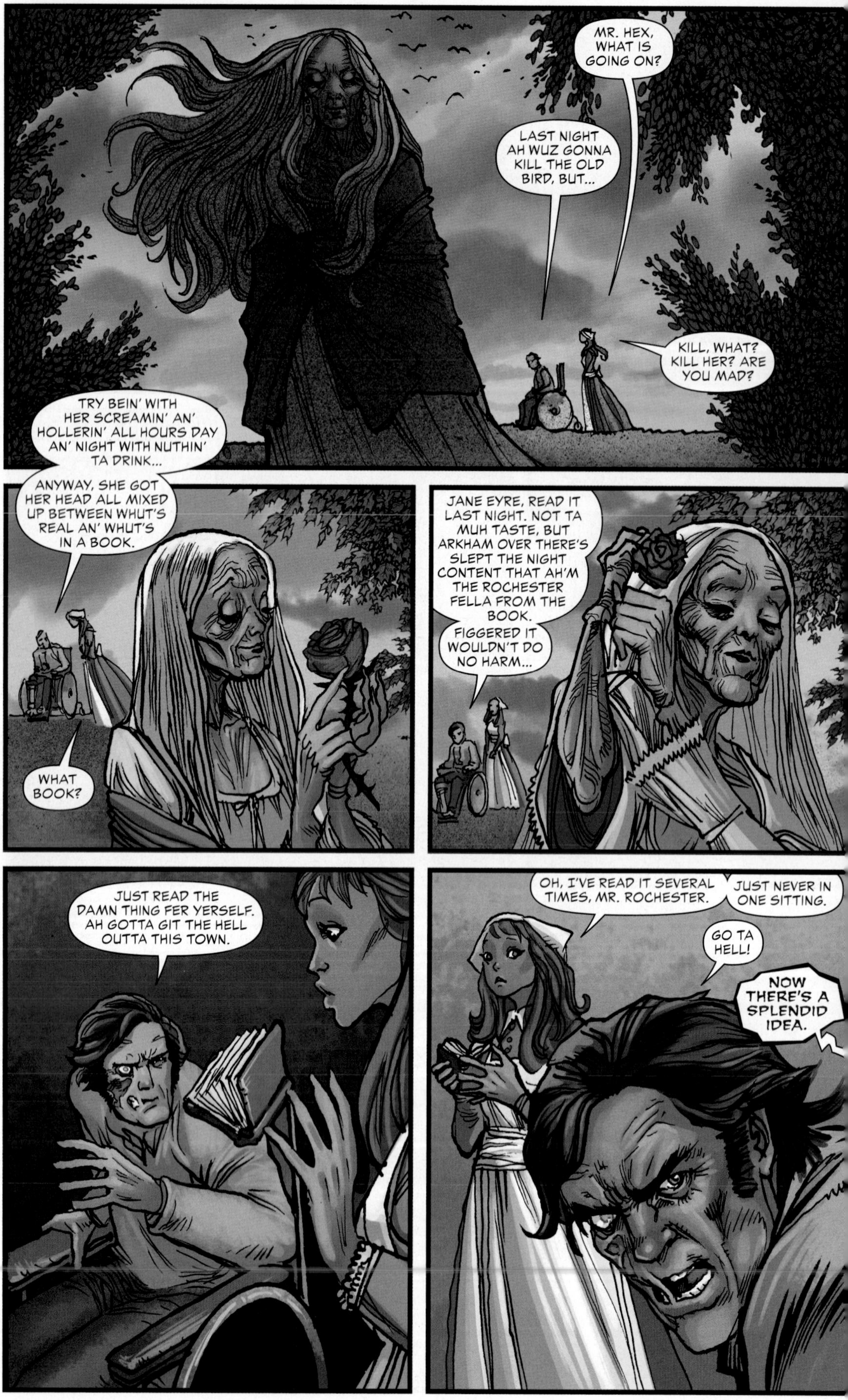
MR. HEX, WHAT IS GOING ON?
LAST NIGHT AH WUZ GONNA KILL THE OLD BIRD, BUT...
KILL, WHAT? KILL HER? ARE YOU MAD?
TRY BEIN' WITH HER SCREAMIN' AN' HOLLERIN' ALL HOURS DAY AN' NIGHT WITH NUTHIN' TA DRINK...
ANYWAY, SHE GOT HER HEAD ALL MIXED UP BETWEEN WHUT'S REAL AN' WHUT'S IN A BOOK.
WHAT BOOK?
JANE EYRE, READ IT LAST NIGHT. NOT TA MUH TASTE, BUT ARKHAM OVER THERE'S SLEPT THE NIGHT CONTENT THAT AH'M THE ROCHESTER FELLA FROM THE BOOK.
FIGGERED IT WOULDN'T DO NO HARM...
JUST READ THE DAMN THING FER YERSELF. AH GOTTA GIT THE HELL OUTTA THIS TOWN.
OH, I'VE READ IT SEVERAL TIMES, MR. ROCHESTER.
JUST NEVER IN ONE SITTING.
GO TA HELL!
NOW THERE'S A SPLENDID IDEA.

TOMAHAWK

JIMMY PALMIOTTI & JUSTIN GRAY writers **PHIL WINSLADE** artist

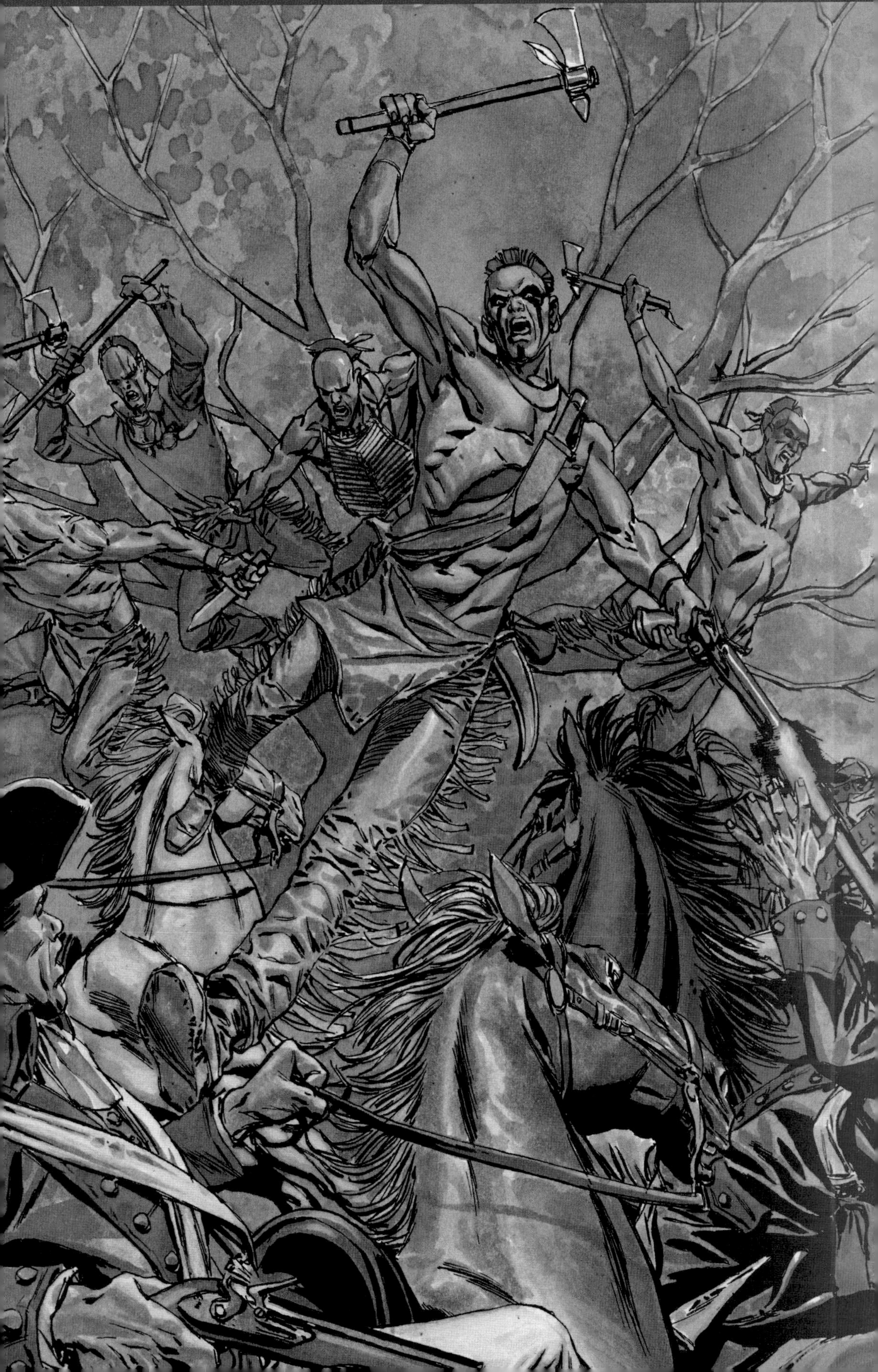

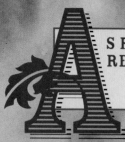

AS PART OF THE TREATY THAT BROUGHT THE AMERICAN REVOLUTION TO A CLOSE, GREAT BRITAIN SURRENDERED THE LANDS OVER THE APPALACHIAN MOUNTAINS AS FAR WEST AS THE MISSISSIPPI RIVER.

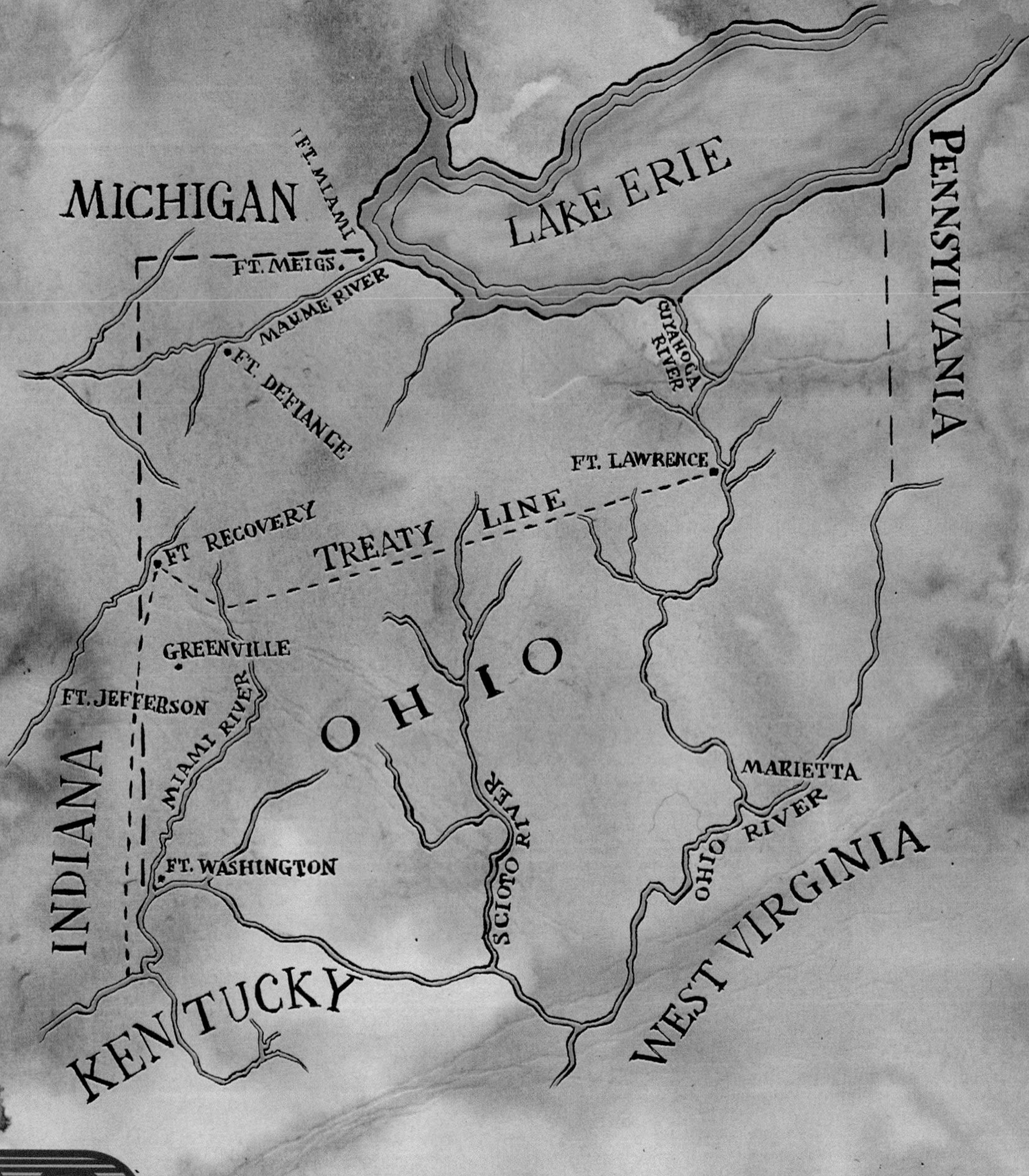

MICHIGAN
FT. MIAMI
LAKE ERIE
PENNSYLVANIA
FT. MEIGS
MAUMEE RIVER
FT. DEFIANCE
CUYAHOGA RIVER
FT. LAWRENCE
TREATY LINE
FT. RECOVERY
GREENVILLE
OHIO
FT. JEFFERSON
MIAMI RIVER
INDIANA
SCIOTO RIVER
MARIETTA
OHIO RIVER
FT. WASHINGTON
WEST VIRGINIA
KENTUCKY

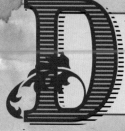

DURING THE LAST QUARTER OF THE 18TH CENTURY, WAR WAS BREWING BETWEEN THE NATIVE AMERICAN TRIBES IN THE NORTHWEST TERRITORIES AND THE AMERICAN SETTLERS WHO, BY GOVERNMENT MANDATE, WERE EXPANDING DEEP INTO INDIAN TERRITORY.

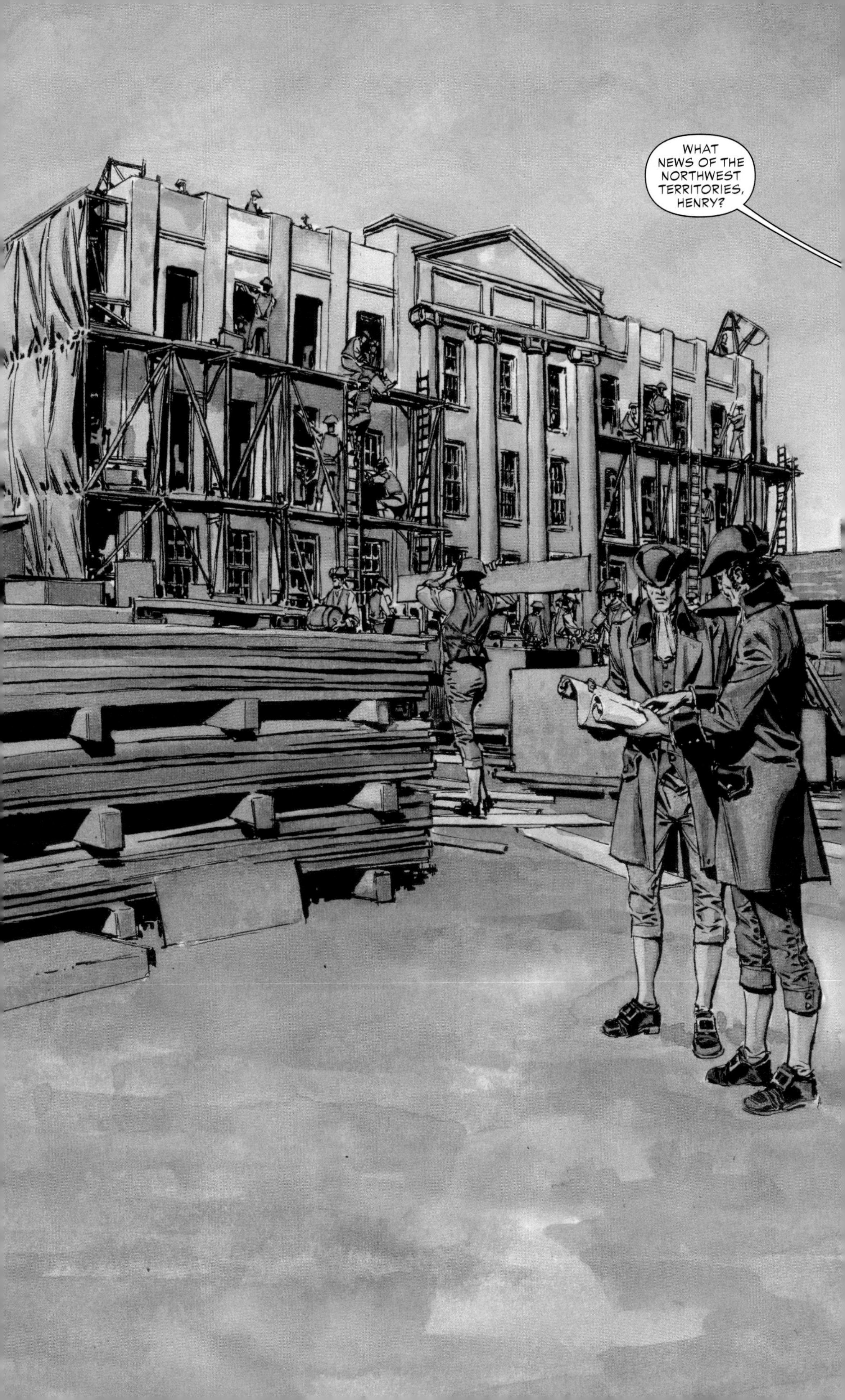
WHAT NEWS OF THE NORTHWEST TERRITORIES, HENRY?

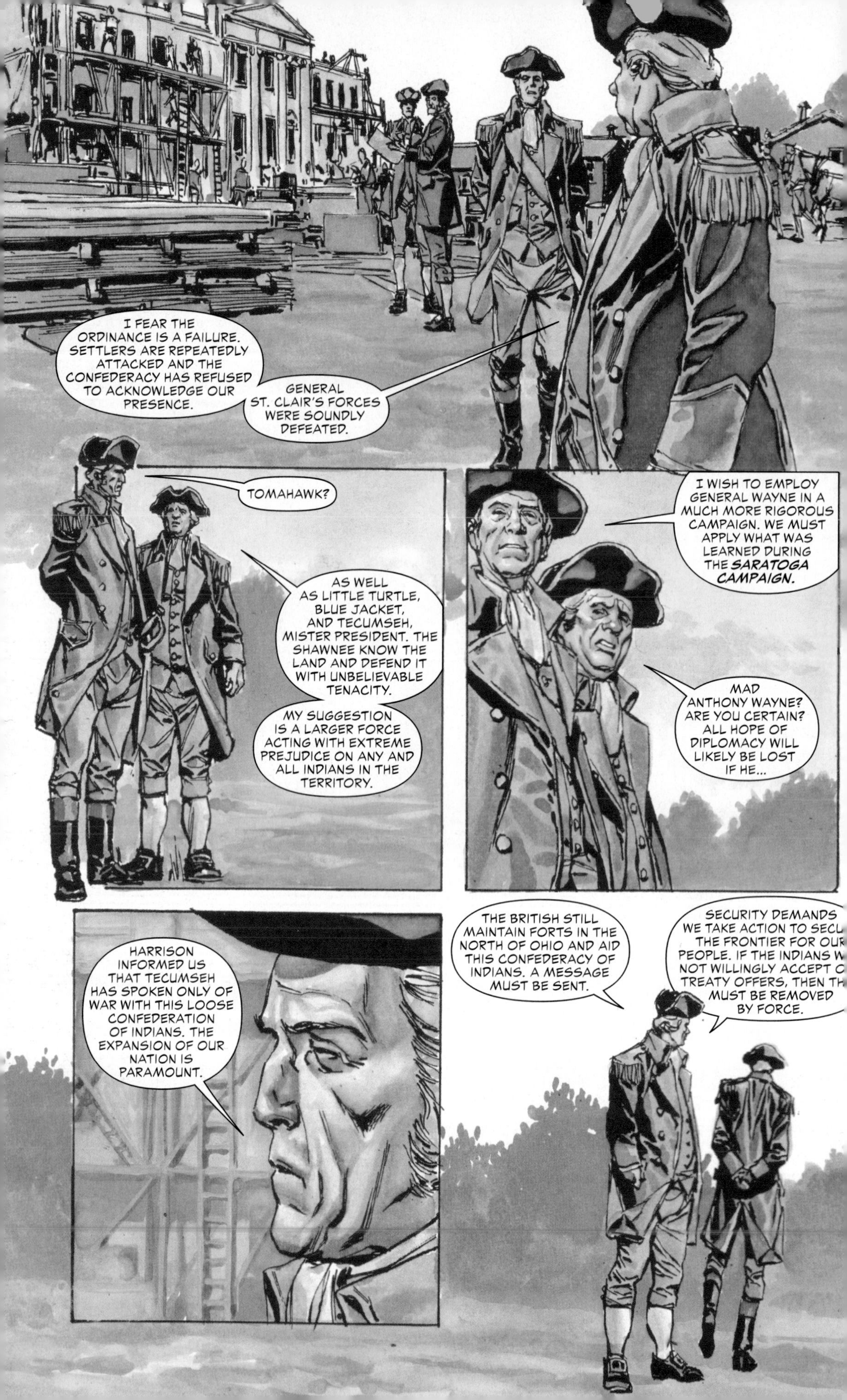
I FEAR THE ORDINANCE IS A FAILURE. SETTLERS ARE REPEATEDLY ATTACKED AND THE CONFEDERACY HAS REFUSED TO ACKNOWLEDGE OUR PRESENCE.
GENERAL ST. CLAIR'S FORCES WERE SOUNDLY DEFEATED.
TOMAHAWK?
AS WELL AS LITTLE TURTLE, BLUE JACKET, AND TECUMSEH, MISTER PRESIDENT. THE SHAWNEE KNOW THE LAND AND DEFEND IT WITH UNBELIEVABLE TENACITY.
MY SUGGESTION IS A LARGER FORCE ACTING WITH EXTREME PREJUDICE ON ANY AND ALL INDIANS IN THE TERRITORY.
I WISH TO EMPLOY GENERAL WAYNE IN A MUCH MORE RIGOROUS CAMPAIGN. WE MUST APPLY WHAT WAS LEARNED DURING THE *SARATOGA CAMPAIGN.*
MAD ANTHONY WAYNE? ARE YOU CERTAIN? ALL HOPE OF DIPLOMACY WILL LIKELY BE LOST IF HE...
HARRISON INFORMED US THAT TECUMSEH HAS SPOKEN ONLY OF WAR WITH THIS LOOSE CONFEDERATION OF INDIANS. THE EXPANSION OF OUR NATION IS PARAMOUNT.
THE BRITISH STILL MAINTAIN FORTS IN THE NORTH OF OHIO AND AID THIS CONFEDERACY OF INDIANS. A MESSAGE MUST BE SENT.
SECURITY DEMANDS WE TAKE ACTION TO SECU THE FRONTIER FOR OUR PEOPLE. IF THE INDIANS W NOT WILLINGLY ACCEPT O TREATY OFFERS, THEN TH MUST BE REMOVED BY FORCE.

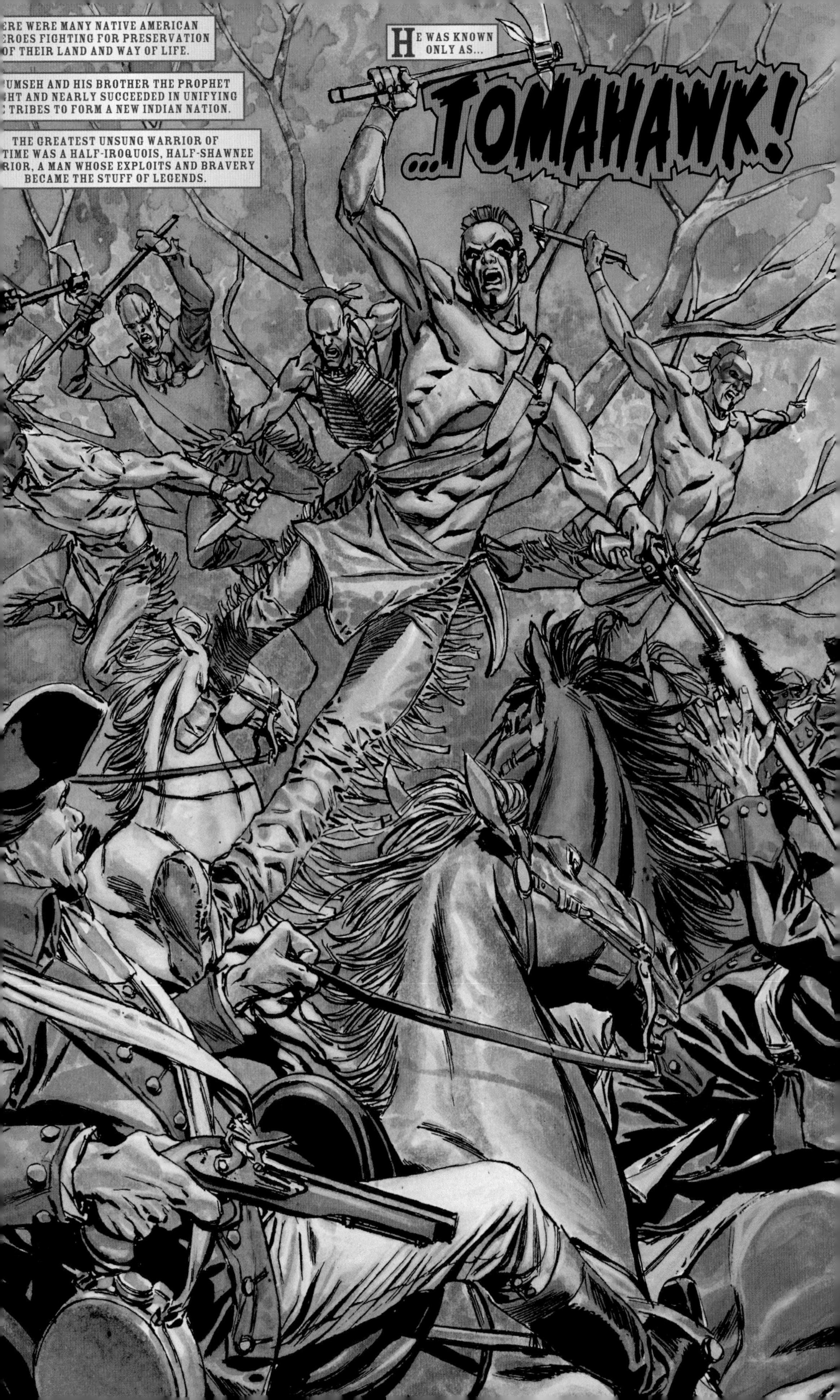

ERE WERE MANY NATIVE AMERICAN
EROES FIGHTING FOR PRESERVATION
OF THEIR LAND AND WAY OF LIFE.
UMSEH AND HIS BROTHER THE PROPHET
HT AND NEARLY SUCCEEDED IN UNIFYING
TRIBES TO FORM A NEW INDIAN NATION.
THE GREATEST UNSUNG WARRIOR OF
TIME WAS A HALF-IROQUOIS, HALF-SHAWNEE
RIOR, A MAN WHOSE EXPLOITS AND BRAVERY
BECAME THE STUFF OF LEGENDS.
HE WAS KNOWN ONLY AS...
...TOMAHAWK!

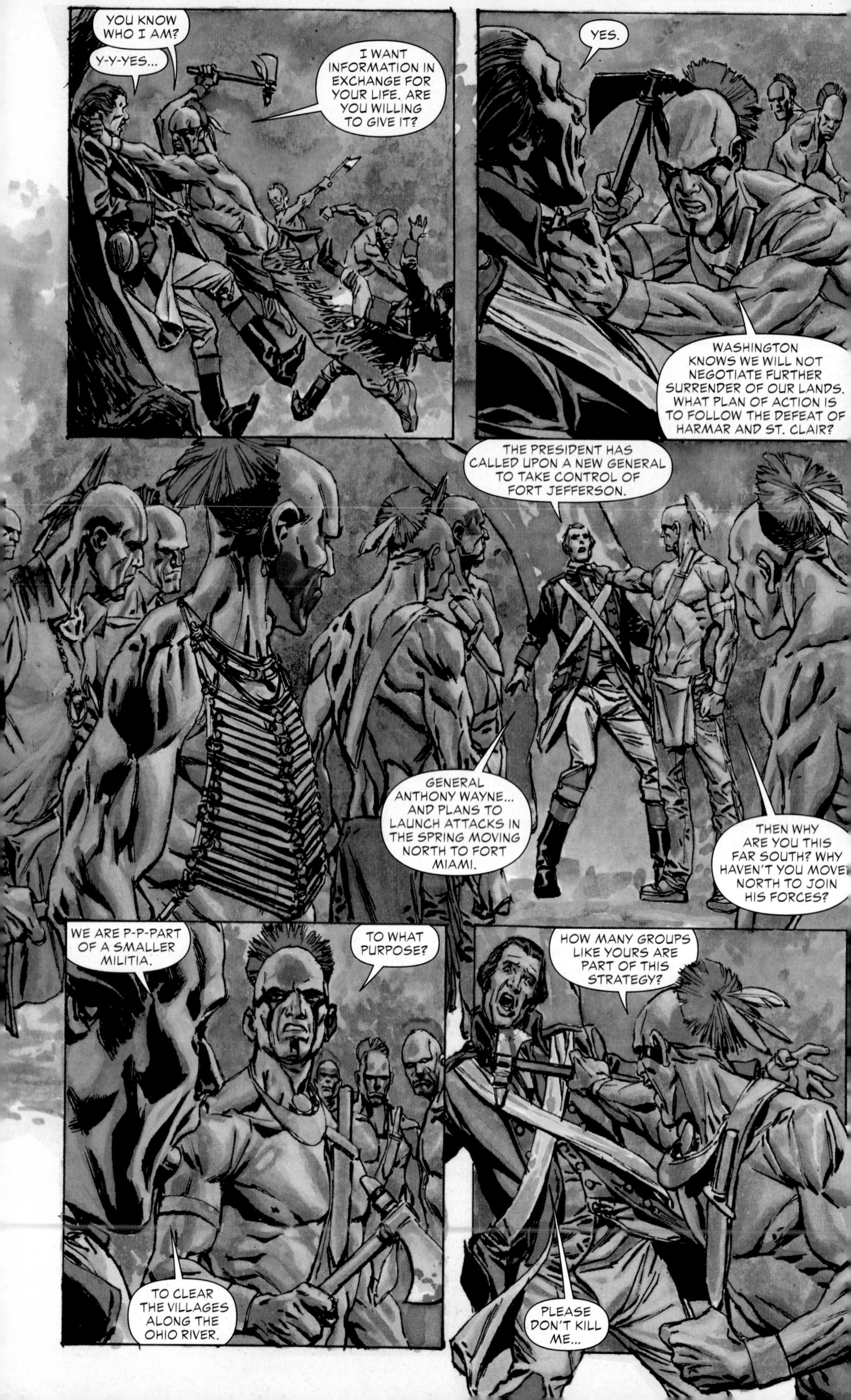

YOU KNOW WHO I AM?
Y-Y-YES...
I WANT INFORMATION IN EXCHANGE FOR YOUR LIFE. ARE YOU WILLING TO GIVE IT?
YES.
WASHINGTON KNOWS WE WILL NOT NEGOTIATE FURTHER SURRENDER OF OUR LANDS. WHAT PLAN OF ACTION IS TO FOLLOW THE DEFEAT OF HARMAR AND ST. CLAIR?
THE PRESIDENT HAS CALLED UPON A NEW GENERAL TO TAKE CONTROL OF FORT JEFFERSON.
GENERAL ANTHONY WAYNE... AND PLANS TO LAUNCH ATTACKS IN THE SPRING MOVING NORTH TO FORT MIAMI.
THEN WHY ARE YOU THIS FAR SOUTH? WHY HAVEN'T YOU MOVED NORTH TO JOIN HIS FORCES?
WE ARE P-P-PART OF A SMALLER MILITIA.
TO WHAT PURPOSE?
TO CLEAR THE VILLAGES ALONG THE OHIO RIVER.
HOW MANY GROUPS LIKE YOURS ARE PART OF THIS STRATEGY?
PLEASE DON'T KILL ME...

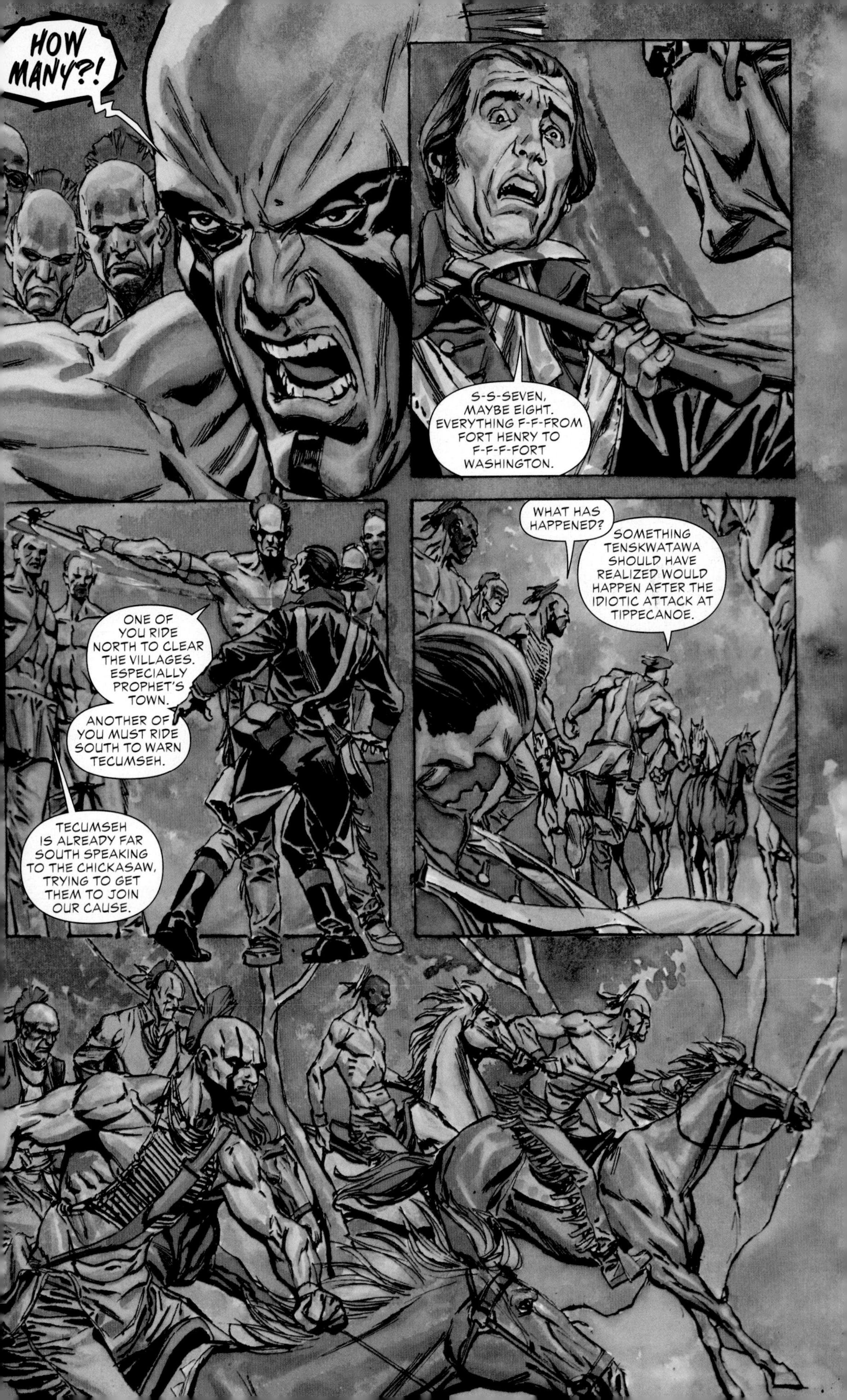
HOW MANY?!
S-S-SEVEN, MAYBE EIGHT. EVERYTHING F-F-FROM FORT HENRY TO F-F-F-FORT WASHINGTON.
ONE OF YOU RIDE NORTH TO CLEAR THE VILLAGES. ESPECIALLY PROPHET'S TOWN.
ANOTHER OF YOU MUST RIDE SOUTH TO WARN TECUMSEH.
TECUMSEH IS ALREADY FAR SOUTH SPEAKING TO THE CHICKASAW, TRYING TO GET THEM TO JOIN OUR CAUSE.
WHAT HAS HAPPENED?
SOMETHING TENSKWATAWA SHOULD HAVE REALIZED WOULD HAPPEN AFTER THE IDIOTIC ATTACK AT TIPPECANOE.

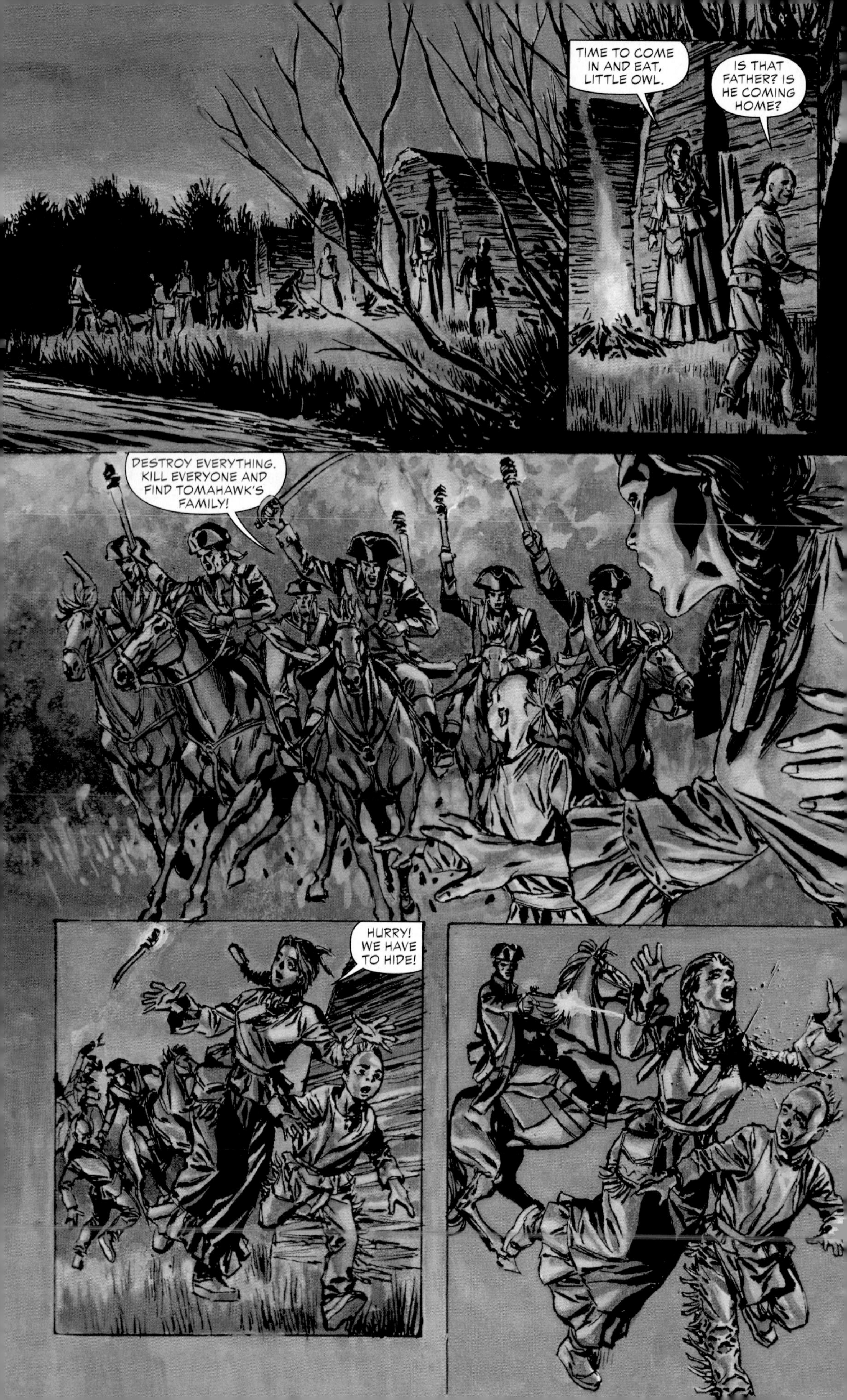
TIME TO COME IN AND EAT, LITTLE OWL.
IS THAT FATHER? IS HE COMING HOME?
DESTROY EVERYTHING. KILL EVERYONE AND FIND TOMAHAWK'S FAMILY!
HURRY! WE HAVE TO HIDE!

WHO ARE YOU?

GET OUTTA HERE, CONSTANCE. TAKE THE OLD BIRD WITH YA.

WHERE'S YOUR SOUTHERN HOSPITALITY, HEX?

YA AIN'T GOT NO QUARREL WITH THEM WOMEN, HYDE.

I LEFT YOU IN QUITE A STATE, DIDN'T I?

DOESN'T REALLY SEEM FAIR TO CALL ON YOU AT THIS TIME, BUT I WAS WONDERING HOW THE LORD OF THE HOUSE WAS FARING.

CONSTANCE, DO AS AH SAY. NOW!

UNHAND ME!

A RATHER PLAIN-LOOKING CREATURE. STILL, SHE IS FAR ABOVE YOUR STATION WITH REGARD TO APPEARANCE.

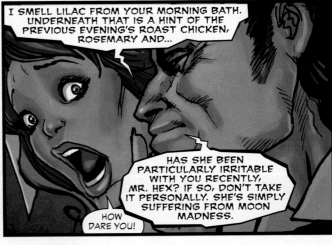

I SMELL LILAC FROM YOUR MORNING BATH. UNDERNEATH THAT IS A HINT OF THE PREVIOUS EVENING'S ROAST CHICKEN, ROSEMARY AND...

HAS SHE BEEN PARTICULARLY IRRITABLE WITH YOU RECENTLY, MR. HEX? IF SO, DON'T TAKE IT PERSONALLY. SHE'S SIMPLY SUFFERING FROM MOON MADNESS.

HOW DARE YOU!

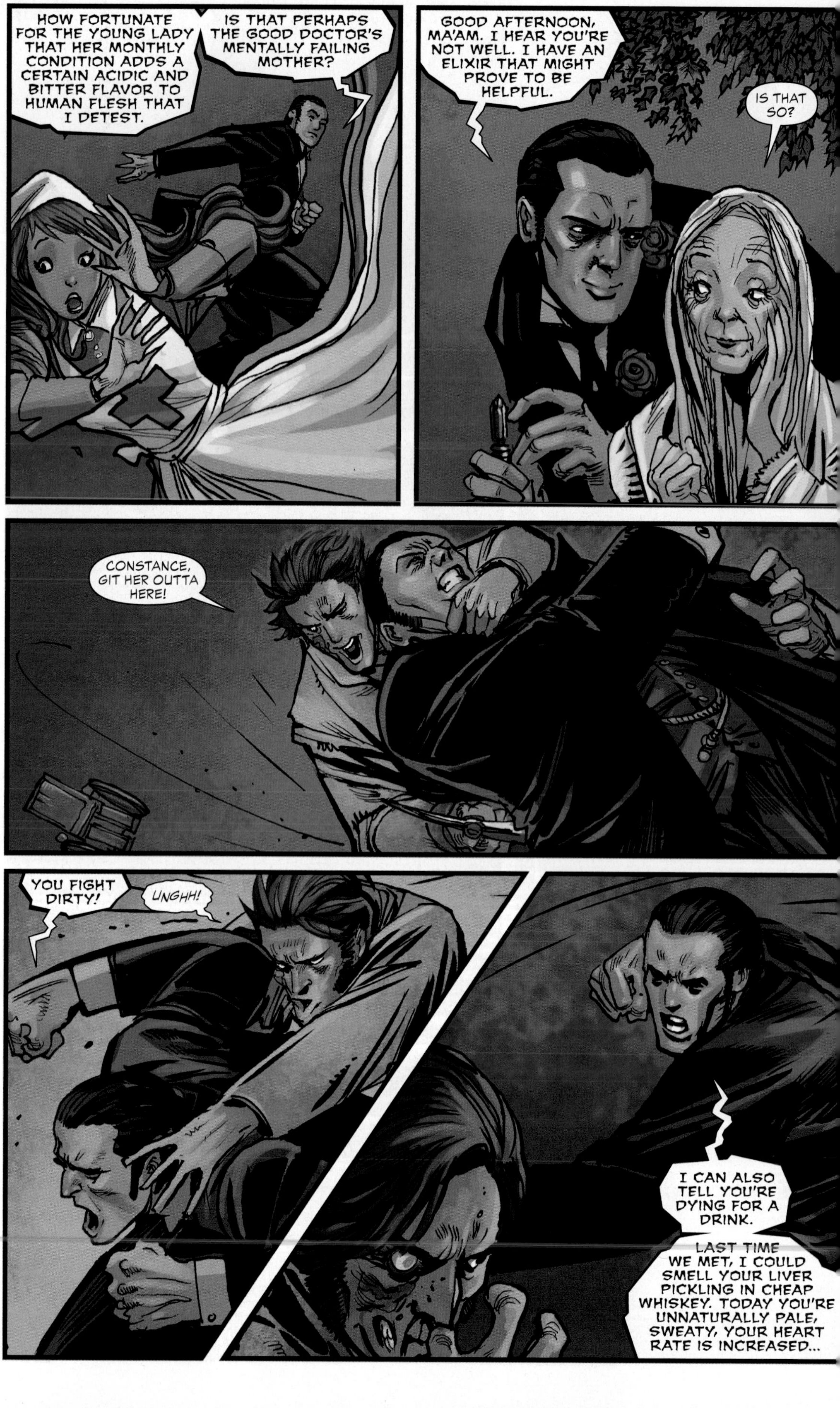
HOW FORTUNATE FOR THE YOUNG LADY THAT HER MONTHLY CONDITION ADDS A CERTAIN ACIDIC AND BITTER FLAVOR TO HUMAN FLESH THAT I DETEST.
IS THAT PERHAPS THE GOOD DOCTOR'S MENTALLY FAILING MOTHER?
GOOD AFTERNOON, MA'AM. I HEAR YOU'RE NOT WELL. I HAVE AN ELIXIR THAT MIGHT PROVE TO BE HELPFUL.
IS THAT SO?
CONSTANCE, GIT HER OUTTA HERE!
YOU FIGHT DIRTY!
UNGHH!
I CAN ALSO TELL YOU'RE DYING FOR A DRINK.
LAST TIME WE MET, I COULD SMELL YOUR LIVER PICKLING IN CHEAP WHISKEY. TODAY YOU'RE UNNATURALLY PALE, SWEATY, YOUR HEART RATE IS INCREASED...

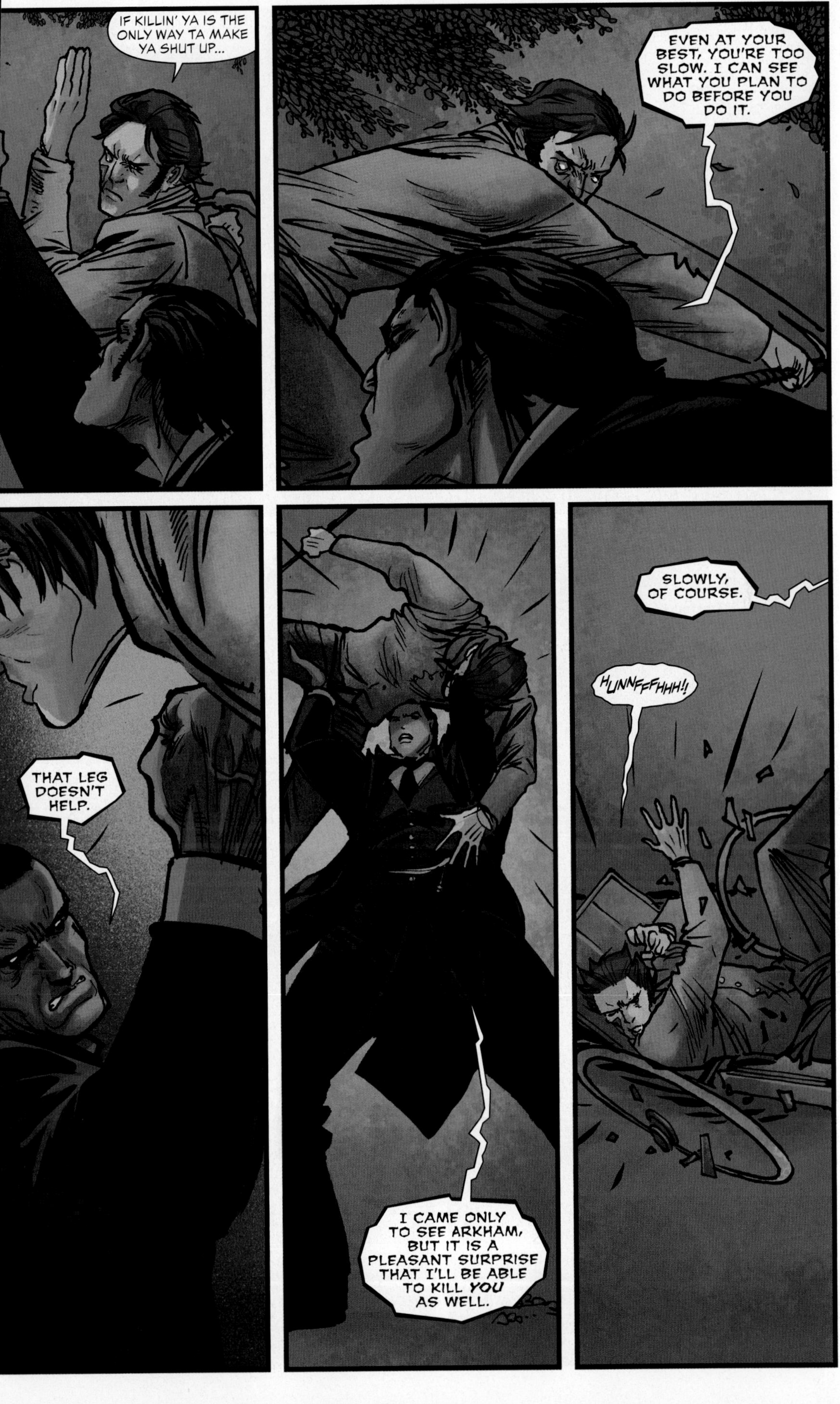
IF KILLIN' YA IS THE ONLY WAY TA MAKE YA SHUT UP...
EVEN AT YOUR BEST, YOU'RE TOO SLOW. I CAN SEE WHAT YOU PLAN TO DO BEFORE YOU DO IT.
THAT LEG DOESN'T HELP.
I CAME ONLY TO SEE ARKHAM, BUT IT IS A PLEASANT SURPRISE THAT I'LL BE ABLE TO KILL *YOU* AS WELL.
SLOWLY, OF COURSE.
HUNNFFFHHH!!

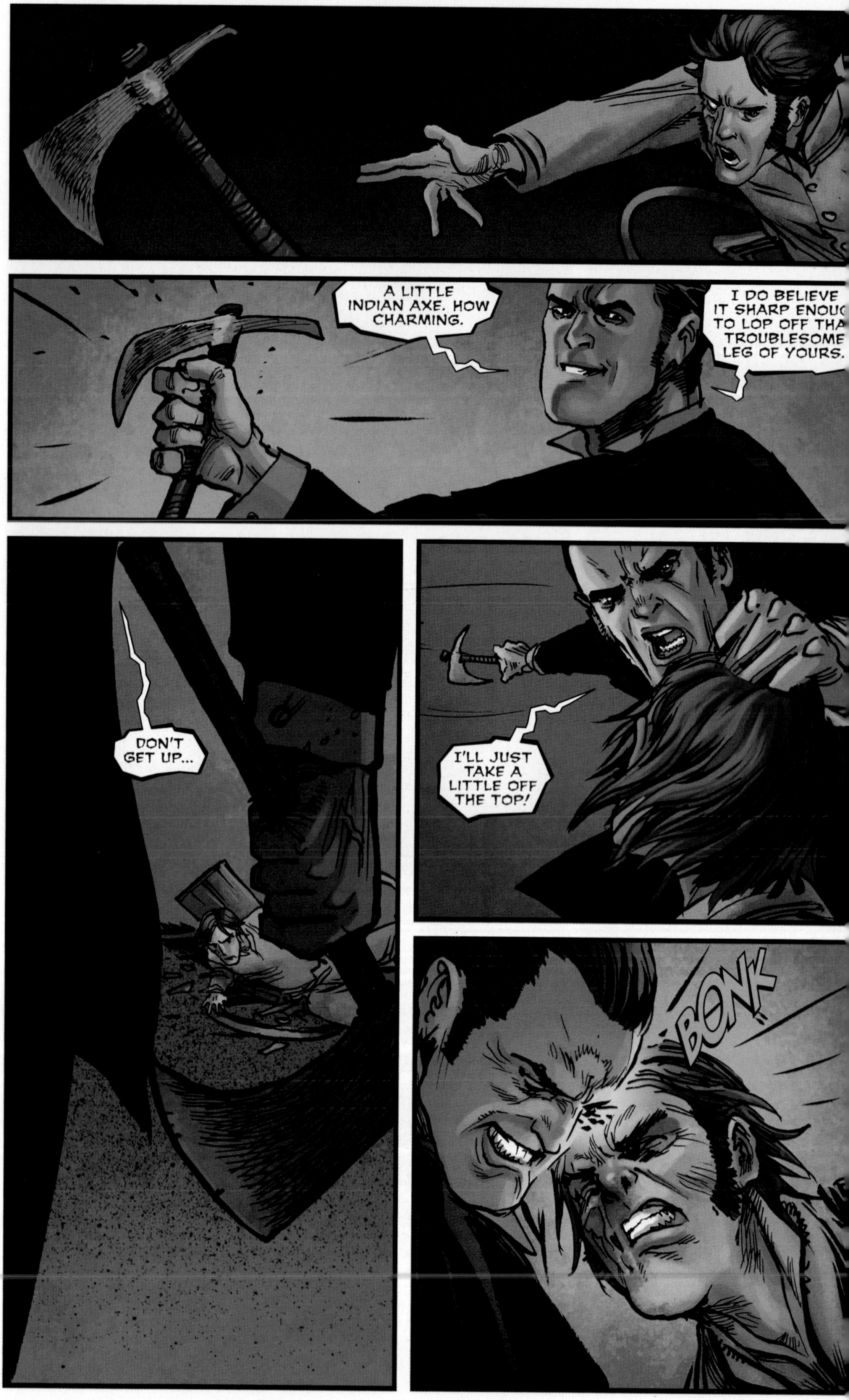

A LITTLE INDIAN AXE. HOW CHARMING.
I DO BELIEVE IT SHARP ENOUG TO LOP OFF THA TROUBLESOME LEG OF YOURS.
DON'T GET UP...
I'LL JUST TAKE A LITTLE OFF THE TOP!
BONK

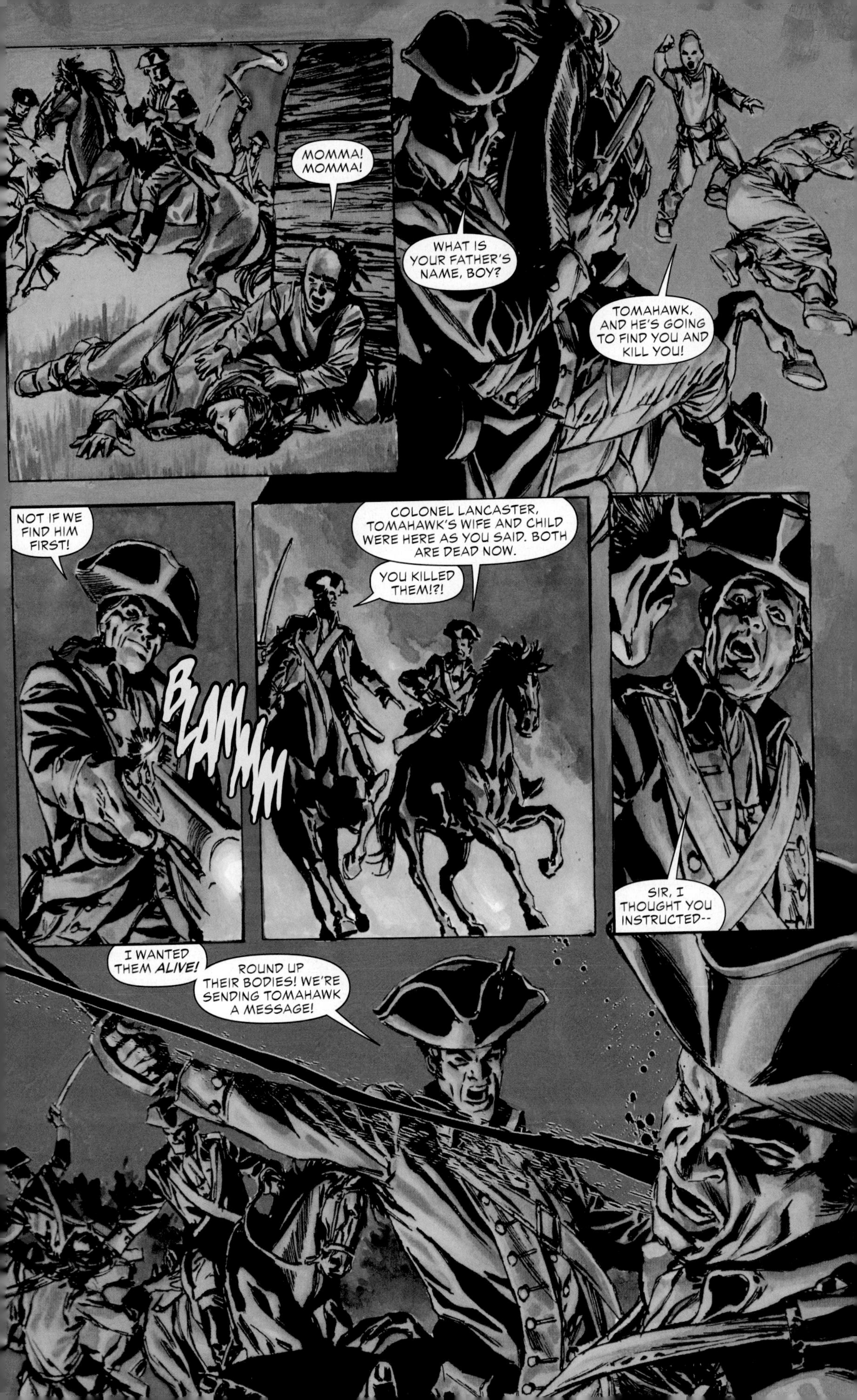
MOMMA! MOMMA!
WHAT IS YOUR FATHER'S NAME, BOY?
TOMAHAWK, AND HE'S GOING TO FIND YOU AND KILL YOU!
NOT IF WE FIND HIM FIRST!
BLAMMM
COLONEL LANCASTER, TOMAHAWK'S WIFE AND CHILD WERE HERE AS YOU SAID. BOTH ARE DEAD NOW.
YOU KILLED THEM!?!
SIR, I THOUGHT YOU INSTRUCTED--
I WANTED THEM *ALIVE!*
ROUND UP THEIR BODIES! WE'RE SENDING TOMAHAWK A MESSAGE!

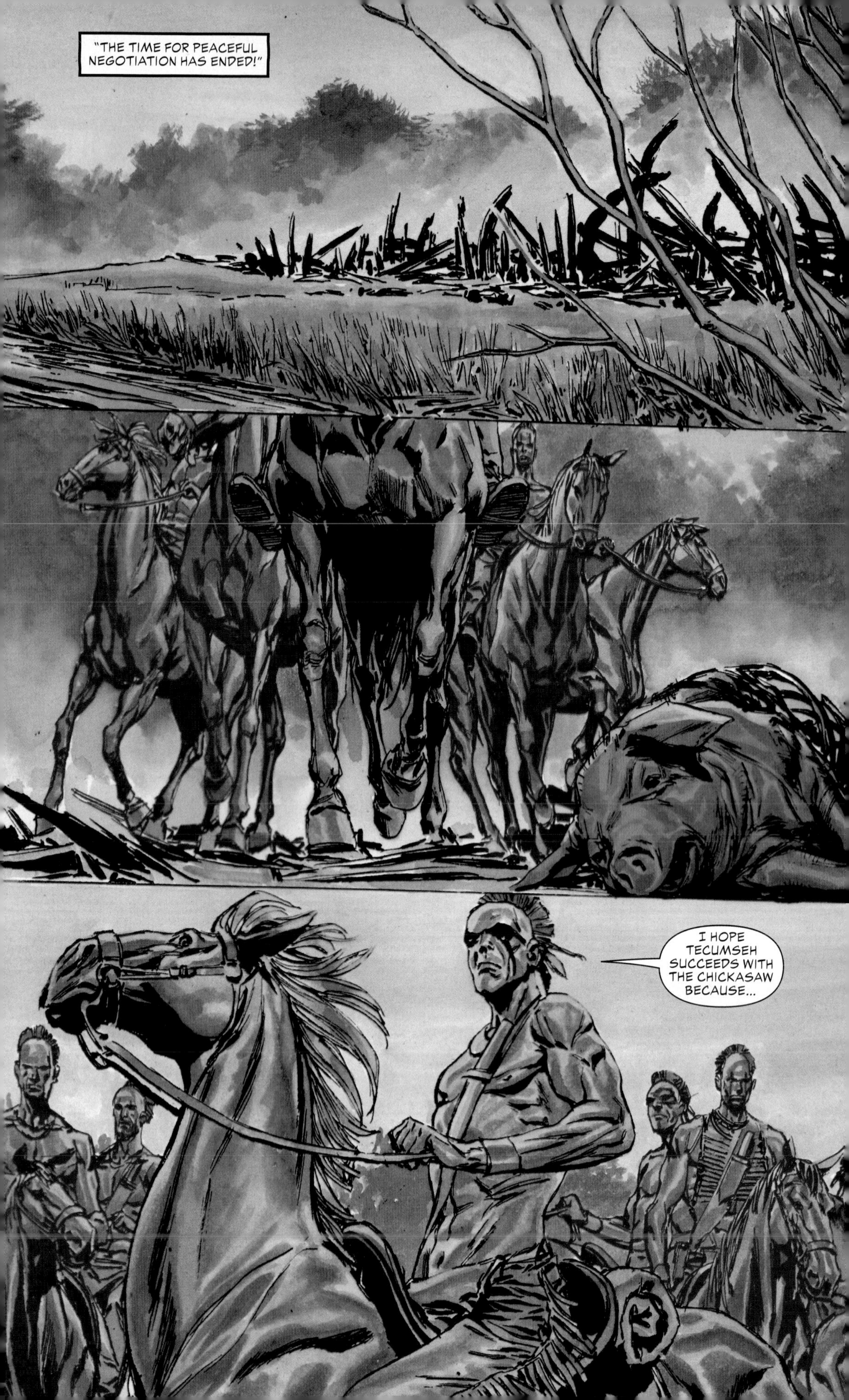
"THE TIME FOR PEACEFUL NEGOTIATION HAS ENDED!"
I HOPE TECUMSEH SUCCEEDS WITH THE CHICKASAW BECAUSE...

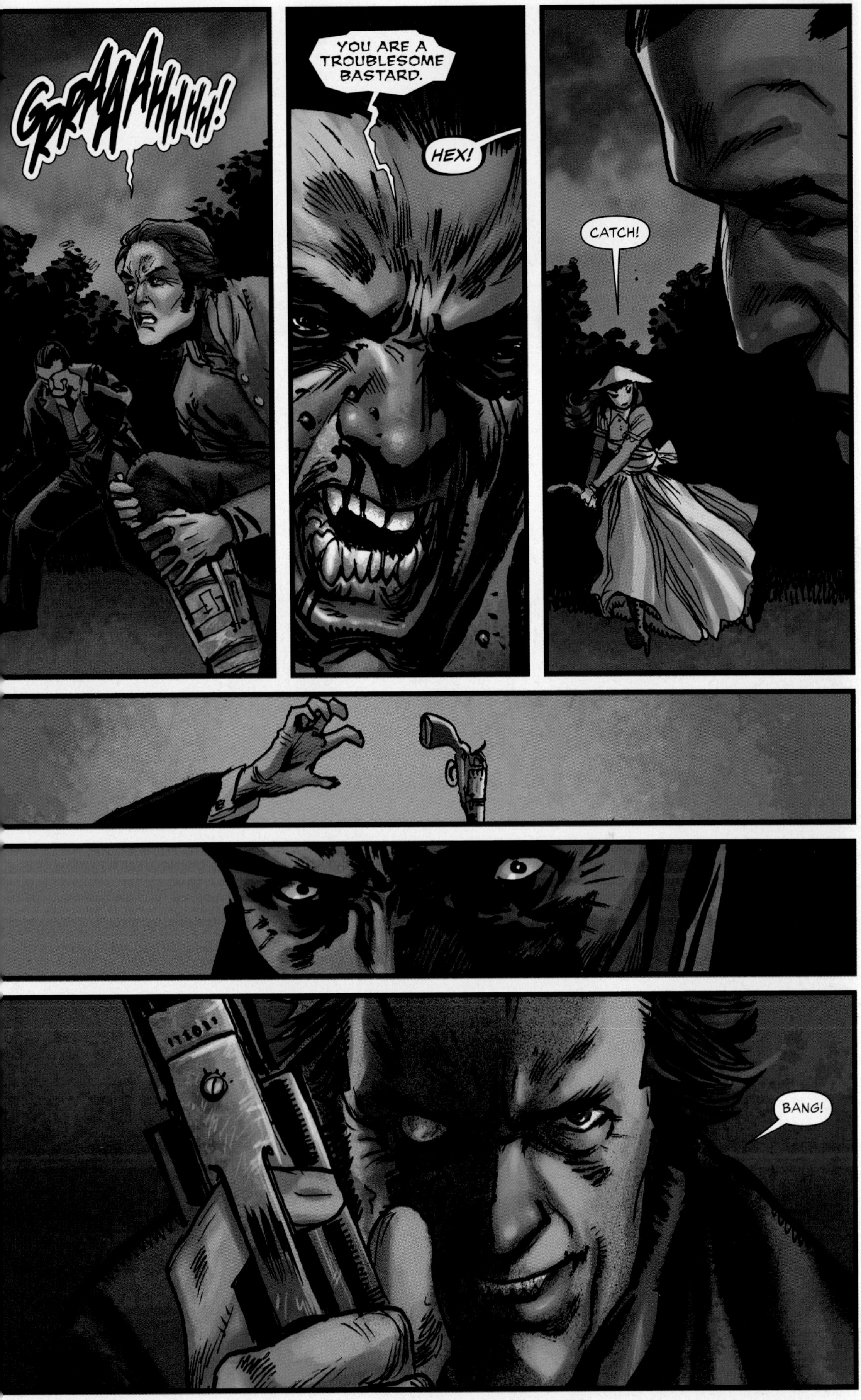

GRRAAAAHHHHH!
YOU ARE A TROUBLESOME BASTARD.
HEX!
CATCH!
BANG!

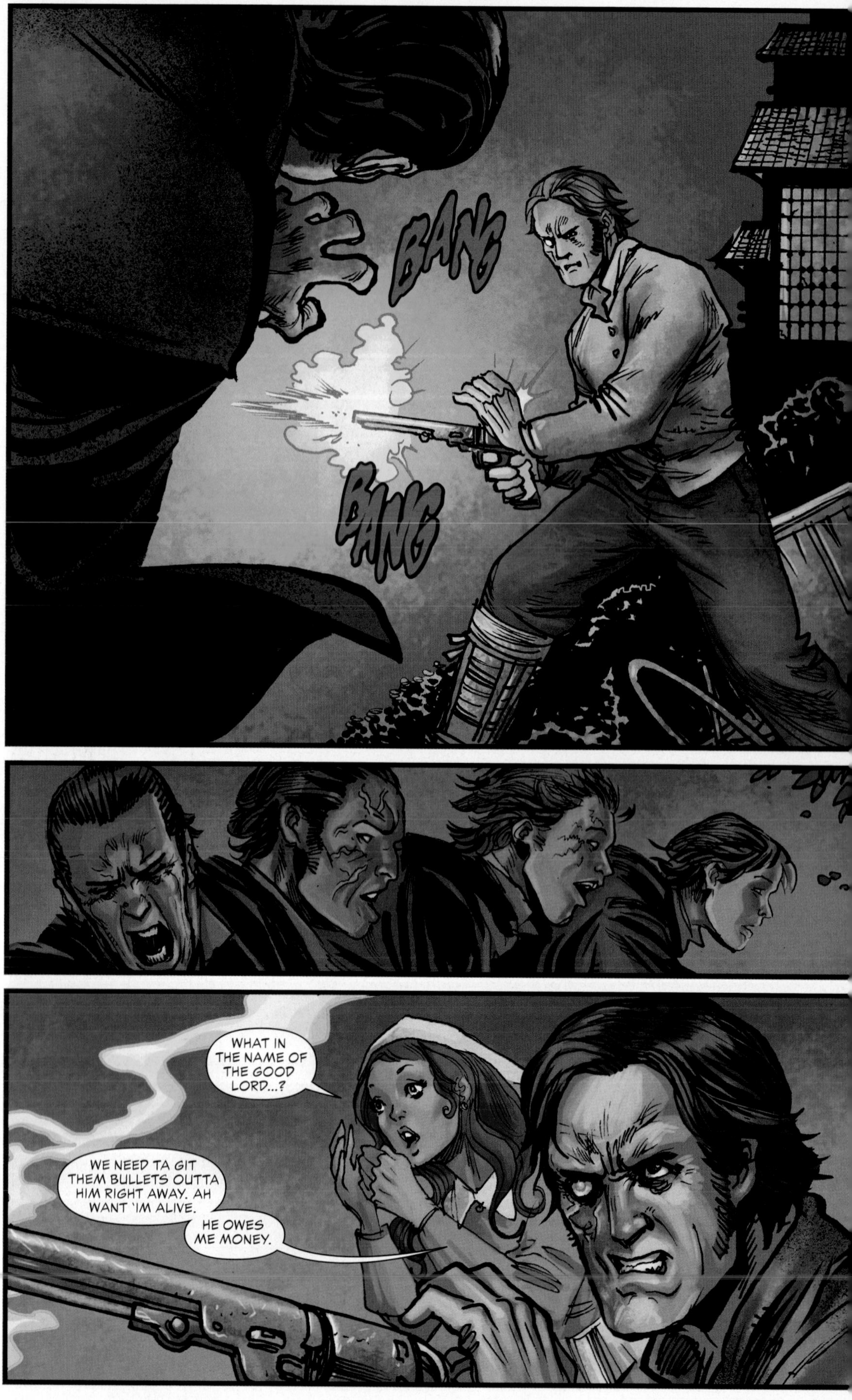
BANG
BANG
WHAT IN THE NAME OF THE GOOD LORD...?
WE NEED TA GIT THEM BULLETS OUTTA HIM RIGHT AWAY. AH WANT 'IM ALIVE.
HE OWES ME MONEY.

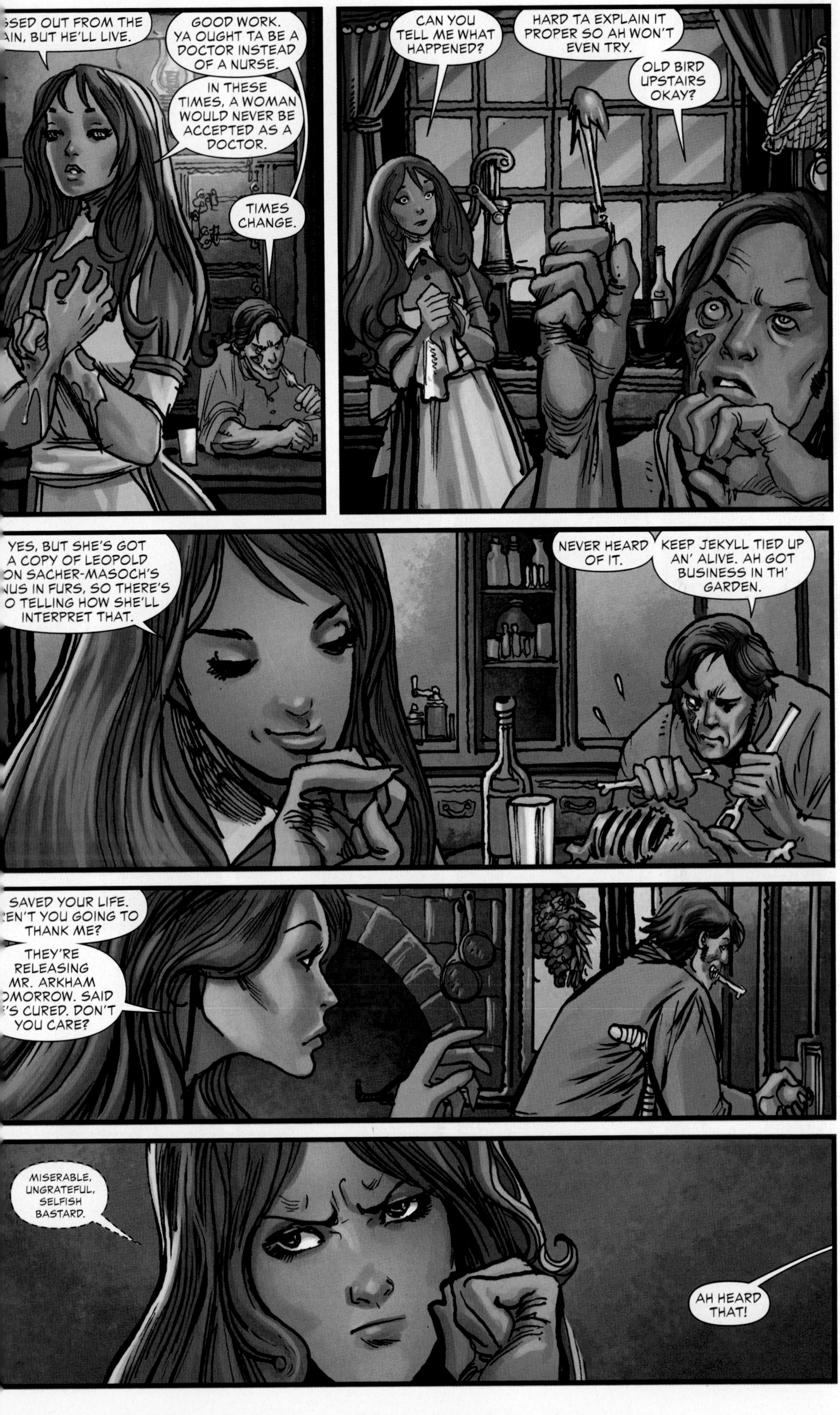

SSED OUT FROM THE
AIN, BUT HE'LL LIVE.
GOOD WORK. YA OUGHT TA BE A DOCTOR INSTEAD OF A NURSE.
IN THESE TIMES, A WOMAN WOULD NEVER BE ACCEPTED AS A DOCTOR.
TIMES CHANGE.
CAN YOU TELL ME WHAT HAPPENED?
HARD TA EXPLAIN IT PROPER SO AH WON'T EVEN TRY.
OLD BIRD UPSTAIRS OKAY?
YES, BUT SHE'S GOT A COPY OF LEOPOLD
ON SACHER-MASOCH'S
NUS IN FURS, SO THERE'S
O TELLING HOW SHE'LL INTERPRET THAT.
NEVER HEARD OF IT.
KEEP JEKYLL TIED UP AN' ALIVE. AH GOT BUSINESS IN TH' GARDEN.
SAVED YOUR LIFE.
EN'T YOU GOING TO THANK ME?
THEY'RE RELEASING MR. ARKHAM
OMORROW. SAID
'S CURED. DON'T YOU CARE?
MISERABLE, UNGRATEFUL, SELFISH BASTARD.
AH HEARD THAT!

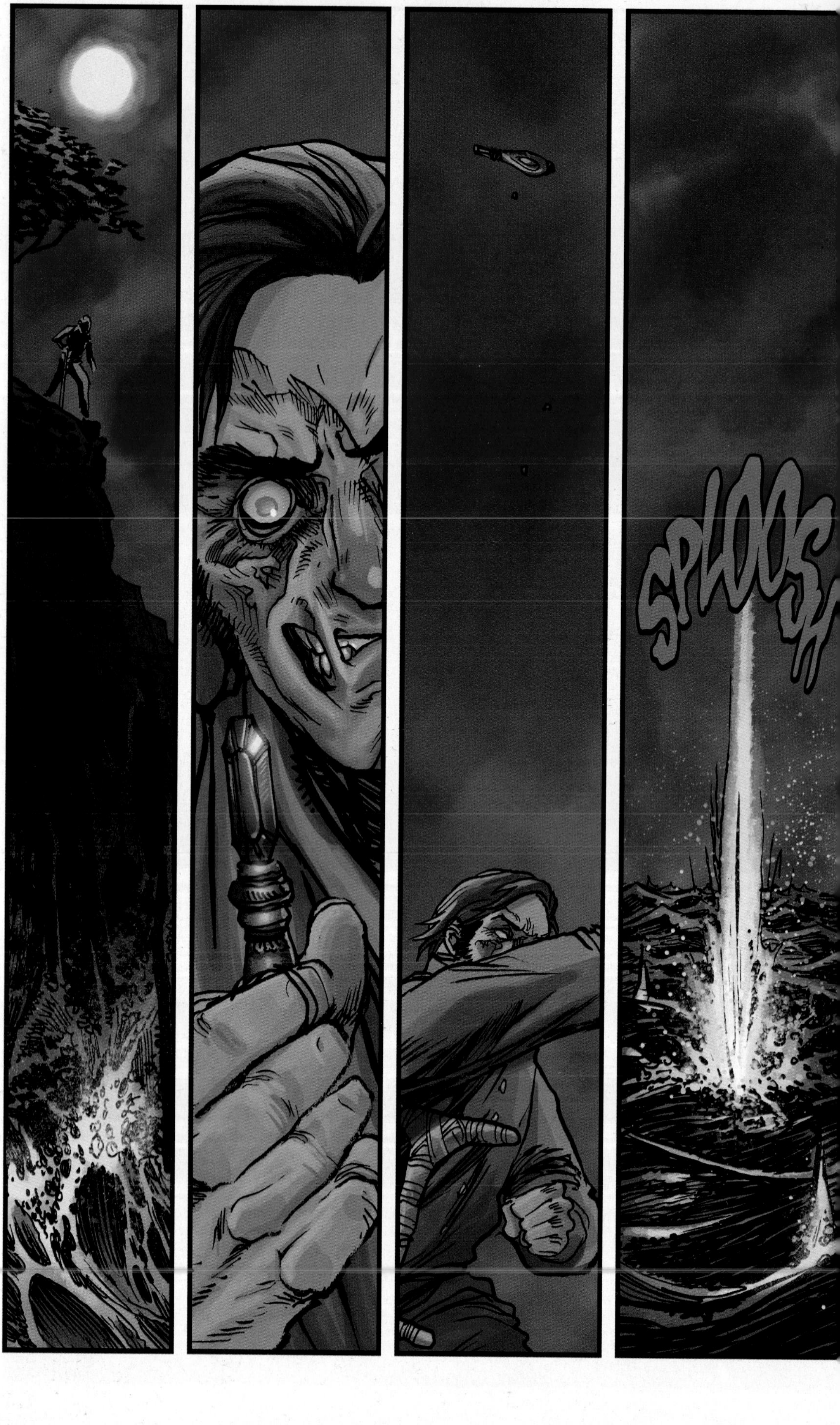
SPLOOS

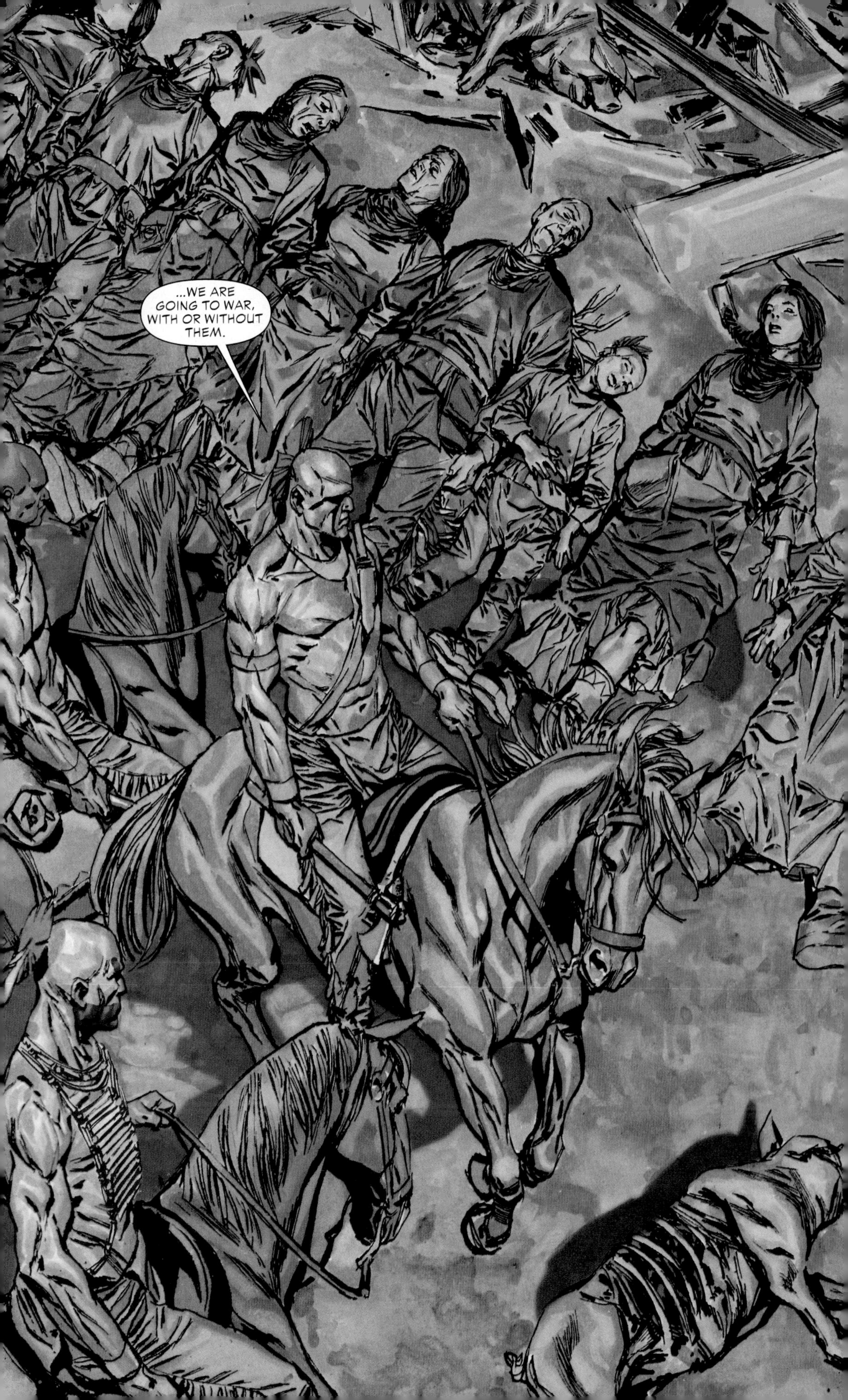
...WE ARE GOING TO WAR, WITH OR WITHOUT THEM.

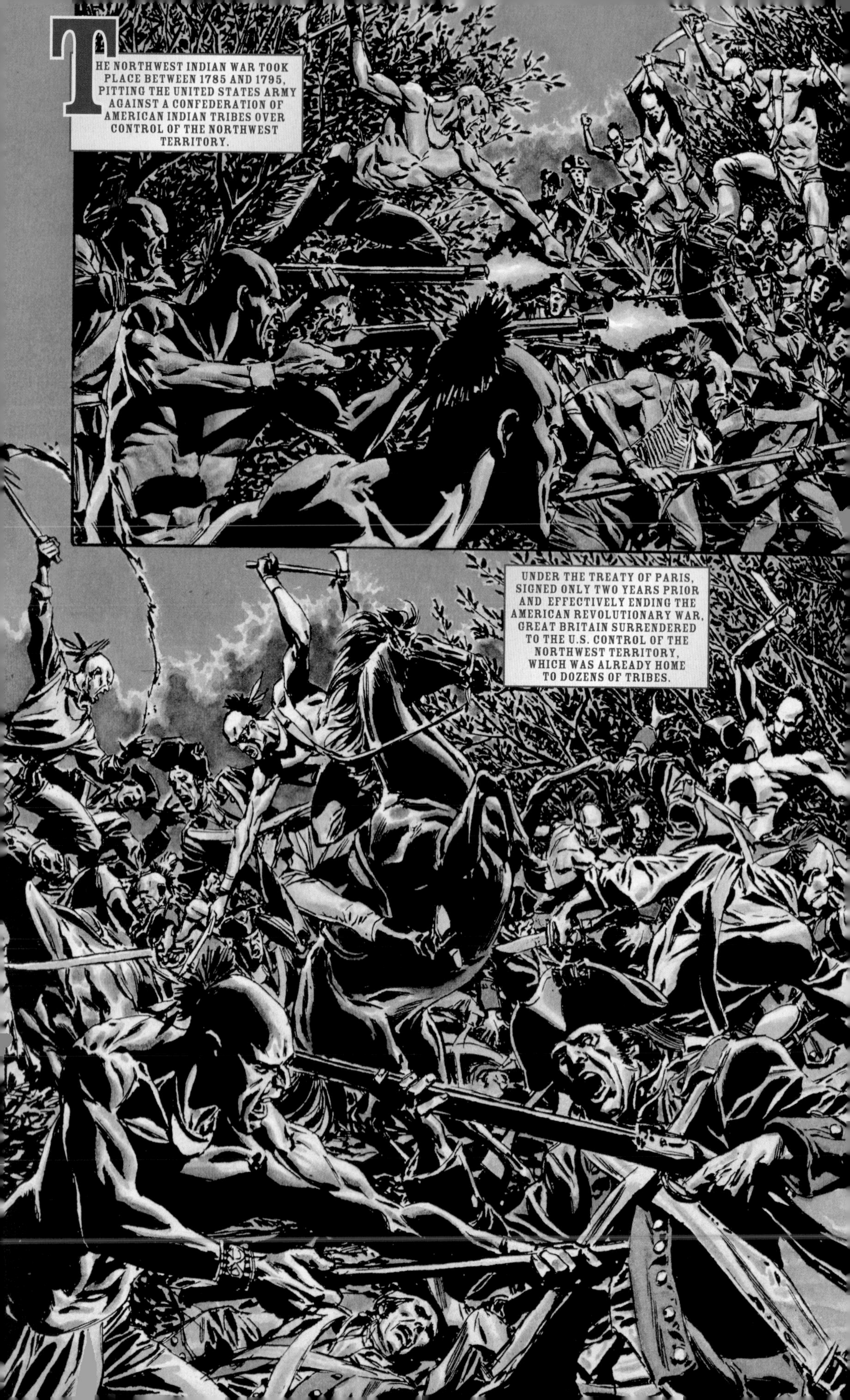
THE NORTHWEST INDIAN WAR TOOK PLACE BETWEEN 1785 AND 1795, PITTING THE UNITED STATES ARMY AGAINST A CONFEDERATION OF AMERICAN INDIAN TRIBES OVER CONTROL OF THE NORTHWEST TERRITORY.
UNDER THE TREATY OF PARIS, SIGNED ONLY TWO YEARS PRIOR AND EFFECTIVELY ENDING THE AMERICAN REVOLUTIONARY WAR, GREAT BRITAIN SURRENDERED TO THE U.S. CONTROL OF THE NORTHWEST TERRITORY, WHICH WAS ALREADY HOME TO DOZENS OF TRIBES.

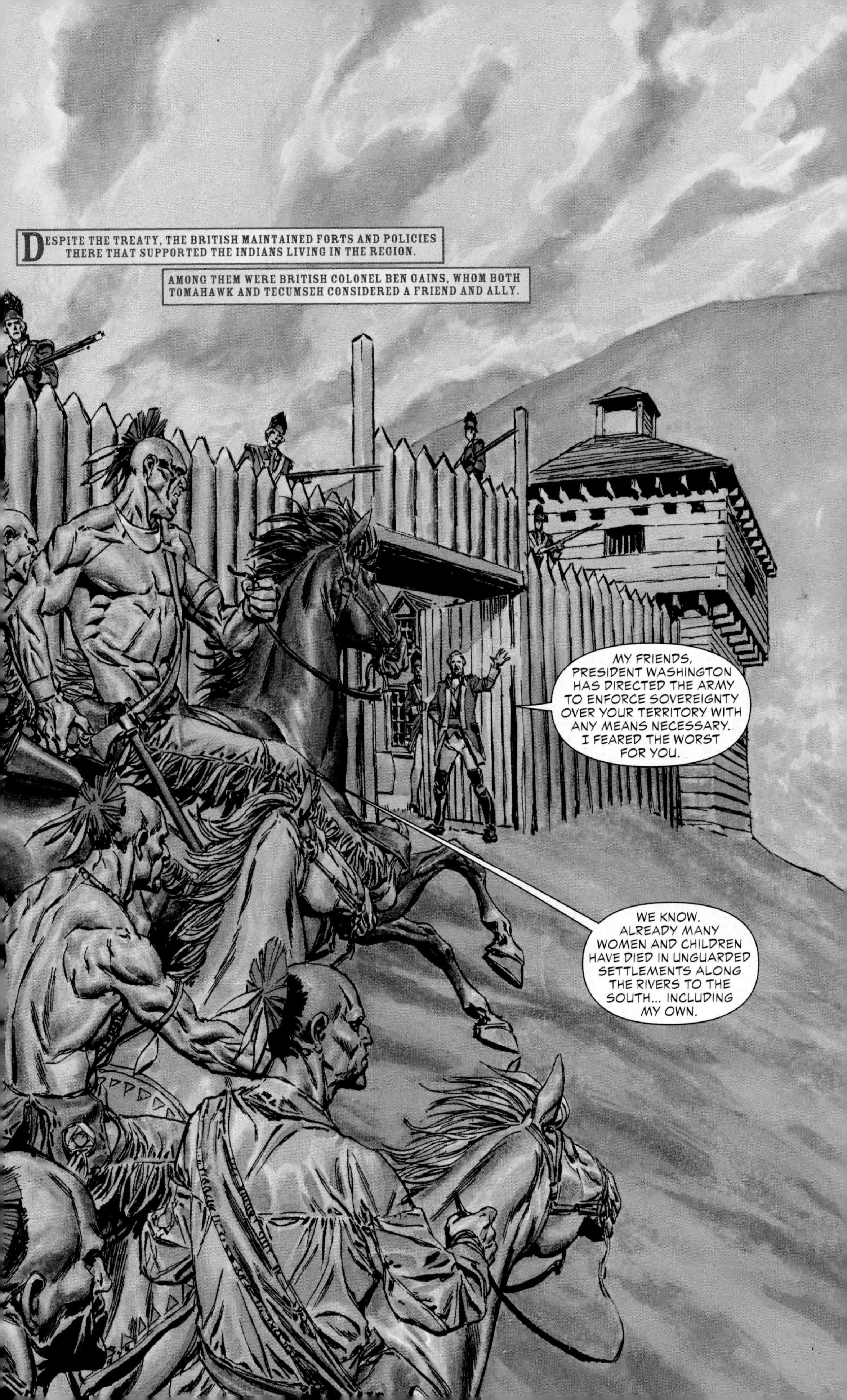
DESPITE THE TREATY, THE BRITISH MAINTAINED FORTS AND POLICIES THERE THAT SUPPORTED THE INDIANS LIVING IN THE REGION.
AMONG THEM WERE BRITISH COLONEL BEN GAINS, WHOM BOTH TOMAHAWK AND TECUMSEH CONSIDERED A FRIEND AND ALLY.
MY FRIENDS, PRESIDENT WASHINGTON HAS DIRECTED THE ARMY TO ENFORCE SOVEREIGNTY OVER YOUR TERRITORY WITH ANY MEANS NECESSARY. I FEARED THE WORST FOR YOU.
WE KNOW. ALREADY MANY WOMEN AND CHILDREN HAVE DIED IN UNGUARDED SETTLEMENTS ALONG THE RIVERS TO THE SOUTH... INCLUDING MY OWN.

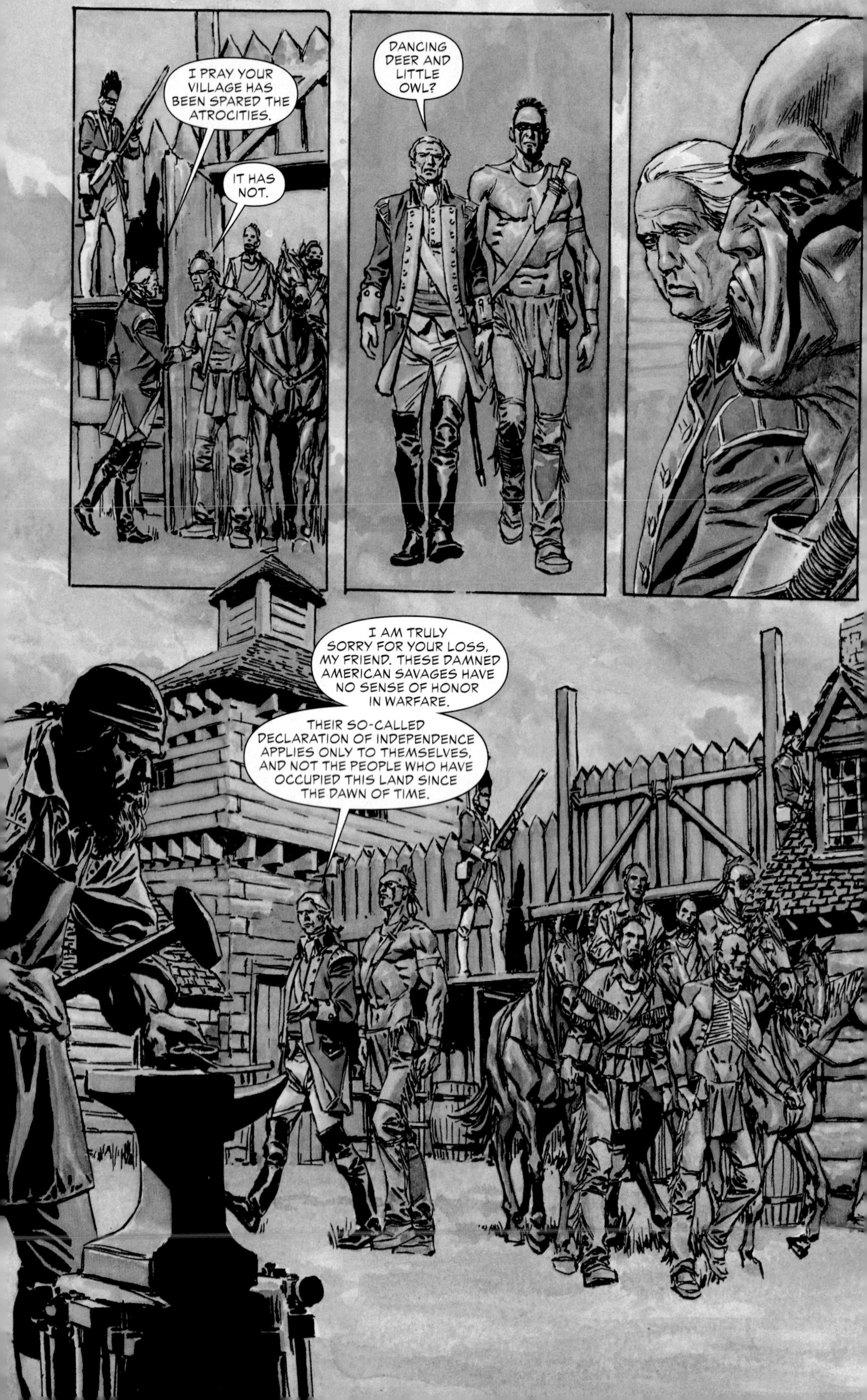
I PRAY YOUR VILLAGE HAS BEEN SPARED THE ATROCITIES.
IT HAS NOT.
DANCING DEER AND LITTLE OWL?
I AM TRULY SORRY FOR YOUR LOSS, MY FRIEND. THESE DAMNED AMERICAN SAVAGES HAVE NO SENSE OF HONOR IN WARFARE.
THEIR SO-CALLED DECLARATION OF INDEPENDENCE APPLIES ONLY TO THEMSELVES, AND NOT THE PEOPLE WHO HAVE OCCUPIED THIS LAND SINCE THE DAWN OF TIME.

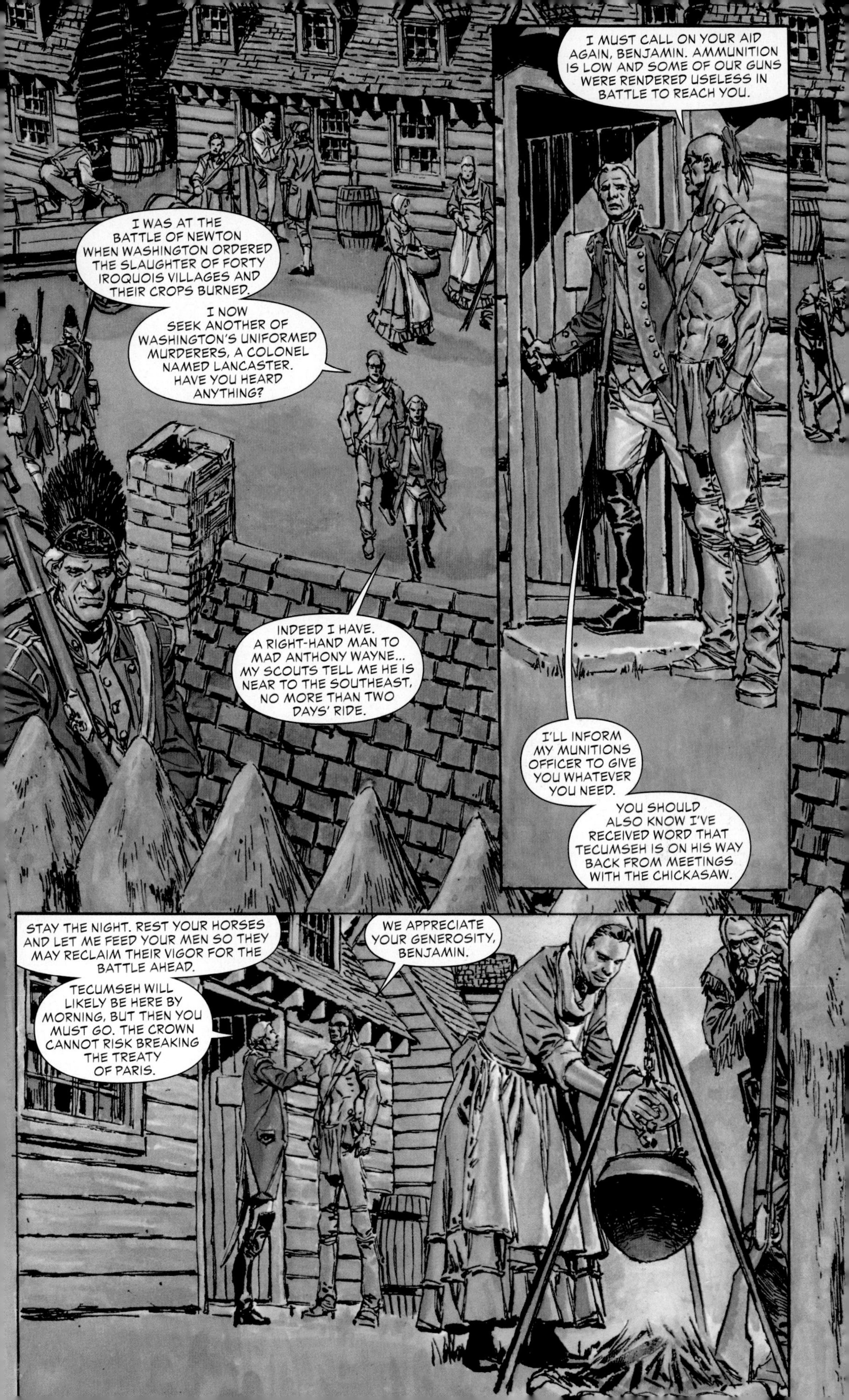
I MUST CALL ON YOUR AID AGAIN, BENJAMIN. AMMUNITION IS LOW AND SOME OF OUR GUNS WERE RENDERED USELESS IN BATTLE TO REACH YOU.
I WAS AT THE BATTLE OF NEWTON WHEN WASHINGTON ORDERED THE SLAUGHTER OF FORTY IROQUOIS VILLAGES AND THEIR CROPS BURNED.
I NOW SEEK ANOTHER OF WASHINGTON'S UNIFORMED MURDERERS, A COLONEL NAMED LANCASTER. HAVE YOU HEARD ANYTHING?
INDEED I HAVE. A RIGHT-HAND MAN TO MAD ANTHONY WAYNE... MY SCOUTS TELL ME HE IS NEAR TO THE SOUTHEAST, NO MORE THAN TWO DAYS' RIDE.
I'LL INFORM MY MUNITIONS OFFICER TO GIVE YOU WHATEVER YOU NEED.
YOU SHOULD ALSO KNOW I'VE RECEIVED WORD THAT TECUMSEH IS ON HIS WAY BACK FROM MEETINGS WITH THE CHICKASAW.
STAY THE NIGHT. REST YOUR HORSES AND LET ME FEED YOUR MEN SO THEY MAY RECLAIM THEIR VIGOR FOR THE BATTLE AHEAD.
TECUMSEH WILL LIKELY BE HERE BY MORNING, BUT THEN YOU MUST GO. THE CROWN CANNOT RISK BREAKING THE TREATY OF PARIS.
WE APPRECIATE YOUR GENEROSITY, BENJAMIN.

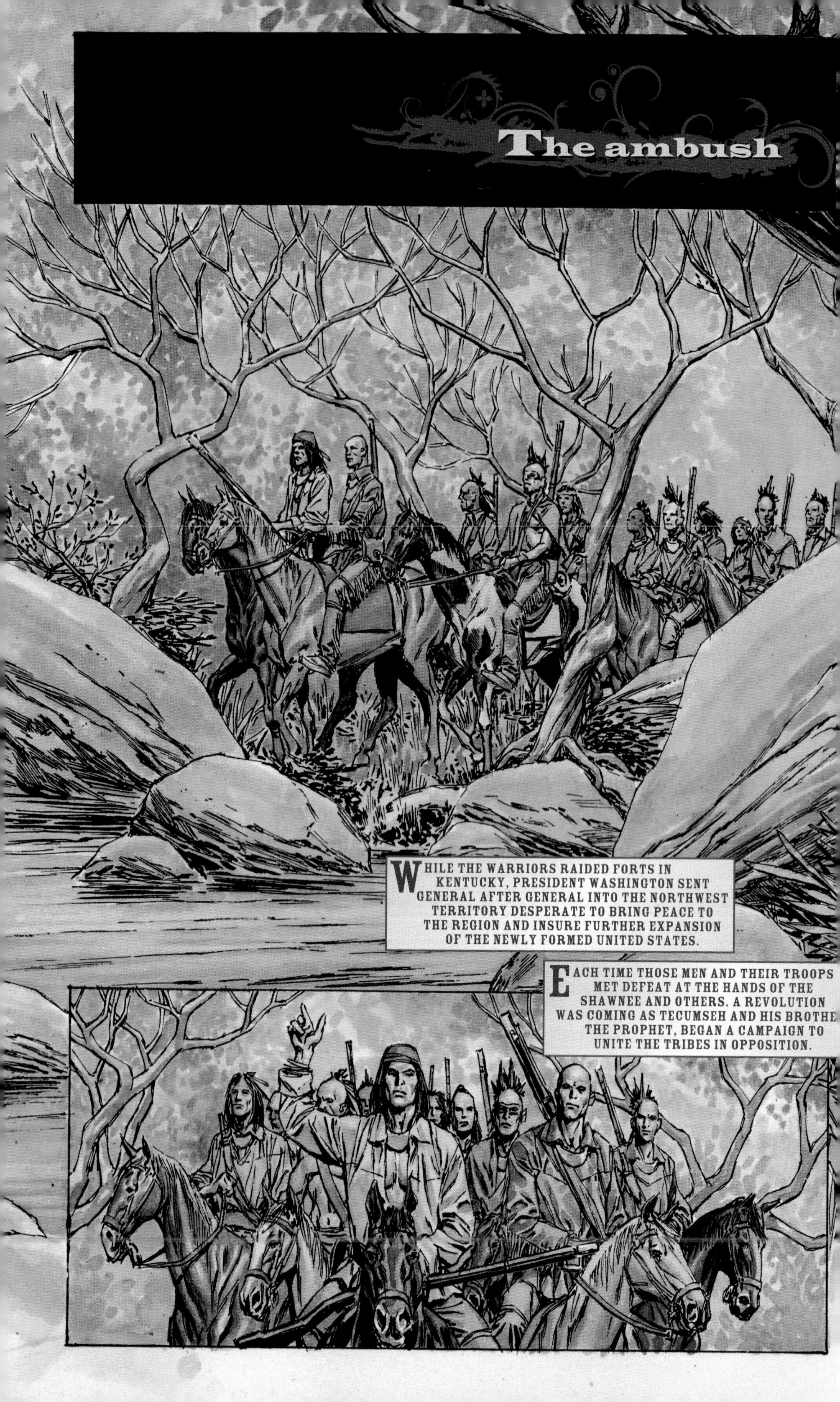

The ambush
WHILE THE WARRIORS RAIDED FORTS IN KENTUCKY, PRESIDENT WASHINGTON SENT GENERAL AFTER GENERAL INTO THE NORTHWEST TERRITORY DESPERATE TO BRING PEACE TO THE REGION AND INSURE FURTHER EXPANSION OF THE NEWLY FORMED UNITED STATES.
EACH TIME THOSE MEN AND THEIR TROOPS MET DEFEAT AT THE HANDS OF THE SHAWNEE AND OTHERS. A REVOLUTION WAS COMING AS TECUMSEH AND HIS BROTHE THE PROPHET, BEGAN A CAMPAIGN TO UNITE THE TRIBES IN OPPOSITION.

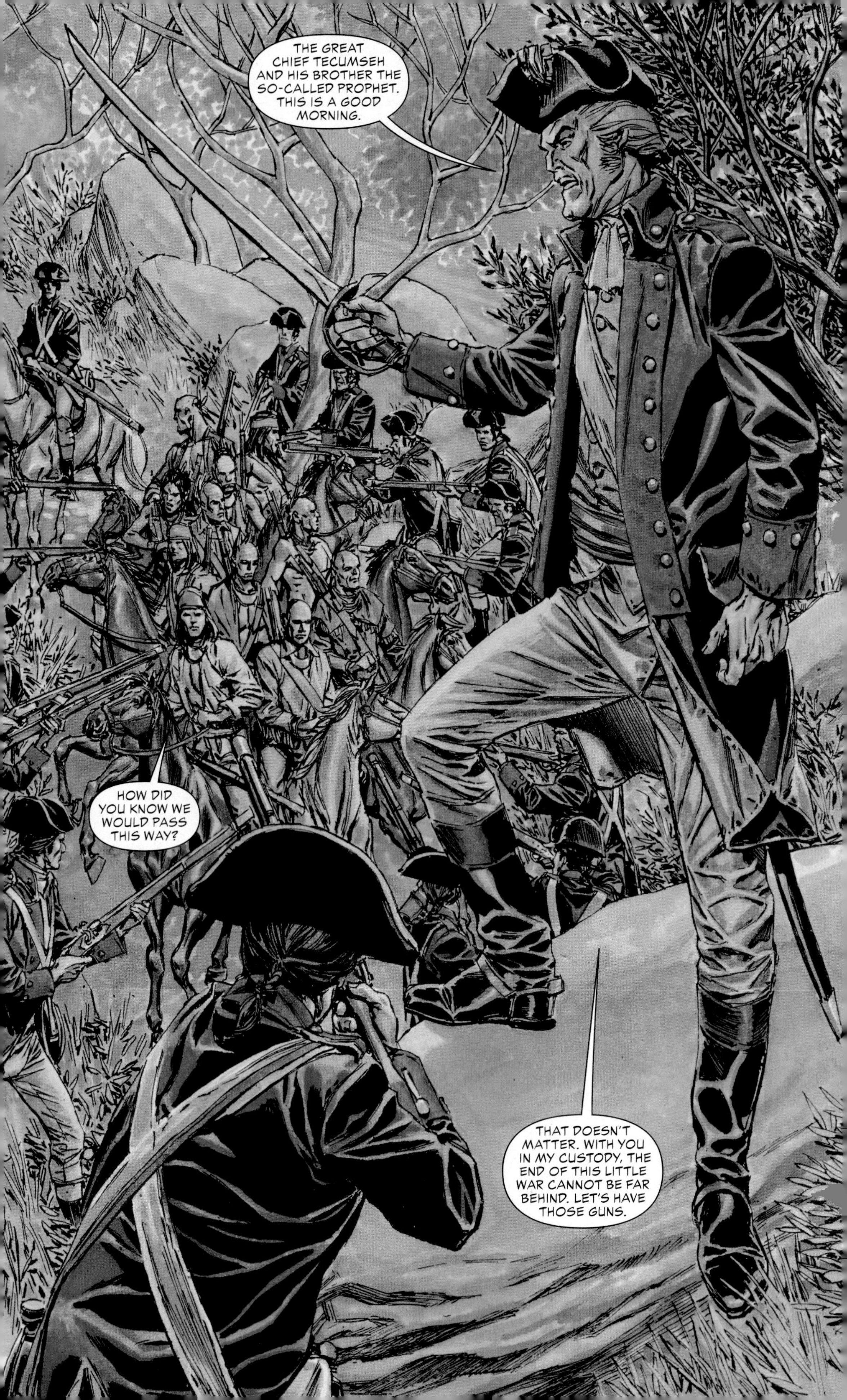
THE GREAT CHIEF TECUMSEH AND HIS BROTHER THE SO-CALLED PROPHET. THIS IS A GOOD MORNING.
HOW DID YOU KNOW WE WOULD PASS THIS WAY?
THAT DOESN'T MATTER. WITH YOU IN MY CUSTODY, THE END OF THIS LITTLE WAR CANNOT BE FAR BEHIND. LET'S HAVE THOSE GUNS.

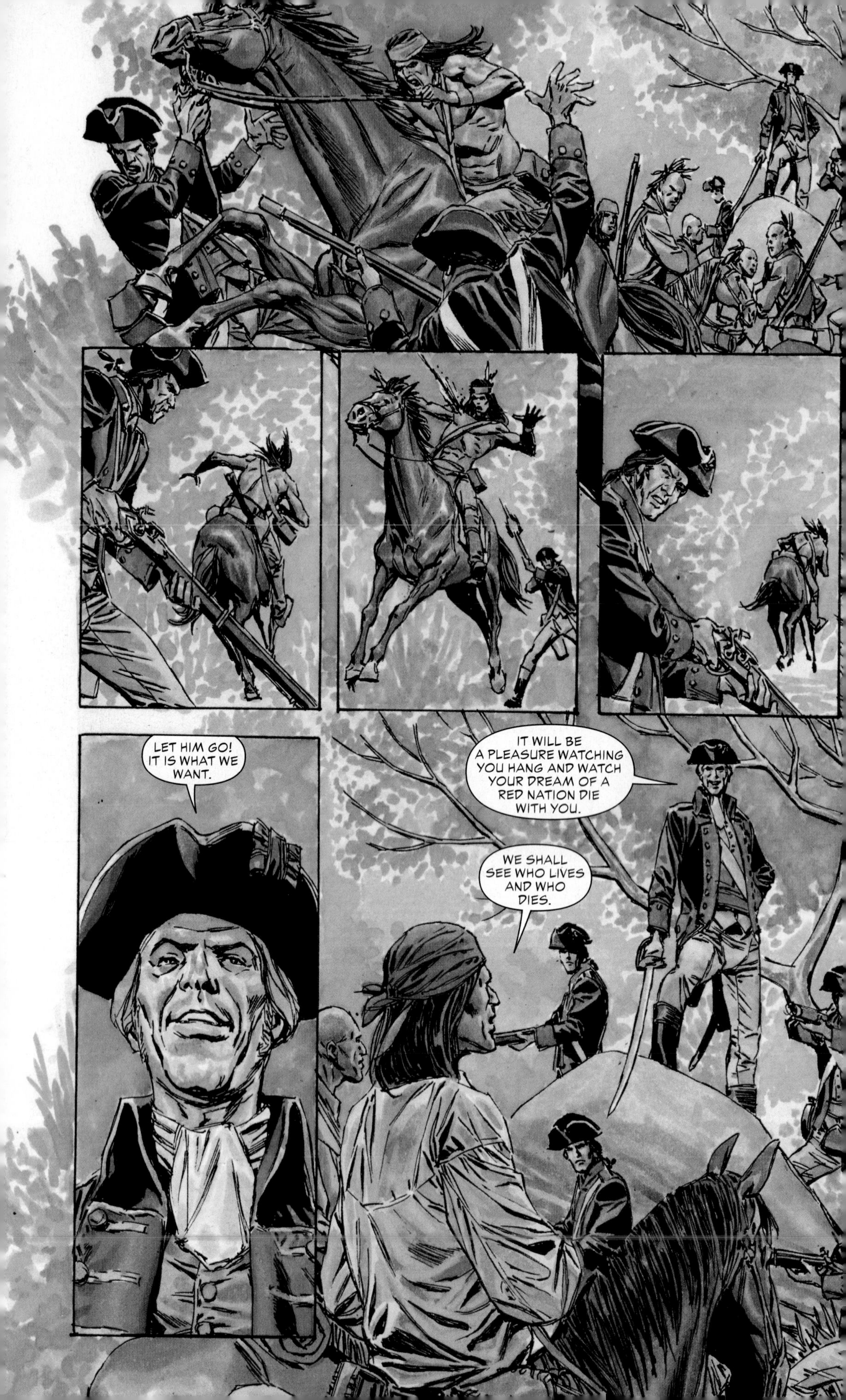
LET HIM GO! IT IS WHAT WE WANT.
IT WILL BE A PLEASURE WATCHING YOU HANG AND WATCH YOUR DREAM OF A RED NATION DIE WITH YOU.
WE SHALL SEE WHO LIVES AND WHO DIES.

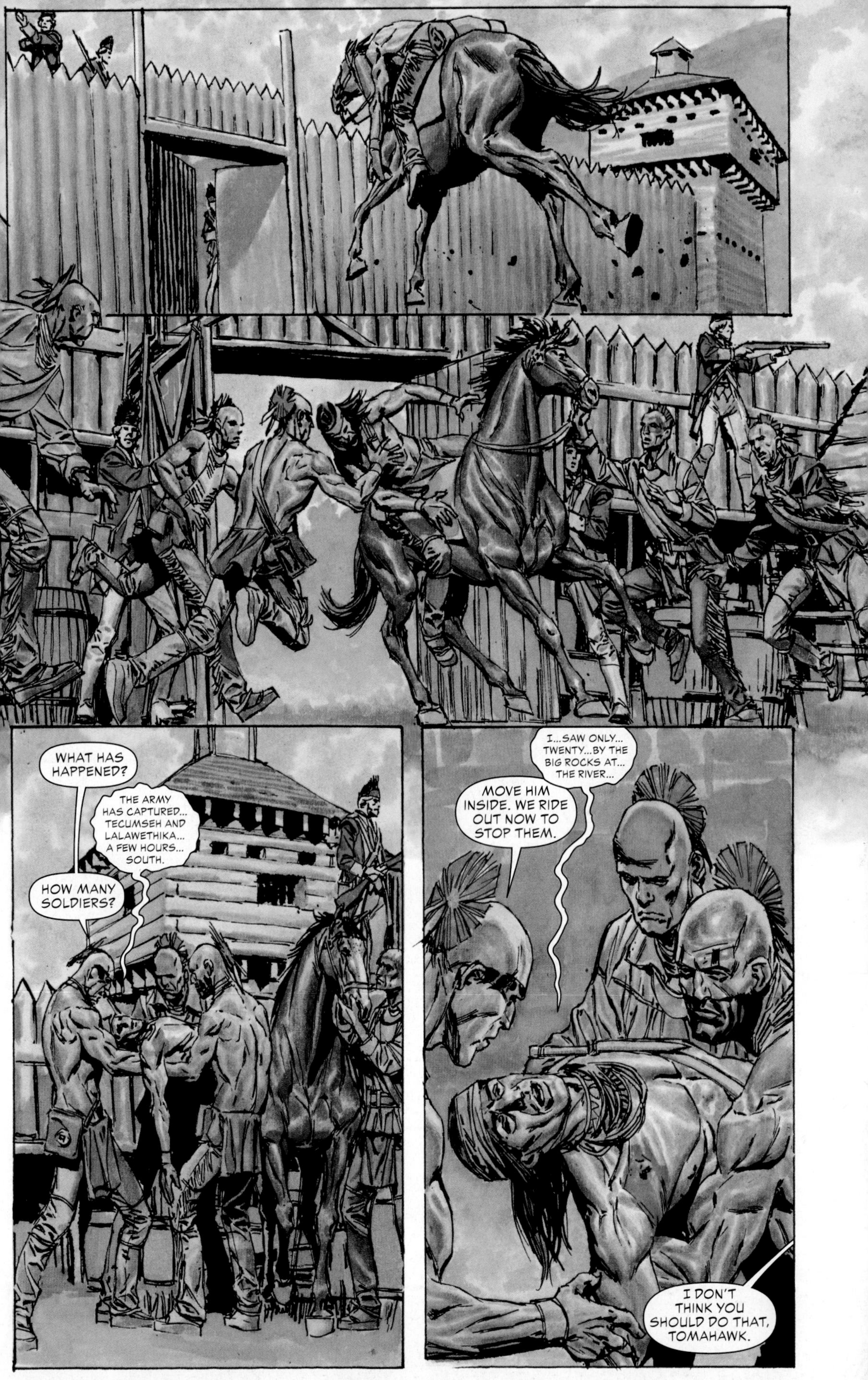
WHAT HAS HAPPENED?
THE ARMY HAS CAPTURED... TECUMSEH AND LALAWETHIKA... A FEW HOURS... SOUTH.
HOW MANY SOLDIERS?
I...SAW ONLY... TWENTY...BY THE BIG ROCKS AT... THE RIVER...
MOVE HIM INSIDE. WE RIDE OUT NOW TO STOP THEM.
I DON'T THINK YOU SHOULD DO THAT, TOMAHAWK.

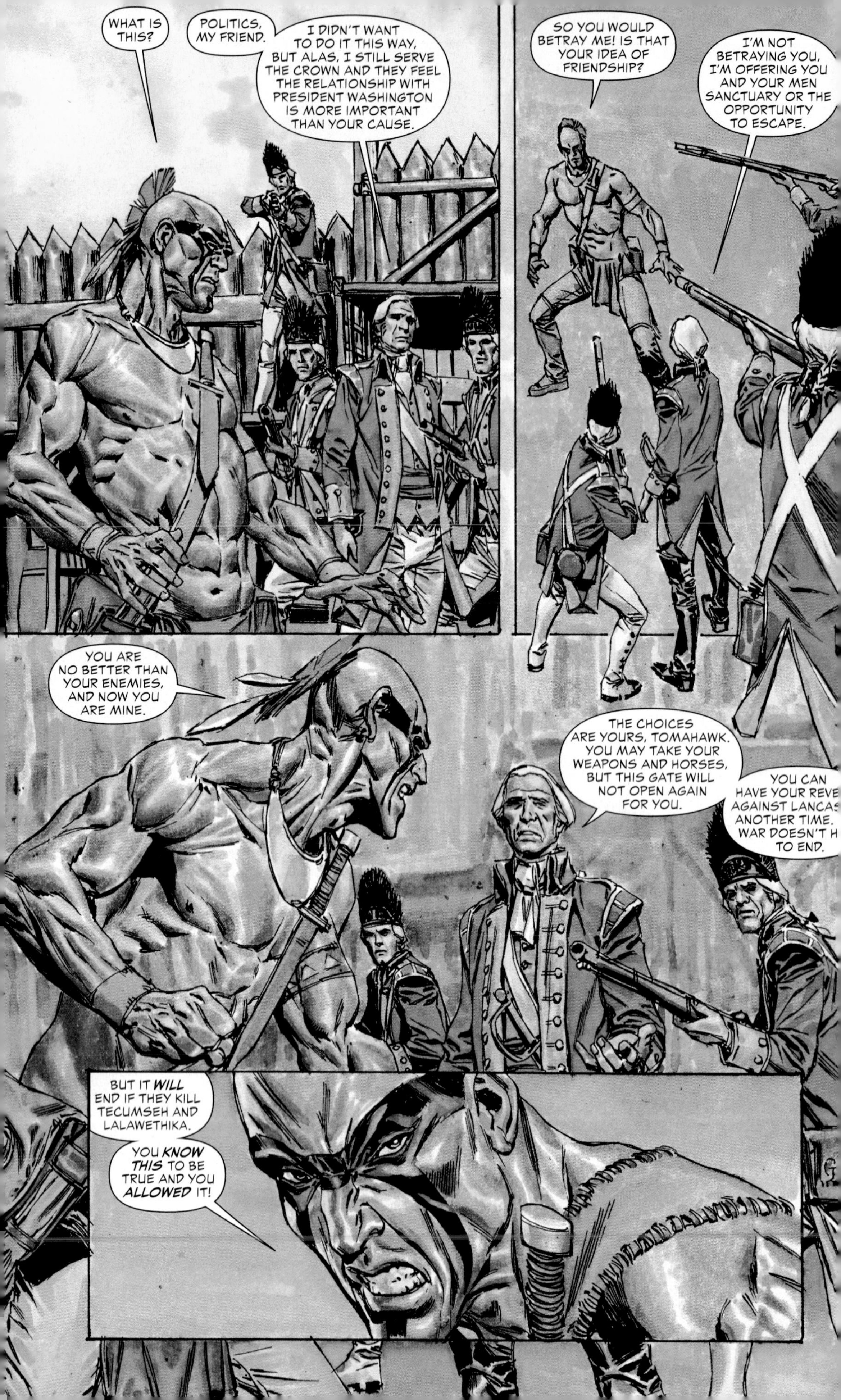
WHAT IS THIS?
POLITICS, MY FRIEND.
I DIDN'T WANT TO DO IT THIS WAY, BUT ALAS, I STILL SERVE THE CROWN AND THEY FEEL THE RELATIONSHIP WITH PRESIDENT WASHINGTON IS MORE IMPORTANT THAN YOUR CAUSE.
SO YOU WOULD BETRAY ME! IS THAT YOUR IDEA OF FRIENDSHIP?
I'M NOT BETRAYING YOU, I'M OFFERING YOU AND YOUR MEN SANCTUARY OR THE OPPORTUNITY TO ESCAPE.
YOU ARE NO BETTER THAN YOUR ENEMIES, AND NOW YOU ARE MINE.
THE CHOICES ARE YOURS, TOMAHAWK. YOU MAY TAKE YOUR WEAPONS AND HORSES, BUT THIS GATE WILL NOT OPEN AGAIN FOR YOU.
YOU CAN HAVE YOUR REVE AGAINST LANCAS ANOTHER TIME. WAR DOESN'T H TO END.
BUT IT WILL END IF THEY KILL TECUMSEH AND LALAWETHIKA.
YOU KNOW THIS TO BE TRUE AND YOU ALLOWED IT!

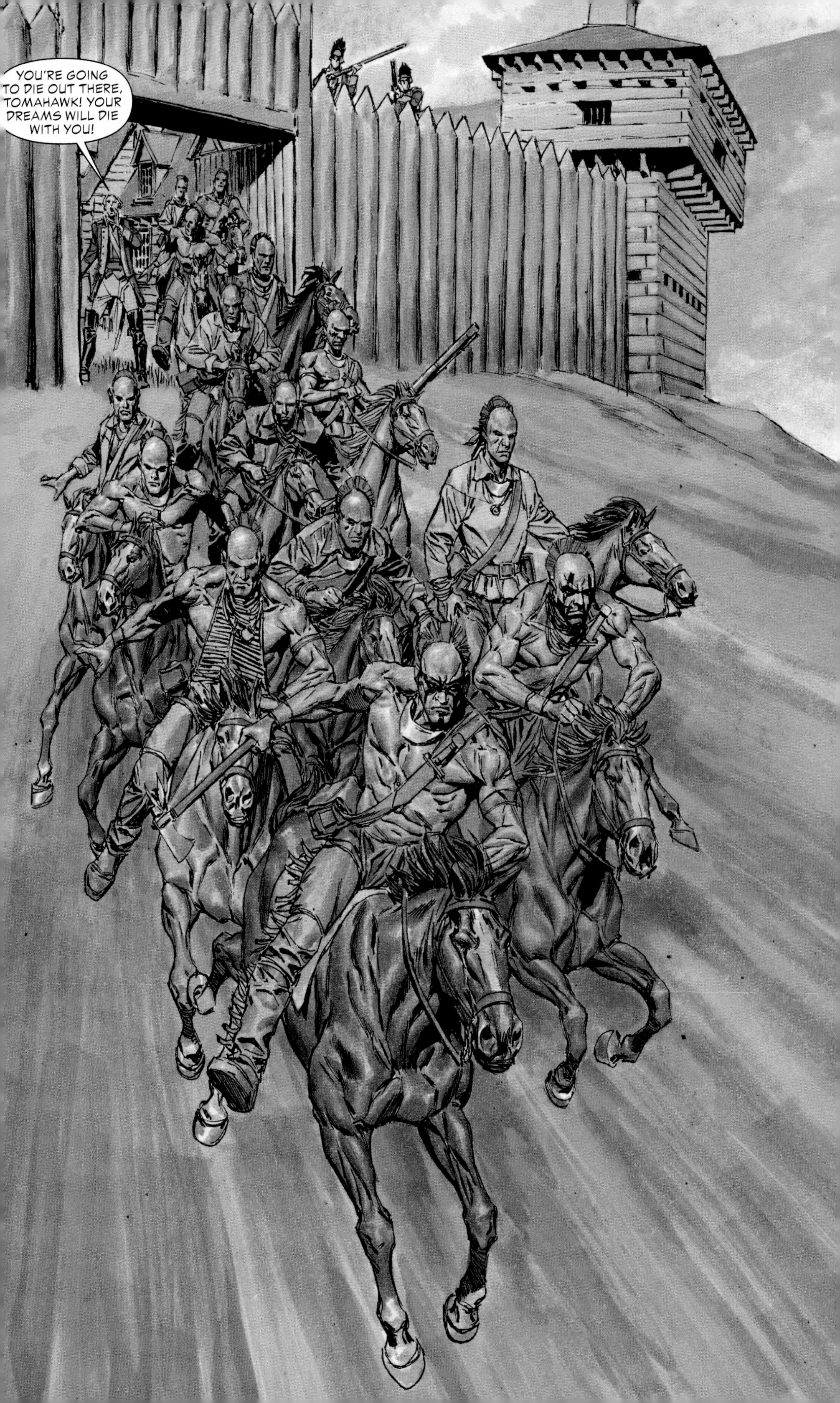
YOU'RE GOING TO DIE OUT THERE, TOMAHAWK! YOUR DREAMS WILL DIE WITH YOU!

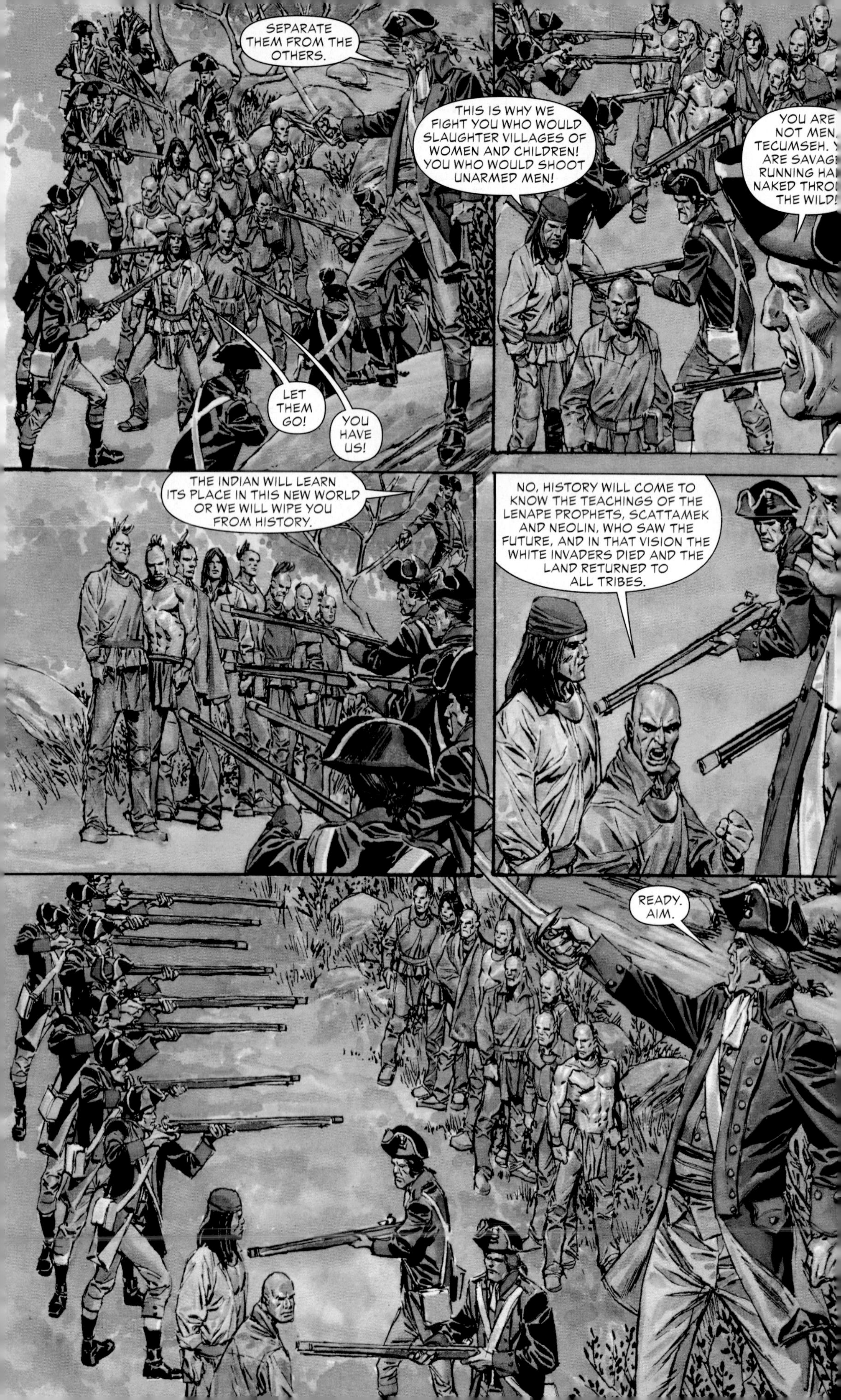
SEPARATE THEM FROM THE OTHERS.
THIS IS WHY WE FIGHT YOU WHO WOULD SLAUGHTER VILLAGES OF WOMEN AND CHILDREN! YOU WHO WOULD SHOOT UNARMED MEN!
LET THEM GO!
YOU HAVE US!
YOU ARE NOT MEN, TECUMSEH. ARE SAVAG RUNNING HA NAKED THRO THE WILD!
THE INDIAN WILL LEARN ITS PLACE IN THIS NEW WORLD OR WE WILL WIPE YOU FROM HISTORY.
NO, HISTORY WILL COME TO KNOW THE TEACHINGS OF THE LENAPE PROPHETS, SCATTAMEK AND NEOLIN, WHO SAW THE FUTURE, AND IN THAT VISION THE WHITE INVADERS DIED AND THE LAND RETURNED TO ALL TRIBES.
READY. AIM.

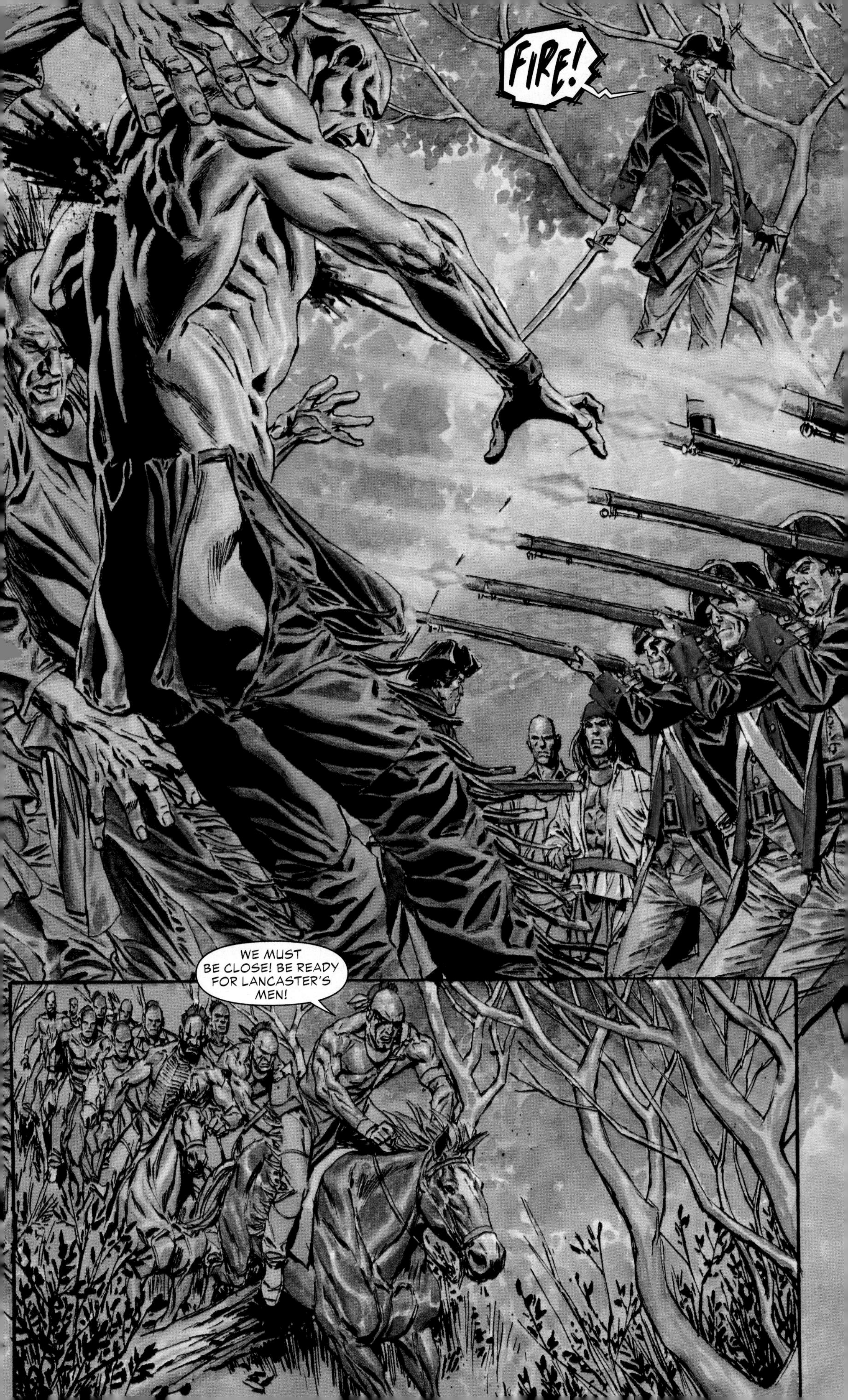
FIRE!
WE MUST BE CLOSE! BE READY FOR LANCASTER'S MEN!

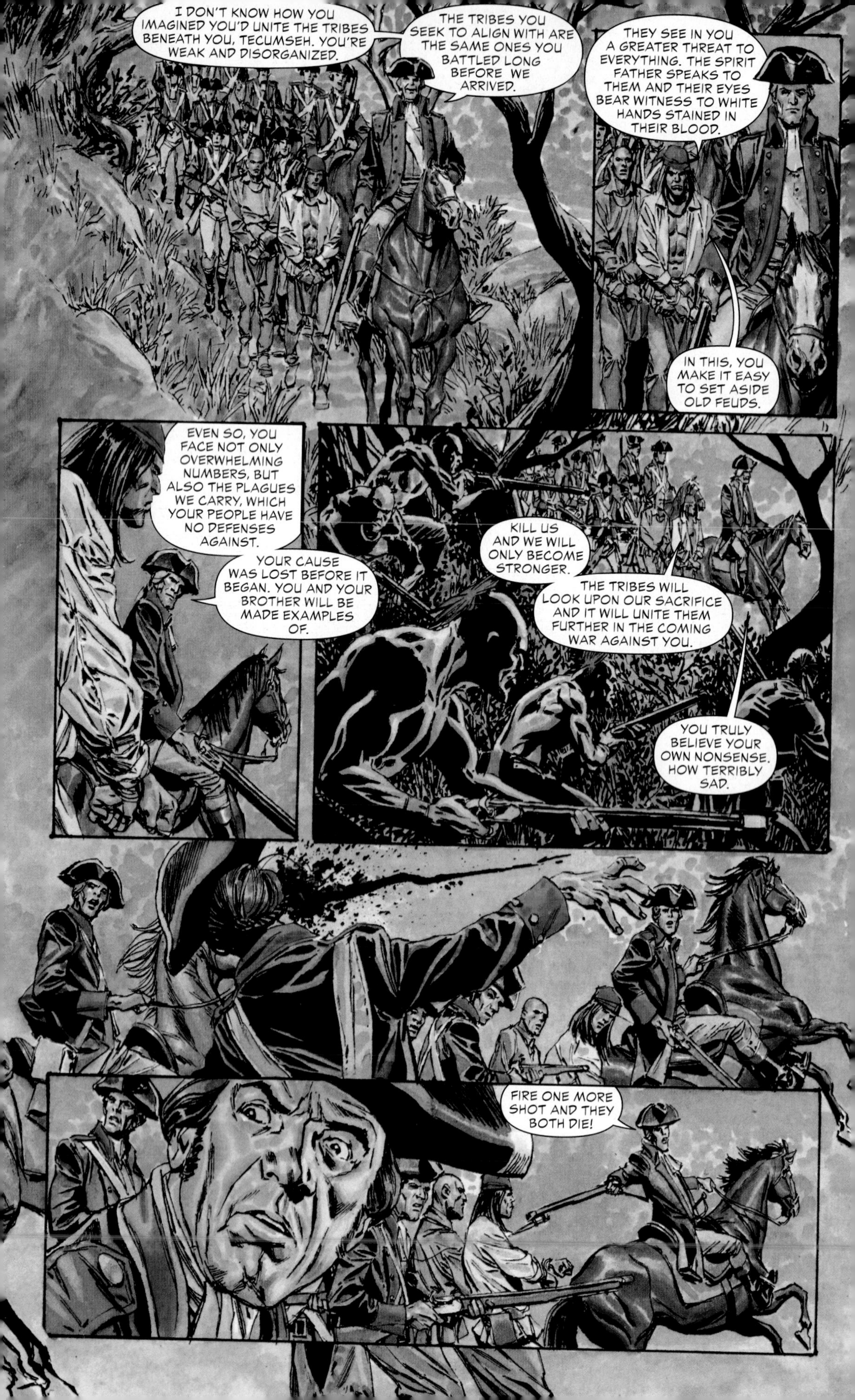
I DON'T KNOW HOW YOU IMAGINED YOU'D UNITE THE TRIBES BENEATH YOU, TECUMSEH. YOU'RE WEAK AND DISORGANIZED.
THE TRIBES YOU SEEK TO ALIGN WITH ARE THE SAME ONES YOU BATTLED LONG BEFORE WE ARRIVED.
THEY SEE IN YOU A GREATER THREAT TO EVERYTHING. THE SPIRIT FATHER SPEAKS TO THEM AND THEIR EYES BEAR WITNESS TO WHITE HANDS STAINED IN THEIR BLOOD.
IN THIS, YOU MAKE IT EASY TO SET ASIDE OLD FEUDS.
EVEN SO, YOU FACE NOT ONLY OVERWHELMING NUMBERS, BUT ALSO THE PLAGUES WE CARRY, WHICH YOUR PEOPLE HAVE NO DEFENSES AGAINST.
YOUR CAUSE WAS LOST BEFORE IT BEGAN. YOU AND YOUR BROTHER WILL BE MADE EXAMPLES OF.
KILL US AND WE WILL ONLY BECOME STRONGER.
THE TRIBES WILL LOOK UPON OUR SACRIFICE AND IT WILL UNITE THEM FURTHER IN THE COMING WAR AGAINST YOU.
YOU TRULY BELIEVE YOUR OWN NONSENSE. HOW TERRIBLY SAD.
FIRE ONE MORE SHOT AND THEY BOTH DIE!

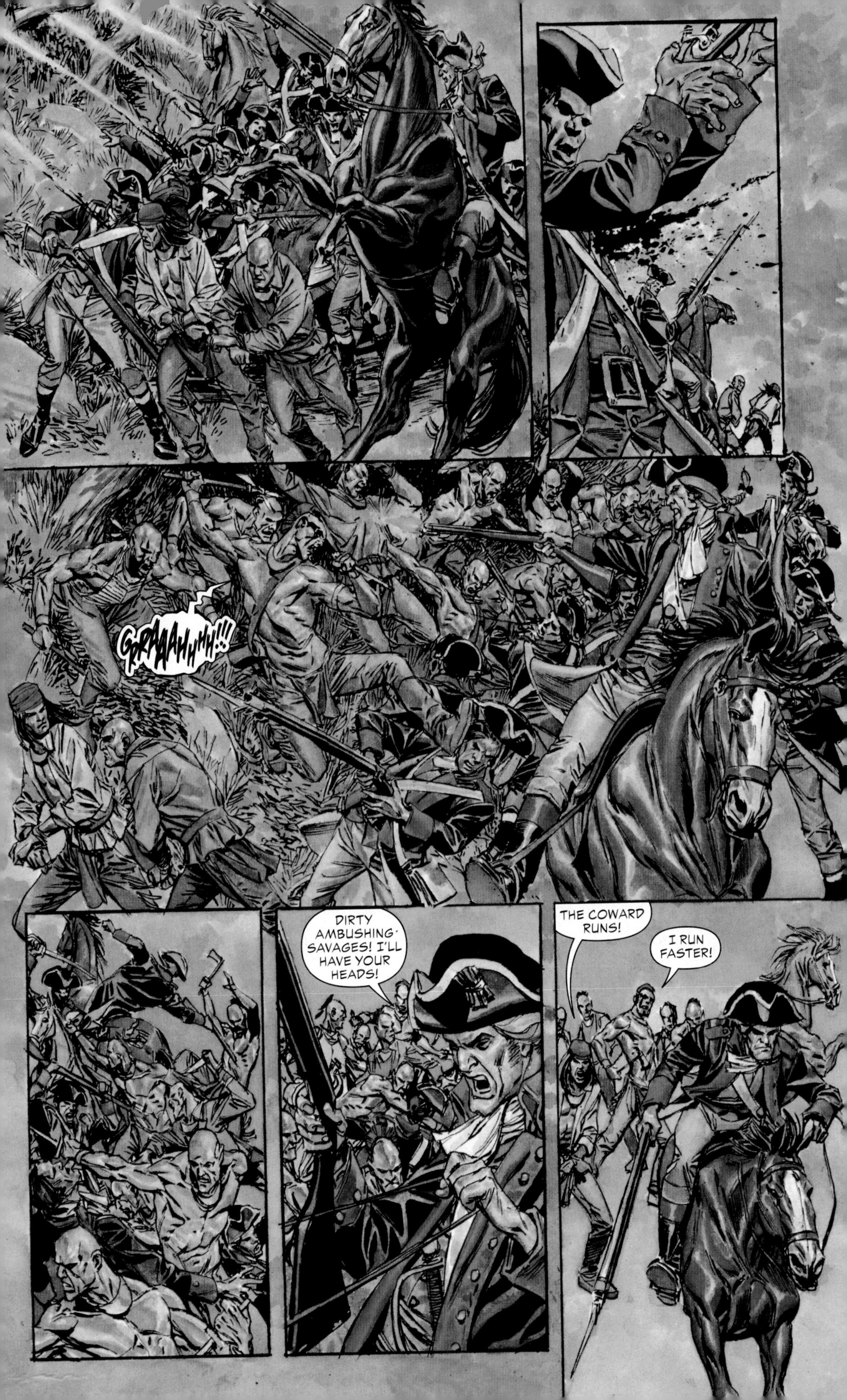
GRRAAAHHHH!!!
DIRTY AMBUSHING SAVAGES! I'LL HAVE YOUR HEADS!
THE COWARD RUNS!
I RUN FASTER!

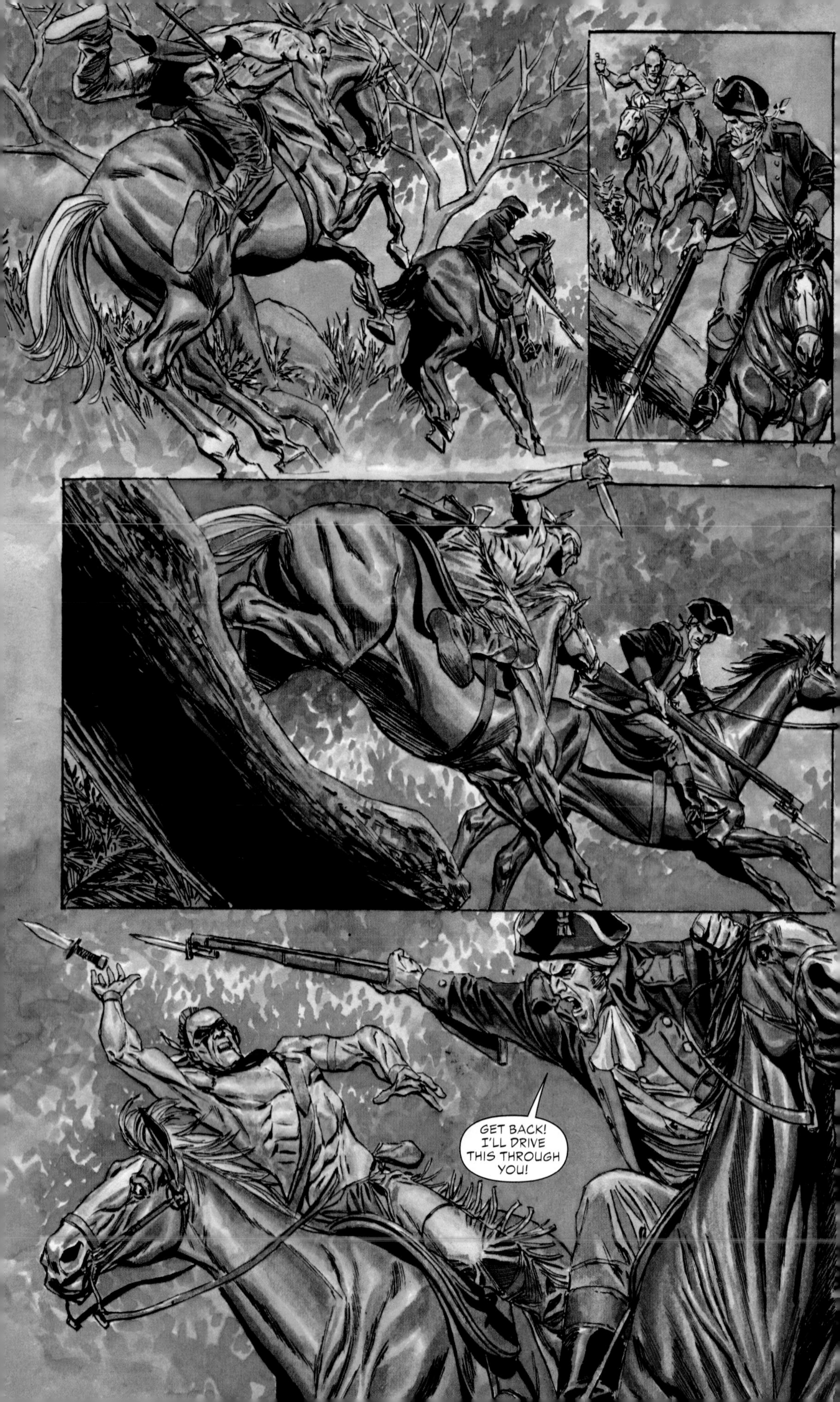
GET BACK! I'LL DRIVE THIS THROUGH YOU!

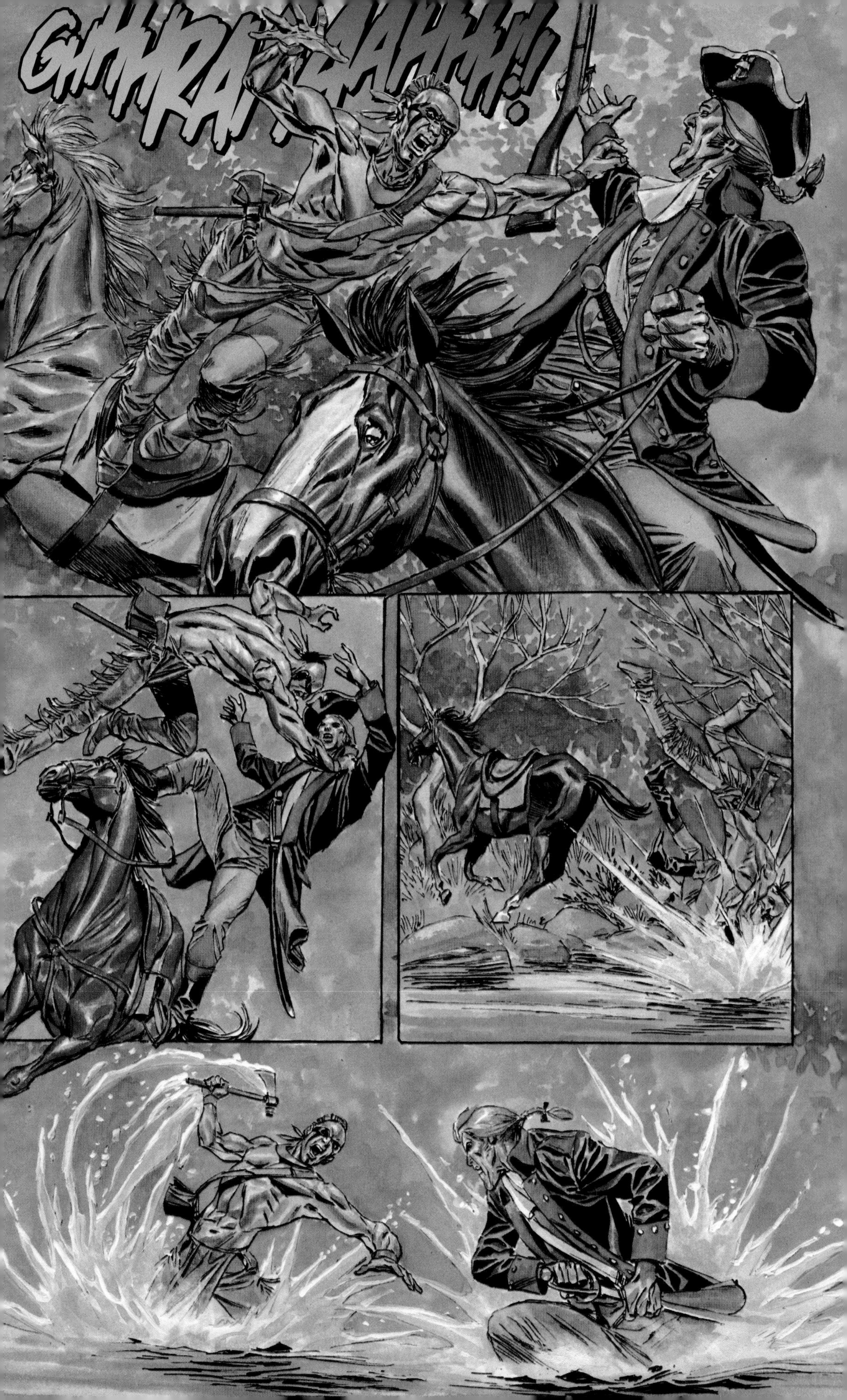
GAHRAAAHHH!

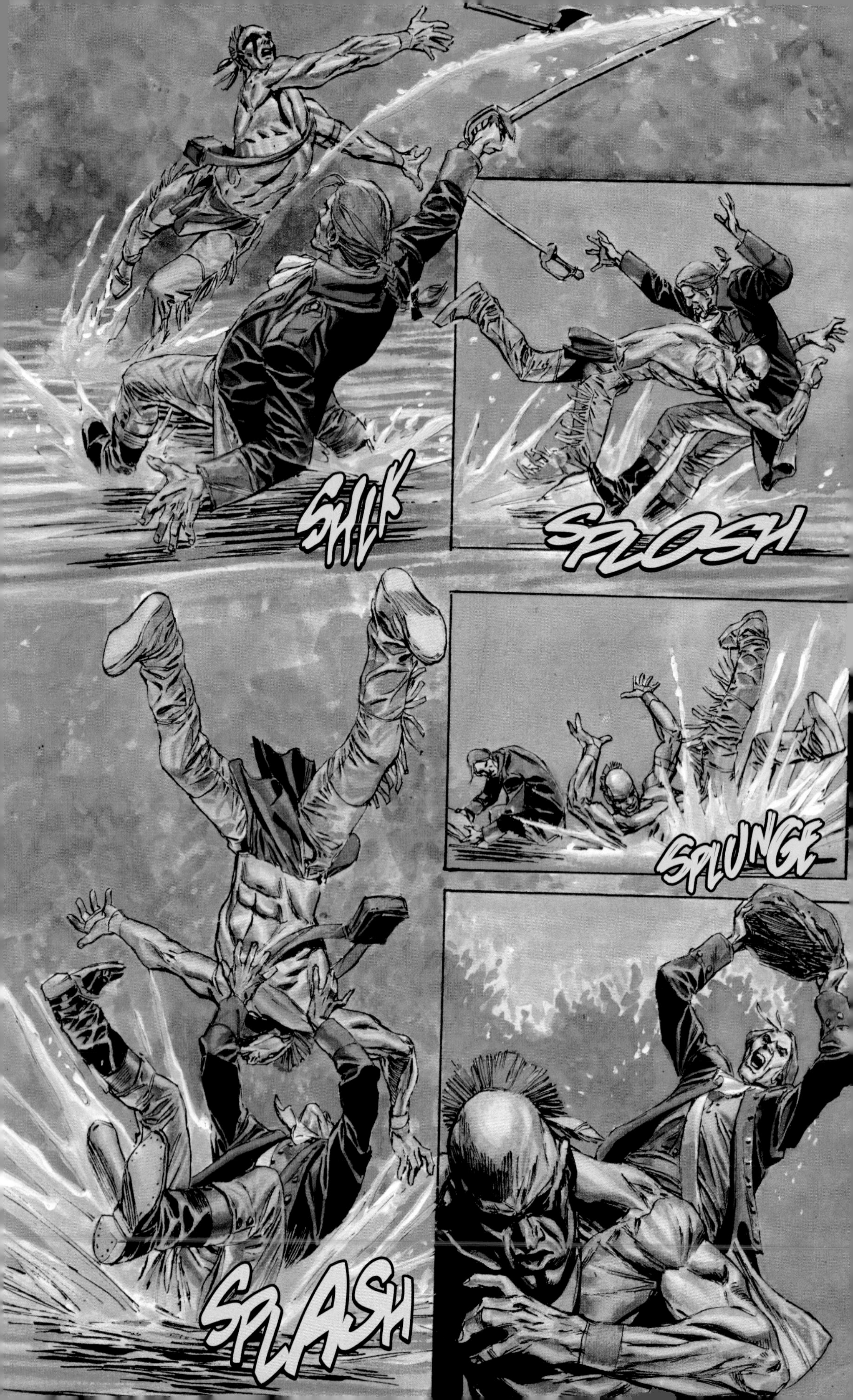
SHLK
SPLOSH
SPLUNGE
SPLASH

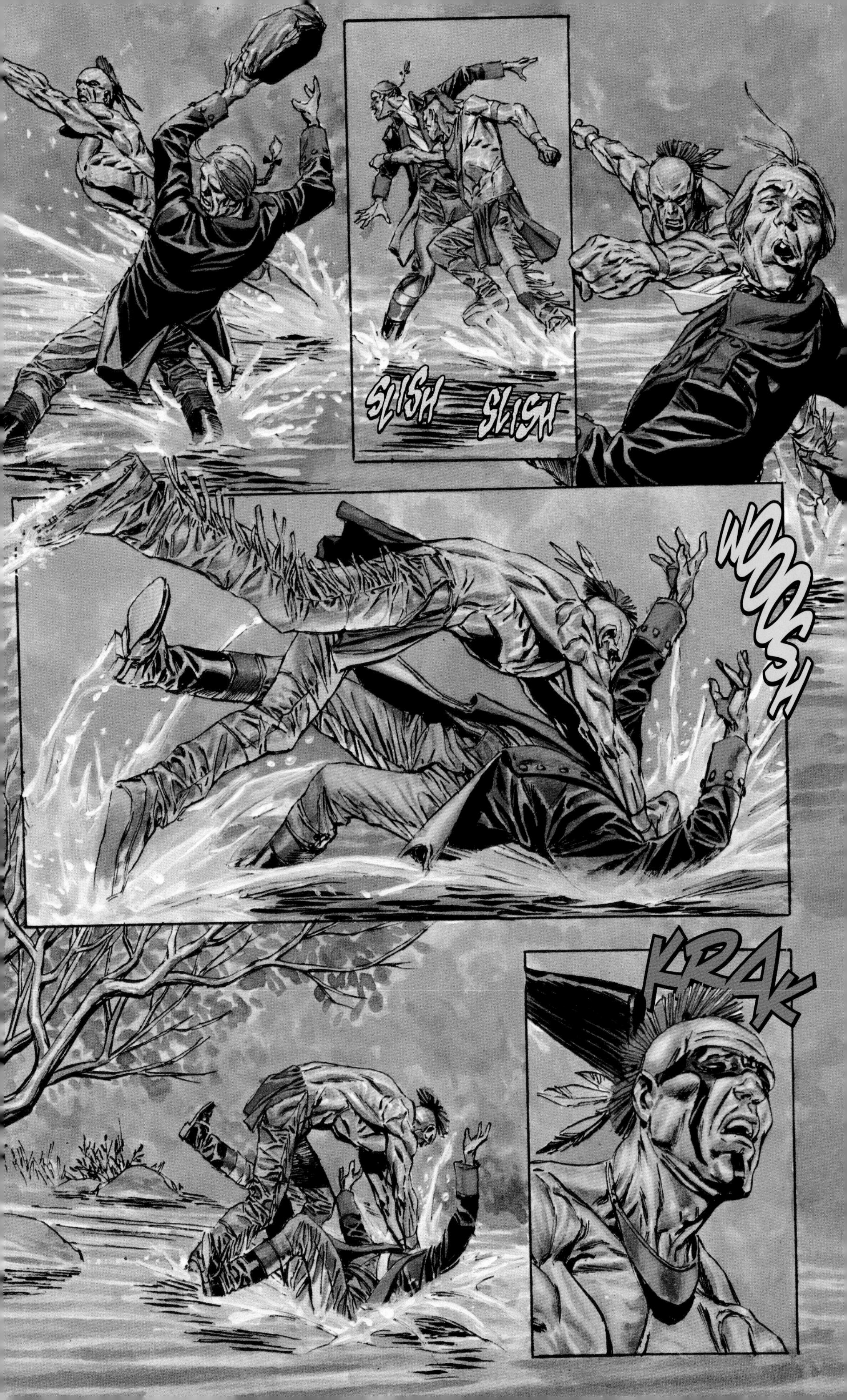
SLISH
SLISH
WOOOSH
KRAK

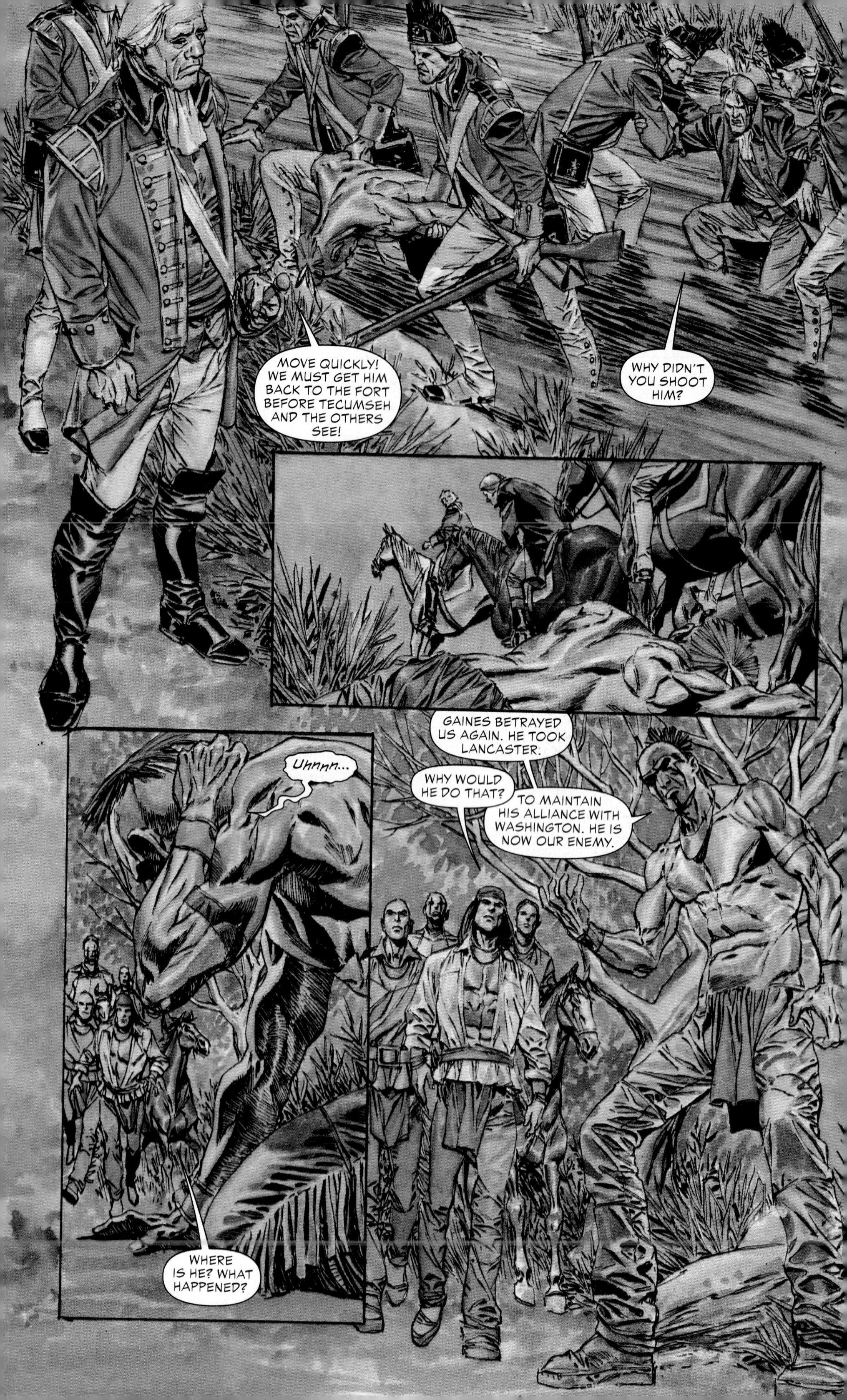
MOVE QUICKLY! WE MUST GET HIM BACK TO THE FORT BEFORE TECUMSEH AND THE OTHERS SEE!
WHY DIDN'T YOU SHOOT HIM?
Uhnnn...
WHERE IS HE? WHAT HAPPENED?
GAINES BETRAYED US AGAIN. HE TOOK LANCASTER.
WHY WOULD HE DO THAT?
TO MAINTAIN HIS ALLIANCE WITH WASHINGTON. HE IS NOW OUR ENEMY.

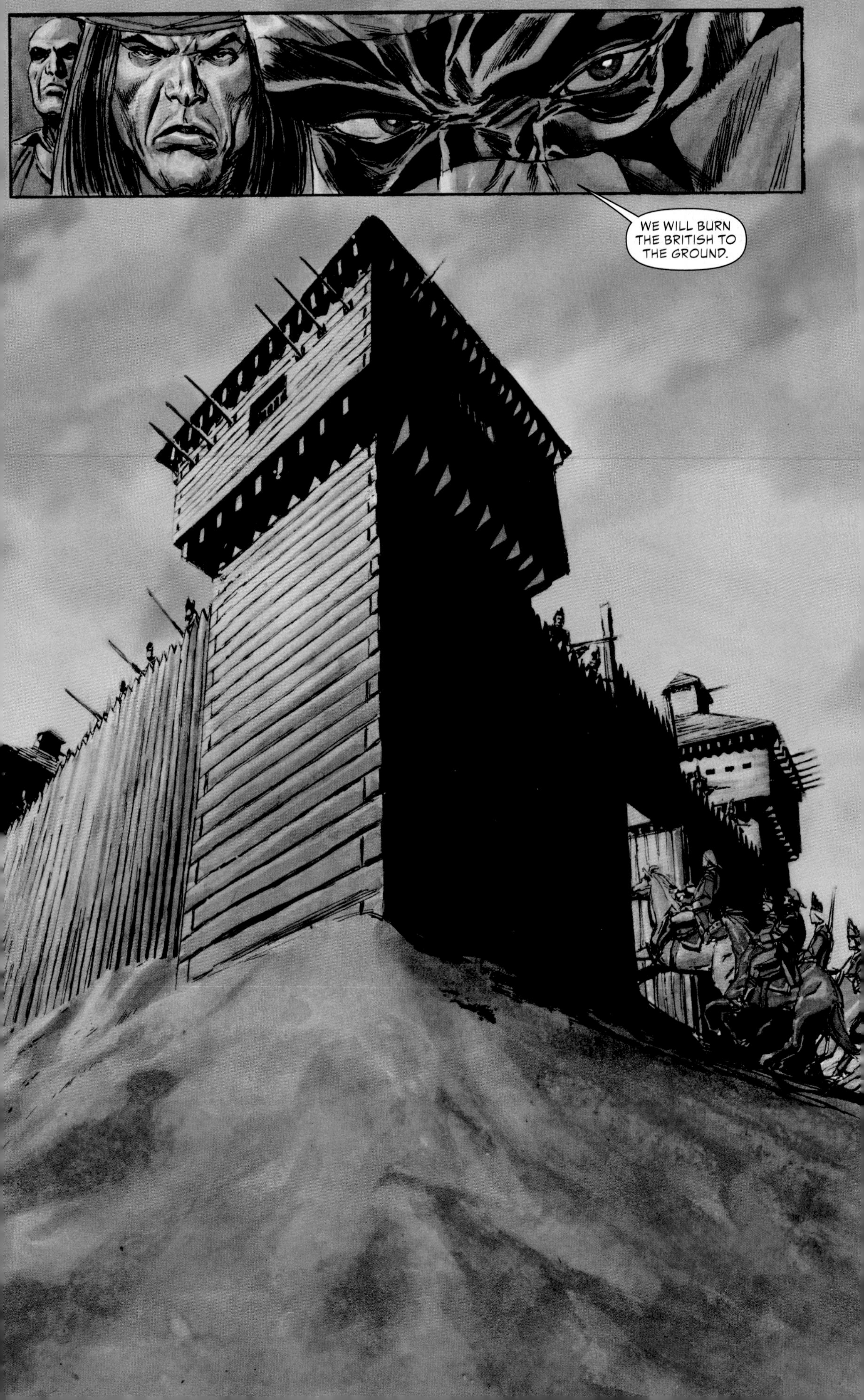
WE WILL BURN THE BRITISH TO THE GROUND.